S0-AGN-689

AMERICAN HISTORY, VOLUME I

Robert James Maddox, *Editor*
Pennsylvania State University
University Park

ANNUAL EDITIONS

The Dushkin Publishing Group, Inc. Sluice Dock, Guilford, Ct. 06437

Volumes in the Annual Editions Series

Abnormal Psychology
- Aging
- American Government
- American History, Pre-Civil War
- American History, Post-Civil War
- Anthropology
Astronomy
- Biology
- Business
Comparative Government
- Criminal Justice
Death and Dying
- Deviance
- Early Childhood Education
Earth Science
- Economics
- Educating Exceptional Children
- Education
Educational Psychology
Energy
- Environment
Ethnic Studies
Foreign Policy

Geography
Geology
- Health
- Human Development
- Human Sexuality
- Management
- Marketing
- Marriage and Family
- Personal Growth and Adjustment
Philosophy
Political Science
- Psychology
Religion
- Social Problems
- Sociology
- Urban Society
- Western Civilization,
  Pre-history – Reformation
- Western Civilization,
  Early Modern – 20th-Century
Women's Studies
World History
- World Politics

● Indicates currently available

© 1981 by the Dushkin Publishing Group, Inc. Annual Editions is a Trade Mark of the Dushkin Publishing Group, Inc.

Copyright © 1981 by the Dushkin Publishing Group, Inc., Guilford, Connecticut 06437

All rights reserved. No part of this book may be reproduced, stored, or transmitted by any means—mechanical, electronic or otherwise—without written permission from the publisher.

Sixth Edition

Manufactured by George Banta Company, Menasha, Wisconsin, 54952

Library of Congress Cataloging in Publication Data
Main entry under title: Annual editions: American history, volume one.

1. United States—History—Periodicals. 2. United States—Historiography—Periodicals. 3. United States—Civilization—Periodicals. I. Title: American history, volume one.
ISBN 0-87967-346-x   973'.05

ADVISORY BOARD

Members of the Advisory Board are instrumental in the final selection of articles for each year's edition of *Annual Editions*. Their review of articles for content, level, and appropriateness provides critical direction to the editor and staff. We think you'll find their careful consideration well reflected in this volume.

William G. Anderson
Suffolk County Community College

Arthur Belonzi
Academy of Aeronautics

Bruce Dudley
Prince Georges Community College

Richard F. Haynes
Northeast Louisiana University

Harry D. Holmes
University of Tennessee
Knoxville

William Hughes
Essex Community College

Harry Russell Huebel
Texas A & I University
Kingsville

Joseph Kudless
Somerset County College

Evelyn Radford
Diablo Valley College

Stephen J. Randall
McGill University

Robert Sterling
Joliet Junior College

James Sweeney
Old Dominion University

AND STAFF

Rick Connelly, Publisher
Ian A. Nielsen, Program Manager
Celeste Borg, Editor
Addie Kawula, Acquisitions Editor
Brenda Filley, Production Manager
Cheryl Kinne, Permissions Coordinator
Charles Vitelli, Designer
Sharon M. Canning, Graphics Coordinator
Libra VonOgden, Typesetter

CONTENTS

*Then the purchafe was agreed, great pr
paffed between us, of kindnefs and good
borhood, and that the Indians and Englif
n love as long as the fun gave light: whi
ier made a fpeech to the Indians in the n
ie Sachamakan [or kings] firft to tell
was done; next to charge and comman*

The New Land

2 Revolutionary America

3

National Consolidation and Expansion

4

The Civil War and Reconstruction

TOPIC GUIDE

This topic guide can be used to correlate each of the articles in *American History-Sixth Edition* to one or more of the topics normally covered by American history books. Each article corresponds to a given topic area according to whether it deals with the topic in a primary or secondary manner. These correlations are intended for use as a general study guide and do not necessarily define the total coverage of any given article.

TOPIC AREA	TREATED AS A PRIMARY ISSUE IN:	TREATED AS A SECONDARY ISSUE IN:
Political History	3. Bacon's Rebellion 6. Trial of Peter Zenger 8. The Revolution as a World Ideal 9. The Spirit of '74 11. England's Vietnam 12. Common Sense 16. The American World Was Not Made for Me 17. George Washington 23. Trail of Tears 26. Sam Houston 27. Jacksonian Democracy 36. How the Lost Cause Was Lost 37. The Tragic Legend of Reconstruction	10. Meet Dr. Franklin 15. The Founding Fathers 19. The Jay Treaty 25. Travels with Tocqueville
Military History	11. England's Vietnam 13. The Revolution Remembered 14. Brave Women 35. Johnny Reb and Billy Yank 36. How the Lost Cause Was Lost 38. The Bluecoats	8. The Revolution as a World Ideal 26. Sam Houston
Diplomatic History	9. The Spirit of '74 11. England's Vietnam 19. The Jay Treaty	1. Christopher Columbus' Quest 10. Meet Dr. Franklin 12. Common Sense
Economic History	29. Eden Ravished	2. Indentured Servants 16. The American World Was Not Made for Me 25. Travels with Tocqueville 27. Jacksonian Democracy
Social History	2. Indentured Servants 5. Battling the Red Death 7. The Great Earthquake 20. Experiment at Nashoba 22. The War Against Demon Rum 24. Our Forefathers in Hot Pursuit 25. Travels with Tocqueville 32. Vanity in the 19th Century 37. The Tragic Legend of Reconstruction	4. The Devil in Salem 6. Trial of Peter Zenger 10. Meet Dr. Franklin 15. The Founding Fathers 18. Do We Care If Johnny Can Read? 30. Lucretia Mott 31. The Green and the Gold 33. Sojourner Truth 35. Johnny Reb and Billy Yank
Religious History	4. The Devil in Salem 7. The Great Earthquake 24. Our Forefathers in Hot Pursuit	1. Christopher Columbus' Quest 5. Battling the Red Death 22. The War Against Demon Rum
Racial History	2. Indentured Servants 15. The Founding Fathers 20. Experiment at Nashoba 21. Gabriel's Insurrection 23. Trail of Tears 34. The Myth of the Underground Railroad 37. The Tragic Legend of Reconstruction 38. The Bluecoats	25. Travels with Tocqueville 30. Lucretia Mott

TOPIC AREA	TREATED AS A PRIMARY ISSUE IN:	TREATED AS A SECONDARY ISSUE IN:
Cultural History	4. The Devil in Salem 8. The Revolution as a World Ideal 14. Brave Women 18. Do We Care If Johnny Can Read? 22. The War Against Demon Rum 28. Melville and Hawthorne 31. The Green and the Gold	1. Christopher Columbus' Quest 29. Eden Ravished 32. Vanity in the 19th Century 34. The Myth of the Underground Railroad 35. Johnny Reb and Billy Yank
Personal History	1. Christopher Columbus' Quest 10. Meet Dr. Franklin 13. The Revolution Remembered 16. The American World Was Not Made for Me 17. George Washington 21. Gabriel's Insurrection 25. Travels with Tocqueville 26. Sam Houston 28. Melville and Hawthorne 30. Lucretia Mott 33. Sojourner Truth	3. Bacon's Rebellion 4. The Devil in Salem 14. Brave Women 24. Our Forefathers in Hot Pursuit 31. The Green and the Gold

PREFACE

To some people history is just "one thing after another." If seen in that light the study of history consists merely of memorizing tariff acts, presidential administrations, and supreme court decisions. A more boring pasttime can scarcely be imagined. If, on the other hand, one tries to learn why things happened the way they did or why people acted and thought the way they did, studying history can be most rewarding. The ideas, customs, and institutions which we accept as commonplace today all had their origins in the past. Understanding these origins can help us decide which aspects of our society we wish to preserve, and which we ought to discard because they are no longer relevant to our needs.

A "sense of history" is not the same as learning multiplication tables. There are several, sometimes many, interpretations of every important issue. But if scholars themselves disagree over these matters, how in the world can students make sense of them? The answer is that they have no choice but to try. It is impossible, for example, to understand the aspirations and frustrations of women or minority groups today without knowing something about their treatment in the past. And to be ignorant of these things leaves one defenseless against the most outrageous myths. It was said long ago that at the very least, studying history will help you to tell "when the other chap is talking rubbish."

The articles in this volume have been chosen for several reasons. Some are analyses of important issues or events written by scholars in the field. Others help to convey a "feel" for the way things were at a given time and place. In both cases there was a conscious effort to combine "history from the top"—accounts of presidents or other important leaders—with essays about more ordinary men and women, and how things seemed to them. New articles are included in this edition, and some of the previous ones have been excluded. The publisher encourages readers to submit suggestions for the next edition. Please share your thoughts with us by completing and mailing the post-paid article rating form included in the back of the book. Your suggestions will be carefully considered and greatly appreciated.

Robert James Maddox
Editor

The Purchase of Pennsylvania
Anno Dom. 1683

"When the purchase was agreed, great promises passed between us, of kindness and good neighborhood, and that the Indians and English must live in love as long as the sun gave light: which done, another made a speech to the Indians in the name of all the Sachamakan *[or kings]* first to tell them what was done; next to charge and command them to love the Christians, and particularly to live in peace with me and the people under my government. That many governors had been in the river, but that no governor had come himself to live, and stay here before; and having now such an one that had treated them well, they should never do him or his any wrong. At every sentence of which they shouted and said Amen, Amen, in their way."

WILLIAM PENN

Extract from a letter written by PENN *to*
The FREE SOCIETY *of* TRADERS~*August 1683*

The New Land

1

Many people hold only a thumbnail sketch of our early history—the details are hazy. Most know that Christopher Columbus "discovered" America in 1492 with the *Niña, Pinta,* and *Santa Maria;* Sir Walter Raleigh had something to do with tobacco in the days before the Surgeon General determined smoking was dangerous to health; Pocahontas saved Captain John Smith's life at Jamestown; the Pilgrims landed at Plymouth Rock—or was it Massachusetts Bay? In any event, having invented Thanksgiving Day, these people and others who followed settled into what became known as the "colonial period" which lasted until the Revolution. To those who know this or a similar version, it comes as a surprise to learn that the United States as a nation has existed only a little longer than the colonial period.

Ronald Leal's essay on Christopher Columbus strips away a number of myths surrounding the man and the times in which he lived. It also provides some insight into the conditions in Europe which stimulated such exploration. An article on indentured servants shows how this institution developed from Jamestown onwards, and how important a role it played in early colonial development. Selections such as these will provide the reader with a better understanding not only of important events, but how and why they took place.

Students should be wary of making comparisons between the past and the present, however, as you read the essay on Bacon's rebellion you might consider whether some of the issues involved have relevance for today. The account of Peter Zenger's trial may also be read in this light, especially since recent Supreme Court decisions have once again reopened questions involving freedom of the press. And finally, though few people today believe in witches, we might question whether fear, prejudice, and ignorance can combine to produce new scapegoats similar to those which occurred in Salem almost two hundred years ago.

The readings in this section are by no means comprehensive, but they raise some broad questions for further study and discussion. Why, for instance, was the system of indenture replaced by that of slavery and what significance did this have for the future? Could the British have learned anything from Bacon's rebellion that might have caused them to treat the colonies differently? What are the issues involved in freedom of the press, and of what importance are they in the evolution towards a free society?

Christopher Columbus' Quest for God, Glory and Gold. And Japan

Admiral of the Ocean Sea . . .a legend brought down to size.

Ronald Leal

The typical secondary school textbook biography of the "discoverer" of America would have us believe that he was a man of divine vision—a man living ahead of his time. These lines from a recent, and favorable, biography are typical: "In 1492 Christopher Columbus crossed the Atlantic Ocean from Palos in Spain to Guanahani, which he renamed San Salvador. Two weeks later he discovered Cuba. In all he made four voyages to the New World, presenting Spain with a vast new empire and, through his discoveries, nearly doubling the size of the known world." True—more or less.

But in many biographies of Columbus there is a recurring theme of "divine providence." In the second-hand copies of his own journals that are available to us, the explorer returned again and again to the idea that God put into his mind the conviction that he could sail west all the way to the Indies; to India and also to Japan, then known to the Western world by the name of Cipangu. Then, of course, we have been taught that no one believed him; that he was a visionary who somehow, perhaps by divine providence, knew that the world was round when all about him men were convinced that it was really flat.

And so the picture emerges of Christopher Columbus sailing out into the Western Sea—with the aid of Queen Isabella—to discover America, and that the world was round. Nothing could possibly be further from the truth. First of all, Columbus believed to his dying day that the earth was a sphere and could never be convinced that he had not sailed to the Indies but had, indeed, landed his three little ships on some islands off the eastern coast of a new world.

Too, very few people in Columbus' time actually believed that the world was flat. The ancient Greeks, two thousand years before Columbus, had concluded that it was not. Sailors of Classic Greece, sailing from Athens and other ports south to Crete and Egypt, had noticed completely new stars rising from the sea in the south, while those familiar ones of the north slipped in the sea behind them. Sailors traveling from south to north observed that the fixed north star seemed to rise out of the sea.

In the sixth century B.C. Pythagoras of Samos suggested that the earth was round and his pupil, Parmenides of Elea wrote a didactic poem called *Nature* in which he presented a geocentric picture of the universe with the earth hanging suspended in the center. He further explained that the earth possessed five climatic zones; a hot zone about the equator, a temperate zone on either side of it, and two cold zones around the poles.

A hundred years later, Eratosthenes measured the circumference of the earth and found it to be 27,750 miles. His estimate was only 2,750 miles in excess of the true circumference. Eratosthenes said: "If the Atlantic Ocean was not so extremely large, we could sail from Iberia (Spain) to India along the same latitude on the other side of the earth. Our inhabited world accounts for about one-third of the circumference of the earth. Along the parallel of Athens, for instance, the entire circumference is about 200,000 stadia. Of these, our inhabited world accounts for about 70,000 (7,700 miles), all the way from Iberia in the west to the remotest Indies in the east. What remains to be traveled by sea in the opposite direction, therefore, is 130,000 stadia (14,400 miles)." One cannot begin to guess how Eratosthenes' theory came so near to the actuality. Alexander the Great apparently believed him when he set out to conquer the

"Christopher Columbus' Quest for God, Glory and Gold," by Ronald J. Schnell, from *Mankind,* The Magazine of Popular History, Vol. 3, No. 10, December 1972.

world and discover new lands. Unfortunately, two thousand years later, Columbus, who certainly must have known about his findings, chose not to believe him. Columbus was convinced that the world was a great deal smaller.

Columbus also chose not to believe Aristotle's theory that there were seven continents in the ocean. If he had, he'd have realized that one of them got in his way on his journey to "the Indies." Nor did he heed Strabo who worked from Aristotle's theory, and suggested there were several continents in the ocean, including a southern one which he called Terra Australis (and when it was finally discovered it was so named) and one in the western ocean which he called Terra Occidentalis. Strabo wrote: "It may be that in the same temperate zone there are in fact two inhabited worlds, or even more, especially along the latitude of Athens, if the parallel is produced in the Atlantic." And of course he was right.

In spite of the fact that he was never convinced that he had, indeed, sailed to a new world, Columbus himself made a free translation of the lines of Seneca, the Roman dramatist, from his play *Medea* suggesting that other worlds existed in the ocean. Columbus wrote his translation of Seneca in his *Libro de las Profecias* (Book of Prophecies): "There will come a time after many years when the Ocean will lose the chains that fetter things, and the great world will lie revealed, and a new mariner, like unto him who was Jason's pilot, called Tiphys, will reveal a new world, and then Thule will not be the most extreme of all lands."

Later both the Greek Stoic philosopher Posidonius, who was not exactly known for original thought, and Marinus of Tyre "corrected" Eratosthenes. Marinus drew up a map of the world on which the land mass occupies 225 of the 360 degrees and calculated that the circumference was 20,000 miles. The geographer Ptolemy thought it was even smaller—and so would Columbus.

During the Dark Ages the Christian philosphers all but rejected the findings of the ancients regarding the size of the world. Basing their theories on the Bible—and the teachings of the ancient Hebrews—they determined that the earth was a rectangular slab, or at best a sphere. Both Cicero and Pliny the Elder suggested that the earth was a disc hanging in space. St. Augustine of Hippo accepted the theory of the sphere. Too, it was completely incompatible with Christian doctrine to suggest that there were lands where men might live who were not descended from Adam and, by extension, that such lands could, therefore, exist.

Geographers and philosophers of the Middle Ages did not concern themselves so much with the shape of the earth as with its size. Such men as the Dominican friar Albertus Magnus and Roger Bacon suggested that there was but a small stretch of water between Spain and India to the west. There were exceptions, such as

the Spaniard Raimundus Lullus, who, in observing the tides, concluded two hundred years before Columbus was to make his voyage that "As on our side there is a portion of the world that we see and know, so there must be on the other side (of the ocean) a continent that we neither know or see." But Raimundus Lullus, for the most part, was ignored—and certainly by Columbus. There is little doubt that Columbus had access to much, if not all, the conclusions of such men. His almost fatal mistake, as we shall see, was that he chose to believe the wrong ones. His notions of geography were purely Ptolemaic. And basing his observations on Ptolemy, he concluded that the world was no more than 14,000 miles in circumference. And like Albertus Magnus and Roger Bacon he also concluded that only a small stretch of water separated Spain from India, or Japan which Columbus had concluded he would reach first if he sailed west.

The notion that Columbus "discovered" America is preposterous. It should go without saying that the Indian militant's slogan, "An Indian Discovered America" is indisputable. The time has long since past for seriously considering all the romantic theories that would have us believe that refugees from Atlantis or lost ships of the Phoenicians, strayed Egyptians, Chinese, Welsh or whatever, wandered into America and brought civilization to the people we know as American Indians. Such theories as that long-lived notion that wandering Israelites were among the founders of the New World civilizations and that (according to the Mormon sacred writings) they came in two waves, an early group of Jaredites who found their way across the Atlantic after the fall of the Tower of Babel and that Lehi led a second from Jerusalem in 600 B.C. cannot be supported by one iota of fact. The American Indians are proto-Mongoloid. They very probably began arriving in America 40,000 years ago and perhaps long before that; they came in a series of waves of migrations almost certainly through Alaska. And they developed their high civilizations independently and probably with very little contact with other worlds.

There can be but little doubt that storm-tossed sailors from Japan, China, India or Malasia—and perhaps from all of those places and more—ended up on the American side of the Pacific. But it is highly unlikely that any of them ever got home again to tell about it. They very probably settled down near where they landed and were quickly absorbed into the dominant society. Surely Polynesians, some of the best seamen the world has ever known, got to the west coast of South America —and it's possible that some of them got home again. The Indian inhabitants of that same west coast, as Thor Heyerdahl has reminded us, were no slouches at sailing either. Perhaps they, in turn, reached some of the Polynesian Islands.

There can be but little doubt that the Vikings reached the American coast of the North Atlantic. After Eric the

1. THE NEW LAND

Red led his colonists to Greenland in the tenth century, the Vikings shuttled back between Norway, Iceland, and Greenland at will. Eric's son Leif sailed from Greenland to "Vinland" which was either Newfoundland or Labrador but if the Vikings did establish a colony in America, it was soon given up or, again, absorbed by the Indians.

The Irish maintain that St. Brendan was the first European to find America, and since the Irish were in both the Faeroes and Iceland long before the Norsemen where, it is probably that at sometime in the dim past some of them did reach the shores of North America. But they left no real record, only rumors. Too, history has all but overlooked a Danish expedition of 1476 that crossed the North Atlantic and reached Labrador. Unlike others, the Danes knew exactly where they were going. Labrador is the Helluland of Norse legend. There is really no way to determine if Columbus knew about the Danish expedition. But according to Fernando Colon, Columbus' son and biographer, his father was in Iceland the following year. Fernando wrote, in the words of his father: "In the month of February, 1477, I sailed one hundred leagues beyond the island of Thule (Iceland), the north part of which lies at latitude of 73 degrees north, and not 63 degrees as some affirm. Nor does it lie on the meridian where Ptolemy says the West begins, but much farther west. And to this island, which is as large as England, the English come with their wares, from Bristol in particular. When I was there, the sea was not frozen, but the tides were so great that in some places the water rose twenty-six fathoms, and fell to the same extent."

As the Swedish biographer Bjorn Landstrom has pointed out, if those are Christopher Columbus's words, he was lying. In those days no one sailed to Iceland in the middle of winter. But the fact remains Columbus knew a great deal about the Atlantic Ocean and what might be found by sailing it. His problem was recognizing it once he'd found it.

Columbus certainly knew about the Portuguese explorations in that direction, under Prince Enrique of Portugal. Known to history as Henry the Navigator, Prince Enrique fought with such extraordinary valor in the 1415 Ceuta campaign that he was granted a dukedom by his father, John I, king of Portugal. The Moroccan campaign inspired Henry to extend his knowledge of Africa and, by extension, the world. In 1415 he founded a naval arsenal at Sangres, using the nearby port of Lagos as a base for exploration. In 1420 one of his navigators rediscovered the Madeira Islands, known to the Romans as *Insulae Purpurariae*. His navy penetrated the Sudan, discovered the Senegal and reached a point near the present Sierra Leone in Africa. The Azores were explored, the Cape Verde Islands were reached and there is evidence, though disputed, that Henry the Navigator's men discovered the West Indies at least half a century before Columbus did.

A map drawn by Zuane Pizzigano in 1424 indicated two large rectangular and five small irregular shaped islands far out in the Atlantic almost exactly in the direction of the West Indies from Portugal. There can be but little doubt that Columbus knew of the Pizzigano map.

Very little is known about Columbus' life before he arrived in Portugal in about 1476. He was born Cristoforo Colombo in Genoa sometime between the end of August and the end of October, 1451, to a family of wool weavers. His mother was Susanna Fontanarossa. His brother Bartolomeo, was was destined to share both his fortune and his misfortune throughout his life was about five years his junior. A second brother, Viovanni, died young and a third, Giacomo, was about seventeen years his junior. A sister named Bianchinetta married a cheesemonger and nothing more was heard of her.

Fernando later wrote that Columbus attended the University of Pavia but Fernando was an outrageous liar especially in matters pertaining to his father. Too, nowhere is Columbus' name contained in the student rolls of that university. And according to Columbus as he calculated in later life, he had first put to sea at the age of nine. That alone would cast some question over Fernando's statement about the college education. While Fernando lied, his father had some trouble remembering: records indicate that he was between the ages of fourteen and eighteen when he went to sea.

At any rate both Cristoforo and Bartolomeo were living in Lisbon in about 1477 and owned a little shop where they made and sold maps. The following year Columbus sailed to Maderia to purchase sugar for the Genoese trading house of Centurione. The following year he married Felipa Moniz de Perestrello e Moniz, whose father was Italian and who was related to the royal house of Braganca through her Portuguese mother. By marrying Felipa, Columbus gained Portuguese citizenship. According to Fernando he also obtained notes and a chart belonging to Felipa's deceased father which inspired him to start thinking about sailing to India via the west. But then Fernando would also have us believe that Felipa's father was a great explorer and had, in fact, rediscovered Madeira himself—a statement that, like many of those made by Columbus' son, does not stand up under historical scrutiny.

But one thing Columbus did obtain while he was living in Lisbon was a copy of Pierre d'Ailly's *Imago Mundi*. Printed in about 1480, *Imago Mundi* was purportedly a description of the entire world. His copy, in which there are marginal notes written in Cristoforo's hand on nearly every page, is at the Biblioteca Columbina in Seville. d'Ailly wrote, and Columbus recopied: "A part of our inhabited world ends in an unknown country . . . towards the rising sun . . . To the south, an unknown country . . . Where the sun sets, an unknown country . . . Note that the Kingdom of Tarshish lies at the end of the Orient, at the end of Cathay (China). It was to that kingdom, to a place called Ophir, that Solomon and Jehosophat sent ships which returned with gold, silver and ivory."

Columbus' notes in both his copy of *Imago Mundi* and his Marco Polo's *Book of Ser Marco Polo* constantly referred to both unknown worlds and riches. In the Marco Polo he underlined the words that he found important: pearls, precious stones, brocades, ivory, pepper, nutmeg, cloves, etc. The dream was born and the only part that discovering unknown lands played in that dream was the matter of what riches might be found in those lands.

Columbus obtained a map from the Florentine physician Paolo dal Pozzo Toscanelli, who had concluded that there was not only a western route to the Orient, but basing his calculations on the work of Posidonius and Marinus, concluded that the route was a short one. That year, 1481, Columbus' son Diego was born in Porto Santo and it is presumed that Felipa died in childbirth or soon afterwards. During the next few years Columbus made several journeys to Guinea. His calculations on those journeys led him to revise his early estimate and decide that the circumference of the earth at the equator was 20,400 miles—and he still believed that most of it was covered by land. Fernando Colon wrote that his father determined that the distance between the Canaries and Cipangu (Japan) was 750 leagues, or 2,760 miles. The actual distance is 12,200 miles.

Columbus attempted to convince John II of Portugal to back his scheme to sail to Japan—not India—to find the riches described by Marco Polo. According to the Portuguese chronicler Barros, Columbus "came to the conclusion that it was possible to sail across the western Ocean to the island of Cipangu and other unknown lands (by) fantastic ideas that he obtained on his continual voyages, and from talks with men who were versed in such matters in this kingdom and had great knowledge of past discoveries . . . He came to King John II, asking him for ships that he might sail away and discover the island of Cipangu in the western Ocean . . . When the King found that this Cristovao Colom was very proud and boastful in presenting his talents, and more fanciful and full of imagination than accurate when speaking of his island of Cipangu, he had little faith in him. But as he would not be put off, the King sent him to Dom Diogo Ortiz, the Bishop of Ceuta, and to Master Rodrigo and Master Josepe, who dealt with such questions of cosmography and discoveries; and all of them found that Cristovao Colom's words were empty, for they were based on fantasy, or such things as Marco Polo's island of Cipangu."

Actually these learned men did not disagree that Japan could be reached by sailing west; they determined that it was a great deal farther away than Columbus thought it was. Later historians have hinted

that King John wanted to steal Columbus' plans and give the assignment to Fernam Dulmo, the Portuguese explorer. But actually the King of Portugal was already in debt from backing expeditions to Guinea that brought little return and was certainly in no mood to ante up for Columbus. Disheartened, Columbus took his son Diego and left Portugal for Castile in 1485, and left behind him a pile of debts and pending lawsuits. If the Portuguese Crown wasn't in the mood to find the Orient, then perhaps the Spanish one would be.

Their Catholic Majesties, Ferdinand and Isabella, had their hands full in trying to drive Boabdil and the Moors out of Granada when Columbus arrived in Spain (see "Boabdil, Sultan of Granada" in MANKIND Volume I, Number 11) and had little inclination to listen to tales of riches in unknown lands. But Isabella was apparently impressed with Columbus' plan or, more likely, that part of his scheme that had to do with unsaved souls in foreign lands as she was a bit fanatic on the subject of heathens. At any rate she attached him to her court on January 20, 1486 and gave him a small donation from the royal coffers—which were just about depleted at the time. While waiting for the King and Queen to return to Cordova in late April, Columbus met and apparently fell in love with Beatriz de Harana. Fernando was born of this union, out of wedlock, in the summer of 1488. But in his biography of his father, Columbus' second son never once mentioned his mother. This union apparently displeased Queen Isabella very much as we shall see.

The Queen did not return to Cordova and meet Columbus until May, 1486. She was impressed enough by her first meeting to arrange for him to become the houseguest of her comptroller of finances and gave him a stipend from the treasury about equal to the pay of a sailor. The stipend continued until shortly before the birth of Fernando when, apparently, Isabella learned of Columbus affair with Beatriz de Harana. A few writers have used that turn of events to suggest that there was more to Columbus and Isabella's relationship than a business arrangement. Actually Isabella was as straitlaced as a nun and her ire was probably over the fact that Columbus had not married his mistress. History has left us with no hint as to why he never legalized the union. And certainly Fernando never said.

Columbus followed the court from Cordova to Salamanca but failed to find additional support from his scheme to sail to Japan. The war with the Moors commanded everyone's attention but Isabella did turn the plan over to a commission for study. The verdict of the commission, delivered finally two years later, like that of King John's, was unfavorable. And for just about the same reasons.

In the meantime Columbus set about gathering friends and supporters close to the crown, among which was Dona Beatrice de Bobadilla, Marquesa de Moya, who was Isabella's close friend and who made the queen aware of the fact that the explorer was awaiting a favorable decision. But the Queen's "holy war" with the Moors continued to command her attention. Finally, in 1488, Columbus returned to Portugal briefly and with his brother, Bartholomeo, again called on John II. This time King John seriously considered Columbus' plans —until he learned that the explorer Bartholomeo Dias had returned from a long voyage during which he had rounded the tip of South Africa and had opened an eastern passage to India for the Portuguese.

Rejected again, Columbus returned to Spain while Bartholomeo set out for England in an attempt to interest Henry VII in the project. Failing at Henry VII's court, Bartholomeo planned to also call on Charles VIII of France but on his way to England he got himself captured by pirates and was held as a prisoner.

Upon arriving in Spain, Columbus learned that the commission had finally rejected his plans. He was about to leave Spain to join Bartholomeo in France when Isabella summoned him to court, now located in Santa Fe, a walled and towered city which Isabella had had constructed in record time for the siege of Granada. He arrived around Christmas, 1491.

He found Isabella and Ferdinand in good spirits. The Moors were all but defeated. Isabella immediately set up a new commission to study Columbus' project which quickly returned a verdict. While this one was not exactly favorable, it was not, on the other hand, as unfavorable as that reached by the first commission. Then on January 2, 1492, Granada surrendered and Columbus witnessed the triumphant entry of the "Catholic Sovereigns" into the bastion of the Moors. The matter of Boabdil and his Moors was out of the way after ten long years. Isabella turned her attentions to Columbus and quickly pledged her support even if it meant pawning her own jewels. Of course there was very little chance of Isabella losing her jewels—and she knew it. The financing of Columbus' expedition was, to a large extent, negotiated through Italian banking interests in Spain. The little financial support that was not Italian came in the form of the *Nina* and the *Pinta* which were furnished by the city of Palos in payment of a fine owed to the Queen.

Columbus was certain that his voyage would greatly enrich Spain and he wanted to make sure that he was adequately compensated. He asked for a tenth of all profits obtained from whatever lands he might "discover" (and it must be remembered that he really intended to "discover Japan and India which were already pretty well discovered.) That request was readily granted by Isabella and Ferdinand as they really had little to lose in light of the fact that they weren't putting up the money. But they balked when Columbus demanded that he and his descendants be given the titles of Admiral of the Ocean Sea and Viceroy and Governor of the newly discovered lands, with all the privileges that went along with those titles. No doubt the idea that Beatriz de Harana's little bastard Fernando might one day inherit those titles galled Isabella. She refused and the negotiations were broken off. Columbus rode off toward La Rábida but was overtaken by a messenger and asked to return. His conditions were accepted and on April 17, 1492, the articles of agreement were signed.

The trials of the Columbus expedition are familiar to us all and we will not go into them here. The fleet weighed anchor in the Rio Tinto at dawn on August 3, and sailed to the island of Salte to wait for a favorable wind. From there they put to sea, eighty-seven officers and men. For the most part the crew were Basques and Andalusians.

A north wind carried the three little ships to the Canary Islands and from there they struck out west on September 6 with the intention of moving westward at latitude $28.3°$ and expecting to find Japan some 2,400 nautical miles away. Had the expedition remained on that course Columbus would have ended up in Florida rather than on San Salvador (Watling Island).

Certainly it was a frightful journey and many of the crew looked back at Ferro, the westernmost of the archipelago, with apprehension and fear. But no doubt they were comforted by the words of Martin Alonso Pizón, commander of the *Pinta,* who had promised them they'd find "houses roofed with gold tiles and come home laden with riches and glory." No consideration seemed to have been made for those persons already in ownership of those houses with gold tiles nor would there be such for inhabitants of the huts they did discover. Those brown *Indios* Columbus found in his Japan (he was convinced that Cuba and Japan were one and the same) were badgered for gold, of which they owned very little, and spices. And six of their number were enslaved and taken back to Spain to be taught Christianity so they might return home and teach the others—a concession Columbus shrewdly made for Isabella. Very shortly they were all enslaved.

In all Columbus made four trips to the New World in search of gold, glory and spices. And Japan. He died refusing to believe that he had, indeed, discovered a new continent, but confusedly insisting that he had explored islands of the Orient.

Indentured Servants

Most colonials got to America by trading seven years of servitude for passage across the Atlantic.

Joseph P. Cullen

Joseph P. Cullen, a regular contributor and consulting editor for this magazine, is in the National Park Service, formerly a historian now director of public relations in the southeastern jurisdiction.

In 1607 three English ships arrived safely at Jamestown, Virginia to found the first permanent English colony in the New World. Most of the passengers, other than the officers and "gentlemen" were indentured to work for the Virginia Company for seven years in return for their passage and keep. At the end of that period they could either return to England or take up land for themselves in Virginia and work for the company as free laborers. Despite the hardships suffered by the colonists in those early years and the high mortality rate, some elected to remain.

It soon became evident, however, that the success of the infant colony depended on more people settling there than the Company's system provided. In a country where land was cheap and plentiful and resources abundant, the paramount need was for a large labor supply. Consequently, a system was adopted whereby people coming from Europe could be indentured to individuals as well as to the Company. As an inducement to the colonists in the early years, for each indentured servant they brought in they were granted a "head-right" of fifty acres of land free.

To many English tenant farmers struggling for maintenance on borrowed land, and to the laborers starving under low wages and miserable living conditions, the opportunity to migrate to the New World as an indentured servant came as a welcome release. And although the practice of granting fifty acres to the importer, and generally to the servant at the end of his period of indenture, gradually died out with availability of cheap land, the system survived for many years and was, in fact, the principal means of peopling the English colonies.

In 1619 eight ships brought 1,261 new settlers to Jamestown, increasing the population to approximately 2,400 people. Many of these newcomers were indentured servants, each of whom signed a contract to work for a master for a specified number of years, usually

three to five, in return for his passage and room and board in the New World, after which he would be given a certain amount of clothes and other provisions to help him begin life on his own, along with various amounts of land if he so desired. One servant wrote that his indenture called for "a pigg to be payd at every years end and in the end of the term to have a Convenient lott," along with "three suits of apparel and six shirts." Another was to receive "meat, drink, lodging and apparell, and double apparell at the end of the term."

In those early years few single women came over indentured, and most of those who did were used as domestic servants until they married, but the supply never could meet the demand despite all attempts to encourage emigration. "The Women that go over . . . as Servants," wrote one contemporary, "have the best luck in any place in the World besides, for they are no sooner on shoar than they are courted into . . . Matrimony."

In 1619 the Virginia Company sent ninety young women to become wives of the planters. These were the first of many groups of "younge, handsome, and honestly educated maydes" sent across the Atlantic for this purpose. They were not indentured, however, but were placed in respectable homes until they "happened upon good matches."

That same year a notorious Dutch slaver stopped at the little colony and exchanged twenty Negroes, including two women, for desperately needed provision. As slavery did not then exist in Virginia either by law or custom, some authorities maintain that these people were indentured servants, not slaves, and when their time was up they became free settlers the same as everyone else.

As the colony grew and prospered, the number of indentured servants continually increased. Out of almost 5,000 settlers in 1635, about half had arrived indentured to furnish the necessary labor to tame the wilderness into farms and plantations. By 1671 the number had grown to 6,000 and ten years later there were 15,000 indentured workers in Virginia alone. With the gradual development of the other colonies the demand increased proportionately, and it is generally estimated that indentured servants comprised over 60

From AMERICAN HISTORY ILLUSTRATED, April 1967. Reproduced through the courtesy of the National Historical Society, Publishers of AMERICAN HISTORY ILLUSTRATED, P.O. Box 1831, Harrisburg, Pa. 17105.

1. THE NEW LAND

percent of all immigrants into the colonies down to 1776.

With the increased demand came abuses and irregularities, however. In 1665 the captain of the ship *Recovery* complained that his only cargo on leaving England was forty passengers, "persons utterly useless to this Kingdom, but rather destructive in their idle course of life." The English courts adopted the policy of transporting felons from the jails and lewd women from houses of correction to the New World to be rid of them, and the demand being so great the plantation owners did not hesitate to accept them. Political prisoners and prisoners of war were also often sent abroad. Unscrupulous captains and crews kidnapped many to be sold to the highest bidder in America. Many of these were being pursued by the law for one reason or another, but the kidnappers generally concentrated on the young, the inexperienced, and the friendless, who were usually lured into taverns and then seized and carried forcibly aboard ship.

Many of those kidnapped it was claimed were "felons condemned to death, sturdy beggars, gipsies, and other incorrigible rogues, poor and idle debauched persons." Historian Beverley, in his famous *"The History and Present State of Virginia"* published in London in 1705, stated that "though the greedy planter will always buy them yet it is to be feared they will be very injurious to the country which has already suffered many murders and robberies."

Many of these were not really criminals, however, in the modern sense of the word. Some had been imprisoned for unpaid debts, while others were guilty of nothing more than stealing a loaf of bread to feed a starving child, or public drunkenness, and there was great demand for them on the part of honest and scrupulous planters. For example, the great distances that necessarily separated plantations made most of them inaccessible to such schools as were established in the southern colonies. Consequently, in many cases plantation owners secured these convicts as indentured servants to be special tutors to their children, particularly if they were well versed in Latin, as was often the case. One contemporary observer reported that two-thirds of the schoolmasters in Maryland just before the Revolution were indentured servants of one kind or another. Tradition has it that George Washington "had no other education than reading, writing, and accounts," which were taught him "by a convict servant whom his father had bought as a schoolmaster."

The establishment of the Royal African Company in 1662, however, with its encouragement and official support of slavery, doomed the indentured servant system in the southern colonies when the tobacco and cotton crops demanded a huge supply of cheap labor which the system could not produce. And slavery also had other major economic advantages. The slave was owned for life, not just a few years, so he would not have

to be continually replaced; all offspring also belonged to the master for life, so the slaves could be bred like animals and the supply thereby increased at relatively little cost; if necessary they could be sold, usually for a profit; and because of their color could be detected more easily if they ran away. Consequently, by 1800 there were virtually no indentured servants in the South.

In the Middle and New England colonies, however, where slavery was not economically feasible, there was a strong demand for indentured servants, particularly during the first half of the 18th century. Massachusetts in 1710 passed an act offering 40 shillings a head to any captain who brought in a male servant from age 8 to 25. Particularly needed were skilled workers such as experienced seamen, carpenters, blacksmiths, silversmiths, coopers, weavers, and bricklayers. Consequently Europeans came by the thousands, particularly Ger-

Early settlers bound for the New World. (Engraved from a drawing by Howard Pyle, in "Harper's Magazine," November 1882).

10

mans, who freely bonded themselves for a number of years in return for learning a trade or even just the language and customs of the new country. Between 1737 and 1746 sixty-seven ships landed 15,000 Germans at Philadelphia alone. Many had sufficient money to pay the passage, but instead saved it to use after their indentures had been served. One contemporary observer noted:

Many of the Germans who come hither bring money enough with them to pay their passage, but prefer to be sold, hoping that during their servitude they may get a knowledge of the language and character of the country and its life, that they may the better be able to consider what they shall do when they have gotten their liberty . . . They launch forth, and, by dint of sobriety, rigid parsimony, and the most persevering industry, they commonly succeed.

He also noted that the "Scotch are frugal and laborious, but their wives cannot work so hard as German women," and the "Irish do not prosper so well; they love to drink and to quarrel; they seem, besides, to labor under a greater degree of ignorance in husbandry than the others."

As the country continued to develop, the demand for apprentices, house servants, farmhands, laborers, settlers for lands the speculators had secured also increased, and with this increased demand came dishonest schemes and abuses. Many who left their homes for the New World started with funds for passage and a little more to live on when they arrived. But for some reason there seems to have been more profit for unscrupulous agents and captains in selling the immigrants upon arrival than in simply transporting them as paying passengers. Consequently, various frauds and deceptions were practiced to relieve the ignorant and unsuspecting of their money at the embarkation points. Their belongings were often stolen outright; they were lured into taverns and robbed; they were subjected to exorbitant charges or sold passage on nonexistent ships; with the result that the only way they could get to America was to agree to sell themselves to pay their passage.

It was remarkable that any of them survived the crossing. Packed into unsafe and unsanitary ships "like so many herrings," they died by the score. The horrible conditions existing aboard many of these floating hells equaled those of the infamous "middle passage" for the African slave trade. Food was totally inadequate and often so rotten as to be inedible. Any unusual delay due to storm or calm threatened death by starvation or thirst. In many instances the immigrants fought for the bodies of rats and mice in order to stay alive. On at least one ship cannibalism was resorted to and the bodies of six dead humans were consumed before another vessel brought relief to the maddened passengers.

Disease and sickness were rife in the filthy holds of the ships as dysentery, smallpox, and typhus swept through them. In one ship 250 out of 400 died; in another 350 out of 400; and in another 250 out of 312. The statistics indicate that in 1711, for example, only one out of three survived the crossing.

This high mortality often caused extra hardship for many of the survivors, as all passengers, living or dead, had to be paid for if possible before the ships' captains would release the immigrants. Thus it was not unusual to see a widow sold to pay for her husband's passage as well as her own, meaning she would have to serve double the normal time of indenture. Children were sold to pay for deceased or unwell parents. Consequently, families were often broken up, just as in the slave trade, never to meet again.

Those fortunate enough to survive the sea passage, however, generally found that the opportunities available to them made the sacrifices worthwhile. In most cases they were well treated. As one observer noted: "There is no master but will allow his servant a parcel of clear ground to plant some tobacco in for himself, which he may husband at those many idle times he hath allowed him, and not prejudice but rejoice his master to see it."

Most of them, particularly in the early years in the South, lived on average farms of from 300-400 acres and cultivated them side by side with the owner and his family. They were generally regarded as members of the family and treated as such; when their indenture was worked out, they might become neighbors of their former owners, although many pushed on farther west as the coastal areas become more populated and land more expensive. In the northern colonies, where they served mostly as house servants and apprentices, they were also usually treated fairly, and after becoming freemen had every opportunity to succeed. A good example was Paul Revere, whose father had come to Massachusetts as an indentured servant.

They were also protected by laws. Most of the colonies passed legislation to improve the legal position of the indentured servant and to safeguard his social condition. Generally, corporal punishment was limited and servants had the right to take complaints against their masters into court. An early statute provided that if any servant had just cause for complaint against his master or mistress for "harsh or unchristianlike usage or otherways for want of diet," he could bring his complaint to the nearest justice of the peace. Another required that "every master shall provide for his servants complete dyett, clothing and lodging, and that he shall not exceed the bounds of moderation in correcting them beyond the meritt of their offenses."

And these laws were not ignored. Sometimes the servants were taken away from cruel masters or mistresses without compensation and the employers were forbidden to own servants again. In rare cases the

Arrival of the young women at Jamestown in 1621. (Drawing by Howard Pyle originally published in "Harper's Magazine" April 1883).

masters were jailed for brutality. "The servants," stated one observer, "live more like Freemen than the most Mechanick Apprentices of London, wanting for nothing that is convenient and necessary, and according to their several capacities, are extraordinary well used and respected."

Despite all this, just as in the South, the system could not furnish the northern colonies with the necessary labor supply, particularly the skilled labor so desperately needed. Skilled craftsmen, even in Europe, were usually not financially helpless and if they did migrate they could generally afford to pay their own passage and come as freemen. Also, by 1770 the colonists found it cheaper to hire native born youngsters as apprentices, rather than pay the passage for indentured servants. As a result, and particularly after the Revolution with its emphasis on equality, the system gradually died out and

by the early 19th century had virtually ceased to exist in the North.

That some of the indentured servants caused serious problems is unquestionable. Running away was the most common offense, particularly among the kidnapped class and the prisoners sent here against their wills. But also among the list of runaway servants were to be found tailors, clothiers, carpenters, and other skilled workers. If caught, they had to serve double their time and were often whipped and branded. Few were ever captured, however, and many became highway robbers and criminals of some sort, or settled around the docks in the cities to prey upon newly arrived immigrants. Here they joined with the penniless, sick, and disabled who could go no farther even had they so desired, and created the first slums in the country.

The presence of both slaves and indentured servants in the southern colonies almost of necessity led to some

Threshing grain with flails—the method used during Colonial days, and one of the chores of indentured servants. From a drawing by F.O.C. Darley in "Scribner's Monthly."

sexual immorality. With white male servants working in the fields side by side with Negresses and deprived of association with white women of their own class, it was inevitable that many would yield to temptation and create the first of the mulatto class in America. Such intercourse was forbidden by law, but as all children born to slaves were also slaves, it is doubtful that the masters were overly concerned. Children born to female indentured servants, however, were born free and punishment here was usually swift and sure, particularly if the father was a Negro. Often the woman was punished by public whipping and forced to serve another full term of indenture. If the father was white, most colonies required the servant "in regard to the losse and trouble her master doth sustain by her having a bastard shall serve two years after her time by indenture is expired."

Regardless of the problems, however, the system of indentured servants filled a dire need in the early years of the New World. Such persons supplied much of the labor necessary for development and growth and in turn became a market themselves for the goods produced by the young nation. With their help the population from 1691 to 1763 increased almost seven times, and instead of the original scattered settlements there was now almost one continuous settlement from Maine to Georgia. They played a major role in pushing the frontier ever westward across the backcountry and even over the mountains, and they carried with them a strong spirit of independence and self-reliance as well as a lack of respect for a government three thousand miles east across the ocean that had done little to help or protect them. They carried with them the seeds of the American Revolution.

Bacon's Rebellion

Joseph P. Cullen

Joseph P. Cullen, an official of the National Park Service, is a frequent contributor to this magazine and to "Civil War Times Illustrated." The following are suggested for additional reading: David Hawke, "The Colonial Experience"; Thomas J. Wertenbaker, "The First Americans"; Wertenbaker, "Bacon's Rebellion"; George F. Willison, "Behold Virginia"; Robert Beverley, "The History and Present State of Virginia."

THE YEAR 1675 was a troubled one for the colonists of Virginia. The price of tobacco, the major economic base of the colony, had fallen drastically, while taxes increased. One official said, "After the taxes . . . shall be deducted, very little remains to a poor man who hath perhaps a wife and children to cloath and other necessities to buy." In addition, the planters along the frontier were being attacked constantly by the Indians, while the Council and House of Burgesses, supposedly the governing body of the colony, were completely under the control of the royal governor, Sir William Berkeley, now almost 70 years old. Only the great mercy of God, one colonist believed, kept the colony from mutiny and confusion.

Since the first settlement at Jamestown in 1607, Virginia had grown and prospered, with no major civil disorders. But now a strong underlying feeling of frustration, resentment, and dissatisfaction existed among many of the 40,000-odd colonists, particularly the small planters, who were squeezed between the rising taxes and the falling price of tobacco. And the landless freemen, mostly former indentured servants who had served out their contracts, were being thwarted by hostile Indians in their attempts to move westward to take up free land. Many of the substantial planters, men such as William Byrd, William Drummond, and Thomas Lawrence, the elite of the colony, shared in the general discontent. Although these well-to-do people were not seriously injured by the high taxes and the low tobacco prices, they strongly resented the autocratic rule of Berkley and his small clique of supporters who controlled all the lucrative political appointments and more important, the highly profitable Indian fur trade.

The House of Burgesses was completely ineffective against this oligarchy, as Berkeley had not allowed an election in almost fourteen years. Consequently, it resembled more a closed corporation than a representative body, responsive only to the will of the governor and not to the needs and wishes of the people. "He hath so fortified his power over us," one member reported, "as of himself without respect to our laws to do what so ever he best pleased." And he bound his favorites to him by granting them great tracts of the best land, with the result that newcomers and landless freemen were forced to either become tenants or seek land on the unprotected frontiers.

SO REBELLION was in the making in Virginia with all the necessary ingredients present, lacking only the spark to set it off. And, as often happens in history, the spark came from a source beyond the control of the rebels or the authorities.

In distant Canada the French were usurping the fur trade from the Seneca Indians. In search of new fur sources, the powerful Senecas pushed southward into territory controlled by the Susquehannocks, who in turn were being pressed by the expansion of the Maryland colony. Threatened from two sides, the Susquehannocks fell back into the country of the Doeg Indians on Virginia's borders. This resulted among other things in a shortage of game and other sources of Indian food, causing the Indians to make frequent raids on Virginia's outlying farms and plantations. And in the process of stealing food it was inevitable that some colonists were killed.

Thus one Sunday morning in July 1675 a Stafford county family riding to church came upon the mutilated body of a planter's overseer. He lived long enough to gasp an accusation against the Doegs. His

From AMERICAN HISTORY ILLUSTRATED, December, 1968. Reproduced through the courtesy of The National Historical Society, publishers of AMERICAN HISTORY ILLUSTRATED, P. O. Box 1831, Harrisburg, Pa. 17105.

Loading tobacco, the colony's prime crop, at a Virginia wharf.

aroused neighbors then exacted reprisals against any Indians they could find, with the result that Susquehannocks as well as Doegs were killed. The embittered Indians broke up into roving bands to seek revenge, and by March 1676 they had killed more than 300 Virginians. Every colonist along the fall-line country lived in constant terror.

BERKELEY, who had claimed that the Indians on Virginia's borders were "absolutely subjected, so that there is no fear of them," now retreated from this stand enough to order out a punitive expedition. But when the chief of the Susquehannocks sent a peace offer, Berkeley suddenly reversed himself again, called off the expedition, and persuaded the assembly to adopt a defensive rather than an offensive policy. The only helpful action of the governor was to authorize the construction of more forts on the Rappahannock, Mattaponi, Pamunkey, James, and Appomattox Rivers.

Perhaps the governor feared his expedition might have provoked a disastrous war with the Indians, and therefore was justified in calling it off. But the hundreds of small planters along the frontier felt that Berkeley was abandoning them and their problems in order to save his own valuable fur trade. Forts could provide only slight protection against the Indians. As one disgusted planter stated, "they [the Indians] quickly found out where the mouse traps were sett [sic], and for what purpose, and so resolved to keep out of the way." Furthermore, the construction of new forts meant more taxes.

SO IT WAS that several hundred planters, including William Byrd, assembled in Charles City County

in April 1676 to consider what action they might take for their own protection. They were soon joined by a newcomer, Nathaniel Bacon, not yet 30 years old. Son of a wealthy squire of Suffolk, he had arrived from England two years before, and bought a plantation at Curles Neck on the James, forty miles above Jamestown.

Educated at Cambridge, Bacon had toured the Continent, traditionally regarded as necessary to put the final polish on a gentleman's education, and had studied law. Described as gay, extravagant, and headstrong, he had married well only to have his wife disinherited by her father for marrying against his wishes. Then when he became involved, innocently or otherwise, in a nefarious scheme to deprive another of his inheritance, Bacon's father decided to let him have a fresh start in the New World.

Bacon was welcomed to Virginia by his cousin, Nathaniel Bacon Sr., a wealthy landowner and member of the Governor's Council. Cousin Nathaniel gave the new arrival much expert advice and influential assistance. Within a few months Berkeley appointed him to the Council, much to young Bacon's surprise. But the governor explained: "Gentlemen of your quality come very rarely into this country, and therefore when they do come are used by me with all respect."

Thus when the group of dissident planters saw the slender, black-haired young aristocrat they set up a cry: "A Bacon! A Bacon!" In him they saw a natural leader—young, eloquent, impetuous, and one who enjoyed the prestige of a seat on the Council. As Bacon was ambitious and arrogant, with "a most imperious and dangerous hidden pride of heart," this expression of admiration was too much for him to resist. He agreed to lead the planters in their fight. He quickly endeared himself to many as a "man of quality and merit, brave and eloquent." And his rough followers listened with approval as he described how he would lead them against the Indians, with or without the governor's permission; then he denounced the government as "negligent and wicked, treacherous and incapable, the laws unjust and oppressive," and demanded reform.

BACON wrote to the governor requesting a commission [license or permit] to attack the Indians, and then, without waiting for a reply, took off into the woods with his followers. Instead of keeping his men in the immediate area to protect the settlements, however, he led them almost 200 miles south to the seat of the friendly Occaneechees, a place known as being a trading center for all Indians within 500 miles.

The Occaneechees welcomed Bacon and his men and even helped them attack and capture a band of Susquehannocks in a nearby fort. But when Bacon

15

demanded for the return journey provisions which the Occaneechees didn't have, and they refused, he started a bloody battle in which Bacon's men plundered and burned the Indian settlement and drove the survivors into the woods. A common saying among the whites of that time was "it matters not whether they be Friends or Foes Soe they be Indians."

Berkeley, on hearing of Bacon's unauthorized actions, immediately dismissed him from the Council, declared him and his followers "rebels and mutineers," and threatened to hang them on sight. The governor then quickly gathered a force of about 300 mounted men, which he sent up the James River to the fall-line to halt the expedition against the Indians. But Bacon eluded them and vanished into the forest with his men. Berkeley, while awaiting Bacon's return, was astonished to learn that the discontented in all parts of the colony were ready to rise up against him. In Bacon they believed they had found a leader who would become the standard bearer for all those who found life under the autocratic governor increasingly intolerable. And they expected the young leader not only to fight the Indians, but to end corruption and favoritism in government, lower taxes, and establish a truly representative government.

To counteract the rising popularity of the brash Bacon, Berkeley quickly made his own bid for popular support. On the advice of his Council he called for a new election of burgesses, the first in over fourteen years. And he extended the franchise for this election to all freemen.

When he returned from the Occaneechee fight just before the election, with the claim that he had killed 150 Indians, Bacon was elated to find himself a popular hero, not only on the frontier but in all parts of the colony. Then he learned of his dismissal from the Council and being branded a rebel. Bacon promptly responded by standing for election as a burgess from Henrico county and won easily. On May 25 he wrote Berkeley: "I am sorry to find that for the expence of our estates and hazard of our lives in the country's service we should by misinformers have our true intentions so falsely represented to you. . . . We have all along manifested our abhorrence of mutiny and rebellion." Then, in a thinly veiled threat, he stated that if he desired revenge on the governor for this, all he had to do was to repeat the stories he heard every day of "your honor's falsehood, cowardice, treachery, receiving bribes."

EARLY in June Bacon, accompanied by only forty armed followers, left by boat for Jamestown, to take his seat in the House of Burgesses. As they came abreast of Jamestown they were fired on by the guns of the fort and quickly retreated farther up the river. That night under cover of darkness Bacon crept into

Jamestown to visit two of his chief supporters, William Drummond and Richard Lawrence, men of influence and respected by all. Drummond, "a sober Scotch gentleman of good repute," had been the first governor of Carolina, but Berkeley had dismissed him and since then they had been at swords' points. Lawrence, a "thinking man" who formerly was of Oxford University, had married a wealthy widow who kept a tavern in Jamestown. He had a personal grievance against the governor because he believed he had been cheated out of a considerable estate on behalf of a corrupt favorite.

After a lengthy conference with Drummond and Lawrence, Bacon returned to his sloop only to be captured by a party from the warship *Adam and Eve* and turned over to the governor. "Now I behold the greatest rebel that ever was in Virginia," the old man exclaimed. Then, after a pause, he added, "Mr. Bacon, have you forgot to be a gentleman?"

"No, may it please your honor."

"Then I'll take your parole."

A few days later at a joint meeting of the Burgesses and Council, Berkeley arose and stated, "If there be joy in the presence of the angels over one sinner that repenteth, there is joy now, for we have a penitent sinner come before us. Call Mr. Bacon."

Bacon stepped forward, fell on his knees, acknowledged his "miscarriages and unwarrantable practices," and promised "good and quiet behavior for one whole year from this date."

"God forgive you! I forgive you!" cried Berkeley.

Thus the governor pardoned Bacon. He promised him a commission to go against the Indians, and restored him to the Council. Later Berkeley admitted that the reason he didn't hang Bacon as he had promised, was that everyone was "frightened with hearing 2000 men were armed to deliver him." Therefore he had put the rebellion leader back on the Council in order to keep him out of the House of Burgesses where he would undoubtedly attempt to carry through reform legislation.

AT THIS POINT it would seem that anyone less stubborn and dictatorial than Berkeley would have granted Bacon his commission, if only to be rid of him, and permitted the burgesses to pass adequate reform measures in order to prevent a general uprising against the government. One colonist, describing the situation, said, "There is not a part of the country free from the infection. Never was there so great a madness as the people generally were seized with."

But Berkeley delayed granting Bacon's commission. When several members in the new House of Burgesses, predominantly hostile to Berkeley, declared they would endeavor to redress several grievances the country then labored under, he let it be known that they should meddle with nothing until the Indian business was finished, and warned the Burgesses against those "two rogues" Lawrence and Drummond.

Bacon was convinced that the burgesses would accomplish nothing. Since he believed his life to be in danger, he returned to Henrico where, as he claimed, the enraged people were shouting that unless Bacon received his commission they would tear down the town. Bacon's angry supporters urged him to go with them to force the governor to grant the commission. And so, it was reported, "the Raging Tummult came downe to Towne."

WHEN the burgesses learned that Bacon and his men were marching on Jamestown, they rushed through a series of reform measures, later to be known as Bacon's Laws, in a desperate, last-minute attempt to appease the aroused colonists. The most important of these measures extended the franchise to all freemen; gave the voters representation in the county courts in assessing taxes; declared that no man could hold more than one public office at one time; fixed the fees of sheriffs, collectors, and other officials; made it illegal for sheriffs to serve more than one year at a time; barred members of the Council from sitting on the county courts; and allowed these courts to appoint their own clerks.

Then on June 23 Bacon's motley band of perhaps 200-300 streamed into Jamestown. "Now tag, rag and bobtail carry a high hand," moaned one colonist. Drawing his "army" up in a double line before the State House, Bacon demanded his commission. At this point Berkeley rushed out and denounced Bacon as a traitor. Waving his arms wildly, he threw back his coat and shouted, "Here, shoot me, 'fore God, fair mark, shoot!" Taken aback by this dramatic gesture, Bacon replied that he did not intend to "hurt a haire of your honor's head," that he sought only a commission to fight "the heathen who daily unhumanely murder us and spill our brethren's blood." Then, in growing anger and frustration, he shouted, "God damne my blood, I came for a commission, and a commission I will have before I go."

The burgesses, crowded about the windows, drew back quickly when Bacon's men pointed their fusils at them and shouted, "We will have it! We will have it!" One frightened burgess shouted back, "For God's sake hold your hands; forbear a little and you shall have what you please."

BACON then entered the Long Room where the burgesses sat, and demanded they give him his commission. When they reminded him that only the governor could grant one, Bacon launched into an im-

passioned harangue that lasted for an hour. He demanded that the burgesses initiate measures to protect the people from the Indians, lower the exorbitant taxes, and redress the other grievances and calamities of their deplorable country. The burgesses replied that they had just enacted new measures to redress their grievances. Bacon was astounded. However, when both the burgesses and the governor asked him to satisfy his men by reading these new laws to them, Bacon refused, and again demanded his commission. Finally he yielded to the entreaties of the burgesses, whereupon the governor granted the commission, but with intense bitterness.

The next day Bacon and his men marched away to prepare for the Indian campaign. He found ready cooperation from the frontier people, who were impatient to get the job finished. Arms, ammunition, and stores were collected quickly, and officers appointed. By late July Bacon had a force of some 1,300 men. Then, just as he was ready to march, he suddenly received word that Berkeley had declared his commission illegal, on the ground that it had been issued under duress. The governor had again denounced Bacon and his men as rebels against the King's authority. Even now he was raising militia in Gloucester to march against them.

Bacon immediately changed his plans, electing to turn back and settle first his score with Berkeley. Here it would appear that Bacon made his first serious mistake—he overestimated the support Berkeley could muster, and his action irrevocably committed both him and his men to open rebellion against a Royal Governor. The report of the affair made later by a royal commission stated: "Now in vaine the Governor attempts raising a force against Bacon, and although the Industry and endeavors he used to effect it was great, yet at this Juncture it was impossible, for Bacon at this time was so much the hopes and Darling of the people that the Governor's interest prov'd but weake, and his Friends so very few that he grew sick of the Essay." Indeed, when Berkeley's men learned they were expected to fight Bacon they immediately deserted, and the governor and his friends were forced to flee for safety to Accomac on the Eastern Shore.

WITH the governor in exile and the Council dispersed, Bacon was now virtually in control of all of Virginia, with the sole exception of the Eastern Shore. Assisted by Drummond and Lawrence, he established his headquarters at Middle Plantation (now Williamsburg). Here he issued a proclamation declaring Berkeley and others in the Council traitors, and threatened to confiscate their estates unless they surrendered within four days. Then he arrogantly called a meeting of the leading planters who had not fled with Berkeley, and demanded that they take

1. THE NEW LAND

three oaths: That they accept his commission to fight the Indians as "lawfull and legally obtained"; that they arrest anyone trying to raise a force against him; and that they would oppose any English troops sent to Virginia until Bacon could plead his case to King Charles II in person. Little objection was voiced to the first two, but the last oath brought on a long and sharp debate. Fighting Indians was one thing; fighting British soldiers was another. But, as the royal commissioners later reported, "many by threats, Force and Feare were feigne to subscribe" to the oath. Bacon then issued a call for a newly elected House of Burgesses to meet later. At last, he marched against the Indians.

Before he left, however, he had a long conversation with a certain John Goode of Henrico, which revealed that Bacon was now thinking in terms of complete independence from England, not only for Virginia but for the other colonies as well. When he was informed that most of the leading citizens would join the redcoats, Bacon replied that he would prevent it.

"Sir, you speak as though you designed a total defection from his Majesty and our country."

"Why, have not many princes lost their dominions so?" Bacon asked, smiling.

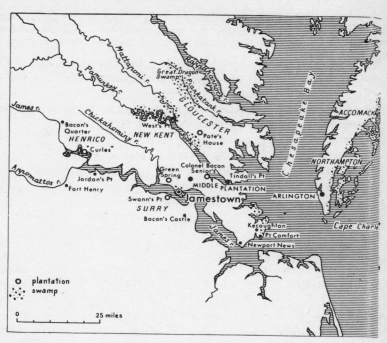

The general area of Bacon's Rebellion, 1676. This map is reprinted from "The Governor and the Rebel" by Wilcomb E. Washburn, published by University of North Carolina Press.

WHEN QUESTIONED about what he would do for supplies, Bacon replied: "For supply I know nothing this country will not be able to provide for itself, withal in a little time, save ammunition and iron, and I believe the King of France or States of Holland would either of them entertain a trade with us."

Goode then reminded him that "your followers do not think themselves engaged against the King's authority, but against the Indians."

"But I think otherwise," replied Bacon, "and am confident of it that it is the mind of this country, and of Maryland and Carolina also, to cast off their governors."

Surprisingly, this was essentially the same plan adopted by the colonies that brought independence just a hundred years later.

Leaving Middle Plantation, Bacon and his men then conducted an indecisive campaign against the Pamunkeys. Berkeley seized this absence as an opportunity to return by water and reoccupy Jamestown. When Bacon learned of this he turned his back on the Indians and again marched on Jamestown with about 200 tired, hungry men. When he found the narrow isthmus, which was the only approach to the town, defended by three heavy guns and the ships in the river, Bacon decided to lay a siege. All night long his men labored to build an entrenchment of trees, brush and earth across the isthmus for protection in case Berkeley sallied out. It also effectively bottled up Berkeley's force in the town.

ON SEPTEMBER 15 Berkeley's troops made a sally. They marched out, formed in front of the entrenchment, and rushed forward in a tight formation. Thus they made an excellent target, and when Bacon's men opened on them those in front threw away their arms and fled. Berkeley's "Accomackians, who, like scholers going to schol, went out with hevie harts but returned home with light heels." Completely disgusted, Berkeley again quit the town and sailed back to Accomac with his followers and most of the inhabitants.

Once more Bacon occupied Jamestown, but now he was uncertain what to do with it. Word reached him that a former supporter of his who had gone over to the governor was raising a force in the northern counties to attack him. If he stayed in Jamestown, he could be caught between the land force and Berkeley's ships in the river. But if he vacated it, Berkeley would undoubtedly return and use it as a base of operations against him. Consequently he decided to burn the town. Lawrence and Drummond applied the torch to their own homes to start the conflagration. They "burnt five houses of mine," Berkeley reported, "and twenty of other gentlemen." Nor did they spare the church, "the first that ever was in Virginia."

TURNING HIS BACK on the ruins, Bacon marched north to meet the new hostile force, which promptly disintegrated on his approach, most of the men being former indentured servants who had been

STRANGE NEWS

FROM

VIRGINIA;

Being a full and true

ACCOUNT

OF THE

LIFE and DEATH

OF

Nathanael Bacon Esquire,

Who was the only Cause and Original of all the late
Troubles in that COUNTRY.

With a full Relation of all the Accidents which have
happened in the late War there between the
Christians and Indians.

LONDON,
Printed for *William Harris*, next door to the Turn-
Stile without *Moor-gate*. 1677.

*The title page of "Strange News from Virginia." Reproduced
from "A History of the American People" by Woodrow Wilson.*

forced into service and had no desire to risk their
lives for the governor. Once again the rebels controlled all of Virginia except the Eastern Shore. Bacon
now "thought it not amiss, but worth his labor, to go
and see how the Accomackians were doing." But "before he could arrive at the perfection of his plans
providence did that which no other hand durst do."
He died unexpectedly of dysentery October 26, 1676.

With Bacon's sudden death and the news that
British troops were on the way, the rebellion collapsed. By the end of the year Berkeley again controlled the colony. The House of Burgesses repealed
most of Bacon's Laws and the governor launched a
vicious program of hanging all the rebel leaders he
could lay his hands on. Drummond, found hiding in
the Chickahominy Swamps, was brought before Berkeley. "Mr. Drummond, you are very welcome," said the
vindictive old man. "I am more glad to see you than
any man in Virginia. Mr. Drummond, you shall be
hanged in half an hour." Lawrence escaped into the
forest and was never heard from again. But more
than twenty others met their fate on the gallows.
Charles II, when he learned of this savagery, is said
to have remarked: "That old fool has hanged more
men in that naked country than I have for the murder
of my father."

Whatever else it may or may not have been, Bacon's
Rebellion was a landmark in the development of
self-government in Virginia. Bacon had been hot-
headed and impetuous, and his judgment was faulty
at times. Also his emotions may have carried him
further than he intended. But he did lead the first
armed uprising in Virginia, not only against the autocratic rule of a royal governor, but also against the
special privileges of the upper classes and the abusive
use of political power.

There was a lesson in this if only those in authority
had been willing to heed. The political relationship
between the Crown and the colonists in general was
evolving too haphazardly. The rebellion pointed up
the inability of the English constitution to provide
for intelligent government for the ever-increasing
number of Englishmen outside the realm. What
should have been a warning, however, was largely
ignored, and the only action taken by the lawmakers
was to strengthen the powers of the royal governors
at the expense of local government, a policy which
led inevitably to the Revolution a century later.

THe DeViL iN SaLeM

Hysteria or demonic possession? Whatever the case, Salem, Massachusetts endured in 1692 a gothic nightmare of fear that saw over 200 convicted of witchcraft, and sent twenty poor souls to meet their master, in Heaven or Hell.

Peggy Robbins

Peggy Robbins is a regular contributor to AHI. For more on Salem and witchcraft, she suggests: Chadwick Hansen, Witchcraft at Salem *(New York, 1969); George Lincoln Burr, ed.,* Narratives of the Witchcraft Cases: 1648-1706 *(New York, 1914): and Marion Starkey,* The Devil in Massachusetts *(New York, 1949).*

It is difficult for the modern mind to understand how the barbaric Massachusetts witch hunts of the late 17th century could have occurred in America, and it is easy to suppose that the shocking accounts of citizens sent to the gallows for the practice of witchcraft have been exaggerated in their telling and re-telling. But records reveal, with facts all too plain, that in Salem Village and its vicinity in 1692, alone, 170 "witches" were imprisoned, and twenty of them were put to death, nineteen on the gallows and one by being pressed under heavy weights until dead.

The Salem witch trials became the most celebrated of all witch hunts even though the number of people who suffered during the Salem hysteria was small in comparison with the thousands who were persecuted in Europe in such outbreaks during the late Middle Ages.

The Massachusetts Bay Colony, from its first settlement, was a likely place for belief in witchcraft as the means by which Satan, through the use of human beings, carried on his war against Heaven. The England from which the colonists emigrated had witnessed, during the decade prior to the 1620 landing at Plymouth, the trial of the Lancashire witches, with ten of the accused sent to the gallows. James I, King of England from 1603 to 1625, had written for the enlightenment of his subjects a treatise on witchcraft called *Demonologie* which served to increase the general fear of witches. Typical of the "investigations" James I reported was one having to do with the cause of tempests which beset his bride on her voyage from Denmark; he found that several hundred witches had taken to sea in a sieve from Leith and caused the storms.

New England in the 17th century was a religious community of fanatically rigid Calvinists. The unknown was categorized as evil and the Devil's power was reckoned to be as strong as God's. Massachusetts Bay settlers were largely Puritans who considered the Devil their particular, personal enemy; since their religion was the true one, it was the one Satan was most anxious to destroy. Doctors, judges, schoolmasters, and particularly ministers, as well as the less learned among the Puritans, were strong believers in witchcraft. Even the most minor occurence was attributed to witchery: if a farmer's cow failed to give milk, or his horse went lame, or his well dried up, it was a witch's doing; if a housewife couldn't get the butter to come, a witch was controlling the churning; if a horse's mane was found tangled, it had been knotted by a witch who had used it as a stirrup to mount for a stolen ride to a witches' Sabbath (a gathering at which witches got instructions from their master the Devil). The Puritan culture, with its strict, tedious, repressed way of life, in which even Christmas

From AMERICAN HISTORY ILLUSTRATED, December 1971. Reproduced through the courtesy of The National Historical

and Mardi Gras were labeled "pagan festivities" and fiercely forbidden, lent itself to the stimulating, unrestrained belief in witchcraft and monotony-breaking witch hunts.

The first recorded American witch hanging was in Boston in 1648. Little is known of the circumstances. In 1656, a quarrelsome Boston widow named Anne Hibbins who was "possessed of preternatural knowledge" was executed as a witch. In 1663, in Hartford, Connecticut, Rebecca Greensmith, who "confessed that she had familiarity with the Devil, which had frequent use of her body," and her husband Nathaniel were hanged; they had been arrested after being "called out against by a person esteemed pious while suffering a violent public fit." As the years passed, a few other accusations of witchcraft in New England resulted in the hanging of "the Devil's advocates."

Then, in 1688, in Boston, the four children of a sober, pious mason named John Goodwin began having strange fits. As the Reverend Cotton Mather, the highly esteemed young minister of Boston's Second Church, later described their symptoms in his *Memorable Providences* "Sometimes they would be deaf, sometimes dumb, and sometimes blind, and often all this at once. One while their tongues would be drawn down their throats; another while they would be pulled out upon their chins to prodigious length. They would have their mouths opened into such a wideness that their jaws went out of joint, and anon they would clap together again with a force like that of a strong spring-lock. The same would happen to their shoulder-blades, and their elbows, and hand-wrists. . . . They would make most piteous outcries that they were cut with knives, and struck with blows that they could not bear. . . . Their heads would be twisted almost around, . . . they would roar exceedingly. Thus they lay some weeks most pitiful spectacles."

The oldest Goodwin child, a teen-age girl, had had a quarrel over some laundry with a slovenly, vile-tongued Irish washerwoman named Glover, and the Goodwins' neighbors began to remember that "the late husband of Goodwife Glover said she was such a scandalous old woman she was undoubtedly a witch." ("Goodwife," often shortened to "Goody," and "Goodman" were much-used forms of address at this period.)

John Goodwin called in Cotton Mather and three other clergymen, who held a day of prayer and fasting in the Goodwin house. It wasn't the first time Mather had "wrestled with the Devil" in "a case of possession, when Satan had entered a human body and spoke through it." In his sermons — he called one "Discourse on Witchcraft" — he told of his bouts with the Devil, often quoting the evil one's exact words, and his congregation thought him a very brave man for personally battling Satan.

After the day with the ministers, the youngest Goodwin child recovered, but the other three continued to be "so seized by the Devil they could not look upon the Bible or the Catechism." Goodwin entered a complaint against Mrs. Glover with the magistrates, and she was arrested and brought to trial under the law making witchcraft a capital offense. She "gave a wretched account of herself," received the sentence of death, and was hanged as a witch.

The oldest Goodwin child continued to be "spelled, bewitched," and Cotton Mather, who was 26 at the time, took her into his home so that he might closely observe her as part of his study of witchcraft. Less than a year later he published his book on witchcraft in general and the Goodwin case in particular. It was a fast best-seller throughout Massachusetts.

At this time there lived in Boston a 36-year-old merchant, Samuel Parris. Parris had studied theology at Harvard but, before completing the course, left to become a trader in the West Indies. Upon returning to Massachusetts he tried a merchant's career, but was not successful in business. In 1689 he decided to return to the ministry; he was unable, however, to find an opening in Boston, where the churches wanted graduate theologians. Finally, late in 1689, Parris accepted a call to the little hamlet north of Boston called Salem Village, which could not afford a regular minister.

Mr. Parris' small library, when he moved with his family from Boston to Salem Village (now Danvers), included a copy of Cotton Mather's book about witchcraft, and Puritan children were encouraged to read everything written by both Cotton and his father, Increase Mather, the president of Harvard University. The latter in 1684 had written a book against witchcraft — against its practice and against permitting it to go unpunished, not against believing in it. It is quite probable that Parris' family, including the younger members, had witnessed the hanging of Goodwife Glover in Boston. Puritans didn't approve of children witnessing frivolous activity but sanctioned their attendance at such "corrective procedures" as hangings.

Preacher Parris' household in Salem Village in early 1692 included his withdrawn, meek wife; his gentle, obedient, 9-year-old daughter Elizabeth, called Betty, who was subject to sudden weeping spells; his

1. THE NEW LAND

11-year-old niece, Abigail Williams, a self-satisfied, restive child bold enough to engage in lusty talk about the Devil; and two slaves Parris had brought from Barbados — John, and his consort Tituba, both Carib Indians.

The aging Tituba was not an enthusiastic worker, but she liked taking care of the children, and she spent much of her time in the parsonage kitchen telling them stories of magic and showing them fortune-telling tricks, with both the slave and the children being careful that the Parrises knew nothing of their talk. Sometime during the cold, gloomy January of 1692, other girls, most of them older than Betty and Abigail, began joining Tituba and her two charges in the Parris kitchen. The young visitors had no trouble getting permission from their parents to visit the parsonage, and, if their elders were aware of the time they spent with Tituba, it must have been assumed the sessions were concerned with cooking and housework. Several of the older girls who worked as servants in Salem Village homes managed to slip by the parsonage for a few exciting moments while on errands.

Tituba's fortune-telling began with palm-reading and continued with involved, mysterious machinations by which the girls supposedly could divine the occupations of their future husbands, and the like. It was later divulged that the two slaves at one point, to break the spell of an unidentified witch, prepared a witch cake of rye meal mixed with the children's urine, baked it and fed it to a particular dog, the belief being that the dog was a "familiar," a messenger

Arresting a witch. Engraving from the painting by Howard Pyle, originally published in "Harper's Magazine" for July 1, 1883.

servant assigned to a witch by the Devil. Obviously, the secret experimentation with magic and superstition in the Parris kitchen was no light matter. There is little doubt that it was there, in the parsonage, that the girls' inherent Calvinist fears of the unknown were sparked into a flame, a flame that lit the stage for the terrible Salem witch hunts.

In February, Betty Parris and Abigail Williams began to have hysterical fits, behaving very much as the Goodwin children had four years earlier in Boston. Soon their friends were similarly affected. Ann Putnam, the daughter of the village's prosperous and highly respected Sergeant Thomas Putnam, a tense 12-year-old who had been one of the most determined of the delvers into the occult under Tituba, was the first to follow Betty and Abigail "into horrible bewitchment." There is indication that Ann's mother was the one adult who knew of Tituba's kitchen magic; one account claims Mrs. Putnam, a sickly woman troubled by dreams, sent Ann to Tituba for dream interpretation. Ann was joined in bewitchment by Mercy Lewis, the sly, untidy, 19-year-old maid servant in the Putnam household.

The Reverend Mr. Parris was baffled and distressed by the affliction of his daughter and niece. When

Tituba and the children. (Bryant's "Popular History of U.S.")

prayer and fasting failed to help them, he called in Salem Village's only doctor, William Griggs. The doctor watched the pair twisting and jerking and listened to their piercing gobberish; he pronounced sadly, "The evil hand is upon them," adding, it being the work of the Devil, that he was powerless to help them. Summoned by Sergeant Putnam to see Ann and Mercy, he repeated the diagnosis: The girls had been afflicted by witchcraft.

Word of this sped through Salem Village and by the next day others were having fits: 16-year-old Mary Walcott, a neighbor of the Parrises; 20-year-old Mary Warren, maidservant to John and Elizabeth Proctor; and 17-year-old Elizabeth Hubbard, niece of Mrs. Griggs, who lived and worked in the doctor's household. Other girls joined the number of afflicted as the days passed. All evidenced "possession" in the same general pattern, which included convulsions, contortions, hysterics, barking, periodic blindness, and complaints of being struck, cut, and bitten.

Today, nearly three centuries later, educated opinions are in complete disagreement as to whether these girls were "caught up in histrionics" and faking symptoms of madness or had actually become mentally ill. One chronicler of the Salem story says that, if Thomas Putnam and Samuel Parris had just given the girls in their households sound spankings, the witchcraft persecutions would never have taken place. Others insist this view makes the girls far more gifted at acting than could have possibly been the case; their behavior was not fraudulent but pathological. It is well to remember there is great witchcraft power in a society that believes in witchcraft.

As soon as the girls were pronounced bewitched, all Salem Village sought to know who the witches were. Under constant badgering, sick little Betty Parris sobbed out something about Tituba; the older girls finally admitted a little about her kitchen magic, and the first witch had been pinpointed. But the girls were uneasy that Tituba was being blamed, although the slave cleverly admitted everything, apparently instinctively aware that confessed witches, for whom there might be salvation, were seldom hanged. The afflicted ones cried that Tituba was not alone in practicing witchcraft and they named two other witches, Sarah Good and Sarah Osburn. Sarah Good was a shiftless, dirty, pipe-smoking tramp who wandered with her ragged children from door to door, begging, and who was suspected of stealing when turned away. Well-to-do Sarah Osburn had been considered respectable, but she was a cross, strange woman, and she had not been inside Samuel Parris' church in a year.

Four "yeomen of Salem Village in the County of Essex," one of whom was Thomas Putnam, appeared before the local magistrates and swore out warrants for the arrest of the three accused women on suspicion of witchcraft. Mrs. Osburn was in bed, ill, when arrested and had to be supported even to stand. They were taken to the nearest prison—there was none in Salem Village—and there they were examined for "witches teats from which Satan sucks blood" and "Devil's marks," accepted evidence of guilt. Tituba was found to have "Devils scars" but the examiners were undecided about the moles on the other two. The three were left in leg chains.

On March 1, 1692, a preliminary examination of the women was made in an improvised courtroom in the village church by magistrates Jonathan Corwin and John Hathorne (great-great-grandfather of Nathaniel, who added a "w" to his name), who had been sent from Salem Town, a much larger community a few miles from Salem Village. Neither of these men had any legal training. Professional lawyers were generally disregarded in the colony and at no time did attorneys figure in the proceedings nor did anyone suggest that an accused witch might have the right of counsel.

With the Reverend Mr. Parris assisting the magistrates, the accused were questioned before a throng that filled every inch of the meeting-house and included all the afflicted girls, who were lined up on the front bench. Both Sarah Good and Sarah Osburn claimed innocence — Mrs. Good defiantly, Mrs. Osburn weakly — but what they tried to say was lost in the screams and noisy movements of the girls, who accused them to their faces. Sarah Good's husband William testified that he had "been afraid she was a witch" and had seen "a strange tit or wart" on her body. Dorcas Good, Sarah's 5-year-old daughter, was encouraged to testify against her; the child declared that her mother had familiars: "three birds, one black, one yellow, and these birds hurt children and afflict people."

As the questioning of Tituba began, the girls became motionless and quiet, hanging on her every word —possibly terrified that she might reveal their part in the experimentation with forbidden magic and make them objects of suspicion.

But Tituba didn't incriminate any of them. She knew what the people of Salem Village wanted to hear, and she told it to them, picking up and enlarging upon each suggestion made by her questioners. Yes, she said, she'd been bidden by the Devil to serve him. Goody Osburn and Goody Good and some other unidentified women had hurt the little girls and Tituba had been made to hurt them, too, although she hadn't wanted to. And there was an evil man from Boston, tall and with white hair, who had a book with nine witch names in it, but she could not tell whose names they were because she could not read. Tituba had been made to see red cats and rats, and huge dogs and hogs, and to listen to them talk, and she had been forced to serve them. She had been to many witches' Sabbaths, flying through the sky with the man from Boston, a hog, two cats, and a yellow, woman-headed dog, the last of which was Goody Osburn's familiar. One of Sarah Good's familiars was a wolf and Tituba had seen Witch Good set the wolf on Elizabeth Hubbard.

Apparently enjoying the rapt attention of the crowd, over whom she was exercising a positive spell, the old slave confessed for three days. Of the small number who doubted the truth of her tale, only a few dared make even mild issue of it — and they were soon sorry. There was a general consensus that anyone expressing skepticism of witchcraft was hiding something and was a witch himself.

The slave John, during Tituba's testimony, succumbed to complete demoniac possession, having roaring fits before witnesses at Ingersoll's Inn across from the meeting-house — thus landing himself in the category of the victims rather than the guilty.

On March 7, the magistrates sent the three women, the first lot of history's "Salem witches," to Boston to be imprisoned until their trial. Two months later, Sarah Osburn died in prison. Sometime during that period, a tiny baby belonging to Sarah Good also died in prison; the records do not tell whether it was born prior to, or during, Mrs. Good's imprisonment.

The jailing of the three witches did not ease the girls' affliction nor lighten their fits. In addition, several married women, including Ann Putnam's mother, began having hysterical seizures. Led by Ann Putnam and Abigail Williams, the afflicted cried out periodically against others of Salem Village: farm woman Martha Corey, who had laughed at the girls' antics as "put-ons"; 71-year-old, deeply pious Rebecca Nurse, whose family had been in a prolonged quarrel with Samuel Parris over a land boundary; little Dorcas Good, who, the girls said, had bitten them; Elizabeth and John Proctor, after John had punished the Proctors' maidservant, Mary Warren, for crying out against Rebecca Nurse; Bridget Bishop, who operated a tavern with a bad reputation; Abigail Hobbs, who "lived like a gypsy"; 80-year-old Giles Corey, Martha's husband; the Reverend George Burroughs, a former minister at Salem, who once bested Ann Putnam's uncle in a lawsuit; and many others. At each examination there were witnesses who testified the accused one was "queer" or "practiseth tricks" or the like, and in each case the girls went into fits. As an example, while

Mrs. Corey was before the magistrates, Abigail Williams jumped up, pointed to the rafter overhead, and screamed, "Suffer to look! There sits Goody Corey on the beam suckling a yellow bird betwixt her fingers!"

In April, Hathorne and Corwin were joined in conducting the examinations by four additional magistrates, including Samuel Sewall of Boston and Thomas Danforth, the colony's deputy governor, who served as presiding magistrate. But this resulted in little change in the examining procedure.

At the examination of Elizabeth and John Proctor, Ann Putnam threw herself on the floor and pleaded pathetically that they be made to stop tormenting her. Judge Sewall wrote in his diary, after referring to this scene, " 'Twas awful to see how the afflicted persons were agitated." Then, later, he added in the margin, as if remorsefully, "Alas, alas, alas!"

Cotton Mather wrote on witchcraft and "wrestled with the Devil." He lived to regret his approval of the Salem witch trials. (Reproduced from "Harper's New Monthly Magazine.")

Captain Alden denounced. (Bryant's "Popular History of U.S.")

The arrest of 70-year-old John Alden, son of Priscilla and John, as Tituba's "tall man from Boston," added to the excitment in Salem. After fifteen weeks in prison, John Alden managed to escape; he stayed far away until the witch hysteria subsided.

During May 1692, the witch hunts were extended to the villages surrounding Salem, and the jails in all of them grew full. The prisoners, from little Dorcas Good to the several aged and infirm, were forced to exist under such conditions that they grew thin and dirty, with wild, matted hair and sullen eyes — they looked like witches!

There had been no formal trials because there was no legally constituted court to try them. But Sir Wil-

liam Phips, the new royal governor, had arrived in Boston on May 14, and he issued a commission for a Court of Oyer and Terminer to be held in Salem Town, appointing the judges on May 27. The seven judges included Samuel Sewall and three others from Boston, John Richards, William Sergeant, and Wait Winthrop; Bartholomew Gedney from Salem; Nathaniel Saltonstall from Haverhill; and the new deputy governor, William Stoughton, the presiding justice, from Dorchester.

The court opened in the solidly packed courthouse in Salem Town on the morning of June 2, with Bridget Bishop the first to face the judges — and the assembled afflicted girls. Witnesses testified the tavernkeeper, filthy now in the red dress once considered offensively flashy, had a "preternatural teat" on her body and that she had wrought mischief upon her neighbors even as her "disembodied shape" had tormented the girls. She was sentenced to be "hanged by the neck until dead" on the tenth of June, and on that day the sheriff took her in a cart to Salem's Gallow's Hill and so hanged her.

The procedure in the Bishop trial, as well as future trials, was little different from the preliminary examinations: in general, convictions were obtained on the old evidence and the continuing afflictions of the girls. There was a jury, but the judges, and particularly the merciless Chief Justice Stoughton, were all-supreme. Cotton Mather, in his account of the Bishop trial, said, "There was little occasion to prove the witchcraft, it being evident and notorious to all beholders."

A heavily controlling feature in convicting the "witches" was the fact that the Court of Oyer and Terminer had decided to accept "spectral evidence," testimony that an accused had appeared as a "shape" or apparition of some sort rather than her recognizable bodily person, just as had been done in the preliminary examinations. Much of the evidence against all the accused was spectral evidence.

Before the second session of the court, Judge Saltonstall, who was troubled about the kind of evidence being accepted, resigned from the court. Although he did so quietly, his reason must have been suspected because some of the afflicted girls promptly claimed to have been tormented by his "shape," which acted mysteriously. Saltonstall hurried to Haverhill, far removed from the witchcraft scene, and stayed there, but he took to drinking heavily — so heavily that Samuel Sewall, hearing about it, wrote him reprovingly. His place on the court was filled by Jonathan Corwin, who had helped hold the first examinations and voiced no complaint about the acceptance of spectral evidence.

When the second court session ended on June 30, all five who had been tried — Sarah Good, Rebecca Nurse, Susanna Martin, Elizabeth Howe, Sarah Wildes — had been condemned to die on July 19. At the gallows that day, the Reverend Nicholas Noyes told Sarah Good she would do well to confess because she knew she was a witch. Her reply was loud enough for all the crowd on Gallows Hill to hear, "You are a liar! I am no more a witch than you are a wizard, and if you take away my life God will give you blood to drink!" Tradition has it that, many years later, Noyes choked to death on his own blood.

The third court session, on August 5, again condemned all who were tried — John and Elizabeth Proctor, John Willard, George Jacobs, Martha Carrier, and George Burroughs — but Elizabeth Proctor, pregnant, was given a stay of execution until after the baby's birth. The other five made the trip to Gallows Hill on August 19. Burroughs, speaking from the scaffold ladder, repeated the Lord's Prayer, which no servant of Satan was supposed to be able to do, but it didn't save him.

Cotton Mather, present at the hanging, was having ever stronger doubts about accepting spectral evidence. He had earlier written Judge John Richards, "Do not lay more stress upon pure Spectre evidence than it will bear — It is very certain that the Devills have sometimes represented the shapes of persons not only innocent, but also very vertuous."

On September 9, the court condemned six witches, and on September 17, nine more. Of these fifteen, eight whom preacher Noyes called "firebrands of Hell" were hanged on September 22 — Martha Corey, Mary Easty, Alice Parker, Ann Pudeator, Margaret Scott, Wilmot Reed, Samuel Wardwell, and Mary Parker. One of the others escaped, one was pregnant, and five confessed in time to be reprieved. Some fifty-

MORE
WONDERS
OF THE
INVISIBLE WORLD:
Or, The Wonders of the
Invisible World,
Display'd in Five Parts.

Part I. An Account of the Sufferings of *Margaret Rule*, Written by the Reverend Mr. *C. M.*
P. II. Several Letters to the Author, &c. And his Reply relating to Witchcraft.
P. III. The Differences between the Inhabitants of *Salem*-Village, and Mr. *Parris* their Minister, in *New-England.*
P. IV. Letters of a Gentleman uninterested, Endeavouring to prove the received Opinions about Witchcraft to be Orthodox. With short Essays to their Answers.
P. V. A short Historical Account of Matters of Fact in that Affair.

To which is added, A Postscript relating to a Book intitled, The *Life of Sir* WILLIAM PHIPS.

Collected by *Robert Calef*, Merchant, of *Boston* in *New-England.*

Licensed and Entred according to Order.

LONDON:
Printed for *Nath. Hillar*, at the *Princes-Arms*, in *Leaden-Hall-street*, over against St. *Mary-Ax*, and *Joseph Collyer*, at the *Golden-Bible*, on *London-Bridge.* 1700.

Title page of Robert Calef "More Wonders of the Invisible World" published in London in 1700. (Rare Book Division, The New York Public Library, Astor, Lenox and Tilden Foundation.)

The Witch House, Salem, Mass. was built in 1642 and was the home of Judge Jonathan Corwin. It was here that Judge Corwin presided over the preliminary examinations of those accused of witchcraft in 1692. In 1945 the Witch House was purchased by Historic Salem, Inc., and its restoration was financed by Historic Salem, Inc. and by the City of Salem. Ownership of the Witch House was transferred in 1948 to the City of Salem. (Photograph by Markham W. Sexton)

five of those who had confessed earlier, including Tituba, had not been scheduled for trial but were still in prison with those protesting innocence.

Giles Corey was also brought before the court on September 17. When asked how he pleaded, he refused to utter a word. Under law, a man who "stood mute" could not be tried; he could, however, be subjected to peine forte et dure — tortured. Corey was taken to a public lot and laid on the ground, and heavy stones were piled on his chest. With each addi-

tion of more weight, he was coaxed to answer to his indictment. He moaned, but said not a word. It took Giles Corey two terrible days to die.

Corey's dramatic protest against witch hunting, added to the uneasiness about accepting spectral evidence which had been steadily building, particularly since the execution of the Reverend Mr. Burroughs, began to still the witchcraft hysteria. Lady Phips, the governor's wife, publicly stated the witchcraft trials were a disgrace to the colony. Then the girls cried out against her, and Sir William, furious, called a halt to the court sessions. On October 29, 1692, he issued an order dissolving the Special Court of Oyer and Terminer.

But there was still the problem of the accused who were in jail and who, by law, had to be tried — some

140; an undetermined number had died in jail. Governor Phips appointed another court which began meeting in Salem in January 1693; it did not admit spectral evidence and, in a series of trials, found no one guilty. In May, Sir William, disgusted with the whole affair, issued a proclamation releasing all accused witches from jail. His action brought loud protest from some of the Puritan ministers, but it ended the Salem witch hunts. Twenty had been put to death, others had died of ill treatment, and many, like little Dorcas Good, had minds and bodies permanently injured by their ordeals. The property of all the accused had been seized at the time of their arrest and few of the victims were able to recover anything.

Parris, who was held responsible by many for the Devil's work in Salem, was ousted from the Salem Village church; he and his family afterward wandered from one small parish to another.

In 1696, a document signed by twelve of the men who had served as jurors in some of the witchcraft cases was presented to the public. It concluded, "We do therefore hereby signify to all in general, and to the surviving sufferers in special, our deep sense of, and sorrow for, our errors, in acting on such evidence to the condemning of any person; and do hereby declare that we justly fear that we were sadly deluded and mistaken. . . . We do heartily ask forgiveness of you all. . . ."

On January 14, 1697, which had been declared a day of prayer and fasting in repentance of sins in the whole of Massachusetts Bay, Samuel Sewall publicly acknowledged personal guilt for his actions as a judge of the witchcraft trials and asked for the forgiveness of God and man. He stood before the congregation of Boston's Third Church while the minister read his statement of deep repentance. But he did not stop there; during his long life, on the anniversary of the fast day, he did penance. As late as 1720, after reading a passage in a New England history about the Salem trials, he wrote in his diary, "The good and gracious God be pleased to save New England and me and my family!" With the exception of Nathaniel Saltonstall, who had early run from the Salem court, Sewall was the only judge at the trials who admitted error.

Of the afflicted girls, Ann Putnam was the only one to express remorse for her actions, so far as is known. In August 1706, Ann, a semi-invalid who was only 26 but who looked much older and had less than ten years of life remaining, "made public confession." Head bowed, she stood in the Salem Village church while the minister read the long confession she had written. She claimed to have acted "not out of anger, malice or ill will," but because of being deluded by Satan. Her confession ended, "I desire to lie in the dust and earnestly beg forgiveness of God and from all those whom I have given just cause of sorrow and offense, whose relatives were taken away and accused."

On January 15, 1697, the day after the Massachusetts fast day, Cotton Mather wrote in his diary that he had been "afflicted last night with discouraging thoughts, as if unavoidable marks of the Divine Displeasure must overtake my family for my not appearing with vigor enough to stop the proceedings of the judges when the inextricable storm from the invisible world assaulted the country. . . ." The Puritans had not reversed their position as to belief in witchcraft; they had just rejected spectral evidence as a means for catching witches.

Battling the Red Death

By introducing inoculations, a Boston minister and his surgeon friend at first were scorned as town menaces but were hailed later as saviors against the dreaded disease, smallpox.

Mary Musser

Mary Musser, a resident of Reading, Pennsylvania, is a writer, teacher, and a published poet. Among sources used in her writing of this article were: A Destroying Angel: The Conquest of Smallpox in Colonial Boston *(1974), by Ola Elizabeth Winslow and* History of Medicine in the United States *(1973), by Francis R. Packard.*

For centuries the Red Death, its beginnings hidden in antiquity, had swept over Asia and Africa and then to Europe, leaving millions dead and many more blinded or brutally scarred. In India the smallpox goddess, an upraised dagger in each hand, was flanked by executioners with red grinning masks and naked scimitars. Her reign was long and gruesome.

In the long fight against this deadly foe, the first effective counterattack came from an unlikely quarter — the fledgling society of colonial America. Boylston Street signs in downtown Boston remind us that Dr. Zabdiel Boylston, prodded by the Reverend Cotton Mather, risked his reputation and his practice when he introduced inoculation against smallpox in 1721.

Prior to Boylston, early folk doctors found that matter from the pustule of a victim, rubbed into a cut in the skin of a healthy person, often produced a mild form of the disease that conferred future immunity.

At least by 1000 A.D. the Chinese were sporadically using such "variolation" (from the Latin for smallpox — *variola*) in a different way. They poked powder made from dried pustules into the nostrils of persons to be immunized.

Still, when smallpox (as distinguished from the "great pox" — syphilis) reached epidemic proportions in Europe, it carried off defenseless victims by the tens of thousands. Although a few folk doctors used variolation, the practice was hardly known in the European medical profession before the 1700's.

Then a British-educated physician in Constantinople, Emanuel Timonius, observed that "old Greek women" were successfully preventing smallpox, variolating by arm and leg incisions. He described their procedure to a member of the Royal Society in London, and his letter was published in the Society's *Philosophical Transactions* in 1714. Two years later the *Transactions* carried an account by Jacob Pylarinus, Venetian consul at Smyrna, detailing a similar practice there. The London physicians were cautious. They talked it over, but took no action.

In Boston, meanwhile, the Reverend Cotton Mather, long interested in medicine, was studying the Timonius account. He already knew about variolation from his African servant Onesimus, who bore an inoculation scar on his arm and said that the "operation" was common among his people, the Guaramantese.

With some impatience, Mather wrote to Dr. John Woodward in London: "How does it come to pass that no more is done to bring this operation, into experiment & into Fashion in England? . . . I beseech you, sir, to move it. For my own part, if I should live to see the Small-Pox again enter our City I would immediately procure a Consult of our Physicians."

But the London physicians still held back. Then in the spring of 1721 Lady Mary Wortley Montagu, wife of the British ambassador returned from Constantinople, initiated action.

Smallpox had killed Lady Montagu's brother and marred her own youthful beauty, leaving her with a pitted face and no eyelashes. Anxious to protect her children from its ravages, she had had a Greek woman in Constantinople inoculate her son in the presence of her

From *American History Illustrated*, November 1977. Reproduced through the courtesy of The National Historical Society, publishers of *American History Illustrated*, P.O. Box 1831, Harrisburg, PA 17105.

own British physician, Dr. Maitland. Now back in London, she persuaded Dr. Maitland to do the same for her small daughter, and she publicized her move.

After further inoculations had been given successfully to half a dozen convicted criminals, promised freedom in return for serving as guinea pigs, and to a group of orphans who had no parents to object, Princess Caroline had the royal grandchildren Amelia and Caroline inoculated with similarly favorable results. Inoculation suddenly came into favor. Then two inoculated persons died, and the practice came to an abrupt halt.

In the meantime, even as Lady Montagu was taking action in London, Cotton Mather in Boston found that smallpox had indeed entered his city. It was by no means an unfamiliar visitor: In 1630 John Winthrop's fleet had carried a child dying from smallpox en route to Boston. Mather himself caught it in the 1678 epidemic, and so did three of his children in its 1702 appearance.

Even earlier, smallpox had taken a fearful toll of the Indians in America, a highly susceptible group. Brought first on Spanish ships, then by colonists to the Atlantic coastal settlements, it nearly eradicated entire Indian nations. The Pemlicos near Charleston, South Carolina were reported to have been completely destroyed. In New York, "The Small Pox desolates them [the Iroquois] to such a degree that they think . . . only of bewailing the dead, of whom there is already an immense number." Meanwhile, "Indeans (on the Coneighticut River) dye like rotten sheep."

Some colonists looked on these losses as a sign of divine Providence. "God ended the [boundary] controversy by sending the smallpox among the Indians of Sangust, who were before that time exceedingly numerous." Often, though, God's pestilential rain fell quite impartially as settlers and Indians carried the disease back and forth.

There was also another source of infection: Slave ships from Africa brought it to plantations like that of William Byrd in Virginia. "The Small pox . . . was brought into my family by the Negro's I recd from Gambo . . . poor Mrs. Brodnax and 3 of my Negros are allready dead & about fifteen more besides my little daughter have them."

When smallpox hit a colonial town, protective reactions came into play. Instinctively, many residents fled to the countryside, some unwittingly carrying infection with them. Others tried preventatives. In a Charleston epidemic, drinking tar water was highly recommended. Barrels of it were sold at exorbitant prices until the promoter of the rumor himself died of smallpox.

Massachusetts Governor Winthrop received a London doctor's recipe for "My black powder against ye plague, small pox . . . In the Month of March take Toades, as many as you will, alive; putt them into a Earthern pott, so it will be half full; Cover it . . . putt charcoales round about . . . and lett it burne out . . .

When it is cold, take out the toades; and . . . pound them very well. . . . Of this [powder] you may give a dragme. . . . For prevention, half a dragme will suffice. . . . There is no danger in it."

Cotton Mather thought he had a better idea.

A Harvard College student by age 12, Mather had found that a speech impediment threatened his aspiration to be a minister. He therefore added a second interest — reading medical literature. It was not an unusual combination. Many of the early colonial clergymen had "read" medicine, and not a few of them practiced it.

As it turned out, Mather overcame his speech difficulty and became pastor of Boston's Second Church, but he kept up with medical progress by his reading, and by a correspondence with members of the Royal Society in London. Although he did not actually practice medicine, except for treating his family and a few friends, he freely expressed opinions on medical matters. Swallowing bullets to cure "the Twisting of the Guts," he thought, was too dangerous a practice. As for tobacco, he suspected that "the caustick Salt in the Smoke may lay Foundations for Diseases in Millions of unadvised people."

Thus, when the ship *Seahorse* brought smallpox from the West Indies to Boston in the spring of 1721, Mather was ready. First, "Because of the destroying Angel standing over the Town," he called on the ministers to lead a day of prayer. Then to the physicians of Boston (ten or twelve in number), he wrote a letter explaining why he felt they should consider inoculation. Of course, it should be "warily proceeded in, under the management, of a Skilful Physician." He recommended that they hold a consultation on the matter.

No such consultation took place. The epidemic worsened until the town officials gave up trying to stop it. They removed the guards from infected houses flying their red cloth warnings and allowed people to go in and out as they wished. Hundreds of refugees fled the city. Business was down. Shops closed. Daily the death toll rose.

Rebuffed in his efforts to get joint action, Mather appealed to his personal friend, Dr. Zabdiel Boylston, an established Boston surgeon. Within two days, Boylston had inoculated his 6-year-old son Thomas, his slave Jack, and the slave's 2½-year-old son.

The town was aghast. That a reputable doctor should deliberately *give* this horrible disease to his own flesh and blood — many people found it shocking beyond belief.

The town's other physicians were almost solidly opposed to Boylston's move. Inoculation was far too risky, they claimed. It could result in complications or in death. It did not always give immunity, and it would only spread the disease still faster.

Chief spokesman for this opposition was Dr. William Douglass, whose prestige was buttressed by a European medical degree. (Most of the other doctors, like Boylston, had been trained by the apprentice system.) Douglass had read of the Turkish inoculations — he had in fact

AN

Hiſtorical ACCOUNT

OF THE

SMALL-POX

INOCULATED

IN

NEW ENGLAND,

Upon all Sorts of Perſons, *Whites, Blacks,* and of all Ages and Conſtitutions.

With ſome Account of the Nature of the Infection in the NATURAL and INOCULATED Way, and their different Effects on HUMAN BODIES.

With ſome ſhort DIRECTIONS to the UN-EXPERIENCED in this Method of Practice.

Humbly dedicated to her Royal Highneſs the Princeſs of WALES, By *Zabdiel Boylston*, F. R. S.

The Second Edition, Corrected.

LONDON:

Printed for S. CHANDLER, at the Croſs-Keys in the *Poultry*. M. DCC. XXVI.

Re-Printed at *BOSTON* in *N. E.* ſor S. GERRISH in *Cornhil*, and T. HANCOCK at the Bible and Three Crowns in *Annſtreet*. M. DCC. XXX.

Title page of Boylston's treatise on smallpox (1726). (Boston Medical Library and The Countway Library, Boston)

lent such material to Mather—but he was not convinced.

"A certain Cutter for the Stone," he wrote disparagingly of Boylston in a letter to the Boston *News-Letter*, "being illiterate [presumably Boylston could not read Latin and Greek] was not capable of duely understanding the writings of those Foreign Gentlemen [Timonius and Pylarinus]." He went on to accuse Boylston of carelessness in treating his patients, and of rashly spreading the infection around town by failing to isolate them.

Led by Mather, six of Boston's prominent clergymen entered the lists on the side of Boylston. "It was a grief to us . . . to see Dr. Boylston treated so unhandsomely . . . we heartily wish than Men would treat one another with decency and charity. . . ." they wrote to the Boston *Gazette.*

Encouraged by this support and by the success of his experiments, Boylston proceeded with his inoculations in the teeth of admonitions from the town's selectmen to refrain. It can hardly be denied that some of his "inocu-

lees," receiving visitors and going about, did indeed spread the infection. People only mildly ill from inoculation themselves could transmit smallpox to others, who might die of it.

However, rumors of horrible results from the inoculations themselves were wildly exaggerated. Just the same, they were widely believed. Accusations and rebuttals flew back and forth in broadsides, pamphlets, and letters to the newspapers.

The popular feeling against inoculation was heightened by a fear that it would imperil not only the body, but the immortal soul. Since God had sent disease into the world as a result of man's sin—

Our healthful days are at an end,
And sicknesses come on
From year to year because our hearts
Away from God are gone

—was it not then disobeying the divine will if one tried to escape smallpox by inoculation? At the least, it showed less trust in God than in the "Machinations of Men."

Not so, responded Mather and his supporters. God had mercifully provided inoculation, as he had provided other ways to save lives by medical treatment.

Boylston and Mather were taking most of the heat generated by the anti-inoculation forces. Boylston found himself vilified as a town menace. Some people even suggested that if any of his inoculated patients died, he should be hanged for murder. Feelings against Mather also ran high, even within his own congregation. "This abominable Town," he wrote in his diary, "treats me in a most malicious and murderous Manner. . . . The People . . . rave, they rail, they blaspheme."

Mather was facing a hard decision in his own family. "What shall I do? what shall I do with regard unto Sammy?" His son Sammy was home from Harvard (closed by the epidemic), begging for inoculation to "save his life." With the public wrath already focused on him, Mather feared that if the procedure miscarried, not only would he lose his son, but his position in the community would become insupportable.

The day Sammy's college roommate died of smallpox, Mather finally had his son inoculated, but secretly, on Grandfather Increase Mather's advice. Whether from the inoculation, or from a previous "natural" exposure, Sammy's reaction was so severe that for several days his life hung by a thread, but he pulled through.

As the epidemic moved toward its peak, emotions boiled over. One night at 3 a.m. a "granado" sailed through Mather's bedroom window. The perpetrator, a disgruntled parishioner, was unaware that Mather had turned over the room to his nephew, Thomas Walter, recuperating there from his inoculation. Fortunately for Walter, the projectile's lighted fuse was torn loose on the window casement and the bomb did not go off. Attached to it was a note: "COTTON MATHER . . . you Dog . . . Damn You, I will Enoculate You with this, with a Pox to you."

A Brief Rule to guide the Common People of *New-England* how to Order themfelves and theirs in the *Small-Pox* and *Meafels*.

THE *Small Pox* (whofe nature and cure the *Meafels* follow) is a difeafe in the blood, endeavouring to recover a new form and ftate.

2. tHIS nature attempts — 1. By Separation of the impure from the pure, thrufting it out from the Veins to the Flefh.— 2. By driving out the impure from the Flefh to the Skin.

3. THE firft Separation is done in the firft four Days by a Feverifh boiling, Ebullition) of the Blood, laying down the impurities in the Flefhy parts which kindly effected the Feverifh tumuit is calmed.

4. THE fecond Separation from the Flefh to the Skin, or *Superficies* is done through the reft of the time of the difeafe,

5. THERE are feveral Errors in ordering thefe fick ones in both thefe Opera-

Brief rule to guide the "common people" of New England, 1721.
(National Library of Medicine)

Noting that certain persons around town not only applauded this action but were encouraging a second try, Mather declared himself prepared: "I am filled with unutterable Joy at the Prospect of my approaching Martyrdom." His joy was premature; no second "granado" arrived.

While the controversy raged, Boylston pushed ahead with his inoculations. After a time, two other physicians followed his example. Further support began to come from some highly placed persons seeking protection for themselves or their families. Boylston's patients included Judge Samuel Sewall's grandson, Judge Josiah Quincy's son, two Harvard faculty members, and a number of Harvard students.

By the following spring the epidemic had spent itself. A tally showed that of nearly 6,000 smallpox cases caught in the "natural" way, 844—about one in seven—resulted in death. Of 280 inoculated persons, only six—one in forty-seven—had died.

Even Douglass came to a grudging acceptance. "How mean or rash soever the beginning of the Practice of Inoculating the Small Pox may have been . . . nevertheless if . . . it prove useful, it ought to be embraced."

Boylston was invited to England by the Royal Society, elected to its membership, and encouraged in publishing his findings.

Cotton Mather could look with satisfaction on the vindication of his controversial idea. Variolation was now recognized as highly effective in reducing the mortality rate during an epidemic.

Its use spread rapidly. Philadelphia began it in 1730 and New York the following year. During the 1738 epidemic in Charleston one doctor alone was said to have inoculated 450 persons. Encouraged by the American experience, London physicians resumed the practice, and by mid-century it was spreading over the continent.

However, had Mather lived on, he would have seen that this breakthrough was not a final victory. Many physicians and lay people retained serious misgivings about variolation. Although it usually produced only a relatively mild case of smallpox, this was nevertheless the real thing, and no one could accurately predict the severity of a particular reaction. When Abigail Adams had herself and her four children inoculated, daughter Nabby broke out all over. "Nabby . . . [has] not a spot but what is so soar that she can neither walk sit stand or lay with any comfort . . . 6 or 7 hundred boils are no agreable feeling."

Nor could one brush aside the risk of a fatal outcome. Jonathan Edwards had himself inoculated by the renowned Dr. William Shippen of Philadelphia immediately after becoming president of New Jersey College (Princeton), but within a few weeks he was dead. A massive eruption of pox in the mouth and throat had prevented him from swallowing.

To inoculate or not could have been a life-or-death decision. Benjamin Franklin, though a strong advocate of the practice, withheld it from his 4-year-old son Francis because the boy was weak from a "flux." Then Francis contracted smallpox and died. Years later Franklin said, "I still regret that I had not given it to him by inoculation."

Then there was the high probability that variolation would spread the disease. Frequently the civil authorities would forbid it until there was no containing an epidemic by quarantine. Some towns set up special hospitals where it could be done under proper restrictions, but since this usually involved paying a fee and losing a month's work, relatively few people availed themselves of it until they were actually faced with an epidemic.

Thus, although inoculation had been proven effective in reducing the death toll, many people remained unprotected against smallpox, and throughout the 1700's it kept recurring. However, at the onset of an epidemic most of those threatened would quickly "take" it by inoculation.

1. THE NEW LAND

Just as the scourge seemed to have come under some measure of control, the Revolutionary War brought a fresh outbreak. In the army were many vulnerable soldiers, especially those from rural areas. "Our Misfortunes in Canada," wrote John Adams to Abigail in 1776, "are enough to melt an Heart of Stone. The Small Pox is ten times more terrible than Britons, Canadians and Indians together." "Nearly one-half our Army [in Canada] are sick, mostly with the smallpox," and the men are "daily dropping off," reported the generals.

General Washington, himself immune to smallpox after an attack at 19, took decisive steps to stem its ravages. When the army encampment at Morristown became a pesthole, he ordered compulsory inoculation for the troops and all arriving recruits, thus preventing the decimation of his forces.

Meanwhile, across the Atlantic in Dorset, England Dr. Edward Jenner was trying out cowpox lymph to immunize against smallpox. Vaccination, he called it, from *vaccinae* — "of the cow." In twenty-three successful experiments he found it superior to variolation. It was neither fatal nor disfiguring, it protected against smallpox, and a person thus vaccinated could not transmit smallpox to another.

When Jenner published his findings in 1798 he ran into a storm of criticism. Opponents declared the cowpox vaccine ineffective. To inject matter from beasts into humans, they argued, was contrary to the ways of God and would mean the deterioration of the human race. Popular rumor even had it that people who underwent vaccination would sprout horns and begin to "moo."

However, Jenner's method proved its superiority and it soon supplanted variolation. In Boston, Dr. Benjamin Waterhouse vaccinated his 5-year-old son Daniel in the summer of 1800 and, along with other physicians, became an ardent advocate of the new method. Thanks to its continued use, the United States was free of smallpox by 1949.

The Trial of Peter Zenger

PEGGY ROBBINS

The 1735 trial in New York City of a German immigrant accused of seditious libel was both the first great step toward freedom of the press in America and the first successful New World application of the philosophy that truth must be accepted as a defense against the accusation of libel.

The defendant, 38-year-old John Peter Zenger, a printer who could not even write good English and who did not even testify at his own trial, was not a shining hero when it was over. He was not even present at the gala victory dinner the evening after his acquittal: Although technically free, he had been taken back to his jail cell to await the payment of funds to cover his keep during the nearly nine months he had been in custody; his wealthy associates made payment the next day. But Zenger's sacrifices and extraordinary courage and determination were vital forces without which the power of a tyrannical British governor could not have been successfully challenged—certainly not four decades before the Declaration of Independence. "The trial of Zenger in 1735," wrote late 18th-century statesman Gouverneur Morris, "was the germ of American freedom, the morning star of that liberty which subsequently revolutionized America."

Peter Zenger came to the New World from the war-torn Rhenish Palatinate with his family in 1710, when he was 13. His mother Hannah was a widow when she arrived in New York with Peter and two smaller children, and it is believed his father was one of the many who had died of typhus during the voyage. Peter was apprenticed to William Bradford, the only printer in New York in 1710, by a legal agreement signed by his mother. Bradford printed almanacs, official reports and speeches, and paper money for the government.

In 1718, when Peter's indenture ended, he traveled through the colonies as a journeyman printer. In Philadelphia he married Mary White and had a son, John Zenger. He moved his family to Maryland, and there was given the task of printing the Colony's laws, assembly proceedings, and other official documents. After Mary's death he moved to New York City, married a Dutch girl named Anna Catherine Maulin, and took root permanently.

Peter Zenger joined William Bradford in a partnership in 1725, the same year Bradford started New York's first newspaper, the *Gazette*, a publication devoted to government notices, government accomplishments, government opinion, and news from England. It was highly approved by the royal officials of the British colony of New York, who frowned on criticism of their corrupt practices.

After a year Zenger dissolved his partnership with Bradford and set up a printing shop of his own. Now, with few profitable jobs, he had difficulty supporting his growing family—he and Anna had three children by 1728, in addition to his son John (and three more were to be added to the family by 1738). To supplement his income he played the organ at the Old Dutch Church for twelve pounds a year. The struggling printer had no idea in the early days of 1732 that he would be swept into a bitter controversy and eventually end up in jail.

Of the Crown appointees who served as governors of New York during the colonial period, some were thoroughly corrupt; greedy, autocratic William S. Cosby, who appeared on the scene in August 1732, was among the worst. Cosby had previously been governor of the Mediterranean island of Minorca, where he had appropriated revenues, confiscated property for his private use, and falsified records until angry Minorcans had forced his recall. Although appointed to fill the vacancy left by the death of New York's Governor John Montgomerie in 1731, Cosby had spent thirteen months between his appointment and his departure for the New World living lavishly in Europe, enjoying the proceeds of his sojourn in Minorca. The colonists knew nothing of this, and they had no idea that he assumed the active governorship of New York with the intention of wringing money from them to replace his squandered funds.

Governor Cosby bullied the New York Assembly into awarding him a gift of 1,000 pounds for his alleged efforts in London to secure repeal of British legislation detrimental to colonial sugar interests. Then he demanded half the wages the assembly had paid honest, hard-working Rip Van Dam, who had served as acting governor from Montgomerie's death until Cosby's arrival. Van Dam refused to turn over the money, Cosby tried to collect it through legal action, and the resulting controversy started the series of events which ended in the Peter Zenger trial.

From *American History Illustrated*, December 1976. Reproduced through the courtesy of The National Historical Society publishers of *American History Illustrated*, P.O. Box 1831, Harrisburg, PA 17105.

1. THE NEW LAND

Cosby, knowing he would have no chance of success in a jury trial, proclaimed the three-judge New York Supreme Court a "court of equity" and presented his case to it. Van Dam's lawyers, James Alexander and William Smith, ignored the dispute about wages and claimed Cosby had no right to use the court for his suit. Two of the judges, James De Lancey and Frederick Philipse, decided against opposing the governor and voted the court procedure legal. But Chief Justice Lewis Morris, who had stood firm against corrupt governors before, ruled against Cosby. The governor wrote Morris an angry, insulting letter, and Morris promptly replied by having a lengthy statement covering his ruling printed for general circulation. Cosby, in a rage, dismissed Morris from office and replaced him with De Lancey, a move which left the Supreme Court with but two justices, both Cosby supporters.

Peter Zenger had printed a few items of mildly anti-administration material, but it was his spring 1733 printing of Morris' ruling against the governor that deeply involved him in the political turmoil. He certainly knew that his action would incur Cosby's wrath and, in light of his future quiet defiance of the governor, there is no doubt that he was motivated by his dedication to the relief of injustice as well as by his need of business. Following Morris' statement, a series of leaflets exposing Cosby's administration came off Zenger's press. For the first time the general public began learning the facts about local government.

The opposition movement against Cosby and his lackeys had as its top activists, in addition to Lewis Morris, his son Lewis Morris, Jr., James Alexander, William Smith, Rip Van Dam, and Councilman Cadwallader Colden, a prominent New York scholar. These men became the leaders of the new Popular party, and Peter Zenger's printing operation became New York's first "people's press."

The so-called Court party, which supported the administration, was led by James De Lancey's very wealthy father, Stephen De Lancey, "New York's leading merchant prince." This party had two areas of particularly great strength: The royal governor's word was almost always law, and William Bradford's *Gazette* was well established and obedient. Bradford did not dare object when the governor sent one of his most notorious henchmen, Francis Harison, to assume complete editorial control of the newspaper. Harison filled it with praises of the administration and false charges against the Popular party.

The opposition forces, recognizing the need of a crusading newspaper to inform the people of the true state of affairs in New York, planned and financed the New York *Weekly Journal* and hired Peter Zenger to publish it. Though Alexander, Smith, Morris, and Colden wrote the *Journal*'s editorials and articles, and Alexander served as its editor, for political reasons their names did not appear anywhere in the paper. Zenger's did: "Peter Zenger, Printer."

The first issue of the *Journal*, on November 5, 1733, told of the corruption of the ballot box at the Eastchester village green a week earlier by the man in charge, High Sheriff Nicholas Cooper, one of the governor's henchmen. The election was for a Provincial Assembly position, with Popular party candidate Lewis Morris running against Cosby-selected William Forster. The latter held a commission as Clerk of the Peace and Common Pleas—a commission he had acquired, according to the *Journal*, by payment of 100 pistoles (Spanish coins worth about $4 each) to the governor. When the first polling on the village green showed Morris the winner, Cooper conducted a "re-polling" during which he denied the ballot to many Morris supporters. Among them were thirty-eight Quakers who affirmed but refused to swear that they owned property (in colonial New York ownership of property was a prerequisite to voting rights); no swearing demands were made of two Friends who supported Forster. Even against such odds, Lewis Morris won the election. Zenger's *Journal* told the whole story; Bradford's *Gazette* did not even mention that there had been an election.

As the first politically independent publication in America, the New York *Weekly Journal* fought for freedom of the press from its second issue, on November 12, 1733: "The Liberty of the Press is a Subject of the greatest Importance, and in which every Individual is as much concern'd as he is in any other Party of Liberty. . . ." James Alexander was making sure New Yorkers were informed not only about the misconduct of the current administration but about the *Journal*'s right to give them such information.

In attacks that varied from light satire to harsh condemnation, the paper called Cosby "Nero," "rogue," "a fellow only one degree better than an idiot." It accused him of misdemeanors, deceits, and "crimes against our people" and said, "He has nothing human but the shape." It condemned officials who held themselves above the law with "Schemes of General Oppression and Pillage, Schemes to Depreciate or evade the Laws, Restraints upon Liberty and Projects for Arbitrary Rule." It went so far as to accuse Cosby of destroying a deed given by the Mohawks to the city of Albany, as well as allowing the French, under the guise of a trading expedition, to map and sound New York harbor.

The *Journal*, which sold for three shillings per quarter, grew rapidly in circulation and greatly strengthened the popular support of the opposition movement. Governor Cosby invited the New York Assembly and a grand jury to take action in his behalf, but both agencies declined. Then he brought hard political pressure to bear against the Council, a government agency which filled the combined function of a governor's cabinet and a legislative body, to do something. In the name of "His

Majesty's Council," four issues of "John Peter Zenger's journals, entitled *The New York Weekly Journal* . . . were ordered to be burned by the hands of the common hangman or whipper near the pillory in this city. . . ." It was further ordered that the mayor and magistrates of the city were to witness the burning.

Francis Harison outlined plans and gave directions for making the ceremonial burning a big affair, but something went wrong. Nearly all the collected copies of the four condemned issues suddenly disappeared, and neither city officials nor citizenry showed up at the hour scheduled for the affair; even the hangman was missing. Only Harison, the sheriff, and the sheriff's black slave were there, with a few soldiers standing off at a distance. At Harison's order, the Negro set four copies of the *Journal* afire, and Harison and the sheriff (the *Journal* called them "Cosby's spaniels") stood in the empty street and watched the little blaze. New Yorkers laughed about "Cosby's folly."

Governor Cosby finally decided to vent his wrath against the only *Journal* associated person he could reach—John Peter Zenger. He had a warrant issued "in the name of the King," calling upon the sheriff to take the printer into custody. Zenger could readily have protected himself by revealing the names of the *Journal*'s authors, but he refused to do so. So it was against him alone that the administration's legal forces moved. He was arrested on November 17, 1734 on the charge of having printed "several Seditious Libels . . . having in them many Things, tending to raise Factions and Tumults, among the People of the Province, inflaming their minds with Contempt of His Majesty's Government."

Zenger was held in jail on the third floor of New York's City Hall (now Federal Hall) and at first was not allowed visitors. James Alexander and William Smith immediately came forward to defend him. After their demand that he be freed under a writ of *habeas corpus* failed, they requested his release on bail. The judge to whom these applications had to be made was the governor's man, James De Lancey. Justice De Lancey asked Zenger how much he was worth and the printer replied, "No more than 40 pounds," whereupon the court promptly set bail at 800 pounds, an outrageously unreasonable and legally unjustified amount.

The excessive bail kept Zenger in jail, but it did not stop publication of the *Journal*. Zenger's wife Anna, with the help of her sons and a printing assistant, got the weekly out. Its contributors were the same citizens who had been writing for it all along, and its policy of denouncing Cosby remained unchanged.

The *Journal* told the public about Zenger's "illegal arrest and cruel bail." It announced that Zenger's lawyers, Alexander and Smith, had been disbarred for questioning the authority of the governor's hand-picked court to hear the case. It pointed out that although a grand jury had refused to indict the imprisoned man because it could find no valid charge against him, he had been

illegally held in jail for two more months before Attorney General Richard Bradley formally filed against him for "false, scandalous, malicious and seditious libels."

The *Journal* gave an account of Governor Cosby trying for a packed jury: By law, the jury for the Zenger case had to be chosen from the Freeholders Book, which listed property-owning, voting citizens. But the list of jurors produced by the court clerk was mostly of non-property owners and included men to whom the governor had given commissions, as well as his tailor, baker, shoemaker, and candlemaker. The situation was so flagrantly illegal that John Chambers, Zenger's court-appointed attorney, dared to complain to Justice De Lancey, who ordered the "error" corrected and a proper jury list drawn up.

Peter Zenger was finally brought to trial on August 4, 1735 in the courtroom on the second floor of City Hall. The room was packed, and there was no doubt about the sympathy of the observers being with the defendant. But Zenger's position seemed most precarious with Alexander and Smith disbarred and with British common law and previous court decisions against him.

Attorney General Bradley read to the court from the offensive *Journal* articles. According to law, Bradley said quite correctly, only the fact of publication by Zenger needed to be proved to establish his guilt. There were three witnesses—Zenger's assistant printer and two of his sons—subpoenaed to testify to that.

John Chambers based his feeble defense of Zenger largely on the premise that the *Journal*'s printer should not be the one held accountable for the paper's editorial policy. There seemed little remaining in the case except for the prisoner, who still stubbornly refused to name the *Journal*'s authors, to be found guilty.

Then, suddenly, the thing happened that was to make "The Zenger Trial" famous and August 4, 1735 a momentous day in American history. In the rear of the courtroom an elderly, elegantly attired, magnificently wigged gentleman arose and walked toward the judge's bench. With great dignity he informed the court that he was present to act in behalf of the accused publisher. Probably few of the spectators recognized the man; certainly every member of the court knew he was Andrew Hamilton, a member of the Pennsylvania Council and the Philadelphia Assembly, and the most famous lawyer in all the colonies. A great political independent, he had been vigorous in opposing governmental injustice and yet had retained the confidence and esteem of major proprietary interests. His illustrious career had included achievements as an architect (he designed the Pennsylvania State House, later to be known as "Independence Hall") as well as legal and political triumphs, but his greatest lasting fame would come from his defense of Peter Zenger, printer.

James Alexander, with the knowledge of other members of the opposition movement in New York, had quietly asked for Hamilton's help, knowing the Cosby court would not dare disbar *him*. Hamilton's courtly but commanding personality, particularly in contrast to the consternation and confusion of Cosby's justices and the attorney general, dominated Zenger's day in court.

Andrew Hamilton introduced a completely new approach to the issue. He admitted Zenger's responsibility for publication of the alleged libels but denied they were false and defended Zenger's right to print truth. The defendant had simply exercised his freedom to expose a wretched administration.

Hamilton pointed out to the jury that the issues being tried involved much more than the guilt or innocence of Peter Zenger, and that the freedom of every colonist would be either enhanced by Zenger's acquittal or endangered by his conviction. The eloquent lawyer pleaded, in part:

> The loss of liberty, to a generous mind, is worse than death. . . . I cannot but think it my, and every honest man's duty that (while we pay all due obedience to men in authority) we ought at the same time to be upon our guard against power wherever we apprehend that it may affect ourselves or our fellow subjects. . . . It is not the cause of one poor printer . . . which you are now trying. . . . It is the cause of liberty. And I make no doubt but your upright conduct this day will not only entitle you to the love and esteem of your fellow citizens, but every man who prefers freedom to a life of slavery will bless and honor you as men who have baffled the attempt of tyranny, and by an impartial and uncorrupt verdict have laid a noble foundation for securing to ourselves, our posterity, and our neighbors, that to which nature and the laws of our country have given us a right — the liberty of both exposing and opposing arbitrary power . . . by speaking and writing truth.

Attorney General Bradley wanted no discussion about truth as it related to Governor Cosby; he contended that Hamilton, by acknowledging the fact of publication, had himself branded Zenger guilty. Chief Justice De Lancey agreed, saying that the truth of the accusations against Cosby was irrelevant. He told the jurors not to be concerned with the laws of libel, which were in the province of the justices, and instructed them to reach a verdict wholly on the basis of whether or not the defendant had published the offensive material—which was simply an order to find Peter Zenger guilty.

It did not take the twelve jurymen long to decide between the rights of colonists to fight despotism, as presented by Hamilton, and the demands of British law, as expounded by a partisan court. In less than ten minutes they filed back into the courtroom with a verdict of "not guilty."

The liberty-loving New Yorkers crowded in the courtroom went wild. They continued to cheer after they reached the streets. Andrew Hamilton, who had been offered but had refused payment for his defense of Zenger, was honored at a victory dinner at the Black Horse Tavern. Zenger was not present but he later wrote the lawyer a warm letter of gratitude.

Printed copies of Hamilton's lengthy plea in the Zenger case were widely read in both the American colonies and England. Some historians today claim it had more effect on American history than any other document of record prior to 1750; others class it as the "greatest oratorical triumph won in the colonies prior to the speech of James Otis against writs of assistance" in Boston in 1761.

As soon as Peter Zenger was released, he returned to his printing shop to continue the attack on the corrupt Cosby administration. The next year he published *A Brief Narrative of the Case and Tryal of John Peter Zenger,* edited by James Alexander. It became the text used in behalf of anyone faced with censorship. With one possible exception, "this narrative was," says one authority, "the most widely known source of libertarian thought in the English-speaking world during the eighteenth century."

Both Alexander and William Smith were reinstated to the New York bar. Alexander wrote a four-part essay, published in both Benjamin Franklin's *Pennsylvania Gazette* and Zenger's New York *Journal*, stressing that constitutional government and freedom of the press needed each other for survival.

Governor Cosby never recovered from the humiliation of his defeat in the Zenger trial. He died discredited and rebuked, but still governor of New York in March 1736. The Crown appointed Councilman George Clarke, a more conscientious administrator, as the new governor, and relative calm settled on the New York political scene. Lewis Morris was named governor of New Jersey and Lewis Morris, Jr. became Speaker of the New York Assembly.

Peter Zenger became an official printer for New York in 1737 and, the next year, for New Jersey as well. Support for his family was no longer a problem, and he enjoyed a busy, quiet life until his death in July 1746. For two years Anna Zenger continued to publish his *Weekly Journal,* and then Peter's oldest son John took it over. John Zenger's death in 1751 lowered the curtain on the relatively brief but highly significant existence of the New York *Weekly Journal.*

In Federal Hall and in many museums and libraries in several states, one may see handsome portraits of leading figures in the Zenger case — Lewis Morris, Rip Van Dam, Cadwallader Colden, James Alexander, William White, Andrew Hamilton, James De Lancey, Frederick Philipse, William Bradford, William Cosby, and even Governor Cosby's "head spaniel," Francis Harison, who was finally run out of the colonies and died in England, penniless. But there is no portrait of John Peter Zenger among them. About his appearance we can only wonder.

The Great Earthquake

Jourdan Houston

Shortly before dawn tne five-inch pine spindle of the Faneuil Hall wind vane snapped, dislodging the thirty-pound gilded cricket that spun ten feet above Boston's marketplace roof. Early risers first heard the baying of dogs, then the roar. Beneath the autumn moon, fifteen hundred chimneys swiveled and spewed bricks; the gable ends of brick houses that had survived the fire of 1747 collapsed onto cobblestone. As the contents of their homes toppled or migrated, families fled into the streets with shrieks attributed by one observer less to their embarrassment at "seeing their neighbors, as it were naked" than to their fears of confronting Judgment Day at last, and in nightclothes.

His Majesty's regiments, camped at Lake George, a day's march west of Vermont's Green Mountains, felt the violence; so, presumably, did the one hundred and fifty French regulars gathered within scouting distance of the demoralized British troops. Newly arrived Samuel Chandler of Gloucester, Massachusetts, later recorded the time as four o'clock on the clear morning of November 18, adding, "2 soldiers died" in skirmishes that same day.

Settlers in Prince George County, Virginia, took note of it, while the captain of a westbound ship seventy leagues off the New England coast felt such a report beneath his vessel that he assumed he had struck a wreck or a sandbar. But when he lowered a lead, the measure sank to fifty fathoms—three hundred feet—in waters that soon began beaching dead fish miles away on the Massachusetts coastal tip of Cape Ann. Unaware, the captain and his crew had passed over the sea-covered epicenter of the first major earthquake in the recorded geological history of North America, and still one of the most powerful within historic memory.

The Cape Ann earthquake of 1755 shook the sleeping New World from Nova Scotia to South Carolina, evoking the greatest awe, damage, and contrition in the heavily populated northern colonies. "It was a terrible night," wrote the Reverend Mather Byles of Boston, "the most so, perhaps, that ever NEW ENGLAND saw." The tremors, followed by several more in ensuing days, signaled Divine displeasure to many. But they suggested Divine restraint once the colonies learned—about four weeks later—of the devastation of Lisbon by earthquake on November 1. At least thirty thousand died in the busy European port, many of them while worshiping in the churches on All Saints Day morning. The rest were swept away in the tidal wave that followed the violent shaking, which was felt as far north as Amsterdam.

From the rubble of Lisbon came the political ascent of the ruthless Marquês de Pombal, heightened religious recrimination, and Voltaire's *Candide*, a biting satire of the prevailing optimistic creeds of such philosophers as Leibnitz. Out of the earthquake in the English colonies grew an earnest (if temporary) examination of contemporary morality. And, although a formal science of geology lay a generation in the future, the Cape Ann tremors left the inchoate discipline its first empirical accounting of a North American earthquake and provoked an energetic debate over the natural causes of such phenomena.

"The subject is curious, and at present engages the attention of many persons," said John Winthrop IV, Harvard professor and occupant of only the second scientific chair in the colonies (the first was established in 1711 at William and Mary College). Eight days after the earthquake, which, in his words, had "spread terror and threatened desolation throughout New-England," he attempted to reassure a nervous crowd in the college chapel, acknowledging that never had "so much damage [been] done to our buildings as by the last great shock."

It was not the first earthquake in the continent's known history. That record goes back to 1558 by way of the oral tradition of the native Pequot and Narraganset tribes in Rhode Island. Their members recounted their earthquake chronology to Roger Williams, the renegade province's governor, after the first earthquake of the colonial era in 1638. "The younger natives are ignorant of the like," Williams wrote to John Winthrop, founder of Boston and great-grandfather of the Harvard professor, "but the ellder informe me that this is the 5t within these 4 score yeare in the land." A *Naunaumemoauke*, as the natives called such a tremor, was inevitably the precursor to "either plague or pox or some other epidemicall disease," Williams noted.

The "great and fearfull" earthquake of 1638, America's first documented tremor, occurred on a sunny June afternoon throughout the English plantations. Recognized as coming from "the uninhabited parts of this Wilderness," it is, in fact, now believed to have originated in the St. Lawrence valley.

Although the colonies proceeded to rock several times in the mid-1600's, most notably in 1663, the cruelest earthquakes of the epoch were occurring abroad. In 1692 Jamaica's Port Royal was alternately shaken and inundated by an earthquake that opened huge chasms into which townspeople fell. "Some who were swallowed quite down, rose again in other Streets," wrote the Reverend Thomas Prince, one of the chroniclers of later American earthquakes, "being cast up

©1980 American Heritage Publishing Company, Inc. Reprinted by permission from *AMERICAN HERITAGE* (September, 1980)

with great quantities of Water." Americans read of other tremors that killed some ten thousand Neapolitans in 1688 or swallowed sixteen hills whole, supposedly, in Batavia, on the Island of Java, in 1699.

Sensitive to such a fate, American colonists responded to their next severe earthquake with something less than equanimity. The 1727 earthquake, now believed also to have been centered at sea off Cape Ann, was a brief but noisy event, beginning with "a pounce like great guns," as a Newbury record notes.

But by the time the last aftershocks subsided, the worst reminders of a violent evening were broken stone walls and chimneys in New England and a pervading smell of sulfur, known better in those times as brimstone and widely believed to provoke earthquakes. "There's certainly a trail of sulfur under the earth from Lima to Lisbon," Voltaire's demoralized Candide learned as the optimist Pangloss assessed the benefits of the Lisbon horror. The Reverend John Burt of Bristol, Rhode Island, adopted the Panglossian perspective about the American tremors. "What a happy Effect had the Earthquake in 1727," he told his congregation, "to awaken the Secure, to reform the Vicious and to make all solicitous about their spiritual and everlasting Concerns."

The effect must have worn off, because for about four minutes in 1755, the earth's violent activity bound disparate American colonies of more than one million people in fear. It was the year in which General Edward Braddock had led British-American troops to an embarrassing July defeat at Fort Duquesne, nine months before the formal declaration of the French and Indian War. Preoccupied by the advances of their allied opponents, the colonists reflected somberly on the meaning of the November earthquake and catalogued its causes and effects, both physical and metaphysical.

The earthquake of 1755 announced itself at the waning edge of a calm, windless night. In Boston, cattle began to low and dogs to howl. Birds flew randomly in the moonlight. The vibrations approached with a sound "like the noise of many cartloads of paving stones thrown together." A correspondent for the Boston *Gazette* recorded the time as 4:21 A.M., acknowledging that his own watch read 4:31, but that "most watches in Boston tend to be set at least 10 minutes too fast."

Buildings shook as far north as Port Annapolis, Nova Scotia. The Reverend Joseph Smith of Portland, Maine, gauged the shock at two minutes, long enough to "seem as if it would shake the house to pieces, and then [it] threw down near one hundred bricks to our chimney, and did the same to many other chimneys in town." The residents of Newington, in New Hampshire province, claimed that a "frightful chasm" two feet wide and sixty rods long—nearly one thousand feet—had opened near the town meetinghouse.

In Connecticut, Canterbury preacher James Cogswell identified a "dismal sound" before the onset of the "terrible ague," adding, "Had the Shock been a few Degrees more heavy, or (perhaps), continued much longer in the same Degree, we might have been buried in the Darkness." Benjamin Trumbull, future chronicler of Connecticut's

history, was a freshman at thirty-seven-year-old Yale College when he reflected "*de terribeli teramotu*" in his diary. "The earth seemed to wave like the waves of the sea," he wrote, and, as buildings rocked, he saw students and villagers "rush from their couches with trembling and fear."

The ground undulated visibly. In the Massachusetts coastal town of Scituate, where ten "cart loads" of white, floury earth spewed from chasms, citizens saw the earth "wave like the swelling of the sea," while the sea itself engaged in a "commotion and roaring . . . no less terrible." The sea's response was not confined to the northern Atlantic, although mainland colonists would not know it until the January return of ships from the West Indies. Voyagers reported that at two in the afternoon of November 18, the sea withdrew from St. Martin's harbor, leaving vessels aground in water normally twenty-four feet deep.

At the same time in Barbados, northeast of the Venezuelan coast, a violent tide began to ebb and flow from the island every six or seven minutes, not diminishing in energy until early evening. No one could recall the placid Barbados current "ever to set so strong as 2 miles in an hour," reported Benjamin Franklin's *Pennsylvania Gazette*. (The West Indies commotions may have had a different source, an earthquake that occurred on November 18 in Morocco, killing three thousand. Tradition has credited Cape Ann, however.)

The most pronounced damage from the American disruption occurred in New England, from New Haven to Portland. Accounts focused on Boston, probably because of its population of fifteen thousand, some of whom insisted they had heard Gabriel's trumpet blow before the bricks began bouncing off their roofs. "The effects of the earthquake are very considerable in the town," a reporter for the Boston *Gazette* wrote. The Reverend Charles Chauncey noted that, beyond the "breaking of our brittle wear and the bruising of our pewter," the damage to structures in just one part of the region was "set, moderately computing, at about 50 thousand pounds in the common way we reckon money," in a day when a barrel of West Indies rum cost three shillings sixpence, or a barrel of beef forty shillings.

Fortunately, the effects were worst where the concentration of residences was least—near the docks and warehouses on the "low, loose Ground, made by the Encroachments in the Harbour," where one witness described his passage impeded by "large quantities of mortar and rubbish." Although the large-scale filling of the waters around the original peninsula of Boston did not begin until 1804, the city had already begun to creep into the harbor with the building of wharves such as the fifty-four-foot-wide Long Wharf which stretched 1,586 feet into Town Cove. Atop the fill and pilings were a road and merchant houses vulnerable to earthquake. The original residential settlement of Trimountain, as Boston was called in 1630, covered Beacon Hill, which is geologically stable bedrock less responsive to earthquakes than silted sites.

"Never was such a scene of distress in *New England* before," the voluble Thomas Prince reported. Dr. Prince, who managed to publish a small book on past earthquakes within a week of the Boston shock, quoted an acquaintance who went through the tremor while lying in bed "under the best Composure of Mind I could bring myself to." When he emerged to examine the damage, he encountered a populace of "ghastly" faces, traced with "an Awe and Gloom . . . as would have checked the gay airs of the most *intrepid Libertine* among us."

Disturbed twice more by the return of a trembling earth felt as far south as Pennsylvania on November 24 and December 19, and soon mindful of the Lisbon debacle, New Englanders took to prayer and fasting to ward off further manifestations of what the Bay Colony's Lieutenant Governor Spencer Phips publicly pronounced God's "righteous Anger against the heinous and provoking Sins of Men." How directly Divine Providence participated in the events was a matter of considerable discourse.

The Reverend Mather Byles of Boston, who would be banished from his pulpit as a Tory after the Revolution, espoused the popular mechanistic philosophy of the day, under which cause and effect are considered intricately geared to events everywhere. If the world were analogous to a clock, the seventeenth-century chemist Robert Boyle observed, then God, who created the mechanisms and stood back watching them work, was the Divine Watchmaker. If the mechanistic attitude considered *how* an event occurred, the alternative philosophy of the day subscribed to the so-called teleological view, under which events are purposeful means to prescribed ends. The teleological approach is to ask, "What for?"

Thus, a teleological—and tedious—thirty-six-verse anonymous poem distributed after "the great earthquake" saw Divine intent, explaining:

In seventeen hundred and fifty-five,
When vice its empire did revive,
Consuming fire, a jealous GOD
Call'd on New-England with his rod.

But the mechanistic Reverend Byles proved more sanguine. "No Doubt natural Causes may be assigned for this *Phaenomenon*," he told a group of colonists at Point Shirley, across Boston harbor. "An imprisoned Vapour too closely pent or too strongly compressed in the Caverns beneath, will thro, a natural Elasticity, abhor confinement, dilate and expand, swell and heave up the Surface of the earth, producing a tremor and Commotion." Or, he conjectured, the mass of "Sulphureous and Combustible materials" underground meets with a spark and explodes. "How thin the Arch which interposes between us and a Furnace of Flame," he exclaimed.

Elements of a nascent science of geology appear in the Americans' analysis of their worst earthquake. Advances in chemistry, physics, and the concept of scientific method had followed the work of the Boyles and Newtons and Bacons of the seventeenth century, supporting a departure from such geologic convention as the biblical assertions that the earth was roughly eight thousand years old, that its crust had been shaped by the great flood, and that earthquakes—as Psalm 18

or Revelations 15 told it—were a fundamental tool of God's wrath.

In 1749 Georges Leclerc, Comte de Buffon, of Paris had suggested an age of seventy-five thousand years for the earth, which he speculated had been created from solar matter after the collision of a comet and the sun. The long-standing assertion that the earth's surface had been created from the condensation of minerals suspended in the Mosaic flood would soon face an opposing view that subterranean fire shaped the earth's crust. Known as the Neptunists and the Vulcanists (or Plutonists), both schools were partly right.

Fire, and occasionally water, dominated the speculation about earthquake causes that arose in the colonies after the 1755 shocks, which produced the first attempts to probe such an event with scientific inquiry. Dr. Thomas Prince, who was pastor of Old South Church, acknowledged hypotheses by "the projecting Sort of Philosophers both ancient and modern" over "a central *Concave of fire* [or] a vast internal *Abyss of Waters*." Then he projected his own theory, adding the phenomenon of electricity, lately described by Benjamin Franklin, to his list of earthquake causes.

God, Dr. Prince explained, had created an earth "of very loose Contexture," in which existed numerous caverns filled with "*Sulphurious, nitrous, fiery, mineral* and *other Substances* such as those in the Clouds, which are the natural Causes of Thunder and Lightning." The underground collision of these substances meant an explosion and, hence, an earthquake.

But earthquakes formed merely "a Twentieth Part of our imminent danger," Prince announced. Citing Robert Boyle's law of the pressure of gases, he warned that the "terrible atmosphere" blanketing the earth presses the ground with a weight of 2,592 pounds per square foot. After a subterranean explosion, he said, vapors escape, leaving a vacuum. The menacingly heavy air around us, "this astonishing Weight, besides that of the Earth, immediately bares away everything before it into the Space below." Entire hills and cities had thus been pressed underground by the air.

Prince further refined his theory of electrical causes of earthquakes by suggesting that Boston had suffered worse shocks because of its abundance of lightning rods, then called iron points. The rods had been installed after 1751 at Benjamin Franklin's suggestion, in a city that had last been ravaged by fire as recently as 1747. Prince suggested that they conveyed extra electricity into the earth from the sky and thus imperiled Boston.

Enter an incredulous Harvard professor. "Philosophy, like everything else, has had its fashions," John Winthrop IV scoffed in response to Prince, "and the reigning mode of late has been to explain everything by ELECTRICITY. . . . Now, it seems, it is to be the cause of earthquakes." The earth, he noted, was barred by simple laws of physics from creating electricity And as for Prince's lightning-rod theory, Winthrop answered, "I cannot believe that in the whole town of BOSTON, where so many iron points are erected, there is so much as one person, who is so weak, so ignorant, so foolish, or, to say all in one word, so atheistical, as ever to have entertained a single thought, that it is possible, by the help of a few yards of wire, to 'get out of the mighty hand of GOD.' "

Winthrop, Hollisian professor of mathematics and natural philosophy at Harvard, continued his public tiff with Prince, whom he often referred to as "the Rev. Divine," for several months. Colonists looked to the two of them for answers to the Cape Ann earthquake—which both men incorrectly believed to have come from the northwest. Winthrop, who had introduced Newton's fluxions, or calculus, to the United States and opened the nation's first experimental physics laboratory, was probably the most scholarly of colonists to contribute to the earthquake literature, if not the most prescient.

Flame and pent vapors, he believed, promoted earthquakes, a likelihood he supported by observing the abundance of tremors near volcanoes. Like Prince, he believed the quaking earth exhaled pent vapors, but, citing Newton, Winthrop suggested that the vapors might supply the atmosphere with "true, permanent air," a mysterious but revitalizing substance.

Winthrop's contribution to the imminent science of geology stems more from his careful, empirical descriptions and calculations of the Cape Ann earthquake events. By measuring effects, he carefully deduced the chronology and characteristics of the shock, applying physical maxims whenever he could. He documented the existence of both horizontal and vertical motion during a tremor, comparing the generation of earthquake "waves" to that of the vibrations of a struck musical chord, where an instrument's strings bend broadly at first and then vibrate increasingly rapidly in returning to their stationary positions.

Winthrop told his Harvard Chapel audience that, like many others, he was forced to stay in bed, listening to the beams of his house crack in the violence, for at least the first two minutes of the earthquake. When he arose to seek his watch, it read 4:15 A.M. In examining his mantel clock, which he had earlier synchronized with his watch, he found that it had stopped at 35 seconds past 4:11. A test tube that Winthrop had placed inside the clock case "for security" after an experiment had toppled onto the clock's pendulum, probably with the first tremor. Therefore, Winthrop concluded, the earthquake of 1755 lasted at least four minutes.

To determine the speed of the sway of the region's buildings in the earthquake, he relied on the travels of a key tossed from his mantel and measured the distance that one of his chimney bricks had been thrown—thirty feet from a thirty-two-foot-high chimney. By calibrating the known speed of a falling object—thanks to Newton—he could show that his brick had probably traveled twenty-one feet in one second. The clue of the key, which had apparently not traveled so forcefully, suggested to him that the velocity of moving objects during an earthquake varied, depending on height.

From the northwesterly direction that the key flew, he ascertained that the course of the earthquake had been from northwest to southeast and calculated that it had occurred "at some considerable distance from this place," since he had heard the earthquake about thirty seconds before he had felt it. If the speed of sound is about thirteen miles an hour, he reasoned, then earthquake vibrations traveled at some speed slower than sound.

He arrived, correctly, at a conviction that earthquakes were emitted in an undulating motion. During an aftershock felt the night after the November 18 tremor, Winthrop was sitting at a hearth with his feet on the bricks. As the tremor passed, his feet were lifted directly upward by a series of individual bricks, moving one at a time. "It was not a motion of the whole hearth together," he explained to his audience, "either from side to side, or up and down; but of each brick separately by itself. Now as the bricks were contiguous, the only motion, which could be communicated to them separately, was in perpendicular direction . . . and this shock, I apprehend, was occasioned by one small *wave of earth* rolling along."

But if Winthrop was the consummate observer of an earthquake in practice, a lesser known compatriot proved the more insightful theoretician. John Perkins was a Boston physician who, in his personal journals, freely indulged in scientific speculation, some of it—as in the origins of coal from plant matter—startlingly accurate. In 1758 he published an anonymous tract in the *New American Magazine* on the causes and effects of the 1755 earthquake, which he suspected had originated in the White Mountains of New Hampshire. Perkins recognized features in the earth and earthquakes that would not emerge as commonplace for generations.

Perkins' suggestions were disarmingly reasonable. It was apparent, he noted, that because earthquakes often occurred near volcanic activity, there may be some relationship between heat and earthquakes. But that evidence had created a popular assumption that fire and rarefied vapors were a universal cause of earthquakes. In nonvolcanic regions, the concept was often supported by the occasional spewing up of sulfurous material. But any heat at these nonvolcanic sites may be misleading, he cautioned; it might be the effect of friction, of the earthquake itself, and not be a cause at all.

Instead, he said, "the settlement of high lands may sometimes be the first moving cause of earthquakes." Imagine, he proposed, "what might be the consequence, by the infinitely greater force produced by the weight of a continent land, upon any quantity of matter put in motion under it." Such settling was more likely to occur, he said, where caverns or channels "weaken the stability of the foundation supporting the earth." Noting that earthquakes often occurred on continental coasts, he conjectured that they took place when the higher lands settled and forced the emergence of new coast land. The agitation of the sea that one saw during earthquakes was the effect of the spreading of the coast. Perkins' theories are surprisingly close to the now commonplace awareness that stress, faults, and the collision of expanding tectonic plates contribute to earthquakes.

The Cape Ann earthquake of 1755 remained the premier in the United States until 1811, when a series of earthquakes struck the Mississippi River embayment at New Madrid, Missouri, and was followed by more than one thousand aftershocks. But on the East Coast, no earthquake would match the Cape Ann tremor until the 1886 Charleston, South

Carolina, tremor that severely damaged that community. No earthquake east of the Rockies in the twentieth century has matched the Cape Ann disturbance or those two that followed.

At its sea-covered epicenter, the Cape Ann event (scientists now believe) would have been ranked 8.0 or 9.0 on a scale of 1.0 through 12.0, known as the modified Mercalli scale that measures the visible effects of earthquakes. On land, the earthquake might have registered a Richter scale magnitude of 6.0. The 1886 Charleston earthquake has been given a Mercalli intensity of 9.0 to 10.0, while the San Francisco earthquake reached 8.3 on a Richter rating with a Mercalli index of 11.0

Geologists are still puzzled by the dynamics of the 1755 quake. Unlike California—where the Pacific plate meets the North American plate, and essentially dives under it—the Eastern area is not at the earthquake-prone edge of such plates. But more than two hundred years after colonial scientists initiated the investigation, answers may be starting to emerge.

A study of New England's magnetic field recently revealed a highly magnetic and circular underwater geologic formation at Cape Ann, probably a mass of gabbro, a rock denser than the granite known to surround it. Scientists suggest that this is a pluton, a huge rock cylinder descending into the earth. Similar plutons had been identified ashore—in the White Mountains—and when geophysicists compared notes, they found that plutons with matching characteristics existed in the same sites as the major historic earthquakes of the region. It may be that stress at the boundaries of these pillars caused not only the Cape Ann earthquake but also many of those that followed in the eastern United States.

Were an earthquake of the same intensity to recur at Cape Ann today, geologists have told the U.S. Congress, the damage, especially in the filled areas that now make up half of Boston, would be considerable, with lives lost. But in 1755, more sparsely settled Americans could give thanks for having been spared, newly mindful of the wages of sin. Considering the paucity of earthquakes for the next one hundred and thirty years, at least a few of them must have mended their ways.

Revolutionary America

As noted in the previous unit, the American colonial period lasted a very long time. This fact alone helped to shape relations between Americans and the British. Many colonists were of Dutch, German, or other ancestry, and had no English background at all. Even for those of British stock, however, the passage of time altered their perceptions and loyalties. Those who originally settled were Englishmen in a foreign land, but most members of subsequent generations never even saw the mother country. Though they might have considered themselves loyal subjects of the crown, they were Americans first whose strongest ties were with the local community and with the colony. Indeed, a number of scholars have argued that the passage of time and the distance involved made separation from the mother country inevitable.

The divergence of interests between colonists and their kinsmen was obscured by the British policy of "salutory neglect." What this meant in practice was that, in the decades before 1763, the individual colonies had for all practical purposes become autonomous insofar as their domestic affairs were concerned. And, though theoretically part of the British imperial system of trade and commerce, they had considerable latitude in that area as well. There were specific grievances against England from time to time, but most political and economic problems were internal as various interest groups and classes struggled for influence within a colony.

All that changed in 1763. What Americans referred to as the French and Indian war resulted in the expulsion of the French from the continent. The war had almost bankrupted England, however, and to regain economic health she tried, among other things, to shift part of the burden to the colonies. New duties, taxes, and regulations were enacted, and the means of enforcing existing ones were beefed up. What seemed fair to the British constituted an outrage to the colonists who had grown accustomed to "salutary neglect." That this should have come about at a time when Americans no longer had to fear the French made the situation that much worse.

Perhaps, given the circumstances, separation was inevitable. But individuals play a role as well as circumstances. Had British policymakers been more sympathetic towards American complaints, some scholars believe, events might have turned out differently. And what about the colonial leaders? Did they fail to understand Britain's plight, or were they merely exploiting a situation to gain their own ends? Economic grievances alone do not explain the revolution satisfactorily; questions over political rights and religious considerations also played a part.

Battles and campaigns aside, what was the revolutionary war really like for those who fought in it? The selection of reminiscenses presented in this unit provide some insights. Was the goal merely to gain independence, or did some people genuinely hope to create a new society? If so, how well was this aspiration realized? What kinds of men were our founding fathers, and how well did they cope with the problems they had to confront? And finally, what impact did the American Revolution have on other societies at the time and later?

The Revolution as a World Ideal

To their everlasting credit, the Founding Fathers spoke for mankind, not just for Americans and their fledgling nation.

Henry Steele Commager

The men who fought the Revolution and created the new American nation were children of the Enlightenment. They shared the Enlightenment conviction that mankind was one, that men were everywhere alike— subject to the same laws, responding to the same impulses, animated by the same passions, and entitled to the same rights. They believed in the sovereignty of reason and in the universality of those laws which reason could command and in the ability to achieve those ends which reason dictated as just and sound. When they set up their own commonwealths, they based these on laws they thought universal and permanent, and they took it for granted that men and nations everywhere must eventually follow where they led.

They embraced, with a kind of exultation, the opportunity to set the standards and provide the models that others would of necessity follow. With Patrick Henry they were confident that America had "lighted the candle to all the world." With John Adams they rejoiced that the Revolution was fought "for future millions, and millions of millions," and that it would "spread Liberty and Enlightenment everywhere in the world." The poet Joel Barlow spoke for them when he asserted that the American example "would excite emulation throughout the kingdoms of the earth, and meliorate the conditions of the human race," and so, too, did Tom Paine, who was confident that "we Americans have it in our power to begin the world again . . . the birthday of a new world is at hand." It was Paine, too, who said that "the cause of America is the most honorable that man ever engaged in." No one else proclaimed this gospel more insistently than Thomas Jefferson. "We feel," he wrote to his friend Joseph Priestley, "that we are acting under obligations not confined to the limits of our own society. It is impossible not to be sensible that we are acting for all mankind."

That was the theme, too, of his Farewell Address:

> Trusted with the destinies of this solitary republic of the world, the only monument of human rights and the sole depository of the sacred fire of freedom and self-government, from hence it is to be lighted up in other regions of the earth. . . .All mankind ought, then, to rejoice in its prosperous and sympathize in its adverse fortunes, as involving everything dear to man.

A few more years and Jefferson was writing to his new-found friend John Adams:

> Old Europe will have to lean on our shoulders and hobble along by our side under the monkish trammels of priests and kings as best she can. What a colossus shall we be when the southern continent comes up to our mark! What a stand will it secure as a ralliance for the reason and freedom on the globe!

And he struck that note again in the last letter before the pen fell from his gallant hand: it was his salute to the "Argonauts" who had launched the Declaration and the nation:

> May it be to the world. . .the signal of arousing men to burst the chains under which monkish ignorance and superstition had persuaded them to bind themselves, and to assume the blessings and security of self-government. . . .All eyes are opened, or opening, to the rights of man. The general spread of the light of science has already laid open to every view the palpable truth that the mass of mankind has not been born with saddles on their backs, nor a favored few booted and spurred, ready to ride them legitimately, by the grace of God.

It is sobering to reflect that in celebrating both the Centennial and the Bicentennial of the Revolution, Americans have been content to substitute rhetoric for policy and have even been willing to permit the policy to betray the rhetoric. The Revolutionary generation translated its rhetoric—the term is inadequate—not only into policy but also into institutions. Nothing, indeed, was more impressive in that generation than its ability "to realize the writings of the wisest writers"— that is, to take ideas and principles to which philosophers had subscribed for centuries and institutionalize them. And what is most remarkable is that the institutions which they created were not parochial. As the Founding Fathers drew upon the great heritage of the past, from Greece to 17th-century England, for their inspiration, so they contrived institutions that were valid everywhere and that spread over the globe.

"The Revolution as a World Ideal," Henry Steele Commager, *Saturday Review*, December 13, 1975. Copyright ©1975 Saturday Review, Inc.

Bettmann Archive

Signing the U.S. Constitution—"Nowhere else on the globe—except perhaps in some of the Swiss cantons—had the principle of democracy been institutionalized."

First they created a nation—something no other people had ever done before, for heretofore nations had simply grown. And they did so without benefit of all the insignia and stigmata of Old World nationalism—a monarch, a ruling class, an established church, an army and navy, and even a historical past. What is more, they cast the nation into Republican form—something Montesquieu had asserted was quite impossible except in a small territory or a city-state.

They solved, almost overnight, two of the most intractable problems in the history of government: colonialism and federalism. No Old World nation had known what to do with colonies except to exploit them for the benefit of the mother country. The new United States was born the largest nation in the Western world and was, from the beginning and throughout the 19th century, a great colonizing power with a hinterland that stretched westward to the Mississippi and, eventually, to the Pacific. By the simple device of transforming "colonies" into states, and admitting these states into the union on the basis of absolute equality with the original states, the Founding Fathers taught the world a lesson which it has learned only slowly and painfully down to our own day.

That generation solved, too, the problem of federalism—a problem that had baffled statesmen in the ancient Greek confederacies, in medieval Italy of the Lombard League, in the confederations of Helvetia and of the Low Countries, in the Holy Roman Empire, and in the British Empire. In little more than a decade, Americans worked out the proper principles of federalism and welded together a federal union which is today the oldest and the most successful in history.

They had declared that all government derives its powers from the consent of the governed—a principle ancient in history but never before translated into practice and one which, even today, is not generally conceded. How were the governed to give their "consent"; how were they to "alter or abolish" government and "institute" new government? Nowhere else on the globe—except perhaps in some of the Swiss cantons—had the principle of democracy been institutionalized. The Founding Fathers invented the constitutional convention as the appropriate instrument for making, altering, abolishing, and remaking government; that is, they legalized revolution. And, like federalism, the constitutional convention has spread throughout the globe.

For the first time, too, the Americans institutionalized the familiar principle that government was limited. As late as 1766 the British Parliament had proclaimed the right to bind the colonies "in all cases whatsoever," and it was a commonplace of history that kings and princes had the right to bind their subjects. But the Founding Fathers insisted that no government had all power, and they proceeded, then, to place on government such checks, balances, limits, restrictions, and prohibitions as would make sure that government coud not indeed exercise any powers but those assigned to it by the people. What a congeries of inventions and devices to achieve this end: written constitutions, the federal system, the separation of powers, bicameral legislature, annual elections, and, to top them all, bills of rights that were part of fundamental law and that protected men in their freedom of religion, of speech, of the press, and of assembly—something not even the English Bills of Rights attempted to do. This principle, too—that government was limited—spread into every continent. It has not conquered the globe, and it is competing, even now, for the allegiance of men everywhere. But that the area of freedom is larger today than it was in 1776 owes something to the American demonstration that men can make and that men can limit government.

Thus this generation—incomparably the most creative in our history—was responsible for launching the most important political institutions of modern history: the constitutional convention, the written constitution, federalism, the coordinate state, limited government, substantive bills of rights, judicial review, and even the political party (for the parties that emerged in the 1790s have some claim to be the first modern parties in history). Equally significant—and equally influential—were the innovations in the realm of social institutions.

Thus for the first time, Americans of the Revolutionary generation not only established complete religious toleration but also separated church and state with its corollary principle of voluntarism in religion. Thus—for the first time in modern history—they formally subordinated the military to the civilian authority. They realized the principle that men were

Culver
Patrick Henry—"America had 'lighted the candle to all the world.'"

Culver
Thomas Paine—"'We Americans have it in our power to begin the world again.'"

"created equal" in a larger measure than did any other Western society, though they failed, tragically, to extend that principle to blacks: their failure here was a failure not so much of leadership as of following. It is sobering to reflect that their successors did not solve this problem until almost a century later, and then by violence, and that another century was to elapse before Americans were prepared to concede even formal equality to the black race.

It was good fortune rather than principle which accounted for a greater degree of material well-being in the early Republic than could be found elsewhere on the globe, but it was principle that made that good fortune available to almost all who were white and that kept open the doors for the peoples of the Old World. And, to assure the continuation of all this, Americans embarked upon what we may call, for want of a better name, the Jeffersonian program of the conquest of ignorance by providing schools and colleges on a lavish scale open to all; Americans encouraged learning and science by establishing freedom of the press; they were even so romantic as to write guarantees of happiness into their Constitution.

In all this the Founding Fathers were animated by a sense of obligation, and of mission, not only to the peoples of the world but also to posterity. It was for posterity that they fought and planned and built; it was the needs of posterity that were constantly uppermost in their minds. This concern was sometimes exaggerated—as it was in Jefferson's "land enough for our descendants to the thousandth and ten-thousandth generation," but it was never merely rhetorical. Here is Tom Paine's plea for support to the war for independence: "tis not the concern of a day, a year, or an age; posterity are virtually involved in the contest and will be . . . affected by it to the end of time." Here is John Adams writing his beloved Abigail the day he had signed the Declaration: "Through all the gloom I can see the rays of ravishing light and glory. Posterity will triumph in that day's transaction." Here is Benjamin Rush recalling that "I was animated constantly by a belief that I was acting for the benefit of the whole world, and of future ages."

Washington, who had no posterity of his own and was father only to his country, in his Newburgh address to the officers of the Continental Army said that "you will, by the dignity of your Conduct, afford occasion for Posterity to say, speaking of the glorious example you have exhibited to Mankind, had this day been wanting, the World had never seen the last stage of perfection to which human nature is capable of attaining." Or listen to Jefferson, at the close of his life, writing to his old comrade-in-arms James Madison: "It has been a great solace to me to believe that you are engaged in vindicating to posterity the course we have pursued, of preserving to them, in all their purity, the blessings of self-government which we had assisted in acquiring for them."

Nowhere else is the contrast between the Revolutionary generation and our own non-revolutionary (or counter-revolutionary) generation more conspicuous than in the passing of the sense of fiduciary obligation. We give lip service to posterity, but by plundering the natural resources of land and water, recklessly polluting the environment, building immense nuclear armaments, fostering racial and national animosities, and piling up almost limitless debts, we systematically betray it.

There is a moving passage in William Story's biography of his father, Justice Joseph Story, which recalls one of the lectures the great jurist gave at the Harvard Law School, which was almost his creation and his lengthened shadow. Moved by the occasion, the young Story tells us, his father:

> spoke of the hopes for freedom with which America was freighted; of the anxious eyes that watched it in its progress; of the voices that called from land to land to enquire of its welfare; closing in an exhortation to the students to labor for the furtherance of justice and free principles . . . and to seek in all their public acts to establish the foundations of right and truth.

This American Revolution was indeed a moving spectacle, the first of its kind in history and the most successful, and contemporaries everywhere saw at once its implications for the rest of mankind. How appropriate that it should be Tom Paine—a recent emigrant from Britain and the most ubiquitous revolutionary of his day—who saw this most clearly:

> O, ye, that love mankind! Ye that dare oppose not only tyranny but the tyrant, stand forth. Freedom hath been hunted round the globe. . . . Asia and Africa have long expelled her. Europe regards her like a stranger and England hath given her warning to depart. O, receive the fugitive, and prepare in time an asylum for mankind.

8. The Revolution as a World Ideal

The American Revolution was a catalytic agent everywhere in the Western world. "All Europe is on our side," wrote Franklin—with pardonable exaggeration—from Paris; ". . . 'tis a common observation here that our Cause is the Cause of all Mankind, and that we are fighting for their Liberty in defending our own." Certainly, all the European liberals, were on the American side—even in Britain, even in British Hanover. The war divided British opinion as sharply as the Vietnam War divided American, but its opponents were more outspoken and more courageous than were the opponents of the Tonkin Bay Resolution or the opponents of the destruction of Vietnam and Cambodia. English *philosophes* like Dr. Price and Dr. Priestley openly championed the American cause; statesmen like Chatham and Shelburne, Rockingham and Grafton, warned that the war was folly; and 19 Lords signed a protest against the proclamation of rebellion.

Lord Frederick Cavendish, who was a lieutenant general, refused to apply for command; Lord Jeffrey Amherst, highest ranking officer in the British army, rejected active command; Admiral Keppel refused to accept service in American waters; and young Lord Effingham informed the King that "I could not, without reproach from my conscience, consent to bear arms against my fellow subjects in America." The war, the American victory, and the American example immensely stimulated popular efforts to reform the British political system—to broaden the suffrage, end the scandal of rotten boroughs, and encourage annual meetings of Parliament: all in vain, for the almost paranoid reaction against the French Revolution, which found classic expression in Edmund Burke's *Reflections,* inaugurated something like a reign of terror in Britain.

Elsewhere, too, the American example was infectious: in France, where Jefferson helped draft the Declaration of the Right of Man and where Tom Paine served in the constituent assembly; in Italy, where the fiery Alfieri celebrated the American cause in five odes to liberty and countless dramas; in the Netherlands, where stout revolutionaries like van der Capellen and van der Kemp fought—again in vain—to reconstruct the aristocratic government of those provinces; in the Germanies, where Christoph Ebeling was certain that "America must give an example to the world" and dedicated himself to writing the most comprehensive history of the new nation to appear before Bancroft; even in despotic Denmark, where, as Henrick Steffens remembered, "all the ships flew flags and pennants and every ship with cannon saluted the new nation."

Nor was the influence of the Revolution confined to the Old World. The struggle for the independence of Latin America derived more from the French than from the American Revolution, but the Latin Americans knew, after all, that the French Revolution had ended in the despotism of a Napoleon and the American in the

Culver
Benjamin Franklin—" 'Our Cause is the Cause of all Mankind.' "

Culver
Benjamin Rush—" 'I was acting for the benefit of the whole world.' "

birth of a free republic, and it was the American example they sought to emulate. And the power of that example was to emerge again and again on the stage of history, even into our own time, when both Rhodesia and North Vietnam borrowed the language, if not the spirit, of the Declaration of Independence to justify their own revolutions.

Revolution, independence, nation-making, new political institutions—all these set examples and standards which excited and encouraged imitation around the globe. More important, however, was the impact of what was going on in the great social and economic laboratory of America—the spectacle not only of successful self-government but also of economic opportunity and social equality and religious liberty and the potentialities of private voluntary associations, all available to ordinary men and women. What excited Europeans in the 19th-century was what had excited the Founding Fathers in the 18th—the chance to escape from Europe and to create a new order of society. Jefferson put it well in his letter to Joseph Priestley in 1801: "We can no longer say there is nothing new under the sun. For this whole chapter in the history of man is new. The great extent of our Republic is new. His sparse habitation is new. The mighty wave of public opinion which has rolled over it is new." What caught the imagination of the Western world was the chance to join in this new enterprise—the chance to start life anew and under circumstances more auspicious than any others in the history of man.

The American farmer, Hector St. John de Crevecoeur, saw this at the very outset of the American experiment. The European, he said, becomes an American:

by being received in the broad lap of our great *Alma Mater.* Here individuals of all nations are melted into a new race of men, whose labors and posterity will one day cause great changes in the world. Americans are the Western pilgrims who are carrying along with them that

49

great mass of arts, sciences, vigour, and industry which began long since in the east; they will finish the great circle.

And he added what was to be of crucial importance in transforming the European into the American, that:

> Europe contains hardly any other distinctions but lords and tenants; this fair country alone is settled by freeholders, the possessors of the soil they cultivate, members of the government they obey, and framers of their own laws. . . . There is room for everybody in America. . . . Instead of starving he will be fed; instead of begin idle he will have employment; and these are riches enough for such men as come over.

What Crèvecoeur described became the stuff of Tocqueville's philosophy: that *equality*—he used the term *democracy*—was the distinguishing feature of American life and that it was, if not precisely the mission, then the destiny of America, by her example and by her attraction, to spread equality throughout the Old World.

In these analyses both Crevecoeur and Tocqueville left out slavery (they were to recognize and lament that curse elsewhere in their writings), but in their recognition that the American Revolution meant—what its motto proclaimed—a new order of the ages (*novus ordo saeclorum*) socially and morally as well as politically, they were one with the Americans who had carried through both revolutions.

There is an elegiac quality about all this. We are no longer a revolutionary people. We are no longer creative in politics and government: every major political institution that we have today was invented before the year 1800; none has been invented since then. We no longer open our doors to the poor and the oppressed of the world. We no longer think of our mission as primarily that of lifting the burdens from the shoulders of men, and when we undertake to spread our way of life, it is through force, not through moral example. Perhaps a realization of what we once stood for, what we once accomplished, and what we once meant to mankind may yet lead us back to those paths which we were the first to tread. Listen to Tom Paine, as he rejoices in the triumph of "the greatest and completest revolution the world ever knew, gloriously and happily accomplished":

> Never had a country so many openings to happiness as this. Her setting out in life, like the rising of a fair morning, was unclouded and promising. Her cause was good. Her principles just and liberal. Her temper serene and firm. Her conduct regulated by the nicest steps, and everything about her wore the mark of honor. It is not every country that can boast so fair an origin.

The Spirit of '74

Thomas Fleming

Two hundred years ago, the 4th of July was a date which had no meaning whatsoever for Americans. The big celebration days were June 4, the birthday of "the Father of the country," King George III, and Jan. 18, the birthday of his consort, homely, prolific Queen Charlotte. But Americans of 1774 did share one thing with Americans of 1974—a state of profound political uneasiness. The turbulence began in the last month of 1773, when a group of Bostonians disguised as Mohawk Indians threw 342 chests of British East India Company tea worth £9,659 6s 4d into their harbor.

It was this event and the reaction to it in England and America that makes 1774 a watershed year, 12 momentous months when the confrontation we will celebrate in 1976 really took place. It was in 1774 that men in both countries saw the shocking dimension of the differences between Englishmen and Americans, differences that many sensed went much deeper than politics. It was in 1774 that the tangle of suspicion and countersuspicion, resentment and arrogance that had confused and irritated people on both sides of the Atlantic for more than a decade blossomed into a conflict of awesome proportions—a war that eventually exploded around the world and shook western civilization to its foundations.

The Boston Tea Party was no mere gesture of defiance. Nine thousand pounds was a large sum of money in 1774—the equivalent of perhaps 250,000 contemporary dollars. A shock wave of disbelief and alarm ran through America. Men of "sense and property," such as George Washington, deplored the Boston Tea Party. Virginians and their Maryland neighbors had, after all, imported record amounts of British tea in 1772 and paid the threepence tax per pound on it without fussing.

Everyone knew that Parliament had kept the tea duty to maintain its right to tax the colonists—a right that almost every American strenuously refused to concede. They shared the opinion that George Washington graphically expressed to a friend. "The Parliament of Great Britain hath no more right to put their hands into my pocket, without my consent, than I have to put my hands into yours for money." But a threepence tax on tea, paid by merchants in distant ports, did not make Washington or most other Americans, who were farmers like him, feel the parliamentary hand acutely enough to fight about it.

Only in the seaports of America—notably New York, Philadelphia and Charleston—did substantial voices cheer Boston's act of destruction. The cheerers were the so-called "popular leaders" who had played prominent and often riotous roles in previous resistance to British taxation. Now they hastened to form Committees of Correspondence in response to Boston's call to unify American resistance. But in every city the committees were dominated by conservatives and moderates. Neither the spark of violence nor even much of a spirit of resistance showed signs of leaping the boundaries of Massachusetts.

In 1774, Boston's cupidity and bigoted religiosity gave the city a low reputation south of Connecticut. One New Yorker described the place as the "common sewer of America." Bostonians had taken the lead in earlier agitation against British attempts to tax Americans without their consent, but the city had forfeited this leadership in 1770, when Boston's merchants had abandoned the policy of boycotting English imports without informing merchants in other colonies. Worse,

Chicago Historical Society

"The Bostonians Paying the Excise-Man," a 1774 cartoon printed in London, from a current exhibit of the National Portrait Gallery of the Smithsonian.

From *The New York Times Magazine*, June 30, 1974. ©1974 by The New York Times Company. Reprinted by permission.

2. REVOLUTIONARY AMERICA

Bostonians had become conspicuous for their failure to stop drinking English tea. In 1771, they had imported 265,000 pounds of it, with one of their more prominent merchants, John Hancock, paying duties on 45,000 pounds.

At the end of February, 1774, New York's "Sons of Liberty," as the popular leaders and their followers called themselves, were glum. Ruefully they admitted to the Boston Committee of Correspondence that they dared not suggest a total boycott of English tea, "least it might divide us." When two tea ships finally arrived in April, the tea aboard one was dumped into the Hudson River because the captain had tried to conceal it. The other captain, who confessed his cargo and agreed to return it to England, was escorted to the pilot boat by the Committee of Correspondence while a band played "God Save the King."

In England, the reaction to Boston's tea party was totally different. The news reached London on Jan. 19, 1774, aboard the Hayley, owned by that prominent tea shipper, John Hancock. Indignation was instantly the order of the day in the imperial capital. The King's First Minister, bland, amiable Lord North, and his pious, gentle half-brother, Lord Dartmouth, the Colonial Secretary, wanted no trouble with the Americans or anyone else. But other members of the Cabinet were spoiling for a fight with the Americans. So was the real head of the Government, 36-year-old George III, who had learned a lot about politics since he came to the throne in 1760, a badly frightened postadolescent with absurd ideas about purifying English society. With £800,000 a year to spend as he pleased, the King guaranteed North some 200 votes in the House of Commons, a nice foundation on which to build a majority. Bought off, outspent at the polls, the opposition was reduced to a shadow.

As the King and most of the Cabinet saw it, the tea party was no isolated incident. It was one more in a decade-long series of acts of defiance. The whole thing was a plot. Independence was the goal and Boston the center of the conspiracy. It was time to teach these obstreperous Puritans a large unforgettable lesson. The business could begin almost immediately, here in London, where a scapegoat was at hand—Benjamin Franklin, the agent for the Massachusetts Assembly.

Except for one brief trip to America to help install his son William as Royal Governor of New Jersey, Franklin had been living in London since 1757. World-famous for his discoveries in electricity, he enjoyed England and was a self-confessed admirer of the British Empire. But the 68-year-old Franklin also remained an unreconstructed American. In 1766, his testimony had played a key role in persuading Parliament to repeal the Stamp Act, the first British attempt to tax America, which had aroused the colonists to widespread rioting and defiance. Recently, Franklin had taken to mocking the Government directly in the newspapers with devas-

tating satires, such as "Rules by Which the Great Empire May Be Reduced to a Small One."

Even more irritating was what the Government learned by intercepting Franklin's letters to America— something it had been doing for several years. He told popular leaders in Massachusetts that in his opinion Parliament had no power over America—the only common tie was allegiance to the King. On one of Franklin's letters, a Colonial Office official had written: "Very remarkable and requires no commentary."

Worst of all, from the Ministers' point of view, Franklin seemed deeply involved in the latest agitation in Massachusetts. A few weeks before the news of the Boston Tea Party arrived, he had submitted to the King's Privy Council a request to remove the Royal Governor of Massachusetts, Thomas Hutchinson, and his Lieutenant Governor, Andrew Oliver, because they had supposedly lost the confidence of the people.

These men, both born in Massachusetts, had lost this confidence because Franklin had sent back to Massachusetts letters they had written years earlier to a minor British official, severely criticizing the popular party in Massachusetts and urging the Government to take a harsher line, including "some abridgement of what is called English liberty." Franklin claimed, somewhat ingenuously, that he had sent the letters in the hope of persuading the popular leaders to take a milder attitude toward the British Government. British officials were being misled, he argued, by Hutchinson, Oliver and their clique. The letters had produced a bristling confrontation between the Governor and the Assembly, which led to the petition for Hutchinson's removal. By a nice coincidence, the Privy Council had a hearing on the petition scheduled for Jan. 29. Lord North and his friends decided to turn it into an auto-da-fé.

When Franklin arrived for the hearing in the Cockpit, a section of Whitehall Palace, he was amazed to discover the room was jammed with lords and ladies in gorgeous finery, with greedily excited looks on their faces. It was obvious, Franklin later wrote, that they had all been invited "as to an entertainment."

The entertainer was Alexander Wedderburn, Solicitor General of England. He was a lean, mean Scot who had, Lord North once remarked, "the invaluable gift of an accommodating conscience." Representing a Government that made a habit of opening personal mail, Wedderburn ferociously denounced Franklin for stealing private letters of Hutchinson and Oliver. (Actually, copies of the letters had been leaked to Franklin, probably by Thomas Pownall, a former Governor of Massachusetts, an old Hutchinson enemy. Franklin claimed that they had been freely passed around London for some time.) Franklin, sneered Wedderburn, was nothing but a thief. Worse, he had become drunk with absurd notions of power. He had begun to think of himself as the minister for "the great American Republic."

Along with Franklin's swollen ego there was another more vicious motive, Wedderburn howled. He wanted the governorship of Massachusetts for himself. What kind of government would he create? A tyranny greater than the Roman, Wedderburn bellowed. Had they not heard in the past few days the latest news from the "good men of Boston"?

The Cockpit rocked with laughter at Wedderburn's best sallies. For almost an hour Franklin stood, in the words of an eyewitness, "the whole time like a rock . . . abiding the pelting of the pitiless storm."

For Franklin it was the end of his belief that he could remain a good American and a citizen of the empire. On the way out of the room, according to one report, he found himself walking beside Wedderburn. Gently Franklin took the Solicitor General by the arm and whispered in his ear, "I will make your master a little king for this."

The ministry's attack on Franklin was an act of incredible stupidity. It was compounded within the next 24 hours by his dismissal as Deputy Postmaster General for America. The British Government thus alienated the one man who could do it the most good— or the most harm—in America. Franklin was also the agent for the colonies of New Jersey and Georgia and, most important, for Pennsylvania. His network of contacts with newspapermen and postmasters up and down the continent from South Carolina to Boston, his fame as a scientist and his long sojourn in England gave everything he said enormous impact. Americans soon heard that Franklin was "at a loss to know how peace and union are to be maintained or restored between the different parts of the empire."

Alienating Franklin was only the first step in a headstrong course on which the King's Government was now embarked. On March 14, Lord North told Parliament that George III was asking for power, first, "to put an end to the present disturbances in America," and, second, "to secure the just dependence of the colonies on the Crown of Great Britain." It was no longer a question of whether Parliament had the right to tax America, North cried, the issue now was "whether or not we have any authority."

North could have said nothing more inflammatory to the swing vote in Parliament, the independent country gentlemen. They never ceased grumbling about the high taxes they paid (about 10 per cent of their incomes) and acutely resented the fact that Americans paid fewer taxes than any other people in the civilized world. Almost to a man, the country gentlemen supported North's Boston Port Bill, which closed the city's harbor until the ruined tea was paid for and "peace and obedience" were visible in the city streets.

The opposition did not even bother to call for a formal vote on the Boston Port Bill, so hopeless was any chance of defeating it. It passed as readily through the House of Lords and was signed by the King on March 31, 1774.

If the Government had stopped with the Port Bill, it might have won its hard-line gamble in America. We have already seen how little support the town of Boston had in other colonies. But the Government was not satisfied with punishing Boston. It was determined to settle the entire Massachusetts problem by remodeling the colony's government to guarantee that "just dependence" on the Crown that Lord North had designated as a primary royal goal.

The changes North recommended for Massachusetts gave the Royal Governor (who was appointed by the King) virtually unchecked power. Except for the annual spring elections, town meetings could be held only with his permission. Judges, sheriffs and all other law-enforcement officials were to be appointed by him alone. No longer could local constables summon juries. The Governor's Council, which functioned as a kind of senate, had traditionally been elected by the Massachusetts Assembly. Henceforth it would be appointed by the King.

With this bill came a companion piece called the Administration of Justice act. It gave the Governor power to send to England for trial any public official indicted for murder while attempting to suppress a riot or enforce the customs laws. The opposition in Parliament objected to these measures more vigorously than it had fought the Boston Port Bill. These struck at fundamental rights enjoyed by Americans in all the colonies—rights which Parliament had never before dared to threaten. The North administration and its supporters defended them in the same hysterical tone. North declared that the Americans had "denied all obedience to your laws and authority . . . whatever may be the consequence, we must risk something; if we do not, all is over."

The opposition suggested giving up the tax on tea to show the Government's good will. "If you give up this tax, you will be required to give up much more, nay, to give up all," Alexander Wedderburn roared, resting Parliament's entire case for legislative supremacy on a tea leaf. The repeal of the tea tax was buried, 182-49.

Still the Government hawks were not satisfied. They amended the Quartering Act, giving British military commanders power to inflict their troops on Americans in their homes. For a final flourish they introduced another bill—the Quebec Act. In many ways it was a sensible measure, which dealt realistically with the realities of French Canada. It guaranteed religious freedom—in effect acknowledging the dominant role of the Roman Catholic Church—and created a government modeled more or less along French colonial lines. There was no elective assembly. But in the context of the confrontation with Massachusetts, all of these measures looked ominous to Protestant Americans. Why this sudden caressing of their traditional enemies?

2. REVOLUTIONARY AMERICA

Was the elimination of an assembly a first step toward the elimination of all colonial assemblies?

For a fillip, the North Government chose Maj. Gen. Thomas Gage, commander of the British Army in America to be the new Governor of Massachusetts. Thomas Hutchinson had asked for a leave of absence, confessing that he had become so unpopular he could no longer govern the province. No one in the North Government seemed even slightly aware of the folly of appointing a military man to a civil post in such an explosive political situation and backing him with a 4,000-man army. Nor did they seem to care that Hutchinson's recall admitted that the petition for which Benjamin Franklin had been so savagely abused was substantially correct. Constitutionality, consistency, no longer seemed to concern the aroused King and his ministers.

The Americans heard about the Coercive Acts in the late spring and early summer of 1774. (The Quebec Act was not passed by Parliament until June 16.) Boston's popular leaders at first declared themselves overjoyed. One wrote to a friend in New York that "at length the perfect crisis of American politics seems to have arrived." But Boston's call for an immediate cessation of trade with Britain received very little support. Most merchants in other ports—and even some in Boston— urged the town to pay for the ruined tea. The idea was militantly rejected by the Boston town meeting. But this did not prevent the Philadelphia Committee of Correspondence, firmly controlled by moderates and conservatives, to reiterate the advice.

In Virginia, that decidedly unradical gentleman, George Washington, demonstrated conclusively the impact of the Coercive Acts by calling the cause of Boston "the cause of America." Popular leaders such as Richard Henry Lee and Patrick Henry, the Cicero and Demosthenes of America in the fond opinion of their supporters, urged immediate total defiance. But their rhetoric failed to ignite the largest colony. Everyone agreed that Britain had no right to tax America and Boston must be backed somehow, but there was no agreement whatsoever on halting trade with England. A similar attitude prevailed in South Carolina where fiery Christopher Gadsden found his rhetoric cooled by conservative caution.

Outside New England, this was the pattern in virtually every colony. The dominant conservative-moderate coalition and the aggressive popular leaders clashed vigorously on practical action. Almost invariably, the conservatives' solution was to delay doing anything until a Continental Congress could be assembled to speak for all Americans. The popular leaders reluctantly agreed to this proposition and in most colonies delegations were soon elected with a delicate balance of popular and conservative spokesmen.

Many conservatives frankly hoped that the Congress would never meet. But moderate men like George Washington no longer agreed. In late August he told a friend he would not "undertake to say where the line between Great Britain and the colonies should be drawn; but I am clearly of opinion, that one ought to be drawn, and our rights clearly ascertained."

On Sept. 5, 1774, 56 wary men from 12 colonies (Georgia was absent) gathered in Philadelphia's Carpenter's Hall. At first it looked like the conservatives had nothing to worry about. John Adams's diary records his dismay at the pervasive suspicion of New Englanders and especially of Massachusetts men. Small-state delegates quarreled with men from the three large states, Massachusetts, Pennsylvania and Virginia, who claimed that Congress should vote by population. (They lost.) George Washington's wish to "draw a line" designating the limits of British power over America was clearly the dominant motive of most delegates. But where and how that line should be drawn quickly split Congress into two warring camps.

The popular leaders backed the idea that Parliament had no power whatsoever and American rights were based on the law of nature. This last phrase awakened images of anarchy in the minds of conservatives, who insisted that the British Constitution, common law and colonial charters were a more than adequate foundation for American rights. Delegate after delegate made windy speeches on each side of the question and the men from Massachusetts became very impatient.

Above all else, they wanted Congress to make a statement of decisive support for Massachusetts. The Adamses and their colleagues had been striving mightily to lessen prejudice and suspicion against their colony. In conservation they breathed moderation and reconciliation. In the opening discussions, they had been more than content to let the popular orators from South Carolina and Virginia take the lead.

Now, Sam Adams decided, it was time to prevent Congress from becoming a constitutional debating society. Into Philadelphia thundered that doughty, dust-covered horseman, Paul Revere, with a set of resolves from the County of Suffolk, which included Boston. They had been written by Dr. Joseph Warren. Sam Adams's right-hand man, and they were nothing less than a declaration of war. They denounced Great Britain as "the parricide which points the dagger to our bosoms," declared the streets of Boston "were thronged with military executioners" and avowed that the compact between George III and the people of Massachusetts, whose rights were based on nature, was "totally wrecked, annulled and vacated." The Coercive Acts were denounced and "no obedience" was "due from this province to either or any part" of them. Finally came a call for an immediate stoppage of all trade with England, Ireland and the West Indies, and a proposal for Americans to stop paying all taxes, to ignore the courts, and to organize the militia for defense.

Sam Adams's timing proved to be superb. Moderates like Washington were bored with the debates and they joined the popular leaders in approving the Suffolk Resolves and ordering them printed in the newspapers. John Adams gleefully informed his diary that "America will support the Massachusetts or perish with her."

But Adams was soon wondering if he might have to eat these words. The conservatives launched a strong counterattack. Their leader was Joseph Galloway, for many years the most powerful politician in Pennsylvania, and long one of Benjamin Franklin's closest friends. Galloway proposed a totally different solution to the crisis—a written constitution for North America which would formally unite Britain and America. It would create a continental legislature, a "Grand Council" which would be composed of members elected by the existing colonial legislatures. This American Parliament would have the power to veto any law passed by England's Parliament affecting the colonies. Conversely, the British Parliament could veto legislation passed by the Grand Council and delegations from the two legislatures would then confer and work out a compromise. In North America, the Council would operate as a federal government, dealing with matters of "general concern" to the continent. The individual colonies would retain control of their internal affairs.

James Duane of New York enthusiastically seconded Galloway's proposal. To everyone's astonishment, Edward Rutledge of South Carolina, previously a popular firebrand, rose to agree, calling it "almost a perfect plan."

The popular leaders waffled. For the first time they were forced to reveal what lay behind their rhetoric— the conviction that no compromise with Great Britain was possible. The Coercive Acts had convinced them of what they had long suspected—there was a plot among the men who ruled England to deprive Americans of their traditional rights, their freedom step by devious step.

The closest anyone came to a serious reply to Galloway's Plan of Union, as it was called, was Patrick Henry and his claim that the American legislature would be corrupted by the British. John Jay of New York dared Richard Henry Lee of Virginia to point out one American liberty or right that the Galloway plan did not protect or enhance. Lee did not even try to answer him.

At the end of a day of inconclusive debate, a popular-party man shrewdly suggested putting off a vote on Galloway's plan for the time being. The conservatives furiously opposed the action, keenly aware that to table the plan was tantamount to killing it. By a hairline, six states to five, with Rhode Island's two-man delegation splitting, Congress voted to table the plan. It was the high-water mark of the attempt of those Americans who

certainly represented a majority of the country in 1774 to work out an accommodation with England.

Thereafter, the popular leaders were in control of Congress—a control which they maintained by carefully muting their rhetoric and decorating it with respectful apostrophes to the King in a declaration of American rights and a petition for the redress of American grievances. Far more important, Congress voted to create a continental association which promised to cease all imports from Great Britain on Dec. 1, 1774, and all exports to Great Britain on Sept. 10, 1775.

Only once did the popular leaders cast aside their moderate cover and reveal their awareness of their minority position. They persuaded Congress to expunge from the official records all mention of Galloway's Plan of Union. As historian Merrill Jensen has wryly pointed out, this maneuver was the first American example of "managed news."

In Boston, Gov. Gen. Thomas Gage was soon telling his superiors in England that "the proceedings of the Continental Congress astonish and terrify all considerate men." But Gage was gloomily certain that they would have the virtual force of law in America because there "does not appear to be resolution and strength enough among the most sensible and moderate people in any of the provinces openly to reject them." Gage had long since given up looking for assistance from sensible and moderate men in Massachusetts. By this time he was a frankly frightened man. He realized there was a distinct possibility that he and his 4,000-man army might be massacred.

On Sept. 1, 1774, he had sent a detachment of 250 men to seize 125 barrels of gunpowder stored at Cambridge. The task was accomplished without resistance—but news of the Governor's act swept through the province and an astonishing number of armed men—some said as many as 20,000—converged

EXPLANATION

A political print designed and used by Benjamin Franklin on his stationery during the Stamp Act controversy. Franklin, then a resident of London, was employed as a colonial agent.

55

on Boston to do battle. The popular leaders managed to persuade them to go home without firing a shot. But the shaken Gage began fortifying the narrow neck which connected Boston to the mainland of Massachusetts.

In England, George III, buoyed by recent elections which gave the North Government a hefty majority in Parliament, read Gage's reports and grimly wrote to Lord North that he was "not sorry that the line of conduct seems now chalked out, which the enclosed dispatches thoroughly justify; the New England governments are in a state of rebellion. Blows must decide whether they are to be subject to this country or independent."

Lord North and Colonial Secretary Lord Dartmouth did not share the satisfaction of their pugnacious sovereign. They were appalled to discover that Americans were supporting Boston and Massachusetts with apparent unanimity. The prospect of war with America dismayed them. England's traditional enemies, France and Spain, were almost certain to exploit her embarrassment by entering the conflict one way or another in the hope of acquiring some lucrative pieces of the far-flung empire. Even the prospect of economic warfare with America was alarming. Well over half of England's imports of raw material came from America and a fifth of her exports—an average of £2,790,000 a year—went to the colonies.

Secretly, Dartmouth, with the probable approval of North, turned to the one man who might yet rescue the situation—Benjamin Franklin. They approached him through a screen of intermediaries, among whom were Dartmouth's Quaker doctor, and Admiral Lord Richard Howe, head of a prominent military family known for its friendly attitude toward America. Franklin reluctantly cooperated—and the negotiations continued until he sailed for home early in March of 1775. Even though Howe frequently dangled the "favors" of the British Government before him as a thinly veiled bribe, Franklin never wavered in his insistence that Parliament had to disclaim all power to tax America or interfere in her internal affairs in any way whatsoever.

How little chance the negotiations had can be glimpsed from Franklin's reaction to Galloway's Plan of Union, which that unhappy politician sent him early in 1775. Franklin himself had proposed a not dissimilar plan at the Albany Congress in 1754. Now he told his friend: "When I consider the extreme corruption prevalent among all orders of men in this old rotten state, . . . I cannot but apprehend more mischief than benefit from a closer union." Yet on his last day in England, Franklin broke down and wept at the thought of war "with such near relations." By the time he would reach Philadelphia, blood would have already spilled on Lexington green and Concord bridge.

Early in December Lord Dartmouth had received from Benjamin Franklin the Continental Congress's petition to the King. It would be ignored by Parliament when it reconvened in 1775. Dartmouth was well aware of this, and as 1774 waned, the one man in the Cabinet who really wanted peace suggested that Britain send commissioners to America to confer with colonial delegates. The King coldly rejected the idea. He said it would make the "Mother Country look more afraid of the continuance of the dispute than the colonies." The King added that he did not wish to drive the Americans to despair. "Submission" was all he wanted.

In America a furious war of words raged in pamphlets and newspapers between conservatives and popular leaders over the decisions of the First Continental Congress, with the advocates of defiance growing bolder every day. Significantly, some of the venom spilled over onto the "father of the country," George III. One Philadelphia writer called the history of kings the history of the depravity of human nature. The American children were growing more and more obstreperous.

On Dec. 14, New Hampshiremen, led by John Sullivan, broke into Fort William and Mary, in Portsmouth, frightened the tiny garrison into submission and carried off the guns and gunpowder. On Dec. 22, in Gloucester, N.J., a shipment of tea stored in a warehouse went up in flames. In Massachusetts, confident men were singing a song written by Sam Adams's lieutenant, Dr. Joseph Warren.

> *Torn from a world of*
> *tyrants*
> *Beneath his western*
> *sky*
> *We formed a new*
> *dominion*
> *A land of liberty*
> *The world shall own*
> *we're masters here;*
> *Then hasten on*
> *the day*
> *Huzza, huzza, huzza,*
> *huzza*
> *For free America. . . .*
> *Some future day shall*
> *crown us*
> *The masters of the*
> *main,*
> *Our fleets shall speak in*
> *thunder*
> *To England, France*
> *and Spain;*
> *And the nations over the*
> *oceans spread*
> *Shall tremble and*
> *obey.*
>
> *The sons, the sons, the*
> *sons, the sons*
> *Of brave*
> *America. . . .*

Meet Dr. Franklin

"So convenient a thing it is to be a *reasonable creature,* since it enables one to find or make a reason for everything one has a mind to do"

RICHARD B. MORRIS

Richard B. Morris, Gouverneur Morris, Professor of History at Columbia University, is a prolific author and frequent contributor. The foregoing essay is part of a book comprised of biographical sketches that suggest new insights into the Founding Fathers.

As bedfellows they were curiously mismatched. Yet Benjamin Franklin and John Adams once shared a bed at a crowded New Brunswick inn, which grudgingly provided them with a room to themselves hardly larger than the bed itself. The room had one small window. Adams, who has recorded the night's adventure, remembered that the window was open. Afraid of the mild September night air, he got out of bed and shut it.

"Don't shut the window. We shall be suffocated," Franklin remonstrated. Adams explained his fears of the night air, but his senior companion reassured him: "The air within the chamber will soon be, and indeed is now, worse than without doors. Come, open the window and come to bed, and I will convince you. I believe you are not acquainted with my theory of colds." With misgivings Adams agreed to open the window. While Franklin continued to expound his theory of the causes of colds, Adams fell asleep, remembering that the last words he heard were spoken very drowsily. For this one night the testy Adams, who never relished being crossed or losing an argument, yielded to the diplomatic blandishments of Franklin, whose scientific experimentalism extended even to his code of personal hygiene. Neither caught colds that night.

Out of choice neither Adams nor Franklin would have picked the other as a companion with whom to spend that or any other night, but they had no choice. Dispatched in the late summer of 1776 by the Continental Congress, along with Edward Rutledge, the young Carolinian, they were en route to a rendezvous with Lord Richard Howe, the British admiral, and Sir William Howe, the general, on Staten Island for an informal peace conference. The hour was late for reconciliation. On the second of July the Congress had voted independence. At the end of August a vast amphibious force had routed the rebels on Long Island and was readying the trap for Washington's forces defending Manhattan. The three congressmen contested for space with soldiers thronging the Jersey roads to join Washington. What the Howes had to offer at the peace conference finally held on September 11 was no more than a pardon for those who had rebelled. It was too little and came too late. The war would be fought to a finish.

No one, least of all an Adams, could really get to know Franklin after a single night in bed with him. While Adams was to become increasingly disenchanted with the man with whom he was to work abroad for a number of years, he could take satisfaction in the knowledge that his prejudices were shared by a whole party in Congress which well knew that Dr. Franklin was up to no good. To the rest of mankind (British officialdom and Tories excepted, of course) Franklin embodied the most admirable traits and was a truly great man.

Deceptively simple and disarmingly candid, but in reality a man of enormous complexity, Franklin wore many masks, and from his own time to this day each beholder has chosen the mask that suited his fancy. To D.H. Lawrence, Franklin typified the hypocritical and bankrupt morality of the do-gooder American, with his stress upon an old-fashioned Puritan ethic that glorified work, frugality, and temperance—in short, a "snuff-coloured little man" of whom "the immortal soul part was a sort of cheap insurance policy." F. Scott Fitzgerald quickly fired off a broadside of his own. In *The Great Gatsby* that literary darling of the Jazz Age indicted *Poor Richard's Almanack* as midwife to a generation of bootleggers.

If Lawrence and Fitzgerald were put off by Franklin's common-sense materialism, which verged on crassness, or if Max Weber saw Franklin as embodying all that was despicable both in the American character and the capitalist system, if they and other critics considered him as little more than a methodical shopkeeper, they signally failed to understand that man of many masks. They failed to perceive how Franklin's materialism was transmuted into benevolent and humanitarian ends; how that shopkeeper's mind was stimulated by a ranging imagination that set no bounds to his intellectual interests and that continually fed an extraordinarily inventive and creative spark. They failed to explain how the popularizer of an American code of hard work,

Reprinted from *American Heritage*, December 1971, by permission of the author.

As American minister to France in 1778, Franklin, though no pioneer, wore a fur hat to build an impression of democratic simplicity—one of the protective guises devised and enjoyed by his complex mind.

frugality, and moral restraint had no conscientious scruples about enjoying high living, a liberal sexual code for himself, and bawdy humor. They failed to explain how so prudent and methodical a man could have gotten caught up in a revolution in no small part of his own making.

Franklin would have been the first to concede that he had in his *Autobiography* created a character gratifying to his own vanity. "Most people dislike vanity in others, whatever share they have of it themselves," he observed, "but I give it fair quarter where I meet it." Begun in 1771, when the author had completed a half dozen careers and stood on the threshold of his most dramatic role, the *Autobiography* constitutes the most dazzling success story of American history. The penniless waif who arrived in Philadelphia dishevelled and friendless, walking up Market Street munching a great puffy roll, had by grit and ability propelled himself to the top. Not only did the young printer's apprentice manage the speedy acquisition of a fortune, but he went on to achieve distinction in many different fields and greatness in a few of them. In an age when the mastery of more than one discipline was possible, Franklin surpassed all his contemporaries as a well-rounded citizen of the world. Endowed with a physique so strong that as a young man he could carry a large form of type in each hand "when others carried but one in both hands," a superb athlete and a proficient swimmer, Franklin proved to be a talented printer, an enterprising newspaper editor and publisher, a tireless promoter of cultural institutes, America's first great scientist, whose volume on electricity turned out to be the most influential book to emerge from America in the eighteenth century, and second to none as a statesman. Eldest of the Founding Fathers by a whole generation, he was in some respects the most radical, most devious, and most complicated.

From the available evidence, mainly provided by the subject himself, Franklin underwent two separate identity crises, those periods when, as modern-day psychoanalysts suggest, the subject struggles for a new self and a new conception of his place in the world. In adolescence Franklin experienced a psychological crisis of the kind that Erik Erikson has so perceptively attributed to personages as disparate as Martin Luther and Mahatma Gandhi. Again, Franklin, the middle-aged man seeking a new image of himself, seems the prototype of Swiss psychiatrist Carl Jung's classic case. As regards the first crisis, the *Autobiography* reveals a sixteen-year-old rebelling against sibling rivalry and the authority of his household, using a variety of devices to maintain his individuality and sense of self-importance.

Born in Boston in 1706, the tenth son of Josiah and Abiah Folger Franklin and the youngest son of the youngest son for five generations, Franklin could very easily have developed an inferiority complex as one of the youngest of thirteen children sitting around his father's table at one time. Everything about the home reduced Franklin's stature in his own eyes. When his father tried to make a tallow chandler and soap boiler out of him, he made it clear that his father's trade was not to his liking. His father then apprenticed the twelve-year-old lad to his brother James, who had started a Boston newspaper, the *New England Courant,* in 1721. For the next few years Benjamin was involved in one or another kind of rebellion.

Take the matter of food. Benjamin, an omnivorous reader, devoured a book recommending a vegetarian diet. Since his brother James boarded both himself and his apprentices at another establishment, Franklin's refusal to eat meat or fish proved an embarrassment to his elder brother and a nuisance to the housekeeper. Franklin, to save arguments, which he abhorred, worked out a deal with his brother, who agreed to remit to him half the money he paid out for him for board if he would board himself. Concentrating on a frugal meatless diet, which he dispatched quickly, Franklin, eating by himself, had more time to continue his studies. While eating one of his hastily prepared meals, he first feasted on *An Essay Concerning Human Understanding,* by John Locke.

A trivial episode indeed, but this piece of self-flagellation forecast a lifelong pattern of pervasive traits. Benjamin Franklin did not like to hurt anyone, even nonhuman creatures. He was prone to avoid hostilities. Rather than insisting upon getting the menu he preferred, he withdrew from the table of battle and arranged to feed himself. This noncombative nature, masking a steely determination, explains much of Franklin's relations with others thereafter. Even his abandonment of the faddish vegetarian diet provides insights into the evolving Franklin with his pride in rational decision. On his famous voyage from Boston to Philadelphia, he tells us, his ship became becalmed off Block Island, where the crew spent their idle moments catching cod. When the fish were opened, he saw that smaller fish came out of the stomachs of the larger cod. "Then, thought I," he confessed in his *Autobiography,* "if you eat one another, I don't see why we mayn't eat you." With that he proceeded to enjoy a hearty codfish repast and to return at once to a normal flesh-eating diet. With a flash of self-revelation, he comments, "So convenient a thing it is to be a *reasonable creature,* since it enables one to find or make a reason for everything one has a mind to do."

Franklin's rebellion against authority and convention soon assumed a more meaningful dimension. When, in 1722, his brother James was jailed for a month for printing in his newspaper critical remarks about the authorities, the sixteen-year-old apprentice pounced on the chance to achieve something on his own. He published the paper for his brother, running his own name on the masthead to circumvent the government. Continually quarrelling with his overbearing brother, Franklin determined to part company with his job, his family, and Boston, and to establish himself by his own efforts, unaided. The youthful rebel set forth on his journey to Philadephia, arriving in that bustling town in October, 1723, when he was little more than seventeen years of age.

To carve out a niche for himself in the printing trade Franklin had to keep a checkrein on his rebellious disposition. For weeks he bore without ill temper the badgering of his master, Samuel Keimer. When the blowup came, Franklin, rather than stay and quarrel, packed up and lit out. Once more he was on his own. "Of all the things I hate altercation," he wrote years later to one of his fellow commissioners in Paris with whom he was continually at odds. He would write sharp retorts and then not mail the letters. An operator or negotiator par excellence, Franklin revealed in his youthful rebellion against family and employers the defensive techniques he so skillfully utilized to avoid combat. Yet there was little about Franklin's behavior

that we associate with neurotics. He was a happy extrovert who enjoyed the company of women and was gregarious and self-assured—a striking contrast to Isaac Newton, a tortured introvert who remained a bachelor all his life. Suffice it to say that Franklin never suffered the kind of nervous breakdown that Newton experienced at the height of his powers, and as a result his effectiveness remained undiminished until a very advanced age.

If Franklin early showed a inclination to back away from a quarrel, to avoid a head-on collision; if his modesty and candor concealed a comprehension of his own importance and a notably persistent deviousness, such traits may go far to explain the curious satisfaction he took in perpetrating hoaxes on an unsuspecting and gullible public. The clandestine side of Franklin, a manifestation of his unwillingess to engage in direct confrontation, hugely benefited by his sense of humor and satirical talents. An inveterate literary prankster from his precocious teens until his death, Franklin perpetrated one literary hoax after another. In 1730, when he became the sole owner of a printing shop and proprietor of the *Pennsylvania Gazette,* which his quondam boss, Keimer, had launched a few years earlier, Franklin's paper reported a witch trial at Mount Holly, New Jersey, for which there was no authority in fact.

Franklin's greatest hoax was probably written in 1746 and perpetrated the following year, when the story ran in London's *General Advertiser.* It was quickly reprinted throughout England, Scotland, and Ireland and in turn picked up by the Boston and New York papers. This was his report of a speech by Polly Baker before a Massachusetts court, in defense of an alleged prosecution for the fifth time for having a bastard child. "Can it be a crime (in the nature of things I mean) to add to the number of the King's subjects, in a new country that really wants people?" she pleaded. "I own it, I should think it as praiseworthy, rather than a punishable action." Denying that she had ever turned down a marriage proposal, but contrariwise was betrayed by the man who first made her such an offer, she compared her role with that of the great number of bachelors in the new country who had "never sincerely and honourably courtet a woman in their lives" and insisted that, far from sinning, she had obeyed the "great command of Nature, and of Nature's God, *Encrease and Multiply.*" Her compassionate judges remitted her punishment, and, according to this account, one of them married her the very next day.

That so obviously concocted a morality tale as that one could have gained such wide credence seems incredible on its face. Yet the French sage, the Abbé Raynal, picked it up for his *Histoire Philosophique et Politique,* published in 1770. Some seven years later, while visiting Franklin at Passy, Raynal was to be disabused. "When I was young and printed a newspaper," Franklin confessed, "it sometimes happened, when I was short of material to fill my sheet, that I amused myself by making up stories, and that of Polly Baker is one of the number."

When, some years later, Franklin's severe critic John Adams listed Polly Baker's speech as one of Franklin's many "outrages to morality and decorum," he was censuring not only Franklin's liberal sexual code but his evident inability to throw off bad habits in old age. Franklin's penchant for pseudonymous writing, abundantly displayed in the Revolutionary years, was one side of his devious nature and evidenced his desire to avoid direct confrontation. . . .

The image of himself Franklin chose to leave us in his unfinished *Autobiography* was of a man on the make who insincerely exploited popular morality to keep his printing presses running. Yet he himself, perhaps tongue-in-cheek, would have said that the morality of *Poor Richard* was foreshadowed by the plan of conduct Franklin had put down on paper in 1726 on a return voyage to Philadelphia from London, where he had spent almost two years in an effort to be able to buy equipment to set himself up as a printer. Later in life Franklin praised the plan as "the most remarkable, as being formed when I was so young, and yet being pretty faithfully adhered to quite through to old age." The plan stressed the practice of extreme frugality until he had paid his debts, as well as truthfulness, industry, and the avoidance of speaking ill of others.

Franklin, the sixteen-year-old apprentice, absorbed the literary styles of his brother James and other New England satirists running their pieces in the *Courant* and clearly used the *Spectator* as his literary model. He produced the Silence Dogood letters, thirteen in a row, until, he admitted, "my small fund of sense for such performances was pretty well exhausted." Until then even his own brother was not aware of the identity of the author.

If the Dogood letters satisfied Franklin's itch for authorship, *Poor Richard* brought him fame and fortune. Lacking originality, drawing upon a wide range of proverbs and aphorisms notably found in a half dozen contemporary English anthologies, Franklin skillfully selected, edited, and simplified. For example, James Howell's *Lexicon Tetraglotton* (London, 1660) says: "The greatest talkers are the least doers"; *Poor Richard* in 1733 made it: "Great talkers, little doers." Thomas Fuller's *Gnomolonia* (London, 1732) advises: "The way to be safe is never to be secure"; this becomes, in *Poor Richard,* 1748, "He that's secure is not safe." Every so often one of the aphorisms seems to reflect Franklin's own views. Thus *Poor Richard* in 1747 counselled: "Strive to be the *greatest* Man in your Country, and you may be disappointed; Strive to be the *best,* and you may succeed: He may well win the race that runs by himself." Two years later *Poor Richard* extols Martin Luther for being "remarkably *temperate* in meat and drink"— perhaps a throwback to Franklin's own adolescent dietary obsessions—with an added comment, "There

was never any industrious man who was not a temperate man." To the first American pragmatist what was moral was what worked, and what worked was moral.

If there was any priggish streak in the literary Franklin, it was abundantly redeemed by his bawdy sense of humor and his taste for earthy language. Thus, to *Poor Richard,* foretelling the weather by astrology was "as easy as pissing abed." And: "He that lives upon hope, dies farting." The bawdy note of reportage guaranteed a good circulation for Franklin's *Gazette.* Thus in 1731:

We are credibly inform'd, that the young Woman who not long since petitioned the Governor, and the Assembly to be divorced from her Husband, and at times industriously solicited most of the Magistrates on that Account, has at last concluded to cohabit with him again. It is said the Report of the Physicians (who in Form examined his *Abilities,* and allowed him to be in every respect *sufficient*) gave her but small Satisfaction; Whether any Experiments *more satisfactory* have been try'd, we cannot say; but it seems she now declares it as her Opinion, That *George is as good as de best.*

Franklin's ambivalent views of women indubitably reflected his own personal relations with the other sex. In his younger days he took sex hungrily, secretly, and without love. One of his women—just which one nobody knows for sure—bore him a son in 1730 or 1731. It was rumored that the child's mother was a maidservant of Franklin's named Barbara, an accusation first printed in 1764 by a political foe of Franklin, reputedly Hugh Williamson. Whether it was this sudden responsibility or just the boredom of sowing his wild oats, Franklin came to realize that "a single man resembles the odd half of a pair of scissors." Having unsuccessfully sought a match with a woman who would bring him money, Franklin turned his thoughts back to Deborah Read, the girl he had first courted in Philadelphia and then jilted. He "took her to wife, September 1st, 1730." The illegitimate child, William, whether born before or after Franklin's common-law marriage to Deborah, became part of the household, a convenient arrangement for Franklin while a constant reminder to Deborah of her spouse's less than romantic feelings about her. Soon there arose between Deborah and William a coldness bordering on hostility.

The married Franklin's literary allusions to women could be both amicable and patronizing; he could treat them as equals but show downright hostility at times. He stuffed his *Almanack* with female stereotypes, perhaps charging off his own grievances to the sex in general. He frequently jabbed at "domineering women," with Richard Saunders the prototype of all hen-pecked husbands. A woman's role in life, he tells us, is to be a wife and have babies, but a man has a more versatile role and therefore commands a higher value.

With the sexual revolution of the twentieth century and the modern penchant for pornographic vocabulary,

Franklin's letter on marriages and mistresses has attained respectability and wide circulation. In essence, Franklin, in a letter dated June 25, 1745, commended marriage as the state in which a man was "most likely to find solid happiness." However, those wishing to avoid matrimony without forgoing sex were advised to prefer "old women to young ones." Among the virtues of older women he listed their more agreeable conversation, their continued amiability to counteract the "diminution of beauty," the absence of a "hazard of children," their greater prudence and discretion in conducting extramartial affairs, and the superiority of their techniques. "As in the dark all cats are gray, the pleasure of corporal enjoyment with an old woman is at least equal, and frequently, superior, every knack being by practice capable of improvement." Furthermore, who could doubt the advantages of making an old woman "happy" over debauching a virgin and contributing to her ruin. Finally, old women are "so grateful!!"

How much this advice reflected Franklin's own marriage of convenience remains for speculation. *Poor Richard* is constantly chiding cuckolds, scolding wives, and suggesting that marital infidelity is the course of things: "Let thy maidservant be faithful, strong, and homely"; "She that paints her face, thinks of her tail"; "Three things are men most liable to be cheated in, a horse, a wig, and a wife." Or consider poor Lub lying on his deathbed, both he and his wife despairing, he fearing death, she "that he may live." Or the metaphor of women as books and men the readers: "Are Women Books? says Hodge, then would mine were an Almanack, to change her every year."

Enough examples, perhaps, have been chosen to show that Franklin's early view of women was based on a combination of gross and illicit sexual experiences and a less than satisfying marriage with a wife neither glamorous nor intellectually compatible.

Abruptly, at the age of forty-two, Franklin retired from active participation in his printing business. He explained the action quite simply: "I flattered myself that, by the sufficient tho' modest fortune I had acquir'd, I had secured leisure during the rest of my life for philosophical studies and amusements." These words masked the middle-age identity crisis that he was now undergoing. Seeking to project himself on a larger stage, he did not completely cut his ties to a less glamorous past—including a wife who was a social liability—but conveniently evaded it. Now he could lay aside the tools of his trade and the garments of a petit bourgeois and enter the circles of gentility. Gone were the days when he would sup on an anchovy, a slice of bread and butter, and a half pint of ale shared with a companion. His long bouts with the gout in later life attest to his penchant for high living—Madeira, champagne, Parmesan cheese, and other continental delicacies. Sage, philanthropist, statesman, he became, as one critic has remarked, "an intellectual trans-

vestite," affecting a personality switch that was virtually completed before he left on his first mission (second trip) to England in 1757. Not that Franklin was a purely parochial figure at the time of his retirement from business. Already he had shown that passion for improvement that was to mark his entire career. Already he had achieved some local reputation in public office, notably in the Pennsylvania assembly. Already he had displayed his inventive techniques, most notably with his invention of the "Pennsylvania Fireplace," and had begun his inquiries into the natural sciences.

Now, on retirement from private affairs, he stood on the threshold of fame. In the subsequent decade he plunged into his scientific investigations and into provincial politics with equal zest. Dispatched to England in 1757 to present the case of the Pennsylvania assembly against the proprietor, he spent five of the happiest years of his life residing at the Craven Street residence of the widowed Margaret Stevenson. Mrs. Stevenson, and especially her daughter Mary, provided for him a pleasant and stimulating home away from home. Reluctantly he returned to Philadelphia at the end of his five-year stay, so enraptured by England that he even contemplated settling there, "provided we can persuade the good woman to cross the seas." Once more, in 1764, he was sent abroad, where he stayed to participate in all the agitation associated with the Grenville revenue measures. Snugly content in the Stevenson menage, Franklin corresponded perfunctorily with his wife back in Philadelphia. Knowing that Deborah was unwilling to risk a sea voyage to join him in London, Franklin did not insist. And though he wrote his wife affectionate letters and sent her gifts, he never saw her again. She died of a stoke in December, 1774, without benefit of Franklin's presence.

It was in France after the American Revolution had broken out that Franklin achieved more completely the new identity that was the quest of his later years. There the mellow septuagenarian, diplomat, and peacemaker carried out a game with the ladies of the salon, playing a part, ironic, detached but romantic, enjoying an *amitié amoureuse* with Mme. Brillon, his impressionable and neurotic neighbor in Passy, flirting in Paris with the romantically minded Comtesse d'Houdetot, and then in the rustic retreat of Auteuil falling in love with the widow of Claude Adrien Helvétius, whom he was prepared to marry had she been so inclined. In the unreal world of the salon Franklin relished the role of "papa." Still he avoided combat or confrontation even in his flirtation. Where he scented rejection, he turned witty, ironic, and verbally sexual.

He found time, while engaged in the weighty affairs of peacemaking during the summer of 1782, to draw up a treaty of "eternal peace, friendship, and love" between himself and Mme. Brillon. Like a good draftsman, Franklin was careful to preserve his freedom of action, in this case toward other females, while at the same time insisting on his right to behave without inhibitions towards his amiable neighbor. Some months before, he wrote her:

I often pass your house. It appears desolate to me. Formerly I broke the Commandment by coveting it along with my neighbour's wife. Now I do not covet it any more, so I am less a sinner. But as to his wife I always find these Commandments inconvenient and I am sorry that they were ever made. If in your travels you happen to see the Holy Father, ask him to repeal them, as things given only to the Jews and too uncomfortable for good Christians.

Franklin met Mme. Brillon in 1777 and found her a beautiful woman in her early thirties, an accomplished musician, married to a rich and tolerant man twenty-four years her senior. To Mme. Brillon, Franklin was a father figure, while to Franklin she combined the qualities of daughter and mistress. Part tease, part prude, Mme. Brillon once remarked: "Do you know, my dear papa, that people have criticized the sweet habit I have of sitting on your lap, and your habit of soliciting from me what I always refuse?" In turn Franklin reminded her of a game of chess he had played in her bathroom while she soaked in the tub.

If Franklin was perhaps most passionately fond of Brillon, other ladies of the salon set managed to catch his eye, among them the pockmarked, cross-eyed Comtesse d'Houdetot, who made up in sex appeal what she lacked in looks. Unlike Rousseau, who cherished for the Comtesse an unrequited passion that was publicized in the posthumously printed *Julie, ou La Nouvelle Héloise,* Franklin had a relationship with her that never seemed to border on intimacy. Contrariwise, Franklin carried on a long flirtation with the widowed Madame Helvétius. Abigail Adams, John's strait-laced wife, was shocked at the open intimacies between the pair. Franklin complained that since he had given Madame "so many of his days," she appeared "very ungrateful in not giving him one of her nights." Whether in desperation or because he really felt the need to rebuild some kind of family life, he proposed to her. When she turned him down, he wrote a bagatelle recounting a conversation with Madame's husband in the Elysian Fields as well as his own encounter with his deceased wife Deborah. He then dashed into print with the piece, an odd thing to do if he were deadly serious about the proposal. As Sainte-Beuve remarked of this episode, Franklin never allowed himself to be carried away by feeling, whether in his youth or in old age, whether in love or in religion. His romantic posture was almost ritualistic. He almost seemed relieved at the chance to convert an emotional rebuff into a literary exercise.

Despite his casual attitude toward sexual morality, Franklin was far from being a playboy. The old Doctor, an irrepressible activist and dogooder, embodied in his own career the blend of practicality and idealism that has characterized Americans ever since. Convinced from early youth of the values of self-improvement and self-education, Franklin on his return to Philadelphia from his first trip to England organized the Junto, a society half debating, half social, attesting both to the sponsor's belief in the potentialities of continued adult education and to his craving for intellectual companionship not provided in his own home. Then came the subscription library, still flourishing in Philadelphia. Franklin's plans for a Pennsylvania academy, drawn up in 1743, reached fruition a decade later and were a positive outgrowth of his conviction that an English rather than a classical education was more suitable to modern man and that most colleges stuffed the heads of students with irrelevant book-knowledge. Then, too, the task of organizing a Pennsylvania hospital—hospitalization being defended by him as more economical than home care—drew upon his seemingly inexhaustible fund of energy. So did his organization of a local fire company, and his program for a tax-supported permanent police watch, and for lighting, paving, sweeping, draining, and de-icing the streets of Philadelphia. Convinced of the virtues of thrift and industry, Franklin could be expected to take a dim view of poor relief, and questioned "whether the laws peculiar to England which compel the rich to maintain the poor have not given the latter a dependence that very much lessens the care of providing against the wants of old age." Truly, this revolutionary, if he returned to us today, might well be aghast at the largess of the modern welfare state with its indifference to the work ethos. That the oldest of American revolutionaries should be committed to controlled, orderly change takes on larger significance when one seeks explanations as to why the American Revolution did not pursue the violent, even chaotic, course of the French. . . .

A man of the Enlightenment, Franklin had faith in the power and beneficence of science. In moments snatched from public affairs during the latter 1740's and early 50's—moments when public alarms interrupted his research at the most creative instant–he plunged into scientific experimentation. While his lightning kite and rod quickly made him an international celebrity, Franklin was no mere dilettante gadgeteer. His conception of electricity as a flow with negative and positive force promoted further theoretical development in the theory of electromagnetism. His pamphlet on electricity, published originally in 1751, went through ten editions, including revisions, in four languages before the American Revolution. Honors from British scientists were heaped upon him; and when he arrived in England in 1757 and again in 1764 and in France in 1776, he came each time with an enlarged international reputation as a scientist whom Chatham compared in Parliament to "our Boyle" and "our Newton."

Pathbreaking as Franklin's work on electricity proved to be, his range of scientific interest extended far beyond theoretical physics. He pioneered in locating the Gulf Stream, in discovering that northeast storms come from the southwest, in making measurements of heat absorption with regard to color, and in investigating the conductivity of different substances with regard to heat. A variety of inventions attested to his utilitarian bent—the Franklin stove, the lightning rod, the flexible metal catheter, bifocal glasses, the glass harmonica, the smokeless chimney. Indefatigable in his expenditure of his spare time on useful ends, he made observations on the nature of communications between insects, contributed importantly to our knowledge of the causes of the common cold, advocated scientific ventilation, and even tried on a number of occasions electric shock treatment to combat palsy.

To the last Franklin stoutly defended scientific experimentation that promised no immediate practical consequences. Watching the first balloon ascension in Paris, he parried the question, "What good is it?" with a characteristic retort, "What good is a newborn baby?"

Committed as he was to discovering truth through scientific inquiry, Franklin could be expected to be impatient with formal theology. While not denigrating faith, he regretted that it had not been "more productive of good works than I have generally seen it." He suggested that, Chinese style, laymen leave praying to the men who were paid to pray for them. At the age of twenty-two he articulated a simple creed, positing a deistic Christian God with infinite power that He would abstain from wielding in arbitrary fashion. His deistic views remained unchanged when, a month before his death, Ezra Stiles asked him his opinion of the divinity of Jesus. Confessing doubts, Franklin refused to dogmatize or to busy himself with the problem at so late a date, since, he remarked, "I expect soon an opportunity to knowing the truth with less trouble."

Unlike the *philosphes* who spread toleration but were intolerant of Roman Catholicism, Franklin tolerated and even encouraged any and all sects. He contributed to the support of various Protestant churches and the Jewish synagogue in Philadelphia, and, exploiting his friendship with the papal nuncio in Paris, he had his friend John Carroll made the first bishop of the Catholic Church in the new United States. He declared himself ready to welcome a Muslim preacher sent by the Grand Mufti in Constantinople, but that exotic spectacle was spared Protestant America of his day.

Although he fancied the garb of a Quaker, a subtle form of reverse ostentation that ill accorded with his preachments about humility, Franklin was no pacifist. Following Braddock's disastrous defeat in December, 1755, Franklin as a civilian committeeman marched into the interior at the head of an armed force, directing an improvised relief program for the frontier refugees who had crowded into Bethlehem and seeing about the

fortifying of the Lehigh gap. Once again, almost a decade later, he took command of a military force—this time to face down a frontier band known as the Paxton Boys, who in 1764 set out on a lawless march to Philadelphia to present the government with a demand for protection against the Indians. Franklin issued a blazing pamphlet denouncing the Paxton Boys for their attacks on peaceful Indians and organized and led a force to Germantown, where he confronted the remonstrants and issued a firm warning. The Paxton Boys veered off, and order was finally restored. "For about forty-eight hours," Franklin remarked, "I was a very great man, as I had been once some years before in a time of public danger."

Franklin's brief exposure as a military figure, combined with his leadership of the antiproprietary party and his general prominence and popularity had by now made him anathema to proprietor and conservatives alike. Standing out against the Establishment, Franklin was heartened by the enemies he had made. A thorough democrat, Franklin had little use for proprietary privileges or a titled aristocracy. In his Silence Dogood letters written as far back as 1723 he had pointed out that "Adam was never called *Master* Adam; we never read of Noah *Esquire,* Lot *Knight* and *Baronet,* nor the *Right Honourable* Abraham, Viscount Mesopotamia, Baron of Carian; no, no, they were plain Men." Again, *Poor Richard* engaged in an amusing genealogical computation to prove that over the centuries it was impossible to preserve blood free of mixtures, and "that the pretension of such purity of blood in ancient families is a mere joke." With perhaps pardonable inconsistency Franklin took the trouble to trace his own family back to stout English gentry, but his basic antiaristocratic convictions stood the test of time. When, in the post-Revolutionary years, the patrician-sounding Society of the Cincinnati was founded in America, Franklin in France scoffed at the Cincinnati as "hereditary knights" and egged on Comte de Mirabeau to publish an indictment of the society which set off an international clamor against its hereditary character.

For courts and lawyers, defenders of property and the status quo, Franklin reserved some of his most vitriolic humor. His *Pennsylvania Gazette* consistently held up to ridicule the snobbery of using law French in the courts, excessive legal fees and court costs, and the prolixity and perils of litigation. For the lawyers who "can, with ease, twist words and meanings as you please," *Poor Richard* shows no tolerance. Predictably, Franklin took the side of the debtor against the creditor, the paper money man against the hard currency man.

Franklin's support of paper money did not hurt him in the least. As a matter of fact, the Pennsylvania assembly gave him the printing contract in 1731 for the £40,000 in bills of credit that it authorized that year. This incident could be multiplied many times. Franklin ever had an eye for the main chance. Whether as a poor printer, a rising politician, or an established statesman-scientist, Franklin was regarded by unfriendly critics as a man on the make, of dubious integrity.

Accumulating a tidy capital, Franklin invested in Philadelphia townlots, and then, as the speculative bug bit him, plunged into Nova Scotian and western land ventures. His secretive nature seemed ideally suited to such investments, in which he followed a rule he laid down in 1753: "Great designs should not be made publick til they are ripe for execution, lest obstacles are thrown in the way." The climax of Franklin's land speculations came in 1769 when he joined forces with Samuel Wharton to advance in England the interests of the Grand Ohio Company, which was more British than colonial in composition. This grand alliance of speculators and big-time politicians succeeded in winning from the Privy Council on July 1, 1772, a favorable recommendation supporting their fantastic dream of a colony called "Vandalia," to be fitted together from the pieces of the present-day states of Pennsylvania, Maryland, West Virginia, and Kentucky. There Franklin's love of order would replace that frontier anarchy which he abhorred.

Standing on the brink of a stunning success, the Vandalia speculators were now put in jeopardy by Franklin's rash indiscretion in turning over to his radical friends in Massachusetts some embarrassing letters of Governor Thomas Hutchinson that had been given to him in confidence. Indignant at Franklin's disloyalty, the Crown officers refused to complete the papers confirming the grant to the Grand Ohio Company. With his usual deviousness, Franklin, in concert with the banker Thomas Walpole, publicly resigned from the company. In reality Walpole and Franklin had a private understanding by which the latter would retain his two shares out of the total of seventy-two shares of stock in the company. As late as April 11, 1775, Franklin, Walpole, and others signed a power of attorney authorizing land speculator William Trent to act on their behalf with respect to the grant, hardly necessary if Franklin was indeed out of the picture. In the summer of 1778 Franklin had a change of heart and decided to get back his original letter of resignation. When Walpole complied, Franklin added thereto a memorandum asserting: "I am still to be considered as an Associate, and was called upon for my Payments as before. My right to two shares, or two Parts of 72, in that Purchase still continues . . . and I hope, that when the Trouble of America is over, my Posterity may reap the Benefits of them." Franklin's posterity, it should be pointed out, stood a much better chance were England to retain the Old Northwest and the Crown validate the Grand Ohio claim than were title thereto to pass to the new United States, whose claim to that region Franklin would be expected by Congress to press at the peacemaking. Such an impropriety on Franklin's part was compounded by his casual attitude about his carrying on a correspondence with a British subject in wartime while officially an American commissioner to France.

Franklin's critics decried his penchant for nepotism, his padding the postmastership payroll with his relatives, the pressure he exercised on his fellow peace commissioners to have the unqualified Temple Franklin appointed as secretary to the commission, and his willingness to have his grandnephew Jonathan Williams set up as a shipping agent at Nantes. Franklin's conduct of his office in France continued to supply grounds for ugly charges. What is significant is not that Franklin was guilty as charged but rather that the suspicion of conflict of interest would not die down despite his own disclaimer. At best, Franklin in France was untidy and careless in running his office. What can be said about a statesman whose entourage included a secretary who was a spy in British pay, a maitre d'hotel who was a thief, and a grandson who was a playboy! Only a genius could surmount these irregularities and achieve a stunning triumph. And Franklin had genius.

Because of Franklin's prominence in the Revolutionary movement, it is often forgotten that in the generation prior to the final break with England he was America's most notable imperial statesman, and that the zigzag course he was to pursue owed more to events than to logic. As early as 1751 he had proposed an intercolonial union to be established by voluntary action on the part of the colonies. Three years later at Albany, where he presented his grand design of continental union, he included therein a provision for having the plan imposed by parliamentary authority. . . .

Each intensely jealous of its own prerogatives, the colonial assemblies proved cool to the plan, while the Privy Council was frigid. As Franklin remarked years later, "the Crown disapproved it as having too much weight in the democratic part of the constitution, and every assembly as having allowed too much to the prerogative; so it was totally rejected." In short, the thinking of the men who met at Albany in 1754 was too bold for that day. In evolving his Plan of Union Franklin had shown himself to be an imperial-minded thinker who placed the unity and effective administration of the English-speaking world above the rights and rivalries of the separate parts. Had Franklin's Plan of Union been put in operation, it would very likely have obviated the necessity for any Parliamentary enactment of taxes for the military defense and administration of the colonies.

Franklin's pride in the Empire survived his letdown in 1754. In April, 1761, he issued his famous Canada pamphlet, *The Interest of Great Britain Considered,* wherein he argued the case for a plan that would secure for Great Britain Canada and the trans-Appalachian West rather than the French West Indian islands, arguments upon which Lord Shelburne drew heavily in supporting the Preliminary Articles of Peace of 1762 that his sponsor Lord Bute had negotiated with France.

For Franklin, 1765 may be considered the critical year of his political career. Thereafter he abandoned his role as imperial statesman and moved steadily on a course toward revolution. Some would make Franklin out as a conspirator motivated by personal pique, and, while one must concede that Franklin's reticence and deviousness endowed him with the ideal temperament for conspiracy and that his public humiliation at the hands of Crown officials provided him with all the motivation that most men would need, one must remember that above all Franklin was an empiricist. If one course would not work, he would try another. Thus, Franklin as agent in London for Pennsylvania's assembly not only approved the Stamp Act in advance, but proposed many of the stamp collectors to the British government. To John Hughes, one of his unfortunate nominees who secured the unhappy job for his own province, Franklin counselled "coolness and steadiness," adding:

. . .a firm loyalty to the Crown and faithful adherence to the government of this nation, which it is the safety as well as honour of the colonies to be connected with, will always be the wisest course for you and I to take, whatever may be the madness of the populace or their blind leaders, who can only bring themselves and country into trouble and draw on greater burthens by acts of rebellious tendency.

But Franklin was a fast learner. If the violence and virtual unanimity of the opposition in the colonies to the Stamp Act took him by surprise, Franklin quickly adjusted to the new realities. In an examination before the House of Commons in February, 1766, he made clear the depth of American opposition to the new tax, warned that the colonies would refuse to pay any future internal levy, and intimated that "in time" the colonists might move to the more radical position that Parliament had no right to levy external taxes upon them either. Henceforth Franklin was the colonists' leading advocate abroad of their rights to self-government, a position grounded not only on his own eminence but on his agency of the four colonies of Pennsylvania, New Jersey, Massachusetts, and Georgia. If he now counselled peaceful protest, it was because he felt that violent confrontations would give the British government a pretext for increasing the military forces and placing the colonies under even more serious repression. A permissive parent even by today's lax standards, Franklin drew an interesting analogy between governing a family and governing an empire. In one of his last nostalgic invocations of imperial greatness, Franklin wrote:

Those men make a mighty noise about the importance of keeping up our authority over the colonies. They govern and regulate too much. Like some unthinking parents, who are every moment exerting their authority in obliging their children to make bows, and interrupting the course of their innocent amusements, attending constantly to their own prerogative, but forgetting tenderness due to their offspring. The true act of governing the colonies lies in a nut-shell. It is only letting them alone.

Down to the outbreak of hostilities Franklin still clung to his post of absentee deputy postmaster general of the colonies, with all the perquisites thereto attached. All that dramatically changed in the years 1773-74, a final turning point in his career.

Franklin had gotten his hands on a series of indiscreet letters written by Thomas Hutchinson and Andrew Oliver, the governor and lieutenant governor of Massachusetts Bay, respectively, and addressed to Thomas Whately, a member of the Grenville and North ministries. The letters, which urged that the liberties of the province be restricted, were given to Franklin by a person whose confidence he preserved to show him that false advice from America went far toward explaining the obnoxious acts of the British government. Tongue in cheek, Franklin sent the letters on to Thomas Cushing, speaker of the Massachusetts house of representatives, with an injunction that they were not to be copied or published but merely shown in the original to individuals in the province. But in June 1773, the irrepressible Samuel Adams read the letters before a secret session of the house and later had the letter copied and printed.

The publication of the Hutchinson-Oliver letters, ostensibly against Franklin's wishes, caused an international scandal, which for the moment did Franklin's reputation no good. Summoned before the Privy Council, he was excoriated by Solicitor General Alexander Wedderburn. The only way Franklin could have obtained the letters, Wedderburn charged, was by stealing them from the person who stole them, and, according to one account, he added, "I hope, my lords, you will mark and brand the man" who "has forfeited all the respects of societies and of men." Henceforth, he concluded, "Men will watch him with a jealous eye; they will hide their papers from him, and lock up their escritoires. He will henceforth esteem it a libel to be called a man of letters; homo trium literarum!" Of course, everyone in the audience knew Latin and recognized the "three letters" Wedderburn referred to as fur, the word for "thief."

Discounting Wedderburn's animosity, the solicitor general may have accurately captured Franklin's frame of mind at this time when he remarked that "Dr. Franklin's mind may have been so possessed with the idea of a Great American Republic, that he may easily slide into the language of the minister of a foreign independent state," who, "just before the breaking out of war . . . may bribe a villian to steal or betray any state papers." There was one punishment the Crown could inflict upon its stalwart antagonist, and that was to strip him of his office as deputy postmaster general. That was done at once. Imperturbable as was his wont,

2. REVOLUTIONARY AMERICA

Franklin remained silent throughout the entire casti-gation, but inwardly he seethed at both the humiliation and the monetary loss that the job, along with his now collapsed Vandalia scheme, would cost him. He never forgot the scorching rebuke. He himself had once remarked that he "never forgave contempt" and that it "costs me nothing to be civil to inferiors; a good deal to be submissive to superiors." It is reported that on the occasion of the signing of the treaty of alliance with France, he donned the suit of figured blue velvet that he had worn on that less triumphal occasion and, according to an unsubstantiated legend, wore it again at the signing of the preliminary peace treaty by which Great Britain recognized the independence of the United States.

Believing he could help best by aiding Pitt in his fruitless efforts at conciliation, Franklin stayed on in England for another year. On March 20, 1775, he sailed for America, convinced that England had lost her colonies forever. On May 6, 1775, the day following his return to Philadelphia, he was chosen a member of the Second Continental Congress. There he would rekindle old associations and meet for the first time some of the younger patriots who were to lead the nation along the path to independence.

As apocryphal story is told of Franklin's journey from Nantes to Paris, where he would later be the American ambassador. At one of the inns in which he stayed, he was informed that the Tory-minded Edward Gibbon, the first volume of whose *Decline and Fall of the Roman Empire* had been published in the spring of that year, was also stopping. Franklin sent his compliments, requesting the pleasure of spending the evening with the historian. In answer he received a card stating that notwithstanding Gibbon's regard for the character of Dr. Franklin as a man and a philosopher, he could not reconcile it with his duty to his king to have any conservation with a rebellious subject. In reply Franklin wrote a note declaring that "though Mr. Gibbon's principles had compelled him to withhold the pleasure of his conversation, Dr. Franklin had still such a respect for the character of Mr. Gibbon, as a gentleman and a historian, that when, in the course of his writing a history of the *decline and fall* of empires, the *decline and fall* of the British Empire should come to be his subject as he expects it soon would, Dr. Franklin would be happy to furnish him with ample materials which were in his possession."

England's Vietnam:
The American Revolution

Richard M. Ketchum

If it is true that those who cannot remember the past are condemned to repeat it, America's last three Presidents might have profited by examining the ghostly footsteps of America's last king before pursuing their adventure in Vietnam. As the United States concludes a decade of war in Southeast Asia, it is worth recalling the time, two centuries ago, when Britain faced the same agonizing problems in America that we have met in Vietnam. History seldom repeats itself exactly, and it would be a mistake to try to equate the ideologies or the motivating factors involved; but enough disturbing parallels may be drawn between those two distant events to make one wonder if the Messrs. Kennedy, Johnson, and Nixon had their ears closed while the class was studying the American Revolution.

Britain, on the eve of that war, was the greatest empire since Rome. Never before had she known such wealth and power; never had the future seemed so bright, the prospects so glowing. All, that is, except the spreading sore of discontent in the American colonies that, after festering for a decade and more, finally erupted in violence at Lexington and Concord on April 19, 1775. When news of the subsequent battle for Bunker Hill reached England that summer, George III and his ministers concluded that there was no alternative to using force to put down the insurrection. In the King's mind, at least, there was no longer any hope of reconciliation—nor did the idea appeal to him. He was determined to teach the rebellious colonials a lesson, and no doubts troubled him as to the righteousness of the course he had chosen. "I am not sorry that the line of conduct seems now chalked out," he had said even before fighting began; later he told his prime minister, Lord North, "I know I am doing my Duty and I can never wish to retract." And then, making acceptance of the war a matter of personal loyalty, "I wish nothing but good," he said, "therefore anyone who does not agree

with me is a traitor and a scoundrel." Filled with high moral purpose and confidence, he was certain that "when once these rebels have felt a smart blow, they will submit . . ."

In British political and military circles there was a general agreement that the war would be quickly and easily won. "Shall we be told," asked one of the King's men in Commons, "that [the Americans] can resist the powerful efforts of this nation?" Major John Pitcairn, writing home from Boston in March, 1775, said, "I am satisfied that one active campaign, a smart action, and burning two or three of their towns, will set everything to rights." The man who would direct the British navy during seven years of war, the unprincipled, inefficient Earl of Sandwich, rose in the House of Lords to express his opinion of the provincial fighting man. "Suppose the Colonies do abound in men," the First Lord of the Admiralty asked, "what does that signify? They are raw, undisciplined, cowardly men. I wish instead of forty or fifty thousand of these *brave* fellows they would produce in the field at least two hundred thousand; the more the better, the easier would be the conquest; if they did not run away, they would starve themselves into compliance with our measures. . . ." And General James Murray, who had succeeded the great Wolfe in 1749 as commander in North America, called the native American "a very effeminate thing, very unfit for and very impatient of war." Between these estimates of the colonial militiaman and a belief that the might of Great Britain was invincible, there was a kind of arrogant optimism in official quarters when the conflict began. "As there is not common sense in protracting a war of this sort," wrote Lord George Germain, the secretary for the American colonies, in September, 1775, "I should be for exerting the utmost force of this Kingdom to finish the rebellion in one campaign."

Optimism bred more optimism, arrogance more arrogance. One armchair strategist in the House of Commons, William Innes, outlined for the other members an elaborate scheme he had devised for the

©1971 American Heritage Publishing Company, Inc. Reprinted by permission from *AMERICAN HERITAGE* (June, 1971)

2. REVOLUTIONARY AMERICA

conduct of the war. First, he would remove the British troops from Boston, since that place was poorly situated for defense. Then, while the people of the Massachusetts Bay Colony were treated like the madmen they were and shut up by the navy, the army would move to one of the southern colonies, fortify itself in an impregnable position, and let the provincials attack if they pleased. The British could sally forth from this and other defensive enclaves at will, and eventually "success against one-half of America will pave the way to the conquest of the whole. . . ." What was more, Innes went on, it was "more than probable you may find men to recruit your army in America." There was a good possibility, in other words, that the British regulars would be replaced after a while by Americans who were loyal to their king, so that the army fighting the rebels would be Americanized, so to speak, and the Irish and English lads sent home. General James Robertson also believed that success lay in this scheme of Americanizing the combat force: "I never had an idea of subduing the Americans," he said, "I meant to assist the good Americans to subdue the bad."

This notion was important not only from the standpoint of the fighting, but in terms of administering the colonies once they were beaten; loyalists would take over the reins of government when the British pulled out, and loyalist militiamen would preserve order in the pacified colonies. No one knew, of course, how many "good" Americans there were; some thought they might make up half or more of the population. Shortly after arriving in the colonies in 1775, General William Howe, for one, was convinced that "the insurgents are very few, in comparison with the whole of the people."

Before taking the final steps into full-scale war, however, the King and his ministers had to be certain about one vitally important matter: they had to be able to count on the support of the English people. On several occasions in 1775 they were able to read the public pulse (that part of it, at least, that mattered) by observing certain important votes in Parliament. The King's address to both Houses on October 26, in which he announced plans to suppress the uprising in America, was followed by weeks of angry debate; but when the votes were counted, the North ministry's majority was overwhelming. Each vote indicated the full tide of anger that influenced the independent members, the country gentlemen who agreed that the colonials must be put in their place and taught a lesson. A bit out of touch with the news, highly principled, and content in the belief that the King and the ministry must be right, none of them seem to have asked what would be best for the empire; they simply went along with the vindictive measures that were being set in motion. Eloquent voices—those of Edmund Burke, Charles James Fox, the Earl of Chatham, John Wilkes, among others—were raised in opposition to the policies of the Crown, but as Burke said, ". . . it was almost in vain to contend, for

the country gentlemen had abandoned their duty, and placed an implicit confidence in the Minister."

The words of sanity and moderation went unheeded because the men who spoke them were out of power and out of public favor; and each time the votes were tallied, the strong, silent, unquestioning majority prevailed. No one in any position in power in the government proposed, after the Battle of Bunker Hill, to halt the fighting in order to settle the differences; no one seriously contemplated conversations that might have led to peace. Instead the government—like so many governments before and since—took what appeared to be the easy way out and settled for war.

George III was determined to maintain his empire, intact and undiminished, and his greatest fear was that the loss of the American colonies would set off a reaction like a line of dominoes falling. Writing to Lord North in 1779, he called the contest with America "the most serious in which any country was ever engaged. It contains such a train of consequences that they must be examined to feel its real weight. . . . Independence is [the Americans'] object, which every man not willing to sacrifice every object to a momentary and inglorious peace must concurr with me in thinking this country can never submit to. Should America succeed in that, the West Indies must follow, not in independence, but for their own interest they must become dependent on America. Ireland would soon follow, and this island reduced to itself, would be a poor island indeed."

Despite George's unalterable determination, strengthened by his domino theory; despite the wealth and might of the British empire; despite all the odds favoring a quick triumph, the problems facing the King and his ministers and the armed forces were formidable ones indeed. Surpassing all others in sheer magnitude was the immense distance between the mother country and the rebellious colonies. As Edmund Burke described the situation in his last, most eloquent appeal for conciliation, "Three thousand miles of ocean lie between you and them. No contrivance can prevent the effect of this distance in weakening government. Seas roll, and months pass, between the order and the execution; and the want of a speedy explanation of a single point is enough to defeat a whole system." Often the westerly passage took three months, and every soldier, every weapon, every button and gaiter and musket ball, every article of clothing and great quantities of food and even fuel, had to be shipped across those three thousand miles of the Atlantic. It was not only immensely costly and time consuming, but there was a terrifying wastefulness to it. Ships sank or were blown hundreds of miles off course, supplies spoiled, animals died en route. Worse yet, men died, and in substantial numbers: returns from regiments sent from the British Isles to the West Indies between 1776 and 1780 reveal that an average of 11 per cent of the troops was lost on these crossings.

Beyond the water lay the North American land mass, and it was an article of faith on the part of many a British military man that certain ruin lay in fighting an enemy on any large scale in that savage wilderness. In the House of Lords in November, 1775, the Duke of Richmond warned the peers to consult their geographies before turning their backs on a peaceful settlement. There was, he said, "one insuperable difficulty with which an army would have to struggle"—America abounded in vast rivers that provided natural barriers to the progress of troops; it was a country in which every bush might conceal an enemy, a land whose cultivated parts would be laid waste, so that "the army (if any army could march or subsist) would be obliged to draw all its provisions from Europe, and all its fresh meat from Smithfield market." The French, the mortal enemies of Great Britain, who had seen a good deal more of the North American wilds than the English had, were already laying plans to capitalize on the situation when the British army was bogged down there. In Paris, watchfully eyeing his adversary's every move, France's foreign minister, the Comte de Vergennes, predicted in July, 1775, that "it will be vain for the English to multiply their forces" in the colonies; "no longer can they bring that vast continent back to dependence by force of arms." Seven years later, as the war drew to a close, one of Rochambeau's aides told a friend of Charles James Fox: "No opinion was clearer than that though the people of America might be conquered by well disciplined European troops, the country of America was unconquerable."

Yet even in 1775 some thoughtful Englishmen doubted if the American people or their army could be defeated. Before the news of Bunker Hill arrived in London, the adjutant general declared that a plan to defeat the colonials militarily was "as wild an idea as ever controverted common sense," and the secretary-of-war, Lord Barrington, had similar reservations. As early as 1774 Barrington ventured the opinion that a war in the wilderness of North America would cost Britain far more than she could ever gain from it; that the size of the country and the colonials' familiarity with firearms would make victory questionable—or at best achievable only at the cost of enormous suffering; and finally, even if Britain should win such a contest, Barrington believed that the cost of maintaining the colonies in any state of subjection would be staggering. John Wilkes, taunting Lord North on this matter of military conquest, suggested that North—even if he rode out at the head of the entire English cavalry—would not venture ten miles into the countryside for fear of guerrilla fighters. "The Americans," Wilkes promised, "will dispute every inch of territory with you, every narrow pass, every strong defile, every Thermopylae, every Bunker's Hill."

It was left to the great William Pitt to provide the most stirring warning against fighting the Americans. Now Earl of Chatham, he was so crippled in mind and body that he rarely appeared in the House of Lords, but in May, 1777, he made the supreme effort, determined to raise his voice once again in behalf of conciliation. Supported on canes, his eyes flashing with the old fire and his beak-like face thrust forward belligerently, he warned the peers: "You cannot conquer the Americans. You talk of your numerous friends to annihilate the Congress, and of your powerful forces to disperse their army, but I might as well talk of driving them before me with this crutch. . . . You have been three years teaching them the art of war, and they are apt scholars. I will venture to tell your lordships that the American gentry will make officers enough fit to command the troops of all the European powers. What you have sent there are too many to make peace, too few to make war. You cannot make them respect you. You cannot make them wear your cloth. You will plant an invincible hatred in their breast against you . . . "

"My lords," he went on, "you have been the aggressors from the beginning. I say again, this country has been the aggressor. You have made descents upon their coasts. You have burnt their towns, plundered their country, made war upon the inhabitants, confiscated their property, proscribed and imprisoned their persons. . . . The people of America look upon Parliament as the authors of their miseries. Their affections are estranged from their sovereign. Let, then, reparation come from the hands that inflicted the injuries. Let conciliation succeed chastisement. . . ." But there was no persuading the majority; Chatham's appeal was rejected and the war went on unabated.

It began to appear, however, that destruction of the Continental Army—even if that goal could be achieved—might not be conclusive. After the disastrous campaign around Manhattan in 1776, George Washington had determined not to risk his army in a major engagement, and he began moving away from the European battle style in which two armies confronted each other head to head. His tactical method became that of the small, outweighed prizefighter who depends on his legs to keep him out of range of his opponent and who, when the bigger man begins to tire, darts in quickly to throw a quick punch, then retreats again. It was an approach to fighting described by Nathanael Greene, writing of the campaign in the South in 1780: "We fight, get beat, rise, and fight again." In fact, between January and September of the following year, Greene, short of money, troops, and supplies, won a major campaign without ever really winning a battle. The battle at Guilford Courthouse, which was won by the British, was typical of the results. As Horace Walpole observed, "Lord Cornwallis has conquered his troops out of shoes and provisions and himself out of troops."

There was, in the colonies, no great political center like Paris or London, whose loss might have been demoralizing to the Americans; indeed, Boston, New York, and Philadelphia, the seat of government, were all held at one time or another by the British without

2. REVOLUTIONARY AMERICA

irreparable damage to the rebel cause. The fragmented political and military structure of the colonies was often a help to the rebels, rather than a hindrance, for it meant that there was almost no chance of the enemy striking a single crushing blow. The difficulty, as General Frederick Haldimand, who succeeded Carleton in Canada, saw it, was the seemingly unending availability of colonial militiamen who rose up out of nowhere to fight in support of the nucleus of regular troops called the Continental Army. "It is not the number of troops Mr. Washington can spare from his army that is to be apprehended," Haldimand wrote, "it is the multitude of militia and men in arms ready to turn out at an hour's notice at the shew of a single regiment of Continental Troops. . . ." So long as the British were able to split up their forces and fan out over the countryside in relatively small units, they were fairly successful in putting down the irregulars' activities and cutting off their supplies; but the moment they had to concentrate again to fight the Continentals, guerrilla warfare burst out like so many small brush fires on their flank and rear. No British regular could tell if an American was friend or foe, for loyalty to King George was easy to attest; and the man who was a farmer or merchant when a British battalion marched by his home was a militia-man as soon as it had passed by, ready to shoulder his musket when an emergency or an opportunity to confound the enemy arose.

Against an unnumberable supply of irregular forces the British could bring to bear only a fixed quantity of troops—however many, that is, they happened to have on the western side of the Atlantic Ocean at any given moment. Early in the war General James Murray had foreseen the difficulties that would undoubtedly arise. Writing to Lord Barrington, he warned that military conquest was no real answer. If the war proved to be a long one, their advantage in numbers would heavily favor the rebels, who could replace their losses while the British could not. Not only did ever musket and grain of powder have to be shipped across the ocean; but if a man was killed or wounded, the only way to replace him was to send another man in full kit across the Atlantic. And troop transports were slow and small: three or four were required to move a single battalion.

During the summer of 1775 recruiting went badly in England and Ireland, for the war was not popular with a lot of the people who would have to fight it, and there were jobs to be had. It was evident that the only means of assembling a force large enough to suppress the rebellion in the one massive stroke that had been determined upon was to hire foreign troops. And immediately this word was out, the rapacious petty princes of Brunswick, Hesse-Cassel, and Waldeck, and the Margrave of Anspach-Bayreuth, generously offered up a number of their subjects—at a price—fully equipped and ready for duty, to serve His Majesty George III. Frederick the Great of Prussia, seeing the plan for what it was, announced that he would "make all

the Hessian troops, marching through his dominions to America, pay the usual cattle tax, because, although human beings, they had been sold as beasts." But George III and the princes regarded it as a business deal, in the manner of such dubious alliances ever since: each foot soldier and trooper supplied by the Duke of Brunswick, for instance, was to be worth seven pounds, four shillings, fourpence halfpenny in levy money to his Most Serene Highness. Three wounded men were to count as one killed in action, and it was stipulated that a soldier killed in combat would be paid for at the same rate as levy money. In other words the life of a subject was worth precisely seven pounds, four shillings, fourpence halfpenny to the Duke.

As it turned out, the large army that was assembled in 1776 to strike a quick, overpowering blow that would put a sudden end to the rebellion proved—when that decisive victory never came to pass—to be a distinct liability, a hideously expensive and at times vulnerable weapon. In the indecisive hands of men like William Howe and Henry Clinton, who never seemed absolutely certain about what they should do or how they should do it, the great army rarely had an opportunity to realize its potential; yet, it remained a ponderous and insatiable consumer of supplies, food, and money.

The loyalists, on whom many Englishmen had placed such high hopes, proved a will-o'-the-wisp. Largely ignored by the policy makers early in the war despite their pleas for assistance, the loyalists were numerous enough but were neither well organized nor evenly distributed throughout the colonies. Where the optimists in Britain went wrong in thinking that loyalist strength would be an important factor was to imagine that anything like a majority of Americans *could* remain loyal to the Crown if they were not continuously supported and sustained by the mother country. Especially as the war went on, as opinions hardened, and as the possibility increased that the new government in America might actually survive, it was a very difficult matter to retain one's loyalty to the King unless friends and neighbors were of like mind and unless there was British force nearby to safeguard such a belief. Furthermore, it proved almost impossible for the British command to satisfy the loyalists, who were bitterly angry over the persecution and physical violence and robbery they had to endure and who charged constantly that the British generals were too lax in their treatment of rebels.

While the problems of fighting the war in distant America mounted, Britain found herself unhappily confronted with the combination of circumstances the Foreign Office dreaded most: with her armies tied down, the great European maritime powers—France and Spain—vengeful and adventurous and undistracted by war in the Old World, formed a coalition against her. When the American war began, the risk of foreign intervention was regarded as minimal, and the decision to fight was made on the premise that victory

70

would be early and complete and that the armed forces would be released before any threatening European power could take advantage of the situation. But as the war continued without any definite signs of American collapse, France and Spain seized the chance to embarrass and perhaps humiliate their old antagonist. At first they supported the rebels surreptitiously with shipments of weapons and other supplies; then, when the situation appeared more auspicious, France in particular furnished active support in the form of an army and a navy, with catastrophic results for Great Britain.

One fascinating might-have-been is what would have happened had the Opposition in Parliament been more powerful politically. It consisted, after all, of some of the most forceful and eloquent orators imaginable, men whose words still have the power to send shivers up the spine. Not simply vocal, they were highly intelligent men whose concern went beyond the injustice and inhumanity of war. They were quick to see that the personal liberty of the King's subjects was as much an issue in London as it was in the colonies, and they foresaw irreparable damage to the empire if the government followed its unthinking policy of coercion. Given a stronger power base, they might have headed off war or the ultimate disaster; had the government been in the hands of men like Chatham or Burke or their followers, some accommodation with America might conceivably have evolved from the various proposals for reconciliation. But the King and North had the votes in their pockets, and the antiwar Opposition failed because a majority that was largely indifferent to reason supported the North ministry until the bitter end came with Cornwallis' surrender. Time and again a member of the Opposition would rise to speak out against the war for one reason or another: "This country," the Earl of Shelburne protested, "already burdened much beyond its abilities, is now on the eve of groaning under new taxes, for the purpose of carrying on this cruel and destructive war." Or, from Dr. Franklin's friend David Hartley: "Every proposition for reconciliation has so constantly and uniformly been crushed by Administration, that I think they seem not even to wish for the appearance of justice. The law of force is that which they appeal to. . . ." Or, from Sir James Lowther, when he learned that the King had rejected an "Olive Branch Petition" from the provincials: "Why have we not peace with a people who, it is evident, desire peace with us?" Or this, from General Henry Seymour Conway, inviting Lord North to inform members of the House of Commons about his overall program: "I do not desire the detail; let us have general outline, to be able to judge of the probability of its success. It is indecent not to lay before the House some plan, or the outlines of a plan. . . . If [the] plan is conciliation, let us see it, that we may form some opinion of it; if it be hostility and coercion, I do repeat, that we have no cause for a minute's consideration; for I can with confidence

pronounce, that the present military armament will never succeed." But all unavailing, year after year, as each appeal to reason and humanity fell on ears deafened by self-righteousness and minds hardened against change.

Although it might be said that the arguments raised by the Opposition did not change the course of the war, they nevertheless affected the manner in which it was conducted, which in turn led to the ultimate British defeat. Whether Lord North was uncertain of that silent majority's loyalty is difficult to determine, but it seems clear that he was sufficiently nervous about public support to decide that a bold policy which risked defeats was not for him. As a result the war of the American Revolution was a limited war—limited from the standpoint of its objectives and the force with which Britain waged it.

In some respects the aspect of the struggle that may have had the greatest influence on the outcome was an intangible one. Until the outbreak of hostilities in 1775 no more than a small minority of the colonials had seriously contemplated independence, but after a year of war the situation was radically different. Now the mood was reflected in words such as these—instructions prepared by the county of Buckingham, in Virginia, for its delegates to a General Convention in Williamsburg: ". . . as far as your voices are admitted, you [will] cause a free and happy Constitution to be established, with a renunciation of the old, and so much thereof as has been found inconvenient and oppressive." That simple and powerful idea—renunciation of the old and its replacement with something new, independently conceived—was destined to sweep all obstacles before it. In Boston, James Warren was writing the news of home to John Adams in Philadelphia and told him: "Your Declaration of Independence came on Saturday and diffused a general joy. Every one of us feels more important than ever; we now congratulate each other as Freemen." Such winds of change were strong, and by contrast all Britain had to offer was a return to the status quo. Indeed, it was difficult for the average Englishman to comprehend the appeal that personal freedom and independence held for a growing number of Americans. As William Innes put it in a debate in Commons, all the government had to do to put an end to the nonsense in the colonies was to "convince the lower class of those infatuated people that the imaginary liberty they are so eagerly pursuing is not by any means to be compared to that which the Constitution of this happy country already permits them to enjoy."

With everything to gain from victory and everything to lose by defeat, the Americans could follow Livy's advice, that "in desperate matters the boldest counsels are the safest." Frequently beaten and disheartened, inadequately trained and fed and clothed, they fought on against unreasonably long odds because of that slim

71

2. REVOLUTIONARY AMERICA

hope of attaining a distant goal. And as they fought on, increasing with each passing year the possibility that independence might be achieved, the people of Britain finally lost the will to keep going.

In England the goal had not been high enough, while the cost was too high. There was nothing compelling about the limited objective of bringing the colonies back into the empire, nothing inspiring about punishing the rebels, nothing noble in proving that retribution awaited those who would change the nature of things.

After the war had been lost and the treaty of peace signed, Lord North looked back on the whole affair and sadly informed the members of the House of Commons where, in his opinion, the fault lay. With a few minor changes, it was a message as appropriate to America in 1971 as to Britain in 1783: "The American war," he said, "has been suggested to have been the war of the Crown, contrary to the wishes of the people. I deny it. It was the war of Parliament. There was not a step taken in it that had not the sanction of Parliament. It was the war

of the people, for it was undertaken for the express purpose of maintaining the just rights of Parliament, or, in other words, of the people of Great Britain, over the dependencies of the empire. For this reason, it was popular at its commencement, and eagerly embraced by the people and Parliament. . . . Nor did it ever cease to be popular until a series of unparalleled disasters and calamities caused the people, wearied out with almost uninterrupted ill-success and misfortune, to call out as loudly for peace as they had formerly done for war."

For further reading: The British Empire Before the American Revolution, *Vol. 12,* The Triumphant Empire: Britain Sails into the Storm, 1770-1776, *by Lawrence Henry Gipson (Knopf, 1965);* British Politics and the American Revolution: The Path to War, 1773-75, *by Bernard Donoughue (St. Martin's Press, 1965);* The War for America, 1775-1783, *by Piers G. Mackesy (Harvard University Press, 1964);* The First Year of the American Revolution, *by Allen French (Octagon, 1967).*

The Most Uncommon Pamphlet of the Revolution

COMMON SENSE

By BERNARD BAILYN

Common Sense is the most brilliant pamphlet written during the American Revolution, and one of the most brilliant pamphlets ever written in the English language. How it could have been produced by the bankrupt Quaker corsetmaker, the sometime teacher, preacher, and grocer, and twice-dismissed excise officer who happened to catch Benjamin Franklin's attention in England and who arrived in America only 14 months before *Common Sense* was published is nothing one can explain without explaining genius itself. For it is a work of genius—slapdash as it is, rambling as it is, crude as it is. It "burst from the press," Benjamin Rush wrote, "with an effect which has rarely been produced by types and papers in any age or country." Its effect, Franklin said, was "prodigious." It touched some extraordinarily sensitive nerve in American political awareness in the confusing period in which it appeared.

It was written by an Englishman, not an American. Paine had only the barest acquaintance with American affairs when, with Rush's encouragement, he turned an invitation by Franklin to write a history of the Anglo-American controversy into the occasion for composing a passionate tract for American independence. Yet not only does *Common Sense* voice some of the deepest aspirations of the American people on the eve of the Revolution but it also evokes, with superb vigor and with perfect intonation, longings and aspirations that have remained part of American culture to this day.

What is one to make of this extraordinary document after 200 years? What questions, in the context of the current understanding of the causes and meaning of the Revolution, should one ask of it?

Not, I think, the traditional one of whether *Common Sense* precipitated the movement for independence. To accomplish that was of course its ostensible purpose, and so powerful a blast, so piercing a cry so widely heard throughout the colonies—everyone who could read must have seen it in one form or another—could scarcely have failed to move some people some of the way. It undoubtedly caused some of the hesitant and vaguely conservative who had reached no decision to think once more about the future that might be opening up in America.

For it appeared at what was perhaps the perfect moment to have a maximum effect. It was published on January 10, 1776. Nine months before, the first skirmishes of the Revolutionary War had been fought, and seven months before, a bloody battle had taken place on Breed's Hill, across the bay from Boston, which was the headquarters of the British army in America, long since surrounded by provincial troops. Three months after that, in September 1775, a makeshift American army had invaded Canada and taken Montreal. In December its two divisions had joined to attack Quebec, and though that attack, on December 30–31, had failed miserably, the remnants of the American armies still surrounded the city when Paine wrote *Common Sense,* and Montreal was still in American hands.

That a war of some sort was in progress was obvious, but it was not obvious what the objective of the fighting was. There was disagreement in the Continental Congress as to what a military victory, if it came, should be used to achieve. A group of influential and articulate leaders, especially those from Massachusetts, were convinced that only independence from England could properly serve American needs, and Benjamin Franklin, recently returned from London, had reached the same conclusion and had found like-minded people in Philadelphia. But that was *not* the common opinion of the Congress, and it certainly was not the general view of the population at large. Not a single colony had instructed its delegates to work for independence, and not a single step had been taken by the Congress that was incompatible with the idea—which was still the prevailing view—that America's purpose was to force Parliament to acknowledge the liberties it claimed and to redress the grievances that had for so long and in so many different ways been explained to the world. All the most powerful unspoken assumptions of the time—indeed, common sense—ran counter to the notion of independence.

If it is an exaggeration, it is not much of an exaggeration to say that one had to be a fool or a fanatic in early January 1776 to advocate American independence. Militia troops may

Reprinted from *American Heritage*, December 1973 by permission of the author. Copyright ©1973 by Bernard Bailyn.

2. REVOLUTIONARY AMERICA

Thomas Paine

have been able to defend themselves at certain points and had achieved some limited goals, but the first extended military campaign was ending in a squalid defeat below the walls of Quebec. There was no evidence of an area of agreement among the 13 separate governments and among the hundreds of conflicting American interests that was broad enough and firm enough to support an effective common government. Everyone knew that England was the most powerful nation on earth, and if its navy had fallen into disrepair, it could be swiftly rebuilt. Anyone whose common sense outweighed his enthusiasm and imagination knew that a string of prosperous but weak communities along the Atlantic coast left uncontrolled and unprotected by England would quickly be pounced on by rival European powers whose ruling political notions and whose institutions of government were the opposite of what Americans had been struggling to preserve. The most obvious presumption of all was that the liberties Americans sought were British in their nature: they had been achieved by Britain over the centuries and had been embedded in a constitution whose wonderfully contrived balance between the needs of the state and the rights of the individual was thought throughout the western world to be one of the finest human achievements. It was

obvious too, of course, that something had gone wrong recently. It was generally agreed in the colonies that the famous balance of the constitution, in Britain and America, had been thrown off by a vicious gang of ministers greedy for power, and that their attention had been drawn to the colonies by the misrepresentations of certain colonial officeholders who hoped to find an open route to influence and fortune in the enlargement of Crown power in the colonies. But the British constitution had been under attack before, and although at certain junctures in the past drastic action had been necessary to reestablish the balance, no one of any importance had ever concluded that the constitution itself was at fault; no one had ever cast doubt on the principle that liberty, as the colonists knew it, rested on—had in fact been created by—the stable balancing of the three essential socioconstitutional orders, the monarchy, the nobility, and the people at large, each with its appropriate organ of government: the Crown, the House of Lords, and the House of Commons. If the balance had momentarily been thrown off, let Americans, like Britishers in former ages, fight to restore it: force the evildoers out, and recover the protection of the only system ever known to guarantee both liberty and order. America had flourished under that benign system, and it was simply common sense to try to restore its balance. Why should one want to destroy the most successful political structure in the world, which had been constructed by generations of constitutional architects, each building on and refining the wisdom of his predecessors, simply because its present managers were vicious or criminal? And was it reasonable to think that these ill-coordinated, weak communities along the Atlantic coast could defeat England in war and then construct a system of government free of the defects that had been revealed in the almost-perfect English system?

Since we know how it came out, these seem rather artificial and rhetorical questions. But in early January 1776 they were vital and urgent, and *Common Sense* was written to answer them. There was open warfare between England and America, but though confidence in the English government had been severely eroded, the weight of opinion still favored restoration of the situation as it had been before 1764, a position arrived at not by argument so much as by recognition of the obvious sense of the matter, which was rooted in the deepest presuppositions of the time.

In the weeks when *Common Sense* was being written the future—even the very immediate future—was entirely obscure; the situation was malleable in the extreme. No one then could confidently say which course history would later declare to have been the right course to have followed. No one then could know who would later be seen to have been heroes and who weaklings or villains. No one then could know who would be the winners and who the losers.

But Paine was certain that he knew the answers to all these questions, and the immediate impact that *Common Sense* had was in large part simply the result of the pamphlet's ringing assertiveness, its shrill unwavering declaration that all the right was on the side of independence and all the wrong on the side of loyalty to Britain. History favored Paine, and so the pamphlet became prophetic. But in the strict context of the historical moment of its appearance, its assertiveness seemed to many to be more outrageous than prophetic, and rather ridiculous if not slightly insane.

All of this is part of the remarkable history of the pamphlet, part of the extraordinary impact it had upon contemporaries' awareness. Yet I do not think that, at this distance in time and in the context of what we now know about the causes of the Revolution, the question of its influence on the developing movement toward independence is the most useful question that can be asked. We know both too much and too little to determine the degree to which *Common Sense* precipitated the conclusion that Congress reached in early July. We can now depict in detail the stages by which Congress was led to vote for independence—who played what role and how the fundamental, difficult, and divisive problem was resolved. And the closer we look at the details of what happened in Congress in early 1776 the less important *Common Sense* appears to have been. It played a role in the background, no doubt; and many people, in Congress and out, had the memory of reading it as they accepted the final determination to move to independence. But, as John Adams noted, at least as many people were offended by the pamphlet as were persuaded by it—he himself later called it "a poor, ignorant, malicious, short-sighted, crapulous mass"—and we shall never know the proportions on either side with any precision.

What strikes one more forcefully now, at this distance in time, is something quite different from the question of the pamphlet's unmeasurable contribution to the movement toward independence. There is something extraordinary in this pamphlet—something bizarre, outsized, unique—quite aside from its strident appeal for independence, and that quality, which was recognized if not defined by contemporaries and which sets it off from the rest of the pamphlet literature of the Revolution, helps us understand, I believe, something essential in the Revolution as a whole. A more useful effort, it seems to me, than attempting to measure its influence on independence is to seek to isolate this special quality.

2

Certainly the language is remarkable. For its prose alone, *Common Sense* would be a notable document—unique among the pamphlets of the American Revolution. Its phraseology is deeply involving—at times clever, at times outrageous, frequently startling in imagery and penetration—and becomes more vivid as the pamphlet progresses.

In the first substantive part of the pamphlet, ostensibly an essay on the principles of government in general and of the English constitution in particular, the ideas are relatively abstract but the imagery is concrete: "Government, like dress, is the badge of lost innocence; the palaces of kings are built upon the ruins of the bowers of paradise." As for the "so much boasted constitution of England," it was "noble for the dark and slavish times in which it was erected"; but that was not really so remarkable, Paine said, for "when the world was overrun with tyranny, the least remove therefrom was a glorious rescue." In fact, Paine wrote, the English constitution is "imperfect, subject to convulsions, and incapable of producing what it seems to promise," all of which could be "easily demonstrated" to anyone who could shake himself loose from the fetters of prejudice. For "as a man who is attached to a prostitute is unfitted to choose or judge of a wife, so any prepossession in favor of a rotten constitution of government will disable us from discerning a good one."

The imagery becomes arresting in Part 2, on monarchy and hereditary succession, institutions which together, Paine wrote, formed "the most prosperous invention the Devil ever set on foot for the promotion of idolatry." The heathens, who invented monarchy, at least had had the good sense to grant divinity only to their *dead* kings; "the Christian world has improved on the plan by doing the same to their living ones. How impious is the title of sacred majesty applied to a worm, who in the midst of his splendor is crumbling into dust!" Hereditary right is ridiculed by nature herself, which so frequently gives "mankind an *ass for a lion*."

What of the true origins of the present-day monarchs, so exalted by myth and supposedly sanctified by antiquity? In all probability, Paine wrote, the founder of any of the modern royal lines was "nothing better than the principal ruffian of some rest-

COMMON SENSE;

ADDRESSED TO THE

INHABITANTS

OF

AMERICA,

On the following interesting

SUBJECTS.

I. Of the Origin and Design of Government in general, with concise Remarks on the English Constitution.

II. Of Monarchy and Hereditary Succession.

III. Thoughts on the present State of American Affairs.

IV. Of the present Ability of America, with some miscellaneous Reflections.

Man knows no Master save creating HEAVEN,
Or those whom choice and common good ordain.
THOMSON.

PHILADELPHIA;
Printed, and Sold, by R. BELL, in Third-Street.
MDCCLXXVI.

less gang, whose savage manners or preeminence of subtility obtained him the title of chief among the plunderers; and who, by increasing in power and extending his depredations, overawed the quiet and defenseless to purchase their safety by frequent contributions." The English monarchs? "No man in his senses can say that their claim under William the Conquerer is a very honorable one. A French bastard, landing with an armed banditti and establishing himself king of England against the consent of the natives, is in plain terms a very paltry rascally original." Why should one even bother to explain the folly of hereditary right? It is said to provide continuity and hence to preserve a nation from civil wars. That, Paine said, is "the most barefaced falsity ever imposed upon mankind." English history alone disproves it. There had been, Paine confidently declared, "no less than eight civil wars and nineteen rebellions" since the Conquest. The fact is that everywhere hereditary monarchy has "laid . . . the world in blood and ashes." "In England a king hath little more to do than to make war and give away places; which in plain terms is to impoverish the nation and set it together by the ears. A pretty business indeed for a man to be allowed eight hundred thousand sterling a year for, and worshipped into the bargain!" People who are fools enough to believe the claptrap about monarchy, Paine wrote, should be allowed to do so without interference: "let them promiscuously worship the Ass and the Lion, and welcome."

But it is in the third section, "Thoughts on the Present State of American Affairs," that Paine's language becomes most effective and vivid. The emotional level is extremely high throughout these pages and the lyric passages even then must have seemed prophetic:

The sun never shined on a cause of greater worth. . . . 'Tis not the concern of a day, a year, or an age; posterity are virtually involved in the contest, and will be more or less affected even to the end of time by the proceedings now. Now is the seedtime of continental union, faith, and honor. The least fracture now will be like a name engraved with the point of a pin on the tender rind of a young oak; the wound will enlarge with the tree, and posterity read it in full grown characters.

The arguments in this section, proving the necessity for American independence and the colonies' capacity to achieve it, are elaborately worked out, and they respond to all the objections to independence that Paine had heard. But through all of these pages of argumentation, the prophetic, lyric note of the opening paragraphs continues to be heard, and a sense of urgency keeps the tension high. "Everything that is right or reasonable," Paine writes, "pleads for separation. The blood of the slain, the weeping voice of nature cries, 'TIS TIME TO PART." *Now* is the time to act, he insists: "The present winter is worth an age if rightly employed, but if lost or neglected the whole continent will partake of the misfortune." The possibility of a peaceful conclusion to the controversy had vanished, "wherefore, since nothing but blows will do, for God's sake let us come to a final separation, and not leave the next generation to be cutting throats under the violated unmeaning names of parent and child." Not to act now would not eliminate the need for action, he wrote, but only postpone it to the next generation, which would clearly see that "a little more, a little farther, would have rendered this continent the glory of the earth." To talk of reconciliation "with those in whom our reason forbids us to have faith, and our affections, wounded through a thousand pores, instruct us to detest, is madness and folly." The earlier harmony was irrecoverable: "Can ye give to prostitution its former innocence? Neither can ye reconcile Britain and America. . . . As well can the lover forgive the ravisher of his mistress as the continent forgive the murders of Britain." And the section ends with Paine's greatest peroration:

O ye that love mankind! Ye that dare to oppose not only the tyranny but the tyrant, stand forth! Every spot of the old world is overrun with oppression. Freedom hath been hunted round the globe. Asia and Africa have long expelled her. Europe regards her like a stranger, and England hath given her warning to depart. O! receive the fugitive, and prepare in time an asylum for mankind.

In the pamphlet literature of the American Revolution there is nothing comparable to this passage for sheer emotional intensity and lyric appeal. Its vividness must have leapt out of the pages to readers used to greyer, more solid prose.

3

But language does not explain itself. It is a reflection of deeper elements—qualities of mind, styles of thought, a writer's personal culture. There is something unique in the intellectual idiom of the pamphlet.

Common Sense, it must be said, is lacking in close rigor of argumentation. Again and again Paine's logic can be seen to be grossly deficient. His impatience with following through with his arguments at certain points becomes almost amusing. In the fourth and final section, for example, which is on America's ability to achieve and maintain independence, Paine argues that one of America's great advantages is that, unlike the corrupt European powers, it is free of public debt, a burden that was well known to carry with it all sorts of disabling social and political miseries. But then Paine recognizes that mounting a full-scale war and maintaining independence would inevitably force America to create a national debt. He thereupon proceeds to argue, in order, the following: 1) that *such* a debt would be "a glorious memento of our virtue"; 2) that even if it *were* a misery, it would be a cheap price to pay for independence and a new, free constitution—though not, for reasons that are not made entirely clear, a cheap price to pay for simply getting rid of the ministry responsible for all the trouble and returning the situation to what it was in 1764: "such a thought is unworthy a man of honor, and is the true characteristic of a narrow heart and a peddling politician." Having reached that point, he goes the whole way around to make the third point, which is that "no nation ought to be without a debt," though he had started with the idea that the absence of one was an advantage. But this new notion attracts him, and he begins to grasp the idea, which the later federalists would clearly see, that "a national debt is a national bond"; but then, having vaguely approached that idea, he skitters off to the curious thought that a national debt could not be a grievance so long as no interest had to be paid on it; and that in turn leads him into claiming that America could produce a navy twice the size of England's for 1/20th of the English national debt.

As I say, close logic, in these specific arguments, contributes nothing to the force of *Common Sense*. But the intellectual style of the pamphlet is extraordinarily impressive nevertheless, because of a more fundamental characteristic than consistency or cogency. The great intellectual force of *Common Sense* lay not in its close argumentation on specific points but in its reversal of the presumptions that underlay the arguments, a reversal that forced thoughtful readers to consider, not so much a point here and a conclusion there, but a wholly new way of looking at the entire range of problems involved. For beneath all of the explicit arguments and conclusions against independence, there were underlying, unspoken, even unconceptualized presuppositions, attitudes, and habits of thought that made it extremely difficult for the colonists to break with England and find in the prospect of an independent future the security and freedom they sought. The special intellectual quality of *Common Sense*, which goes a long way toward explaining its impact on contemporary readers, derives from its reversal of these underlying presumptions and its shifting of the established perspectives to the point where the whole received paradigm within which the Anglo-American controversy had until then proceeded came into question.

No one set of ideas was more deeply embedded in the British and the British-American mind than the notion, whose genealogy could be traced back to Polybius, that liberty could survive in a world of innately ambitious and selfish if not brutal men only where a balance of the contending forces was so institutionalized that no one contestant could monopolize the power of the state and rule without effective opposition. In its application to the Anglo-American world this general belief further presumed that the three main socioconstitutional contestants for power—the monarchy, the nobility, and the people—had an equal right to share in the struggle for power: these were the constituent elements of the political world. And most fundamental of all in this basic set of constitutional notions was the unspoken belief, upon which everything else rested, that complexity in government was good in itself since it made all the rest of the system possible, and that, conversely, simplicity and uncomplicated efficiency in the structure of government were evil in that they led to a monopolization of power, which could only result in brutal state autocracy.

Paine challenged this whole basic constitutional paradigm, and although his conclusions were rejected in America—the American state and national governments are of course built on precisely the ideas he opposed—the bland, automatic assumption that all of this made sense could no longer, after the appearance of *Common Sense*, be said to exist, and respect for certain points was permanently destroyed.

The entire set of received ideas on government, Paine wrote, was false. Complexity was not a virtue in government, he said—all that complexity accomplished was to make it impossible to tell where the faults lay when a system fell into disarray. The opposite, he said, was in fact true: "the more simple anything is, the less liable it is to be disordered and the easier repaired when disordered." Simplicity was embedded in nature itself, and if the British constitution had reversed the natural order of things, it had done so only to serve the unnatural purposes of the nobility and the monarchy, neither of which had a right to share in the power of the state. The nobility was scarcely even worth considering; it was nothing but the dead remains of an ancient "aristocratical tyranny" that had managed to survive under the cover of encrusting mythologies. The monarchical branch was a more serious matter, and Paine devoted pages of the pamphlet to attacking its claim to a share in the constitution.

As the inheritor of some thuggish ancestor's victory in battle, the "royal brute of Great Britain," as he called George III, was no less a ridiculous constitutional figure than his continental equivalents. For though by his constitutional position he was required to know the affairs of his realm thoroughly and to participate in them actively, by virtue of his exalted social position, entirely removed from everyday life—"distinguished like some new species"—he was forever barred from doing just that. In fact the modern kings of England did nothing at all, Paine wrote, but wage war and hand out gifts to their followers, all the rest of the world's work being handled by the Commons. Yet by virtue of the gifts the king had at his disposal, he corrupted the entire constitution, such as it was. The king's only competitor for power was the Commons, and this body he was able to buy off with the rewards of office and the intimidation of authority. The whole idea of balance in the British constitution was therefore a fraud, for "the *will* of the king is as much the *law* of the land in Britain as in France, with this difference, that instead of proceeding directly from his mouth, it is handed to the people under the formidable shape of an act of Parliament." Yet, was it not true that individuals were safer in England than in France? Yes, Paine said, they are, but not because of the supposed balance of the constitution: "the plain truth is that *it is wholly owing to the constitution of the people and not to the constitution of the government* that the crown is not as oppressive in England as in Turkey."

This was a very potent proposition, no matter how poorly the individual subarguments were presented, for it was well known that even in the best of times formal constitutional theory in England bore only a vague relation to the informal, ordinary operation of the government, and although penetrating minds like David Hume had attempted to reconceive the relationship so as to bring the two into some-

77

what closer accord, no one had tried to settle the matter by declaring that the whole notion of checks and balances in the English constitution was "farcical" and that two of the three components of the supposed balance had no rightful place in the constitutional forms at all. And no one—at least no one writing in America—had made so straightforward and unqualified a case for the virtues of republican government.

This was Paine's most important challenge to the received wisdom of the day, but it was only the first of a series. In passage after passage in *Common Sense* Paine laid bare one after another of the presuppositions of the day which had disposed the colonists, consciously or unconsciously, to resist independence, and by exposing these inner biases and holding them up to scorn he forced people to think the unthinkable, to ponder the supposedly self-evident, and thus to take the first step in bringing about a radical change.

So the question of independence had always been thought of in filial terms: the colonies had once been children, dependent for their lives on the parent state, but now they had matured, and the question was whether or not they were strong enough to survive and prosper alone in a world of warring states. This whole notion was wrong, Paine declared. On this, as on so many other points, Americans had been misled by "ancient prejudices and . . . superstition." England's supposedly protective nurturance of the colonies had only been a form of selfish economic aggrandizement; she would have nurtured Turkey from exactly the same motivations. The fact is, Paine declared, that the colonies had never needed England's protection; they had indeed suffered from it. They would have flourished far more if England had ignored them, for their prosperity had always been based on a commerce in the necessities of life, and that commerce would have flourished, and would continue to flourish, so long as "eating is the custom of Europe." What in fact England's maternal nurture had given America was a burdensome share of the quarrels of Euro-

pean states with whom America, independent of England, could have lived in harmony. War was endemic in Europe because of the stupidities of monarchical rivalries, and England's involvements had meant that America too was dragged into quarrels in which it had no stake whatever. It was a ridiculous situation even in military terms, for neutrality, Paine wrote, is "a safer convoy than a man of war." The whole concept of England's maternal role was rubbish, he wrote, and rubbish, moreover, that had tragically limited America's capacity to see the wider world as it was and to understand the important role America had in fact played in it and could play even more in the future.

> . . . the phrase *parent* or *mother country* hath been jesuitically adopted by the king and his parasites with a low papistical design of gaining an unfair bias on the credulous weakness of our minds. Europe, and not England, is the parent country of America. This new world hath been the asylum for the persecuted lovers of civil and religious liberty from *every part* of Europe. . . . we claim brotherhood with every European Christian, and triumph in the generosity of the sentiment. . . . Not one third of the inhabitants even of this province [Pennsylvania] are of English descent. Wherefore I reprobate the phrase of parent or mother country applied to England only, as being false, selfish, narrow, and ungenerous.

The question, then, of whether America had developed sufficiently under England's maternal nurture to be able to live independent of the parent state was mistaken in its premise and needed no answer. What was needed was freedom from the confining imagery of parent and child which had crippled the colonists' ability to see themselves and the world as they truly were.

So too Paine attacked the fears of independence not defensively, by putting down the doubts that had been voiced, but aggressively, by reshaping the premises on which those doubts had rested. It had been said that if left to themselves the colonies would destroy themselves in civil strife. The opposite was true, Paine replied: The civil strife that America had known had flowed from the connection with England and was a necessary and in-

escapable part of the colonial relationship. Similarly, it had been pointed out that there was no common government in America, and doubts had been expressed that there ever could be one; so Paine sketched one, based on the existing Continental Congress, which he claimed was so fairly representative of the 13 colonies that anyone who stirred up trouble "would have joined Lucifer in his revolt." In his projected state, people would worship not some "hardened, sullentempered Pharaoh" like George III, but law itself and the national constitution, "for as in absolute governments the king is law, so in free countries the law *ought* to be KING." The question was not whether America could create a workable free constitution but how, in view of what had happened, it could afford not to.

So too it had been claimed that America was weak and could not survive in a war with a European power. Paine commented that only in America had nature created a perfect combination of limitless resources for naval construction and a vast coastal extension, with the result that America was not simply capable of self-defense at sea but was potentially the greatest naval power in the world—if it began to build its naval strength immediately, for in time the resources would diminish. So it was argued that America's population was too small to support an army: a grotesquely mistaken idea, Paine said. History proved that the larger the population the *smaller* and *weaker* the armies, for large populations bred prosperity and an excessive involvement in business affairs, both of which had destroyed the military power of nations in the past. The City of London, where England's commerce was centered, was the most cowardly community in the realm: "the rich are in general slaves to fear, and submit to courtly power with the trembling duplicity of a spaniel." In fact, he concluded, a nation's bravest deeds are always done in its youth. Not only was America now capable of sustaining a great military effort, but now was the *only* time it would *ever* be able to do so, for its commerce was sure to rise, its wealth to increase, and its anxiety for the safety of its property to become all-engrossing.

The vast variety of interests, occasioned by an increase of trade and population, would create confusion. Colony would be against colony. Each being able, would scorn each other's assistance: and while the proud and foolish gloried in their little distinctions, the wise would lament that the union had not been formed before.

So on the major questions Paine performed a task more basic than arguing points in favor of independence (though he did that too); he shifted the premises of the questions and forced thoughtful readers to come at them from different angles of vision and hence to open for scrutiny what had previously been considered to be the firm premises of the controversy.

4

Written in arresting prose—at times wild and fierce prose, at times lyrical and inspirational, but never flat and merely argumentative, and often deeply moving—and directed as a polemic not so much at the conclusions that opponents of independence had reached but at their premises, at their unspoken presumptions, and at their sense of what was obvious and what was not, *Common Sense* is a unique pamphlet in the literature of the Revolution. But none of this reaches its most important inner quality. There is something in the pamphlet that goes beyond both of these quite distinguishing characteristics, and while it is less susceptible to proof than the attributes I have already discussed, it is perhaps the most important element of all. It relates to the social aspects of the Revolution.

Much ink has been spilled over the question of the degree to which the American Revolution was a social revolution, and it seems to me that certain points have now been well established. The American Revolution was not the result of intolerable social or economic conditions. The colonies were prosperous communities whose economic condition, recovering from the dislocations of the Seven Years' War, improved during the years when the controversy with England rose in intensity. Nor

was the Revolution deliberately undertaken to recast the social order, to destroy the last remnants of the *ancien régime*, such as they were in America. And there were no "dysfunctions" building up that shaped a peculiarly revolutionary frame of mind in the colonies. The Anglo-American political community could have continued to function "dysfunctionally" for ages untold if certain problems had not arisen which were handled clumsily by an insensitive ministry supported by a political population frozen in glacial complacency, and if those problems had not stirred up the intense ideological sensibilities of the American people. Yet in an indirect way there was a social component in the Revolutionary movement, but it is subtle and latent, wound in, at times quite obscurely, among other elements, and difficult to grasp in itself. It finds its most forceful expression in the dilated prose of Paine's *Common Sense*.

The dominant tone of *Common Sense* is that of rage. It was written by an enraged man—not someone who had reasoned doubts about the English constitution and the related establishment in America, but someone who hated them both and who wished to strike back at them in a savage response. The verbal surface of the pamphlet is heated, and it burned into the consciousness of contemporaries because below it was the flaming conviction, not simply that England was corrupt and that America should declare its independence, but that the whole of organized society and government was stupid and cruel and that it survived only because the atrocities it systematically imposed on humanity had been papered over with a veneer of mythology and superstition that numbed the mind and kept people from rising against the evils that oppressed them.

The aim of almost every other notable pamphlet of the Revolution—pamphlets written by substantial lawyers, ministers, merchants, and planters—was to probe difficult, urgent, and controversial questions and make appropriate recommendations. The aim of *Common Sense* was to tear the world apart—the world as it was known and as it was constituted. *Com-*

mon Sense has nothing of the close logic, scholarship, and rational tone of the best of the American pamphlets. Paine was an ignoramus, both in ideas and in the practice of politics, next to Adams, Wilson, Jefferson, or Madison. He could not discipline his thoughts; they were sucked off continuously from the sketchy outline he apparently had in mind when he began the pamphlet into the boiling vortex of his emotions. And he had none of the hard, quizzical, grainy quality of mind that led Madison to probe the deepest questions of republicanism not as an ideal contrast to monarchical corruption but as an operating, practical, everyday process of government capable of containing within it the explosive forces of society. Paine's writing was not meant to probe unknown realities of a future way of life, or to convince, or to explain; it was meant to overwhelm and destroy. In this respect *Common Sense* bears comparison not with the writings of the other American pamphleteers but with those of Jonathan Swift. For Swift too had been a verbal killer in an age when pamphleteering was important to politics. But Swift's chief weapon had been a rapier as sharp as a razor and so pointed that it first entered its victim unfelt. Paine's writing has none of Swift's marvelously ironic subtlety, just as it has none of the American pamphleteers' learning and logic. Paine's language is violent, slashing, angry, indignant.

This inner voice of anger and indignation had been heard before in Georgian England, in quite special and peculiar forms. It is found in certain of the writings of the extreme leftwing libertarians; and it can be found too in the boiling denunciations of English corruption that flowed from the pens of such would-be prophets as Dr. John Brown, whose sulfuric *Estimate of the Manners and Principles of the Times* created such a sensation in 1757. But its most vivid expression is not verbal but graphic: the paintings and engravings of William Hogarth, whose awareness of the world had taken shape in the same squalor of London's and the provinces' demimonde in which Paine had lived and in which he had struggled so unsuccessfully. In Paine's pamphlet all of these strains and sets of attitudes combine: the extreme left-wing political views that had developed during the English Civil War period as revolutionary republicanism and radical democracy and that had survived, though only underground, through the Glorious Revolution and Walpole's complacent regime; the prophetic sectarian moralism that flowed from 17th-century Puritan roots and that had been kept alive not in the semiestablished nonconformism of Presbyterians and Independents but in the militancy of the radical Baptists and the uncompromising Quakers whom Paine had known so well; and finally, and most important, the indignation and rage of the semi-dispossessed, living at the margins of respectable society and hanging precariously over the abyss of debtors prison, threatened at every turn with an irrecoverable descent into the hell that Hogarth painted so brilliantly and so compulsively in his savage morality tales—those dramatic "progresses" that depict with fiendish, almost insane intensity the passages people in Paine's circumstances took from marginal prosperity, hope, and decency, through scenes of seduction, cruelty, passion, and greed, into madness, disease, and a squalor that became cosmic and apocalyptic in Hogarth's superb late engraving entitled *The Bathos*.

These were English strains and English attitudes—just as *Common Sense* was an English pamphlet written on an American theme—and they were closer in spirit to the viciousness of the Parisian demimonde depicted in the salacious reportage of Restif de La Bretonne than to the Boston of the Adamses and the Philadelphia of Franklin. Yet for all the differences—which help explain why so many American radicals found *Common Sense* so outrageous and unacceptable—there are similarities too. In subdued form something of the same indignation and anger lurks around the edges and under the surface of the American Revolutionary movement. It is not the essential core of the Revolution, but it is an important part of it, and one of the most difficult aspects to depict. One catches a sense of it in John Adams' intense hatred of the Hutchinson–Oliver establishment in Boston, a hatred that any reader of Adams' diary can follow in innumerable blistering passages of that wonderful book, and that led to some of the main triggering events of the Revolution. It can be found too in the denunciations of English corruption that sprang so easily to the lips of the New England preachers, especially those most sunk in provincial remoteness and closest to the original fires of Puritanism which had once burned with equal intensity on both sides of the Atlantic. And it can be found in the resentment of otherwise secure and substantial Americans faced with the brutal arrogance and irrational authority of Crown officials appointed through the tortuous workings of a patronage system utterly remote from America and in no way reflective of the realities of American society.

Common Sense expresses all of this in a magnified form—a form that in its intensity no American could have devised. The pamphlet sparked into flame resentments that had smoldered within the American opposition to England for years, and brought into a single focus the lack of confidence in the whole European world that Americans had vaguely felt and the aspirations for a newer, freer, more open world, independent of England, which had not, until then, been freely expressed. *Common Sense* did not touch off the movement for a formal declaration of independence, and it did not create the Revolutionary leaders' determination to build a better world, more open to human aspirations, than had ever been known before. But it stimulated both; and it exposes in unnaturally vivid dilation the anger—born of resentment, frustration, hurt, and fear—that is an impelling force in every transforming revolution.

The Revolution Remembered

Newly Discovered Eyewitness Accounts of the War for Independence

Edited by John C. Dann

Shortly before the fighting began in 1775 a British officer based in Boston watched the local militia stumble through its paces and wrote home about it. "It is a Masquerade Scene," he said, "to see grave sober Citizens, Barbers and Tailors, who never looked fierce before in their Lives, but at their Wives, Children or Apprentices, strutting about in their Sunday wigs in stiff Buckles with their Muskets on their Shoulders, struggling to put on a Martial Countenance. If ever you saw a Goose assume an Air of Consequence, you may catch some idea of the foolish, awkward, puffed-up stare of our Tradesmen."

His scorn was understandable, for in his time the profession of soldiering called for training every bit as refined and rigorous as that given, say, a watchmaker. The idea of a citizen army was entirely new and more than a little ludicrous.

Yet just such an army would win the war that was to come, and no documents demonstrate the qualities of its amateur soldiers more vividly than the extraordinary, never-before-published reminiscences on the following pages.

In 1832, Congress passed the first comprehensive Pension Act for veterans of the Revolution. It offered a yearly stipend to any man (or his widow) who could prove service of more than six months in the struggle for independence. Most of the thousands of elderly veterans who applied could offer little documentary evidence of having fought: discharge papers had been lost (or never issued); pay certificates had been sold or thrown away; comrades-in-arms who would have remembered them were long since dead. Their only recourse was to submit what the enabling legislation called "a very full account" of their service and have it sworn to in a court of law.

Accordingly, the old men made their way to the local courthouse and told their stories to a clerk or court reporter. Pension agents sought out others, recorded their memories, and filled out applications for a fee. The narratives thus collected—the results of one of the first and largest oral-history projects ever undertaken anywhere—are recorded on 898 reels of microfilm at the National Archives in Washington. Most have never before been published. Now, Professor John C. Dann of the University of Michigan has performed the mind-numbing task of deciphering them

all, and has chosen seventy-nine to include in his book, The Revolution Remembered, to be published soon by the University of Chicago Press. We, in turn, have selected portions of sixteen narratives to present here.

These are the voices of ordinary men and women— farmers, mainly, but servants, too, and a slave and a shoemaker and a laundress—and their stories are told, for the most part, in the plainest possible language. Some veterans were terse, others garrulous, and here and there a date is muddled or a detail embroidered; it had, after all, been just under half a century since the shooting stopped. But almost all of them retained a fierce—and justifiable— pride in what they had done.

Sylvanus Wood, a shoemaker of Woburn, Massachusetts, was a minuteman when the war came.

I was then established at my trade two miles east of Lexington meetinghouse, on west border of Woburn, and on the nineteenth morn of April, 1775, Robert Douglass and myself heard Lexington bell about one hour before day. We concluded that trouble was near.

We waited for no man but hastened and joined Captain Parker's company at the breaking of the day. Douglass and myself stood together in the center of said company when the enemy first fired. The English soon were on their march for Concord. I helped carry six dead into the meetinghouse and then set out after the enemy and had not an armed man to go with me, but before I arrived at Concord, I see one of the grenadiers standing sentinel. I cocked my piece and run up to him, seized his gun with my left hand. He surrendered his armor, one gun and bayonet, a large cutlass and brass fender, one box over the shoulder with twenty-two rounds, one box round the waist with eighteen rounds. This was the first prisoner that was known to be taken that day.

Ten-year-old Israel Trask of Essex County, Massachusetts, was a regimental cook and messenger in 1776 when he first saw General Washington in the rebel encampment at Cambridge.

"The Revolution Remembered," by John C. Dann, *American Heritage*, April/May 1980. From THE REVOLUTION REMEMBERED: EYEWITNESS ACCOUNTS OF THE WAR FOR INDEPENDENCE, University of Chicago Press, 1980.

2. REVOLUTIONARY AMERICA

A day or two preceding the incident I am about to relate, a rifle corps had come into camp from Virginia, made up of recruits from the backwoods and mountains of that state, in a uniform dress totally different from that of the regiments raised on the seaboard and interior of New England. Their white linen frocks, ruffled and fringed, excited the curiosity of the whole army, particularly . . . the Marblehead regiment, who were always full of fun and mischief. [They] looked with scorn on such an rustic uniform when compared to their own round jackets and fishers' trousers, [and they] directly confronted from fifty to an hundred of the riflemen who were viewing the college buildings. Their first manifestations were ridicule and derision, which the riflemen bore with more patience than their wont, but resort being made to snow, which then covered the ground, these soft missives were interchanged but a few minutes before both parties closed, and a fierce struggle commenced with biting and gouging on the one part, and knockdown on the other part with as much apparent fury as the most deadly enmity could create. Reinforced by their friends, in less than five minutes, more than a thousand combatants were on the field, struggling for the mastery.

At this juncture, General Washington made his appearance, whether by accident or design I never knew. I only saw him and his colored servant, both mounted. With the spring of a deer, he leaped from his saddle, threw the reins of his bridle into the hands of his servant, and rushed into the thickest of the melee, with an iron grip seized two tall, brawny, athletic, savage-looking riflemen by the throat, keeping them at arm's length, alternately shaking and talking to them. In this position, the eye of the belligerents caught sight of the general. Its effect on them was instantaneous flight at the top of their speed in all directions from the scene of the conflict. Less than fifteen minutes time had elapsed from the commencement of the row before the general and his two criminals were the only occupants of the field of action. Here bloodshed, imprisonment, trials by court-martial were happily prevented, and hostile feelings between the different corps of the army extinguished by the physical and mental energies timely exerted by one individual.

James Hawkins of New York met Washington a little later in camp near Kingsbridge, during the bitter winter of 1776–77.

During a part of this time, General Washington . . . was in command, and he [James Hawkins] well recollects a personal interview with him under the following circumstances. He, the said James, and a soldier by the name of Elijah Morehouse, a tent mate of his, being barefooted and having made fruitless applications to their under officers for a furlough to enable them to procure shoes, applied to the commander-in-chief at his quarters. Having been conducted into his presence by a file of soldiers, they found the general surrounded by officers, who rose, and, pointing them to seats, he himself took a chair, and with the utmost condescension and kindness of manners listened to the story of their sufferings. The good general, after

a pause of a few moments, replied, "My brave fellows, you see the condition in which I am placed. Yonder upon the East River is the enemy. Should they advance, and we expect them every moment, I shall need every man of you. My soldiers are my life. Should they retire, call again, and you shall have your furlough."

Jacob Francis, a New Jersey freedman, was helping to build fortifications during the siege of Boston when he encountered General Israel Putnam.

I recollect General Putnam . . . from a circumstance that occurred when the troops were engaged in throwing up a breastwork at Lechmere Point across the river, opposite Boston, between that and Cambridge. The men were at work digging, about five hundred men on the fatigue at once. I was at work among them. They were divided into small squads of eight or ten together and a noncommissioned officer to oversee them. General Putnam came riding along in uniform as an officer to look at the work. They had dug up a pretty large stone, which lay on the side of the ditch. The general spoke to the corporal who was standing looking at the men at work and said to him, "My lad, throw that stone up on the middle of the breastwork."

The corporal, touching his hat with his hand, said to the general, "Sir, I am a corporal."

"Oh," said the general, "I ask your pardon, sir," and immediately got off his horse and took up the stone and threw it up on the breastwork himself and then mounted his horse and rode on, giving directions, et cetera. It was in the winter season, and the ground was froze.

Samuel DeForest of Connecticut witnessed the Battle of Long Island as a frightened eighteen-year-old.

On the twenty-eighth day of August . . . we could see boats passing and repassing from Staten to Long Island loaded with men. After sunrise we returned to our quarters, and after breakfast Colonel Lewis, with some of his officers, among the rest Lieutenant Curtis (being his waiter, I was permitted to follow the company), [climbed] up several flights of stairs, till we reached the top of the roof, from which we [could see] the British soldiers were landing at the foot of a road perhaps three-quarters of a mile south of Brooklyn Ferry. Leading an eastern direction, the road appeared about four rods wide, and the road was constantly filled with men. The road ascended gradually about forty rods and then lay on a level. The motion of the men's bodies while under march, which of course would give motion to the burnished arms which came in contact with the rays of a brilliant morning sun . . . to the eye gleamed like sheets of fire. This road was filled with reinforcements from Staten Island for about six hours, and this time and much longer the battle was fighting.

About eleven o'clock, Colonel Lewis had orders to march his regiment along the dock opposite Brooklyn Ferry, and when there was an officer on horseback, we concluded he was one of the general's aides. He informed us that he was calling for volunteers to turn out and man every watercraft which lay along the dock. "All must know there was dreadful fighting, and if our men were driven to retreat, we wish to be able to bring them over this side."

One Wells Judson and myself turned out. A periauger was committed to our charge, and we landed at Brooklyn Ferry about one o'clock. The thunder of the British artillery, the roaring of the small arms of both armies, was tremendous.

Judson and I walked up the ferry road and lay down under a shade, for it was very warm, and drank some cold water. While we lay under the board fence perhaps an hour, ruminating on the terrors of that day, we heard the tramping of men just over the knoll, but we [had] hardly time to think before they hove in sight, and the road was filled with redcoat regulars, and again we had hardly time for surprise before we saw they were prisoners, and they were hurried over the ferry and through the city and over the Hudson into Jerseys. We concluded there was between two or three hundred of them. The firing ceased a little before sundown, and a number of us got into a small boat and went back to our regiment. We learned soon that the flower of the army was killed and taken prisoners; that General Lord Stirling and General Sullivan and several brigadier generals and between nine and ten thousand soldiers were taken prisoners. The remaining of our army on Long Island retreated and pitched on the best and highest ground just back of Brooklyn and entrenched themselves as suddenly as well as they could. The British army left Flatbush, where the late and dreadful ill-fated battle had been lately fought, and were planting themselves alongside our troops in order soon to give the finishing stroke to Washington's army.

But shortly after, I do not remember how many days, a most wonderful thunderstorm took place. It commenced about one o'clock in the day. The thunder and the lightning was dreadful. The clouds run so low, that they seemed to break over the houses, and the water run in rivers. The darkness was so great that the two armies could not see each other, although within one hundred rods of each other. Through the whole of that stormy afternoon they were crossing as fast as possible, but they themselves did [not] know that they were retreating. They came over to get a little rest, and we [were] to go over and take their places. The sergeant major told us that Colonel Lewis told him we must be prepared to go over the next morning. In one hour after, the sergeant major come to Captain Tomlinson's quarters and warned us all forth to march up to the grand parade in order to pass a review and take further orders. The storm began at one, and it was now five o'clock. It now rained but not so hard. The company would not turn out.

A Mr. Othniel French, a nice and good man, a friend and neighbor to my father, he says to me, "The men will not turn out, Samuel. You are a minuteman. Will you turn out with me and go up to the grand parade and see what is going to be done?"

I says, "Yes, Mr. French, I will go with you."

There was a few in other companies belonging to Colonel Lewis's regiment fell in, and we marched up to the grand parade, and we found three or four hundred men.

There was an officer there, who says to us, "Come, my brave boys, I am glad you are not afraid of a few drops of water." By this time, the rain had subsided. It appeared to be turned into mist and fog. "A picket guard is to be set tonight a little this side [of] Bunker Hill on the Bowery."

Mr. French says to me again, "Samuel, keep close to me."

"I will, sir," and we marched on, and we come to the house where the picket was to be kept, and the sergeants began to distribute the sentinels.

Mr. French says to the sergeant, "I wish you would be so good as to let this young lad stand next to me, for there is none that either of us are acquainted with," and the sergeant placed me close to the guardhouse and Mr. French next. I found out the whole of three or four hundred men who marched with us was to form a line of sentries from the North River to the East River, once in forty feet.

As soon as the sentries were set, an officer on horseback, he rid close to me and says to me, "Let no man pass you this night. Take no countersign nor watchword. If any man come to you, see that he is put under guard. You must keep your station here till morning." There was no more through the night. The fog thickened and all was silent as death. At about twelve o'clock . . . the dogs began to bark, the cattle to low, the Indians to howl and yell. All these noises was from Long Island, by reason of the thick and heavy fog, and all the other dense qualities which conspired to tune the air like an organ. We supposed that the barking of the dogs and the lowing of the cattle and the howling of the Indians was two miles from us. It was said afterwards that perhaps there was three or four hundred Indians attached to our army on Long Island. They made as much noise as the yelling of a thousand under other circumstances. It was said that the Indians was set to yelling that night by the counsel of General Putnam.

About day, the noise was all still, and about sun an hour high, the fog began to go off. At this instant, a man in the appearance of an officer came up to the guardhouse. One of the officers asked him where he was from. He replied, "From Long Island, sir."

"What's the word from there?"

"Our army has all came off the night past."

The officer says, "Gentleman, this man ought to be put under guard."

The gentleman who had just came up said, "You can put me under guard if you please, sir, but I presume that in less than forty minutes, you will find what I tell you is true."

The officer of the guard now says, "Gentleman, if this is true, we shall be all sacrificed. What can hinder the whole British army now on Long Island? Flushed with conquest, thirty or forty thousand can march their army up the island till they get opposite to Kingsbridge in four hours, and their fleet can send them the boats which we see them cross their army from Staten Island to Long Island in as short a time."

By this time, Mr. French and I began to think about hunting up our courageous comrades and to learn whether they had kept themselves dry through the storm. I have but a confused recollection of what passed after this scene—all bustle and preparation to retreat out of the city as soon as possible. Mr. French and I, after the fatigue of the stormy day and standing sentry all night in our wet clothes, was quite sick, and preparations was to leave the city next morning, and he saw a man with a wagon that night from New Rochelle, and he hired him to carry us both to his house. We got our pass and went on, and stopped and recruited, and went as I could. I reached home about the last of September and soon listed under Lieutenant Isaac Burr of old Fairfield into the Black Rock battery service, according to best my memory, for one year.

Black Rock rock or battery lay on the top of a rock alongside of a narrow and crooked channel environed on every side with rocks, which made it dangerous for vessels unacquainted with the channel to enter. I cannot remember how many cannon was placed on the platform. I think six or eight. It belonged to the town of Fairfield and lay about half a mile east of the courthouse and jail. I believe the fortification was kept up till peace. I have forgotten how many men was supported for its defense, whether thirty or forty, I cannot [remember]. There was no particular occurrence took place of notice until about the close of the year 1776.

Near the last of December, Colonel Abel, a patriot and prominent character in the town and county, early in the morning he sent his waiter, a colored man by the name of Bill Molat, with a message to Lieutenant Burr. When Molat had reached within perhaps fifteen rods of the barracks, he began to shout and holler, "*Huzza, huzza, huzza.*" He jumped up, knocked his heels together, and shouted, "Colonel Abel has news from Washington, and he has taken the whole Hessian army." Lieutenant Burr hallooed for Molat to come to the barracks, and when he came, he presented a short, brief statement in print stating that Washington, agreeable to a preconcerted plan, commenced his march at dark through rain, hail, and sleet on Christmas Day evening. He arrived at Trenton the next morning before daylight, and as they had been holding Christmas frolic, drove them out of their bunks and took them all prisoners. Thus the setting sun of the dreadful summer of '76 sheds some rays of light on her horizon and was presageful of better days, and in fact this event was the dayspring to those better days, and the news flew swift through the land.

Abel Potter was one of thirty-six militiamen who slipped onto British-held Rhode Island in 1777, hoping to seize Major General Richard Prescott, the enemy commander. Later in the war, Potter returned to the island and was himself captured.

He was one of the . . . volunteers who took General Prescott from his lodgings in the nighttime from the island of Rhode Island. Colonel [William] Barton commanded at this adventure. His brother James Potter was second in command and he (this applicant) the third in command. . . . His brother James, after the expedition had landed on the island, took the two first sentinels that they passed, and this claimant took the third

and last one who stood at the door of General Prescott's quarters. . . .

They went into the house and the Widow Oberin, who kept the house, cried, "Captain Potter, what's the matter?"

His brother James had been a sea captain . . . and was acquainted with the widow. He said, "You need not be scared, Mrs. Oberin. We are not agoing to hurt you. Where is the general?"

She said he was upstairs.

He and his brother and Colonel Barton went up into the general's lodging room. He had raised up in his bed. He (General Prescott) spoke immediately and said, "Gentlemen, your business requires haste, but do for God's sake let me get my clothes."

Says Colonel Barton, "By God, it is no time for clothes."

They started him immediately and bare-legged through a field of barley, which pricked him some. They went quick to their boat, where a part of their party had remained, and with them went back to their camp. The enemy fired at them as they were crossing back. They saw the shot strike the water around them. None was hurt.

The three sentinels they took with them under guard. . . . The mode in which he took the guard standing at the door was as follows. He answered as a "friend" and then stepped up to him to whisper the countersign in his ear and stooped forward to him, and as the sentinel inclined toward him, he seized the sentinel's piece with his left hand and told him not to speak or he should die, the only words which this claimant spoke while on the island.

The sentinel answered, "I won't," tremblingly. This same sentinel afterward taught school in Pownal, Vermont, and claimant sent a member of his family to school to him. Leaving the island, claimant was the last of the party to get into the boat. They were in a great haste, and he waded to his breast after the boat as it started. . . .

In the fall of '78, he with two others went on to the island of Rhode Island to get apples. The island was in the possession of the British. They were overtaken suddenly by a scout and taken to the British camp. A lieutenant's commission was offered him (the claimant) by the British officers, which he spurned to accept. He told them he had a commission which suited him and which he intended to use again in a few days against them, as he expected to be exchanged. He, however, made his escape by getting his guard drunk and pretending to drink himself. He got outdoors to attend the call of nature, knocked down his guard, and made his escape fifty or sixty rods to floodwood on the shore, where he secreted himself till the first bustle was over (it was in the night) and then got onto a slab and swam across the channel toward his own camp. He almost perished with being chilled.

He was cordially received when he reached his quarters and called on General Cornell and told him he was at his mercy as he had crossed after apples against orders. General Cornell told him to go to his quarters, he should not break him, but should, if he went again, and added, "I knew you would be back again soon. I told 'em, they might as well undertake to keep the *devil* as to keep Potter."

Jehu Grant of Rhode Island was one of several dozen blacks who applied for pensions—and one of thousands who served in the American army. He had run away from his Tory master to join the wagon service, but when he asked for his pension in 1832, the pension office replied that he had been a fugitive slave at the time and was therefore ineligible. His reply is given here in its entirety; despite its bitter eloquence, he never got his money.

That he was a slave to Elihu Champlen who resided at Narragansett, Rhode Island. At the time he left him his said master was called a Tory, and in a secret manner furnished the enemy, when shipping lay nearby, with sheep, cattle, cheese, et cetera, and received goods from them. And this applicant being afraid his said master would send him to the British ships, ran away sometime in August, 1777, as near as he can recollect, being the same summer that Danbury was burnt. That he went right to Danbury after he left his said master and enlisted to Captain Giles Galer for eighteen months. That, according to the best of his memory, General Huntington and General Meigs' brigades, or a part of them, were at that place. That he, this applicant, was put to teaming with a team of horses and wagon, drawing provisions and various other loading for the army for three or four months until winter set in, then was taken as a servant to John Skidmore, wagonmaster general (as he was called), and served with him as his waiter until spring, when the said troops went to the Highlands or near that place on the Hudson River, a little above the British lines. That this applicant had charge of the team as wagoner and carried the said General Skidmore's baggage and continued with him and the said troops as his wagoner near the said lines until sometime in June, when his said master either sent or came, and this applicant was given up to his master again, and he returned, after having served nine or ten months.

Corroborating Letter of 1836

Honorable J. L. Edwards, Commissioner of Pensions:

Your servant begs leave to state that he forwarded to the War Department a declaration founded on the Pension Act of June, 1832, praying to be allowed a pension (if his memory serves him) for ten months' service in the American army of the Revolutionary War. That he enlisted as a soldier but was put to the service of a teamster in the summer and a waiter in the winter. In April, 1834, I received a writing from Your Honor, informing me that my "services while a fugitive from my master's service was not embraced in said Act," and that my "papers were placed on file." In my said declaration, I just mentioned the cause of leaving my master, as may be seen by a reference thereunto, and I now pray that I may be permitted to express my feelings more fully on that part of my said declaration.

I was then grown to manhood, in the full vigor and strength of life, and heard much about the cruel and arbitrary things done by the British. Their ships lay within a few miles of my master's house, which stood near the shore, and I was confident that my master traded with them, and I suffered much from fear that I should be sent aboard a ship of war. This

I disliked. But when I saw liberty poles and the people all engaged for the support of freedom, I could not but like and be pleased with such thing (God forgive me if I sinned in so feeling). And living on the borders of Rhode Island, where whole companies of colored people enlisted, it added to my fears and dread of being sold to the British. These considerations induced me to enlist into the American army, where I served faithful about ten months, when my master found and took me home. Had I been taught to read or understand the precepts of the Gospel, "Servants obey your masters," I might have done otherwise, notwithstanding the songs of liberty that saluted my ear, thrilled through my heart. But feeling conscious that I have since compensated my master for the injury he sustained by my enlisting, and that God has forgiven me for so doing, and that I served my country faithfully, and that they having enjoyed the benefits of my service to an equal degree for the length [of] time I served with those generally who are receiving the liberalities of the government, I cannot but feel it becoming me to pray Your Honor to review my declaration on file and the papers herewith amended.

A few years after the war, Joshua Swan, Esq., of Stonington purchased me of my master and agreed that after I had served him a length of time named faithfully, I should be free. I served to his satisfaction and so obtained my freedom. He moved into the town of Milton, where I now reside, about forty-eight years ago. After my time expired with Esq. Swan, I married a wife. We have raised six children. Five are still living. I must be upward of eighty years of age and have been blind for many years, and notwithstanding the aid I received from the honest industry of my children, we are still very needy and in part are supported from the benevolence of our friends. With these statements and the testimony of my character herewith presented, I humbly set my claim upon the well-known liberality of government.

Most respectfully your humble servant

his

Jehu   X   Grant

mark

In September of 1777, Richard Wallace, a farmer of Thetford, Vermont, marched with Connecticut troops against Fort Ticonderoga—and found himself swimming for his life.

General [Horatio] Gates contrived to cut off the British watercraft on Lake George, and for that purpose sent two detachments of five hundred men each, one on the west side of the lake to the south side of the mountains that lie south of Ticonderoga, where our troops were ordered to halt. I belonged to this detachment.

Directly after halting, Colonel Brown came to me and inquired if I could swim. I told him I was not a great swimmer. He said he wanted me to swim a little way but did not then tell me where or for what purpose. After excusing myself a little, I agreed to swim, [as] he was exceedingly earnest to have me engage. He then said he wanted a man to go with me and inquired who would volunteer in the service. A man by the name of Samuel Webster offered himself and said he was a great swimmer. Colonel Brown engaged him to go with me. This done, Colonel Brown called several officers and some soldiers, and we all set off together and traveled up the mountain a few miles until we came in full view of the British encampment, and after reconnoitering the mountain east and west for about three miles and taking observations, the officers arranged all things for an attack at break of day the next morning. Colonel Brown then called Webster and myself and told us of "the little way" he wished us to swim, which was nothing less than across Lake Champlain, then in view about five miles distant. He accordingly gave us our instructions, both verbal and written, and we made our [way] over rocky mountains and through hurricanes of fallen trees to the lake, where we arrived a little before sunset, so near the enemy's ships that we could see them walk on their decks and hear them talk, and had they seen us they might have reached us with their grapeshot.

With deep anxiety for the event, we undressed, bound our clothes upon our backs, drank a little ginger and water, and entered the cold waters of the lake, here about a mile in width. Webster went forward, and I followed. After proceeding a few rods, I was on the point of turning about. The water was so chilling I thought I could never reach the opposite shore, but when I reflected that the lives of many of my countrymen might depend upon the success of my effort, I resolved at every hazard to go forward, and if I perished, I should die in the best of causes. When we had got into the middle of the lake, the wind blew and dashed the water onto our bundles of clothes and wet them and made them very heavy. And the garter with which I bound on my bundle swelled and got across my throat and choked me and exceedingly embarrassed me. When we had swam about two-thirds across, I found myself almost exhausted and thought I could not proceed further. But at the instant I was about giving up, the Lord seemed to give me new courage and strength, and shifting my manner of swimming a little, I went forward and soon discovered a tree directly before, about twenty rods from the shore. This tree I reached with a struggle and thought I could not have obtained the shore if it had been to gain the world. The tree was large, and I made out to get onto it and adjust my bundle.

At this instant, Webster, who was about twelve rods north of me, cried out, "For God's sake Wallace, help me, for I am a drowning!" The cry of my companion in distress gave me a fresh impulse. I swam to the shore, ran opposite to him, and directly found there poles, which had been washed upon the beach, about twelve or fifteen feet long. I flung one toward him, but it did not reach him. I flung the second without success. The third, I pushed toward him until the further end reached him; he seized it and sunk to the bottom. I then exerted myself with all my might and drew him out, I hardly know how. As soon as he came to a little and could speak, he cried out, "O Lord God, Wallace, if it had not been for you, I should have been in the eternal world." I told him not to make any noise, as the enemy might be watching us in ambush.

I then wrung his clothes and dressed him and put on my own, and we set out to find the American encampment. But it soon became so dark that we lost our way, and in a short time we found ourselves in an open field near the enemy's guard. We then returned into the woods and remained in a secure place until the moon rose, which appeared to rise directly in the west. I, however, told Webster the moon must be right, and we traveled on until we came to the road that led north and south, just as the enemy fired their nine o'clock gun. But we did not know whether to go north or south. Our object was to find General Warner's encampment and deliver our express to him. But we were not certain whether he was north or south of us, and we might fall into the enemy's hands, let us go which way we would, and the whole plan of our officers fail of success. In this trying dilemma, we agreed that one should go north, followed by the other at few rods distant, and risk his life to the best advantage, and if taken by the enemy, the hind one should go south and deliver the express. It fell to my lot to go forward, and, after I had traveled about an hour, I came to a sentry who hailed me and said, "Who comes there?"

I answered, "A friend."

He asked, "A friend to whom?"

I asked him whose friend he was.

He then said, "Advance and give the countersign."

This I could not do, as I did not know the countersign of this detachment. I knew the sentry was an American from his voice, yet he might be a Tory in the British service. I then asked him in a pleasant voice if there was another sentry near and if he would call him. He did so, and to my great joy, I knew the man and informed them at once that I was a friend to America and had brought an express to their commander and requested to be conducted to him immediately, and calling Webster, who was a few rods behind, we were conducted by an officer and file of men to General Warner's quarters and delivered our message, both written and verbal. I also informed General Warner that the British were much nearer than he imagined, and that unless everything was kept still in the camp, the plan would yet fail. He then ordered all lights to be extinguished and no noise to be made. We then retired a little into the woods and lay down cold and wet in blankets furnished us by the commissary, and when we awoke in the morning, all our troops destined to this service on both sides of the lake were in motion. The Indian spies took possession of all the watercraft belonging to the British on Lake George, and about five hundred prisoners were taken.

John Ingersoll of Tuckahoe joined the New Jersey sea service about 1778 in order to avoid being drafted for the militia (he had already served nine months). He might better have stayed on shore.

The seashore was at that time much infested by refugees, who collected in bodies and plundered and annoyed the inhabitants whenever they could. They frequently burned the private dwellings, deprived the families of their stock of provisions, drove off large stocks of cattle from the beaches; in fact, ruin and desolation marked their footsteps wherever they went. It was to protect the coast from their depredations that these lookout boats were fitted out. There were two of said boats started out together. One was commanded by Captain McGee, with a crew of sixteen men. The other was commanded by Captain Willets of Cape May with an equal number of men. To the latter boat I belonged.

We followed along the coast until we came to Barnegat Inlet. We there ran in and landed on Cranberry Beach. We there fell in with a larger body of refugees. They were far superior in number to us, and they succeeded in taking us prisoners. They handcuffed us and conveyed us onto the prison ship then laying in the North River opposite the city of New York, whose name was the *Scorpion.* I remained on board the *Scorpion* about three weeks. It being then in the month of July, I was taken sick with a camp fever, when I was removed out of the *Scorpion* and put on board the *Huntress,* also a prison ship but then converted into an hospital. I was on board the *Huntress* but a short time, when I was attacked with dysentery. Here I thought would be an end to my sufferings, but although death relieved some of my messmates from the horrors of that prison (Captain Willets was among the number who fell a victim to the disease), I was one among those who recovered. The water was bad and the provisions worse. Our allowance was a half pound of mutton per day, but to our surprise, when the mutton came on board, it was only the heads of sheep with the horns and wool thereon. Our bread was oatmeal, neither sifted nor bolted. Our manner of preparing it was as follows: pound up a sheep's head until the bones were all broken, then sink the oatmeal in a bowl of water and float out the hulls; with this we would thicken the broth and thus we kept soul and body together.

I had been on board about two months, sometimes almost famished for the want of provisions, when the officers of the hospital ship made a proposal to me. In case I would keep the cabin clean, boil their tea kettle, black their boots, et cetera, I should have a hammock to sleep in, should be better fed, and should be exchanged when the rest of my company was. I accordingly accepted of the offer. The hospital ship was anchored in what is called Buttermilk Channel with their cables and anchors. The center one was a tremendous chain cable. There were but one gun kept on board said ship, and that was an English musket which the officers kept in the cabin. There were about two hundred prisoners on board said ship, with seven officers and one physician.

I had been doing my duty in the cabin about two weeks, when we laid a plan for our escape. It was as follows. One day while the officers were absent on Long Island, I took down the said musket, poured out the priming, poured water into the barrel of the gun until the load became thoroughly wet. I then wiped the pan thoroughly dry, reprimed her, and put her back in her place. One or two days had elapsed, but we could get no boat wherein to make our escape, for they universally at night chained and locked her fast.

An opportunity at length presented itself, to wit., the officers had a mind to go on shore, and it being tremendous stormy weather, they unlocked their boat from the chain, brought her up alongside, and ordered a boy to get in the boat and bail the water out of her. I had communicated the secret of the gun being out of order to some of my fellow prisoners, and there being at [the] time a heavy storm, with the wind blowing directly upon the Jersey shore together with a thick, dense fog in the air, we considered this a favorable time to make our escape. We accordingly embraced the opportunity which then offered.

Seven prisoners (beside the boy which was in the boat) sprang into the boat. We shoved off, but before we had fairly cut the boat loose, one of the officers came on deck and discovered us. He screamed out for the gun, which he readily obtained, took aim at us, but as he pulled trigger, she only flashed. He reprimed her, but as oft as he pulled trigger, she would only flash. They then abandoned their musket, all ran upon the quarterdeck, hallooed as loud as they could to give the alarm to the fleet then laying at anchor around us, but the wind was blowing so heavy, it was impossible for them to be heard at even so short a distance. They then hoisted a flag on the flagstaff on the stern of the ship as a signal of distress, but the fog being so dense, none of the fleet discovered it. By this time we were pretty nearly over to the Jersey shore, which we reached at length.

We landed on an island in the meadow called Communipaw, between Staten Island and Paulus Hook, but here we were in great danger of being taken up as runaways, for the enemy had possession of the whole country through which we had to travel for some miles at least. We were emaciated with hunger and sickness, and vermin covered our bodies. We were, however, fortunate enough to reach the camp of General Lafayette in safety, who received us joyfully and sent a sergeant of his guard to pilot us on to General Washington's army. We stayed with General Lafayette's army about one day, when we left it and reached General Washington's camp, which was about two miles distant. General Washington's army was then under arms and about to remove from that place of encampment. We marched with his army about two miles further, when he again encamped and furnished us with passes to return to our homes, which I reached in safety. My pass which I received from General Washington at that time I kept for many years, and I was under strong impressions that I had it to this day, but I have had my papers searched, and it cannot be found. What has become [of it], it is impossible for me to say.

John McCasland of Pennsylvania recalls a foray from Valley Forge in the spring of 1779.

[On] one occasion, sixteen of us were ranging about hunting Hessians, and we suspected Hessians to be at a large and handsome mansion house in Bucks County, Pennsylvania, about sixteen miles from Philadelphia. We approached near the house and discovered a large Hessian standing in the yard with his gun, as a sentinel we supposed, and by a unanimous vote of the company present it was agreed on that Major McCorman or myself, who were good marksmen, should shoot him (McCorman was then a private). We cast lots, and it fell to my lot to shoot the Hessian. I did not like to shoot a man down in cold blood. The company present knew I was a good marksman, and I concluded to break his thigh. I shot with a rifle and aimed at his hip. He had a large iron tobacco box in his breeches pocket, and I hit the box, the ball glanced, and it entered his thigh and scaled the bone of the thigh on the outside. He fell and then rose. We scaled the yard fence and surrounded the house. They saw their situation and were evidently disposed to surrender. They could not speak English, and we could not understand their language. At length one of the Hessians came out of the cellar with a large bottle of rum and advanced with it at arm's length as a flag of truce. The family had abandoned the house, and the Hessians had possession. They were twelve in number. We took them prisoners and carried them to Valley Forge and delivered them up to General Washington.

Garret Watts of Caroline County, Virginia, confesses his own terror, fifty-four years after the battle of Camden.

The two armies came near each other at Sutton's about twelve or one o'clock in the night.... The pickets fired several rounds before day. I well remember everything that occurred the next morning: I remember that I was among the nearest to the enemy; that a man named John Summers was my file leader; that we had orders to wait for the word to commence firing; that the militia were in front and in a feeble condition at that time. They were fatigued. The weather was warm excessively. They had been fed a short time previously on molasses entirely. I can state on oath that I believe my gun was the first gun fired, notwithstanding the orders, for we were close to the enemy, who appeared to maneuver in contempt of us, and I fired without thinking except that I might prevent the man opposite from killing me. The discharge and loud roar soon became general from one end of the lines to the other. Amongst other things, I confess I was amongst the first that fled. The cause of that I cannot tell, except that everyone I saw was about to do the same. It was instantaneous. There was no effort to rally, no encouragement to fight. Officers and men joined in the flight. I threw away my gun, and reflecting I might be punished for being found without arms, I picked up a drum, which gave forth such sounds when touched by the twigs, I cast it away.

John Cock of Bedford County, Virginia, survived this random encounter with hostile Indians on the Clinch River to live a long life.

Here he remained for several months, during which time, in the month of December, John English, who lived in the neighborhood and had come to the station for protection, wished to go to his plantation a mile off and got permission of applicant's captain to go with him, as well as one Oxshir [Oxter?] and English's wife. Applicant accordingly went to English's house with him and stayed all night. Their guns were laid away. In the morning, about sunup, the dogs barked exceedingly fierce. Applicant stepped out into the yard to see what they were baying, and got some distance from the door

and discovered four Cherokee fellows, all armed. He ran to the door, but the inmates of the house had by this time discovered the Indians and closed it. They were afraid to open the door to let him in for fear the Indians would also enter. Being thus situated and without his gun, applicant had no hope of safety but by flight. He accordingly ran through a field, the only way he could go, the outlet toward the woods being the direction at which the Indians had gone and where they then were. After he had gone some distance, perhaps two hundred yards, he, as he run, turned his head to see if he was pursued, when to his misfortune he beheld two Indians close to him, each running with their guns presented at him. An effort to escape being hopeless, applicant stopped and signed to them that he would surrender.

Each of the merciless savages instantly drew from their belts their tomahawks and stepped up to him. One of them immediately struck him upon his bare head, for he had left his hat in the house, with the point of his tomahawk and sunk it in applicant's skull and gave him a second lick with the edge of the ax which sunk into his head and touched the brain. Applicant fell lifeless, and the Indians no doubt believed him to be so. They immediately scalped him and pulled his hunting shirt off of him and cut one-half of his waistcoat off and took these with them. In a short time, applicant came to his senses. His neck was entirely limber. He had no use of his left arm or shoulder nor has he ever regained the use of his shoulder or arm. The arm has wasted away. The places where the tomahawk entered his head healed up, but the holes never filled up. They remain yet, and one of them is perhaps two inches long and one wide and about one deep.

North Carolinian Moses Hall recalls the special viciousness of war between rebels and marauding Tories in this account of the Battle of Haw River, February 23, 1781, and its bloody aftermath.

Our troops and this body of Tories and Colonel [Banastre] Tarleton all being in the same neighborhood, our troops on the march met said body of Tories at a place called the Race Paths, and mistaking our troops for Tarleton's, Colonel Lee and officers kept up the deception, and Colonel Lee and his light horse marching in one column or line, and Major or Colonel Dixon's command in another, some interval apart, the Tories passed into this interval between our lines. Or, perhaps which is the fact, the Tories having halted, our lines passed one on each side of them whilst marching along to cover them so as to place them between our said lines. They frequently uttered salutations of a friendly kind, believing us to be British. Colonel Lee knew what he was about and so did Major Dixon. But I recollect that my Captain Hall, perceiving they were Tories and thinking that Colonel Lee did not know it and was imposed upon by their cries of friendship and misunderstood them to be our friends instead of the British, he called to Colonel Lee across the Tories' line and told him, "Colonel Lee, they are every blood of them Tories!" Colonel Lee gave him a sign to proceed on with the execution of the command, which was to march on until a different command was given. In a few minutes or less time, and at the instant they, the Tories, were completely covered by our lines upon both flanks, or front and rear as the case may have been, the bugle sounded to attack, and the slaughter began, the Tories crying out, "Your own men, your own men, as good subjects of his Majesty as in America." It was said that upwards of two hundred of these Tories were slain on the ground. . . .

The evening after our battle with the Tories, we having a considerable number of prisoners, I recollect a scene which made a lasting impression upon my mind. I was invited by some of my comrades to go and see some of the prisoners. We went to where six were standing together. Some discussion taking place, I heard some of our men cry out, "Remember Buford," and the prisoners were immediately hewed to pieces with broadswords. At first I bore the scene without any emotion, but upon a moment's reflection, I felt such horror as I never did before nor have since, and returning to my quarters and throwing myself upon my blanket, I contemplated the cruelties of war until overcome and unmanned by a distressing gloom from which I was not relieved until commencing our march next morning before day by moonlight. I came to Tarleton's camp, which he had just abandoned leaving lively rail fires. Being on the left of the road as we marched along, I discovered lying upon the ground something with [the] appearance of a man. Upon approaching him, he proved to be a youth about sixteen, who, having come out to view the British through curiosity, for fear he might give information to our troops, they had run him through with a bayonet and left him for dead. Though able to speak, he was mortally wounded. The sight of this unoffending boy, butchered rather than be encumbered in the [illegible] on the march I assume, relieved me of my distressful feelings for the slaughter of the Tories, and I desired nothing so much as the opportunity of participating in their destruction.

Benjamin Jones was serving with the Connecticut Line in Westchester County, New York, in the summer of 1781 when his unit learned that British cavalry was near.

He was a scout . . . and went to New Rochelle and came out onto the main road from New York to Boston about eight o'clock, A.M., thinks in the month of July. His officer made a halt. They had been out all night, and while halting, a gentleman rode up and asked where the commander of the scout or party was.

Ensign Smith, who had the command, said, "I am here."

He said, "You have got sixty [British] light horse in a quarter of a mile of you."

Smith said, "I care not for that."

The man rode away. Smith ordered the men to ready, and you saw the light horse coming in sight on full speed. The scouting party struck across the fields, and the light followed, and they formed into a hollow square. They formed around his party, there being only twenty-seven of his party. The commanding officer of the horse told Smith if he would resign himself up he should be used like a prisoner or he would parole him and his men. Smith told him he should not do it.

The officer of the horse said, "If we have to fight and take you, we shall cut you into inch pieces."

Smith said, "You must take us first."

The officer said he would give five minutes to surrender.

Smith said, "Charge and be damned."

Every man was ordered on his right knee and the britch of his gun on the ground, and Smith stood in the center and told his men the first that gave back he would cut his head off with his sword. Then one-quarter of the horse charged on them, and their horses were pricked, and one of the horses was thrown, and the rider fell over into the hollow square. And Smith put his foot onto the horseman's sword and said, "I have got one. I want some more. Charge again."

The horse made another charge and were repulsed. And the third charge was made and repulsed again, and our party took a prisoner and killed a horse, and one of his own men's arm was broken and bayonet was broken. And the horse rode off and formed, and our men all raised on their feet and rested, and the prisoners sat in the center.

Smith then ordered one of the soldiers to take the commander off of the horse as he was parading his men. The soldier drew up and shot him, and he, the officer, fell dead. Then another officer took the command, and he was ordered to be shot, which was done. And the third took command and rode out from the horse and said to Smith, "If you will give up, it shall be well. If not, we will send for one hundred more horse, and have you, we will."

Smith told him to "send and be damned. I want to manure the ground with the Tories, so that it should bear something after the war."

Two of the horse were dispatched immediately. Smith ordered his men into rank and file at two paces distance in front, and rear opposite to the spaces so as to fire through them. Smith ordered the front rank to begin a scattering fire on the right and to fire to the left and then the rear to do the same from the left to right, and every man to take good aim, which was done, which drove the horse off. There were but twenty-four left [on] the field beside the two that had been sent away. The rest were taken or killed or wounded, and their scout went home to their own party.

William Burnett, a fifteen-year-old runaway servant, was a Virginia wagoner to whom the war seems mostly to have been bewildering.

Recollects passing by with the wagon a mountain called Kings Mountain, as they told him. Thinks it was after the battle had been fought there. Also recollects of seeing General Washington twice on the road with his life guard with him and will never forget while he retains his memory the polite bow that the general made to the poor wagoners as he passed them. Also recollects having, at one time when he came to camps with a load of provision, heard of a circumstance that shocked him mightily. That was, as they informed him, his old captain, which was Walker, and several other officers was walking together down the ditch that surrounded their encampment, and Captain Walker happened to raise his head above the ditch, and the Tories fired on him and killed him.

And remembers that one day while resting, he heard a noise like the clashing of arms in an old field, and he left his wagon and run to see, and saw the British and Americans fight. They were all horsemen, and that he was so scared, that he caught hold of a pine and trembled so that he shook the bush mightily. He instantly remembered his wagon and the wagon master and run to the wagon, for fear the wagon master would come and whip him. And that one night he went to steal some sweet potatoes, and while engaged in graveling them, he latched on the fence and saw three men with a piece of white paper on their hats in front. He instantly knew them to be Tories and run and dropped his potatoes at the fence, that he might be able to go the faster. The Tories followed him and run him into the American lines, and they were taken prisoners by the Americans and the next day was hung for being traitors to the American cause.

He cannot recollect the names of many of the places that he was at during his term of service, as he was kept very close to his team and knew but little else, only what related to them. He hardly ever knew when he started where he was going till he arrived at the place of loading, and when he received his loading, he knew not where he had to take it, as the wagon master did not allow the wagoners to question him, and it seldom happened that the wagon guards knew more than the wagoners.

If he started before the twenty-fourth of July into the service, he was not quite fifteen years old, as that is his birthday, and when he found the service of the United States not to be going to be a frolic, he often wished his term of service out and took but little notice of anything else but the time, as it seemed slowly to pass. And, when his term of time was nearly out, he and some other wagoners were ordered back to Prince Edward Courthouse and was there discharged after remaining in the service eighteen months. He was no scholar and had a bad chance to know much about places even through which he traveled.

After he arrived at home and had stayed there, he thinks three or four days, there was a call for men to guard some prisoners. He again volunteered under James Arnold, captain, other officers not recollected, and went into the neighborhood of Prince Edward Courthouse, and while guarding the prisoners, an officer rode up on a panting horse with a cocked hat on and ordered the guards to form a square with the prisoners in the inside, and then the news of the surrender of Lord Cornwallis was read, and remembers that the officer threw his cocked hat up in the air, and almost every American present done the same, and the words "America is ours" seemed to almost rend the air, such was the joy at that time.

Sarah Osborn was married to a sergeant in the 3rd New York Regiment and served at his side throughout the war as a cook and washerwoman. Hers is the only known autobiographical account of a woman traveling with the Continental Army. In the summer of 1781 her husband's regiment reached the American encampment near Yorktown, Virginia.

Deponent's attention was arrested by the appearance of a large plain between them and Yorktown and an entrenchment thrown up. She also saw a number of dead Negroes lying round their encampment, whom she understood the British had driven out of the town and left to starve, or were first starved and then thrown out. Deponent took her stand just back of the American tents, say about a mile from the town, and busied herself washing, mending, and cooking for the soldiers, in which she was assisted by the other females; some men washed their own clothing. She heard the roar of the artillery for a number of days, and the last night the Americans threw up entrenchments, it was a misty, foggy night, rather wet but not rainy. Every soldier threw up for himself, as she understood, and she afterward saw and went into the entrenchments. Deponent's said husband was there throwing up entrenchments, and deponent cooked and carried in beef, and bread, and coffee (in a gallon pot) to the soldiers in the entrenchment.

On one occasion when deponent was thus employed carrying in provisions, she met General Washington, who asked her if she was "not afraid of the cannonballs."

She replied, "No, the bullets would not cheat the gallows," that "it would not do for the men to fight and starve too."

They dug entrenchments nearer and nearer to Yorktown every night or two till the last. While digging that, the enemy fired very heavy till about nine o'clock next morning, then stopped, and the drums from the enemy beat excessively. Deponent was a little way off in Colonel Van Schaick's or the officers' marquee, and a number of officers were present, among whom was Captain Gregg, who, on account of infirmities, did not go out much to do duty.

The drums continued beating, and all at once the officers hurrah'd and swung their hats, and deponent asked them, "What is the matter now?"

One of them replied, "Are not you soldier enough to know what it means?"

Deponent replied, "No."

They then replied, "The British have surrendered."

Deponent, having provisions ready, carried the same down to the entrenchments that morning, and four of the soldiers whom she was in the habit of cooking for ate their breakfasts.

Deponent stood on one side of the road and the American officers upon the other side when the British officers came out of the town and rode up to the American officers and delivered up [their swords, which the deponent] thinks were returned again, and the British officers rode right on before the army, who marched out beating and playing a melancholy tune, their drums covered with black handkerchiefs and their fifes with black ribands tied around them, into an old field and there grounded their arms and then returned into town again to await their destiny. Deponent recollects seeing a great many American officers, some on horseback and some on foot, but cannot call them all by name. Washington, Lafayette, and Clinton were among the number. The British general at the head of the army was a large, portly man, full face, and the tears rolled down his cheeks as he passed along. She does not recollect his name [O'Hara], but it was not Cornwallis. She saw the latter afterwards and noticed his being a man of diminutive appearance and having cross-eyes.

On going into town, she noticed two dead Negroes lying by the market house. She had the curiosity to go into a large building that stood nearby, and there she noticed the cupboards smashed to pieces and china dishes and other ware strewed around upon the floor, and among the rest a pewter cover to a hot basin that had a handle on it. She picked it up, supposing it to belong to the British, but the governor came in and claimed it as his, but said he would have the name of giving it away as it was the last one out of twelve that he could see, and accordingly presented it to deponent, and she afterward brought it home with her to Orange County and sold it for old pewter, which she has a hundred times regretted.

Brave Women

Beverly Utley

Beverly Utley, a member of our editorial staff, will be remembered for her heart-warming article in the December issue dealing with pioneer women of the West. For further reading about women of the Revolution the following works are suggested: Elizabeth F. Ellet, "Domestic History of the American Revolution" and "Women of the Revolution"; Mrs. A. M. Earle, "Colonial Dames and Good Wives"; Nancy Boyd Turner, "Mary Washington Biography"; and "Revolution: 1776" by John Hyde Preston.

This picture entitled "Defending the Stockade" by William L. Taylor depicts the many chores handled by the women of the Revolution in assisting their men in the struggle to open the wilderness. Note the women applying bandages, moulding bullets, and loading rifles. (Copyright, 1902, Curtis Publishing Company)

From AMERICAN HISTORY ILLUSTRATED, October 1968. Reproduced through the courtesy of The National Historical Society, publishers of AMERICAN HISTORY ILLUSTRATED, P. O. Box 1831, Harrisburg, Pa. 17105.

" . . . and their names were Schuyler, Montgomery, and Motte,
Not to mention the hundreds whose names are forgot."
                                                    —Anonymous

I WILL TELL YOU what I have done. My only brother I have sent to camp with my prayers. Had I twenty sons and brothers, they should go. I have retrenched every superfluous expense in my table and family; tea I have not drunk since last Christmas, nor bought a new cap or gown since your defeat at Lexington. I know this—that as free I can die but once; but as slave I shall not be worthy of life. These are the sentiments of all my sister Americans . . . what must glow in the breasts of our husbands, brothers, and sons! They are as with one heart determined to be free. What we fight for is this plain truth: that no man has a right to take our money without our consent. It is written with a sunbeam. . . . We shall be unworthy of the blessings of Heaven if we ever submit."

So wrote a woman of Revolutionary days. Her name is lost; her cause was not.

AT the outbreak of the war, as in the outbreak of any war, no one could foresee what the months and years would bring to the rebelling colonists. The same pluck that brought their grandmothers and great-grandmothers across the Atlantic kept the colonial dames alert to encourage their men, to have faith in their cause. The web of emotions troubling families with Loyalists and Patriots in one bloodline can only be imagined.

The war years exercised all female talents. Women cooked food, nursed thousands of sick and wounded soldiers, and turned their homes into hospitals. They organized spinning and sewing sessions to clothe the Army. They raised funds for supplies. Those women whose homes lay in the paths of the contending armies suffered foraging parties, theft of horses and stock, arrogance and abuse from the enemy. Some were forced to give over their homes as enemy headquarters and watch them burn when vacated. They did not always endure this passively. Frequently women and girls were alert to enemy conversations, and employed deceit, intrigue, stealth, and escape techniques to help the Patriots.

Many wives of officers and soldiers followed their men. Thousands, making homes of hovels, huts, tents, and lean-to's, used any means to have a hot meal for men returning from battle.

Women on the edges of the Indian country occupied a sphere of danger chilling to recall. Many of the Indians, already hostile to the settlers, were easily aroused. When urged by the British to harass the settlers, they complied with gusto. Under Tory leadership or instigation, Indians attacked settlements and forts both east and west of the Alleghenies. The survival rate was low among these frontier women, but in courage and valor they were unequaled.

A thread of readiness united these women. When the unexpected happened they could act, scheme, and decoy; run, ride, or row; dress wounds, mould bullets, or fire guns. They did not hesitate but gave themselves wholly to the cause in whatever capacity called for. And when every effort was exerted and the battle theater moved from their sphere of feeding, nursing, and visiting, they prayed! Calling on the Almighty, their Bibles close at hand, they prayed for protection and victory for their men, never doubting God was on their side or that they were on His.

DURING the Battle of Guilford Court House women members of the Alamance and Buffalo Presbyterian congregations of fighting preacher David Caldwell held prayer meetings as the guns fired and cannon thundered close by. Even when prayers went unanswered and husbands died and armies retreated, women, often with their children, found strength to comb the battlefields for their dead, to claim and properly bury them.

While war evoked virtue, courage, and acceptance in some, it prompted moral decay and greed in others. Wherever British soldiers encamped, from Sir William Howe down to the lowliest British soldier, they had no difficulty finding "a glass, a lass, or a game of cards."

The greatest unsung "heroine" of the Revolution might well have been young, blond Mrs. Joshua Loring, who reportedly made life so lively for Sir William Howe that he seldom pursued American troops so far out of town that he could not quickly get back to her by nightfall. (Sir William gave Joshua an appointment paying lots of money and he stayed out of the way.) A signer of the Declaration of Independence, Francis Hopkinson, whose witty pen is credited with educating the American people for political independence, wrote in his "Battle of the Kegs" ballad:

Sir William, he, snug as a flea,
    Lay all this time a-snoring,
Nor dreamed of harm as he lay warm,
    In bed with Mrs. Loring.

Every camp had its tramps following the soldiers. One description of them: "filthy, slutty, toothless women following behind the supply wagons, hair caked with mud, lice-ridden, cursing, emitting a stench and words so foul that prudent women along the route closed their doors and windows and covered the ears and eyes of their children."

2. REVOLUTIONARY AMERICA

THESE were but incidental women of the time, as they are of any warring time. It was the faithful, loving, devout wives and mothers whose hearthsides abounded with warm foods, babies, churning cream, drying herbs and parching corn—these were the women who sent men off to war. Protecting and preserving such women and children and homes was their Patriot cause, though it was wrapped in the big word "independence."

Washington could never gain an accurate count of his soldiers, for hundreds of them would fade into the night, sneaking home to see their wives and children, lending a hand with the planting or harvesting, then reappearing in camp as others faded away for similar reasons.

It was not uncommon for the women and children to do all the farm work—planting, harvesting, tending the stock, chopping wood, clearing land, and spinning the cloth and sewing. Many women improved their marksmanship enough to kill game for their tables and to protect their homes.

Alexis de Toqueville would write of America seventy-five years later, "If I were asked to what the singular prosperity and growing strength of Americans ought to be attributed, I should reply: To the superiority of their women." The women of the Revolution were busily earning that accolade during the war years.

AMONG wives who stayed at home and served the cause, Mary Draper stands tall. She knew the feeling for independence in New England. Those normally frugal, cautious folk did bold things when riled. When news of bloodshed spread through the upstate community of Dedham, Massachusetts, a man left his plow in the furrow and started for Cambridge without stopping to change clothes. Another, sawing pine logs without a coat, shut down the sawmill, and began walking to Boston in his shirt sleeves. Mary Draper, after strapping blankets and knapsacks onto the backs of her husband and 16-year-old son and sending them off to join the Army, called to her daughter Kate, "Food must be prepared for the hungry; for before tomorrow night hundreds, I hope thousands, will be on their way to join the Continental Army. Some who have traveled far will need refreshment, and you and I must feed as many as we can."

Her husband was a thriving farmer with a full granary. Mary prided herself on her dairy. She spent two days and a night between, baking brown bread in her large ovens. She erected a roadside stand and served bread, cheese, and cider to weary patriots walking toward the Army. When the hungry were fed and no more passed her doors needing food, she set to melting her pewterware into bullets, and fashioning her blankets and sheets into clothing for the soldiers. Mary Draper personified patriotism.

LYDIA DARRAH also remained at home but did her part for the cause. The British were occupying Philadelphia and General Howe's headquarters were on Second Street. Directly opposite lived Lydia and William Darrah, members of the Society of Friends. A British officer, believed to be the adjutant general of Howe's command, often requested one of the Darrah's back rooms for private conferences.

About December 2, 1977, the officer told Lydia that he wanted the room at 7 p.m. and that he would remain late. He asked that the family retire early, adding that he would extinguish fire and candles when he left. Lydia put the family to bed but listened at the keyhole and overheard an order read for all British troops to march out late in the evening of the 4th to attack General Washington's army, which was then encamped at White Marsh. She went to her room and lay down. Soon after, the officers knocked at her door, but she rose only at the third summons, having feigned sleep. Her mind whirled with her knowledge and concern for General Washington.

Telling William they were out of flour, she set out to Frankfort for some. Refusing all offers for a companion to accompany her, she obtained a pass from General Howe to get her through the British lines. Leaving her wheat at the mill, she hurried to the American lines, encountering an American lieutenant whom she knew. Walking a way with him, she told him the secret. He promised not to betray her and sped to General Washington's headquarters. She returned home with her flour and watched the movement of the British troops.

A few days later they returned. The British adjutant came to Lydia's house and sought a private word with her. He asked if any of her family had been up the night of the meeting. She assured him they all retired at 8 p.m. He continued, "I know *you* were asleep, for I knocked at your chamber door three times before you heard me—I am entirely at a loss to imagine who gave General Washington information of our intended attack. When we arrived near White Marsh, we found all their cannon mounted, and the troops prepared to receive us; and we have marched back here like a parcel of fools."

A mild Quaker lady thus helped the cause.

OTHER Philadelphia ladies helped, too. Esther Reed, wife of Pennsylvania's "president," (so-called before "governor" was adopted), organized The Volunteer Association of Philadelphia ladies. Though born in London, she had absorbed the American spirit. Under her direction, ladies sold jewelry, converted trinkets into bullets, bought raw materials, and at the home of Sarah Bache, Benjamin Franklin's daughter, they cut out 2,200 shirts and sewed them for the soldiers.

In Groton, Massachusetts, the women did more than sew shirts. When their local regiment of minutemen departed, the neighboring women donned their husbands' clothes, collected such muskets and pitchforks as were left, elected Mrs. David Wright their commander, and vowed that no foe to freedom should pass their town bridge. This was the bridge over the Nashua River, between Groton and Pepperell. The first horseman to approach the bridge was Captain Leonard Whiting, a noted Tory, bearing a dispatch from Canada to the British in Boston. "Sergeant" Wright and her crew arrested, unhorsed, and searched him. Finding the concealed dispatches in his boot, the "minutewomen" took him to Groton for justice and jail.

This female activism extended to Southern belles, too. Elizabeth Marshall of South Carolina invited her two daughters-in-law to share her home while her husband and two sons fought in the Army. One evening the women learned that a courier carrying important messages for the British army was to pass by, guarded by two British officers. The two young women dressed in their husbands' clothes, held up the courier at a lonely curve in the road, took his dispatch, and paroled the two guards. Ironically, those two stopped off at Elizabeth's house and asked for lodging for the night. At breakfast the next morning, they did not know that the feminine pair waiting on them were the highwaymen of the previous night.

Another South Carolinian, Mrs. Rebecca Motte, allowed her mansion to be set on fire so the British would have to vacate it. As she handed incendiary arrows to the soldiers to shoot at the house, she stoutly proclaimed, "I am gratified with the opportunity of contributing to the good of the country. I shall view the approaching scene with delight." That night she fed the home-burners dinner on a part of her property not destroyed.

RANKING in hospitality with Mrs. Motte was Mrs. Philip Schuyler of Albany, New York. General Schuyler, victorious over General Burgoyne at Saratoga, sent word to his wife that he was bringing home a "prisoner-guest" and to prepare food and lodging. The prisoner, Burgoyne, had previously destroyed an elegant country estate belonging to the Schuylers. When Mrs. Schuyler received him graciously as a friend, he was affected to tears. He sat at supper sighing deeply and said, "Indeed, this is doing too much for the one who ravaged your lands and burned your dwellings."

Mrs. Schuyler had been up to a bit of crop-burning herself. Only days before, she had burned fields of wheat at her husband's direction, to keep them from the enemy.

The Schuyler's 7-year-old son gave tragicomic relief to the evening by pushing the door shut, aiming a toy gun at Burgoyne and his officers, and proclaiming, "You are all my prisoners!"

ONE Southern woman was thwarted in her attempts to make cloth for the Army when the British came through and even stole the cloth still in the loom unfinished. Undaunted, she went deep into the forest, set up her loom among four trees, and wove cloth for the Army in fair weather and covered it with web and cowhides when it rained.

Mary Washington, George's mother, was too feeble to take an active part, but she followed all events with interest, depending on her early training of her son in Christian principles, discipline, and punctuality to influence the country's efforts. After victory had been achieved and battles were over, General Lafayette went to Fredericksburg to say goodbye to the mother of his dear friend before departing for France. A grandson leading him to the house stopped suddenly in the garden and pointing said, "There, sir, is my grandmother."

Lafayette beheld—working in the garden, clad in domestic-made clothes, her gray head covered with a plain straw hat—the mother of the father of the country. The lady saluted him kindly, observing, "Ah, Marquis! You see an old woman, but come, I can make you welcome to my dwelling without the parade of changing my dress." During the visit Lafayette lavished compliments and praise upon her son, George, almost to her embarrassment. She listened and summed up her feelings about the success of the whole Revolution in these motherly words, "I'm not surprised at what George has done, for he was always a good boy."

OF THE women who spent the war years away from home, George Washington's wife, Martha, leads the list. She, who had never been out of Virginia, answered her husband's call to join him at Cambridge, when he was made commander in chief of the Army. Secluded on her Virginia farm, she was unprepared for the agitation that swept the colonies, and for the fervor with which they supported her husband. Starting forth in her coach with its four horses and the postilions in white and scarlet livery, she reacted with mingled feelings of wonder and pride as country people rushed to doors and windows to cheer her, as Continental soldiers escorted her through the towns en route, to the cheering and ringing of bells. This was the first of many trips she took to join her husband in winter quarters.

During the sad winter at Valley Forge, Martha arrived in a rough farm sleigh, for deep snow forced her to abandon her coach at Brandywine. In a cloak and hood she went regularly, all winter, with her basket on her arm, in deep snow from hut to hut,

This old print pictures Mrs. Philip Schuyler burning her wheat fields in a Revolutionary scorched earth policy to prevent their appropriation by Burgoyne's advancing British.

carrying delicacies for the sick, consolation for the dying, and by her very manner stimulating loyalty and courage in the men.

A group of ladies from Morristown came to call one day. Hearing she was a grand lady, they wore their best dresses. They found Mrs. Washington in a plain, homespun dress and checked apron, and with yarn for a sock she was knitting trailing from one pocket. She received them so graciously and so deeply impressed them that they returned to their homes and set about sewing, knitting, and helping the war effort in various ways.

SAUCY, merry Catherine Greene left her comfortable home to winter with Nathanael. Leaving her friends and family, she lived in cold huts and cabins to keep his spirits warm. A gay woman at home who liked to frolic with her children and savor her friendships, she later gained fame by encouraging one young Eli Whitney to invent the cotton gin.

Catherine welcomed any help for Nathanael and the cause. That's why she appreciated young Emily Geiger. General Greene needed to get a message to General Sumter. The country was alive with Tories and no soldier volunteered, but teen-aged Emily Geiger did. General Greene told her the message aloud as he committed it to paper. She set forth on horseback but a British scout, Peter Simons, soon stopped her. He was discreet enough to send for a Tory matron to search her while detaining her in a room of a house. Emily ripped up the message and swallowed it, piece by piece. When she was released, she proceeded, reaching General Sumter the next day and telling him General Greene's wishes. In later life Peter Simon's daughter married Emily Geiger's son, and their farmland was the same on which Emily had been captured.

Another youngster, Beth Moore, volunteered to get a message of danger to a captain encamped upriver from Charleston. She took her little brother and a girl friend on a canoe ride. To the British it looked like three children enjoying a boat ride, but she rowed into the night, found Captain Wallace, and gave him the warning.

Teen-age Revolution heroine Emily Geiger leaves General Greene's cheering camp to carry a message to General Sumter.

Mrs. Clement Biddle, encamped with her husband near Brandywine, received word that General Washington had directed all wives to leave camp immediately because a large British foraging party was near and a skirmish was likely. She asked permission to remain in camp. Then she sent her servant through the neighborhood, gathering food, and spent the day and evening preparing it. The enemy retreated without a fight and the tired and hungry American troops returned late at night to find dinner prepared. Word spread and as men approached they formally bowed and remarked, "Madam, we hear that you feed the army today," which she did until not a crust remained.

IN North Carolina, Jane Thomas overheard, "Tomorrow night the loyalists intend to surprise the rebels at Cedar Spring." Her sons were at Cedar Spring! She slipped away, mounted, and rode two days, covering sixty miles, to warn them. She arrived at night and their campfires flickered on as the men, hearing her message, stole from their blankets and hid among the trees. They had just finished preparations when they heard the cautious advance of the foe. Slowly and warily, the enemy advanced silently until they were within the glare of the blazing fires. They supposed the intended victims wrapped in heavy slumbers; they heard only the crackling of the flames, and the soft murmur of the wind in the pines. At a signal they rushed towards

the fires. Suddenly gun flashes and sharp reports of rifles revealed the hidden Rebels. The Tories were overwhelmingly defeated, about 150 of them against 60 Patriots, thanks to the spirit and courage of a mother of nine, and wife of a colonel.

On another occasion Tories tried to storm Jane's house to seize ammunition from her husband's stores. The defenders, a youth and Jane, fired guns. She organized her daughters and had them reloading swiftly. They kept up such a rapid fire that the Tories withdrew, believing a large force was in the house. The ammunition Jane had saved later became the main supply for Sumter's army in the Battles of Rocky Mount and Hanging Rock, North Carolina.

Just smatterings of memoirs and ledgers remain as mementos of these women of Revolutionary years. It was not the custom in that age to formally record meritorious deeds, especially those of women. Illiteracy and shortages of paper and pen account in part for our scanty knowledge. These women were busy managing farms, harvesting crops, raising families, and sewing for the Army; and while they did brave and daring deeds, the press of duties prevented most of them from sitting down and recording them.

From the few accounts that have come down to us, we can credit hundreds of women with meritorious work, adventure, courage and hardship, sacrifice and service to the Revolutionary cause.

THE frontier women who encountered Indians needed (and some had) a special blend of nerve. It

In Vermont in 1777 Mrs. Richard Wallace, wife of an American soldier-hero, worked her farm singlehanded while her husband was away with his regiment. Roy F. Heinrich drawing. (Courtesy of the National Life Insurance Company of Vermont)

was one thing to outwit or bluff British officers, who had a background and tradition of chivalry. But the savages had no such code. They killed or carried away their female captives.

In East Tennessee, Sarah Buchanan and Susan Everett were returning home from a visit when they saw a hundred yards ahead in their path a party of Indians, armed and painted for war. There was no chance of slipping away unseen. Their only hope was to make a dash for their small stockade, four or five hundred yards distant. Sarah whispered to her companion to follow and do as she did. She instantly swung from riding side saddle to straddle her horse, like a man, and whipped her steed into a headlong gallop. Waving their bonnets and yelling like madmen, the two women rode straight for the Indians, crying out, "Clear the track, you bloody redskins!"

The startled Indians dodged out of the path and fled into the brush. Before the savages recovered their nerve, the two women were safe within the gates of the fort, trembling like frightened fawns at their narrow escape.

Sarah's husband, a major in the Army, commanded the frontier fort. Once in his absence two men came and demanded from Sarah two of his finest horses. She knew they were lawless characters so she pretended to acquiesce, going with them to the stable. But on arriving at the door she suddenly drew a large hunting knife from under her apron, and declared that if either of them dared to enter the stable, she would instantly cut him down. She held her ground against their threats and they left without the horses.

ONE night Indians surrounded the fort and gave a war whoop. Terror-stricken, the nineteen men and seven women in the fort considered surrendering, as many such small garrisons had done during the French and Indian war. One woman gathered her five children to go out and give themselves up. Sarah knew the Indians, knew they would be merciless. She seized the woman by the shoulder saying, "Come back, and let us all fight and die together." An old man cried, "Oh, we shall all be murdered."

"Get up then and go to fighting," snapped Mrs. Buchanan. "I'd be ashamed to sit crouched there, whimpering!"

Major Buchanan arranged his men in the blockhouse so he could rake the Indians with flanking fire. At the same time he poured a galling fire into the head of the assaulting mass. The foe crowded against the gates, their shots coming faster. Now and then some attempted to scale the palisade wall. At length, unable to do this or to force open the well-barred gate, the Indians advanced to the corner blockhouses,

and, standing before them, aimed into the loopholes. Both sides sometimes at the same instant fired through the same opening. Major Buchanan tried to give the enemy the impression that the fort was defended by a large garrison. To do this he had his men fire often, and occasionally in volleys. But a crisis came when a whisper went around, "All is lost. Our bullets are out!"

Scarcely were the words spoken when Sarah passed around with an apronful of bullets which she and Buchanan's sister had moulded during the fight out of her pewter plates and spoons. At the same time she gave to each of the tired soldiers a swallow of brandy which she carried in a basin. Their good humor restored, the men were able to hold through the night. The Indians withdrew, the fort held. Heroic Sarah Buchanan became a legend on the frontier.

AT the siege of Bryant's fortified station near Lexington, Kentucky in August 1782, the water gave out in the fort. A nearby spring held water, but the people in the station knew Indians were lying in ambush behind it, hoping that thirst would force the soldiers to come out into the open.

One of the women in the fort, Jemima Johnson, knew the situation. Her husband was away, and she and her five children had sought refuge in the besieged fort. She gambled on the Indians holding their fire if women went to the spring. But would any woman go? Every morning women brought water to the fort. If the Indians saw them engaged as usual, they would think their ambuscade was undiscovered.

Jemima led the group of women who marched to the spring, within point-blank range of more than 500 Indian warriors. Some of the girls were skittish, but the married women moved with a steadiness and composure that completely deceived the Indians. Not a shot was fired. They filled their pails, one after another, and returned to the fort, their steps admittedly getting faster and faster upon their return.

The Indians attacked later in the day, and the ensuing fight was a rough one. The women had to use part of the precious water to put out fires caused by flaming arrows. One landed on Jemima's baby Richard's cradle, but a sister tossed it off and stamped it. Jemima and her sisters-at-war moulded bullets, loaded rifles, repaired breaches in the palisade, and often took their places at the loopholes.

Richard grew up to command the Kentucky regiment whose charge decided the Battle of the Thames, (War of 1812) in which he was said to have killed Tecumseh, thus breaking the Indian confederacy and causing their final desertion of the English cause.

When a party of British attempted to seize Jacob Bayley, founder of Newbury, Vt., Bayley escaped and, though his son was captured, other members of the household also made good their escape, thanks to the courage of a housemaid who boldly faced the British, holding them at bay and buying time for her employers. Drawing by Roy F. Heinrich. (Furnished courtesy of the National Life Insurance Company of Vermont)

Richard Johnson later became Vice President under Martin Van Buren.

MRS. HENDEE'S husband was away to the war and she was tending the crops in the fields when the Indians burned Royalton, Vermont. She ran home to find that the Indians had seized her children and carried them across White River, there about 100 yards wide and quite deep in some spots. With a mother's love overriding common sense, she resolutely dashed into the river, wading and swimming across. She fearlessly entered the Indian camp, ignored their waving tomahawks, and demanded the release of her children. She upbraided the Indians and persevered in her request until the redmen, understanding her general meaning, granted her request. She carried her children back through the river and landed them safely on the other bank, then returned and begged for the release of the children of her neighbors. Again rewarded, she crossed the stream, pushing and carrying as many as she could. She returned again and again and was allowed to take more children across.

She continued until she had rescued all fifteen of her neighbors' children. On her last return to the camp, the Indians were so struck with her courageous acts that one of them declared that so brave a squaw deserved to be carried across the river, and offered to take her on his back and carry her over. She, in the same spirit, accepted the offer, mounted the back of the gallant savage, and was carried to the opposite bank, where she collected her brood of rescued children and hastened away to restore them to their frantic parents.

JOHN ADAMS wrote to his wife Abigail in August 1777: "I think I have sometimes observed to you, that upon examining the biography of illustrious men, you will generally find some female about them, in the relation of mother, or wife, or sister, to whose instigation a great part of their merits is to be ascribed. You will find a curious example of this in the case of Aspasia, the wife of Pericles. She was a woman of the greatest beauty, and the first genius. She taught him, it is said, his refined maxims of policy, his lofty imperial eloquence, nay even composed the speeches on which so great a share of his reputation was founded. I wish some of our great men had such wives!"

John Adams did have such a wife. The exalted patriotism and the cheerful piety infused into the letters she wrote to him during the long night of political uncertainty that hung over the colonies, strengthened his courage, fired his nobler feelings, nerved his higher purposes, and helped make him Washington's right-hand man.

The women who supported the Revolution were like an army of Aspasias distributed through the new American states. They urged their sons and husbands to the battlefields, but they didn't stop there. Whether they stayed at home to sew, cook, and nurse; whether they went with their men to feed, wash, and comfort; or faced the savagery of the frontier, their courage and devotion helped win the Revolution.

The Founding Fathers and Slavery

William W. Freehling

Only a few years ago, in a historical age now grown as arcadian as Thomas Jefferson himself, no man needed to defend the Founding Fathers on slavery. However serious were their sins and however greedy seemed their pursuits, the men who made the American Revolution were deemed to have placed black slavery at bay. Patriots such as George Washington, historians used to point out, freed their slaves. If Jefferson emancipated few of his, the condemnation of Jeffersonian ideology and the curse of a declining economy were fast driving Virginia's slavery to smash. Only the fabulous profits made possible by Whitney's invention of the cotton gin and the reactionary abstractions perpetuated by Calhoun's repudiation of Jefferson breathed life into the system and waylaid the Fathers' thrust toward peaceful abolition.

This happy tale, once so important and so widely believed, now lies withered by a decade of attack. Scholars such as Robert McColley, Staughton Lynd, William Cohen, and Winthrop Jordan have assaulted every aspect of the old interpretation.[1] Some revisionists write to correct excesses in the former view. Others are driven by a New Leftist contempt for reformers who repudiate radicalism and a modern-day repugnance for liberals contaminated by racism. Whatever their separate reasons and however qualified their individual positions, these scholars, taken together, have hammered out a new image of the Founding Fathers. The image is not attractive. In an era of racial turmoil the racist taints portrayed by Jordan seem even more grotesque than the grasping materialism described by Beard.

The Declaration of Independence, it is now argued, was a white man's document that its author rarely applied to his or to any slaves. The Constitution created aristocratic privilege while consolidating black bondage. Virginia shrank from abolition, for slave prices were too high and race fears too great. Jefferson himself suspected blacks were innately inferior. He bought and sold slaves; he advertised for fugitives; he ordered lashes well laid on. He lived in the grand manner, burying prayers for freedom under an avalanche of debt. In all these evasions and missed opportunities Jefferson spoke for his age. For whatever the virtues of the Founding Fathers, concludes the new view, they hardly put slavery on the road to ultimate extinction. It seems fitting, then, that when Southerners turned their backs on the Declaration and swung toward reaction in the wake of the Missouri crisis, the sage of Monticello himself helped point the way.

Many admirers of Jefferson, aware of a brighter side, scorn this judgment and yearn for a reassessment. The following essay, while in sympathy with their position, is not written for their reasons. More is at stake than Thomas Jefferson; indeed Jefferson's agonized positions on slavery are chiefly

important as the supreme embodiment of a generation's travail. Moreover, the historian's task is not to judge but to explain; and the trouble with the new condemnatory view is not so much that it is a one-sided judgment of the Founding Fathers as that it distorts the process by which American slavery was abolished. The new charge that the Founding Fathers did next to nothing about bondage is as misleading as the older notion that they almost did everything. The abolitionist process proceeded slowly but inexorably from 1776 to 1860: slowly in part because of what Jefferson and his contemporaries did not do, inexorably in part because of what they did. The impact of the Founding Fathers on slavery, like the extent to which the American Revolution was revolutionary, must be seen in the long run not in terms of what changed in the late eighteenth century but in terms of how the Revolutionary experience changed the whole of American antebellum history. Any such view must place Thomas Jefferson and his contemporaries, for all their ironies and missed opportunities, back into the creeping American antislavery process.

If men were evaluated in terms of dreams rather than deeds everyone would concede the antislavery credentials of the Founding Fathers. No American Revolutionary could square the principles of the Declaration with the perpetuation of human bondage. Only a few men of 1776 considered the evil of slavery permanently necessary. None dared proclaim the evil a good. Most looked forward to the day when the curse could be forever erased from the land. "The love of justice and the love of country," Jefferson wrote Edward Coles in 1814, "plead equally the cause of these people, and it is a moral reproach to us that they should have pleaded it so long in vain."[2]

If the Founding Fathers unquestionably dreamed of universal American freedom, their ideological posture was weighed down equally unquestionably with conceptions of priorities, profits, and prejudices that would long make the dream utopian. The master passion of the age was not with extending liberty to blacks but with erecting republics for whites. Creative energies poured into designing a political City on the Hill; and the blueprints for utopia came to be the federal Constitution and American union. When the slavery issue threatened the Philadelphia Constitutional Convention the Deep South's ultimatums were quickly met. When the Missouri crisis threatened the Union Jefferson and fellow spirits beat a retreat. This pattern of valuing the Union more than abolition—of marrying the meaning of America to the continuation of a particular government—would persist, producing endless compromises and finally inspiring Lincoln's war.

The realization of the Founding Fathers' antislavery

 From *American Historical Review*, February 1972. Reprinted by permission of William Freehling.

dream was blocked also by the concern for property rights articulated in their Declaration. Jefferson's document at once denounced slave chains as immoral and sanctioned slave property as legitimate. It made the slave's right to freedom no more "natural" than the master's right to property. Liberty for blacks became irrevocably tied to compensation for whites; and if some proposed paying masters for slaves, no one conceived of compensating South Carolina planters for the fabulous swamp estates emancipation would wreck.

The financial cost of abolition, heavy enough by itself, was made too staggering to bear by the Founding Fathers' racism, an ideological hindrance to antislavery no less important than their sense of priorities and their commitment to property. Here again Jefferson typified the age. As Winthrop Jordan has shown, Jefferson suspected that blacks had greater sexual appetites and lower intellectual faculties than did whites. This racism was never as hidebound as its twentieth-century varieties. Jefferson kept an open mind on the subject and always described innate differences as but his suspicion. Still it is significant, as Merrill Peterson points out, that Jefferson suspected blacks were inferior rather than suspecting blacks were equal.[3] These suspicions, together with Jefferson's painfully accurate prophecy that free blacks and free whites could not live harmoniously in America for centuries, made him and others tie American emancipation to African colonization. The alternative appeared to be race riot and sexual chaos. The consequence, heaping the cost of colonization on the cost of abolition, made the hurdles to emancipation seem unsurmountable.

Jefferson and the men of the Revolution, however, continually dreamed of leaping ahead when the time was ripe. In 1814, while lamenting his own failure, Jefferson urged others to take up the crusade. "I had always hoped," he wrote Edward Coles, "that the younger generation receiving their early impressions after the flame of liberty had been kindled in every breast . . . would have sympathized with oppression wherever found, and proved their love of liberty beyond their own share of it." As late as 1824, five years after his retreat in the Missouri crisis, Jefferson suggested a federally financed postnati abolition scheme that would have ended slavery faster than the plan proposed by his grandson. Thomas Jefferson Randolph, in the famed Virginia slavery debate of 1832.[4]

The ideological stance of Jefferson and other Founding Fathers on slavery, then, was profoundly ambivalent. On the one hand they were restrained by their overriding interest in creating the Union, by their concern for property rights, and by their visions of race war and miscegenation; on the other hand they embraced a revolutionary ideology that made emancipation inescapable. The question is, how was this theoretical ambivalence resolved in practical action?

The answer, not surprisingly, is also ambivalent. Whenever dangers to Union, property, or racial order seemed to them acute, the Founding Fathers did little. In the short run, especially in those Deep Southern states where the going was stickiest, they did almost nothing. But whenever abolition dangers seemed to them manageable Jefferson and his contemporaries moved effectively, circumscribing and crippling the institution and thereby gutting its long-range capacity to endure.

The revisionist view of the Founding Fathers is at its best in emphasizing slavery's short-run strength in Jefferson's South. In Virginia both secure slave prices and frenzied race fears made emancipation a distant goal. Jefferson as legislator did no more than draft abolitionist resolutions, and his revisions of the Virginia slave code did little to ease the lot of slaves and something to intensify the plight of free blacks. Jefferson's proposed clause, requiring a white woman who had a black child to leave the state within a year or be placed "out of the protection of the laws," speaks volumes on why abolition came hard in Virginia. South of Virginia, where percentages of slaves and profits from staple crops ran higher, abolition was more remote. Planters who worked huge gangs of slaves in pestilential Georgia and South Carolina's lowlands never proposed peacefully accepting the end of their world.

The federal Constitution of 1787 also reflected slavery's short-run strength. Garrison's instinct to consign that document to the flames was exactly right, for the Constitution perpetually protected an institution the Fathers liked to call temporary. Safeguards included the three-fifths clause, destined to help make the minority South political masters of the nation for years, and the fugitive slave clause, destined to help return to thralldom men who had risked everything for freedom. Moreover, to lure Georgia and South Carolina into the Union, the Fathers agreed to allow any state to reopen the African slave trade for twenty years. When South Carolina seized the option from 1803 to 1807, the forty thousand imported blacks and their hundreds of thousands of slave descendants paid an awesome price for the creation of the white man's republic.

After the Constitution was ratified, slavery again showed its strength by expanding over the West. "The years of slavery's supposed decline," Robert McColley points out, "were in fact the years of its greatest expansion."[5] In the age of Jefferson black bondage spread across Kentucky and engulfed Alabama and Mississippi. Furthermore, Jefferson as president acquired slave Louisiana, and Jefferson as elder statesman gave his blessings to the resulting diffusion of the system. If in the 1780s Jefferson had believed, as he did in 1819, that diffusing slavery made it more humane, the antislavery clause in the Northwest Ordinance might have been scotched and this essay could not have been written.

Slavery showed its strength not only in Jefferson's Virginia legislature, Philadelphia's Constitutional Convention, and Louisiana's black deltas but also at Monticello itself. By freeing their slaves George Washington and John Randolph lived up to Revolutionary ideals. These men, however, were exceptions. Thomas Jefferson, who freed nine while blithely piling up debts that precluded freeing the rest, was the rule. The plantation life style, with its elegant manner and extravagent tastes, lessened the chance of reducing debts and allowing quick manumission on a massive scale. That life style, in Virginia and thoughout the South, was as integral a part of slavery as was South Carolina's hunger for Africans and the Southwest's commitment to cotton.

2. REVOLUTIONARY AMERICA

The master of Monticello, finally, revealed the towering practical strength of slavery in the notorious case of Sally Hemings, his mulatto house servant. Those who enjoy guessing whether Jefferson sired Sally's many offspring can safely be left to their own speculations. The evidence is wildly circumstantial and the issue of dubious importance. Of greater significance is the way Jefferson and his contemporaries handled the ugly controversy. Alexander Hamilton could cheerfully confess to illicit relations with a white woman and continue with his career. Jefferson's supporters had to ward off all talk of the embarrassing Sally, for interracial sex would ruin anyone's reputation. Nor could Jefferson handle the problem resolutely in the privacy of his own mansion. Firm action would, as Dumas Malone points out, "have looked like a confession that something was wrong on the mountain."[6] Better to look the other way as Sally's light-skinned children multiplied. Better to keep blacks enchained for a time than risk a nation polluted by allegedly lascivious Sallys. Better, in short, to live uneasily in a corrupted City on the Hill than blurt out the full horror of America's nightmare.[7]

The old view, then, that slavery was dying in Jefferson's South cannot withstand the revisionist onslaught. The system was strong and, in places, growing stronger; and the combination of economic interest, concern for the Union, life style, and race prejudice made emancipationists rare in Virginia and almost nonexistent in South Carolina. Jefferson, no immediate emancipationist, refused as president to endorse an antislavery poem that had been sent to him for his approval. He could not, he said, "interpose with decisive effect" to produce emancipation. To interpose at all was to toss away other reforms.[8] Here as always Jefferson reveals himself as the pragmatic statesman, practicing government as the art of the possible. An idealist might fault him for refusing to commit political suicide by practicing utopian politics. But all the evidence of Robert McColley shows that as a practical politician Jefferson accurately gauged impassable obstacles. The point is crucial: long before Garrison, when Jefferson ruled, peaceful abolition was not possible.

What could be done—what Jefferson and his contemporaries did—was to attack slavery where it was weakest, thereby driving the institution south and vitiating its capacity to survive. In a variety of ways the Founding Fathers took positive steps that demonstrated their antislavery instincts and that, taken together, drastically reduced the slavocracy's potential area, population, and capacity to endure.

The first key reform took place in the North. When the American Revolution began slavery was a national institution, thriving both north and south of the Mason-Dixon line. Slaves comprised 14 percent of the New York population, with other figures ranging from 8 percent in New Jersey to 6 percent in Rhode Island and 3 percent in Connecticut and Pennsylvania. In these states, unlike Virginia, percentages of slaves were low enough to permit an unconvulsive variety of reform.

Still, prior to 1776, abolitionists such as John Woolman found the North barren soil for antislavery ideas. As John Jay recalled, "the great majority" of Northerners accepted slavery as a matter of course, and "very few among them even doubted the propriety and rectitude of it."[9] The movement of 1776 changed all this. The humanitarian zeal of the Revolutionary era, together with nonslaveholder hatred of slave competition and universal acknowledgment that the economy did not need slavery, doomed Northern slavery to extinction. In some states the doom was long delayed as Northern slaveholders fought to keep their bondsmen. Slavery was not altogether ended in New York until 1827 and in New Jersey until well into the 1840s. By 1830, however, less than one per cent of the 125,000 Northern blacks were slaves. Bondage had been made a *peculiar* institution, retained alone in the Southern states.[10]

No less important than abolition in old Northern states was the long and bitter fight to keep bondage from expanding. In 1784 Jefferson drafted a congressional ordinance declaring slavery illegal in all Western territories after 1800. The proposed law, keeping bondage out of Alabama and Mississippi no less than Illinois and Indiana, lost by a single vote, that of a New Jerseyite ill in his dwelling. Seldom has a lone legislator lost so good a chance to turn around the history of a nation. "The fate of millions unborn," Jefferson later cried, was "hanging on the tongue of one man, and heaven was silent in that awful moment."[11]

Three years later, in the famed Northwest Ordinance of 1787, Congress decreed slavery illegal immediately in the upper Western territories. The new law left bondage free to invade the Southwest. But without the Northwest Ordinance slavery might have crept into Illinois and Indiana as well, for even with it bondage found much support in the Midwest.

In the years before 1809 Indiana settlers, led by William Henry Harrison and the so-called Virginia aristocrats, petitioned Congress again and again to allow Midwestern slavery. Indiana's pro-Harrison and anti-Harrison parties were both proslavery; they disagreed only on the tactical question of how to force Congress to budge. When Congress refused to repeal the ordinance, the Indiana legislature in 1805 passed a black indentured servitude act, in effect legalizing slavery. Indiana census takers, more honest than the legislature, counted 237 slaves in the territory in 1810 and 190 in 1820.

In 1809, when the part of Indiana that was most in favor of slavery split off as the new territory of Illinois, the battleground but not the issue shifted. The climax to the territorial phase of the Midwestern quest for slavery came in the Illinois Constitutional Convention of 1818, when proslavery forces, after winning a bitterly contested election to the convention, settled for a renewal of the territorial indentured servitude law because they feared that an explicit slavery law might jeopardize statehood.

With statehood secured, the battle over slavery in Illinois continued in the 1820s. The hero of the antislavery forces was Edward Coles, an enlightened Virginian deeply influenced by Madison and Jefferson. Coles, who came to Illinois to free his slaves and stayed to protect the Northwest Ordinance, narrowly defeated his proslavery rival for governor in 1822. In 1824 he helped secure, by the close vote of 6,640-4,973, final victory in a referendum on a proslavery

102

constitutional convention. With Coles's triumph slavery had again been restricted to the South.[12]

The crusade for slavery in Illinois and Indiana, lasting over a quarter of a century and so often coming so close to victory, forms a dramatic example of the institution's expansive potential in the age of the Founding Fathers. The proslavery drive was turned back in part because of race phobias and economic desires that obsessed nonslaveholding Midwestern farmers. But in an area where victory came so hard no one can deny the importance of the Northwest Ordinance and Edward Coles's crusade in keeping slavery away.

A third antislavery victory of the Founding Fathers, more important than Northern abolition and the Northwest Ordinance, was the abolition of the African slave trade. This accomplishment, too often dismissed as a non-accomplishment, shows more clearly than anything else the impact on antislavery of the Revolutionary generation. Furthermore, nowhere else does one see so clearly that Thomas Jefferson helped cripple the Southern slave establishment.

The drive to abolish the African slave trade began with the drafting of the Declaration of Independence. Jefferson, with the concurrence of Virginia and the upper South, sought to condemn King George for foisting Africans on his colonies. South Carolina and Georgia, less sure they had enough slaves, demanded the clause be killed. Jefferson acquiesced. Thus was prefigured, at the first moment of national history, the split between upper and lower South that less than a century later would contribute mightily to the disruption of the republic.

At the Constitutional Convention, as we have seen, lower South delegates again postponed a national decision on slave importations. This time a compromise was secured, allowing but not requiring Congress to abolish the trade after twenty years. A year before the deadline Jefferson, now presiding at the White House, urged Congress to seize its opportunity. "I congratulate you, fellow citizens," he wrote in his annual message of December 2, 1806, "on the approach of the period when you may interpose your authority constitutionally" to stop Americans "from all further participation in those violations of human rights which have been so long continued on the unoffending inhabitants of Africa, and which the morality, the reputation, and the best interests of our country have long been eager to proscribe." Although the law could not take effect until January 1, 1808, noted Jefferson, the reform, if passed in 1807, could make certain that no extra African was dragged legally across the seas.[13] In 1807 Congress enacted Jefferson's proposal.

The new law, although one of the most important acts an American Congress ever passed, did not altogether end African importations. Americans illegally imported approximately one thousand blacks annually until 1860. This is, however, a tiny fraction of the number that could have been imported if the trade had been legal and considered legitimate. Brazil imported over a million and a half slaves from 1807 to 1860, and the Deep South's potential to absorb bondsmen was greater. South Carolina alone imported ten thousand blacks a year in the early nineteenth century, before the law of 1808 went into effect. Louisiana creole planters

sought unsuccessfully to make Jefferson's administration grant them the same privilege.[14] The desire of Virginia slaveholders to keep slave prices high no doubt helped feed the abolition of the trade, just as the desire of Illinois nonslaveholders to keep out blacks helped give Edward Coles his triumph. In both cases, however, the Revolutionary generation's conception of slavery as a moral disaster was of undeniable significance.

The law that closed the trade and saved millions of Africans from servitude on new Southwestern plantations also aided slaves already on those plantations. The great Southwestern boom came after the close of the African trade. Slaves could not be "used up," no matter how fantastic yearly profits were, for the restricted supply kept slave prices high. By mid-nineteenth century, moreover, almost all blacks were assimilated to the Southern way, making possible a paternal relationship between master and slave that could ease exploitation. One does not have to romanticize slave life or exaggerate planter paternalism to recognized that bondage would have been crueler if millions of Africans had been available in Mississippi and Louisiana to escalate profits. The contrast with nineteenth-century South America, where the trade remained open, makes the point with precision. Wherever Latin Americans imported so-called raw Africans by the boatload to open up virgin territories, work conditions reached a level of exploitation unparalleled in the New World. Easy access to fresh recruits led to using up laborers; and the fact that slaves were unassimilated foreigners precluded the development of the kind of ameliorating relationship that was possible between master and bondsman in North America.[15]

The law profoundly affected North American whites as well as blacks. Most notably, it shut off the South's importation of labor during the period when immigrants were pouring into the North and the two societies were locked in mortal combat. If the trade had remained open, the operation of the three-fifths clause would have given the South greater congressional representation, and a massive supply of Africans might well have helped Southerners to compete more successfully in the race to Kansas and the campaign to industrialize. As it was, with the trade closed, fresh immigration fed the Northern colossus by the hour while Southerners fell ever more desperately behind.

Perhaps the most important long-run impact of closing the trade was to help push bondage deeper into the South, thereby continuing the work the Fathers had begun with Northern abolition and the Northwest Ordinance. Now that African markets were closed the new Southwest had to procure its slaves from Northern slave states. By 1860 the resulting slave drain had significantly reduced percentages of slaves and commitments to slavery throughout the border area stretching from Delaware through Maryland and Kentucky into Missouri. Whereas in 1790, almost 20 percent of American slaves lived in this most northern tier of border slave states, the figure was down to 10 percent and falling by 1860. On the other hand, in 1790, the area that became the seven Deep South states had 20 percent of American slaves and by 1860 the figure was up to 54 percent and rising. During the cotton boom the shift was especially dramatic. From 1830 to 1860 the percentage of slaves in Delaware declined from 4 to 1 percent; in Maryland from 23 to 13 percent; in Kentucky from 24 to 19 percent; in Missouri from 18 to 10 percent; and in the counties to become West Virginia from 10 to 5 percent.[16]

By both reducing the economic reliance on slavery and the psychic fear of blacks this great migration had political consequences. Antislavery politicians, echoing Hinton R. Helper's appeals to white racism, garnered thousands of votes and several elections, especially in Missouri, during the 1850s.[17] It was only a beginning, but it was similar to the early stages of the demise of slavery in New York.

While the end of the slave trade indirectly drained slaves from the border South, another Revolutionary legacy, the tradition of individual manumissions, further weakened the institution in the Northern slave states. Although Jefferson did not live up to his dictum that antislavery planters should free their slaves many upper South masters followed precept rather than example in the antebellum years. The Virginia law of 1806, forcing freed slaves to leave the state in a year, did not halt the process as absolutely as some have supposed. Virginia laws passed in 1819 and 1837 allowed county courts to grant exceptions. The ensuing trickle of manumissions was a festering sore to the Virginia slave establishment.[18]

Meanwhile, in two border states, manumission sabotaged the instituion more insistently. Delaware, which had 9,000 slaves and 4,000 free blacks in 1790, had 1,800 slaves and 20,000 free blacks in 1860. Maryland, with 103,000 slaves and 8,000 free blacks in 1790, had 87,000 slaves and 84,000 free blacks in 1860. These two so-called slave states came close to being free Negro states on the eve of Lincoln's election. Indeed, the Maryland manumission rate compares favorably with those of Brazil and Cuba, countries that supposedly had a monopoly on Western Hemispheric voluntary emancipation.[19]

The manumission tradition was slowly but relentlessly changing the character of states such as Maryland in large part because of a final Jeffersonian legacy: the belief that slavery was an evil that must some day be ended. Particularly in the upper South, this argument remained alive. It informed the works of so-called proslavery propagandists such as Albert T. Bledsoe; it inspired Missouri antislavery activists such as Congressman Frank Blair and the mayor of St. Louis, John M. Wimer; and it gnawed at the consciences of thousands of slaveholders as they made up their wills.[20] Jefferson's condemnation of slavery had thrown the South forever on the defensive, and all the efforts of the George Fitzhughs could never produce a unanimously proslavery society.

In summary, then, the Revolutionary generation found slavery a national institution, with the slave trade open and Northern abolitionists almost unheard. When Jefferson and his contemporaries left the national stage they willed to posterity a crippled, restricted, peculiar institution. Attacking slavery successfully where it was weakest they swept it out of the North and kept it away from the Northwest. They left the antebellum South unable to secure more slaves when

immigrants rushed to the North. Most important of all, their law closing the slave trade and their tradition concerning individual manumissions constituted a doubly sharp weapon superbly calculated to continue pushing slavery south. By 1860 Delaware, Maryland, Missouri, and the area to become West Virginia all had fewer slaves than New York possessed at the time of the Revolution, and Kentucky did not have many more. The goal of abolition had become almost as practicable in these border states as it had been in the North in 1776. As the Civil War began, slavery remained secure in only eleven of the fifteen slave states while black migration toward the tropics showed every capacity to continue eroding the institution in Virginia and driving slavery down to the Gulf.

If the Founding Fathers had done none of this—if slavery had continued in the North and expanded into the Northwest; if millions of Africans had been imported to strengthen slavery in the Deep South, to consolidate it in New York and Illinois, to spread it to Kansas, and to keep it in the border South; if no free black population had developed in Delaware and Maryland; if no apology for slavery had left Southerners on shaky moral grounds; if, in short, Jefferson and his contemporaries had lifted nary a finger—everything would have been different. Because all of this was done slavery was more and more confined in the Deep South as the nineteenth century progressed.

No one spied these trends better than the men who made the Southern revolution of 1860-61. Secessionist newspaper editorials in the 1850s can almost be summed up as one long diatribe against Jeffersonian ideology and the policy to which it led. Committed lower South slaveholders knew the world was closing in on them at the very time the more Northern slave states could not be relied on. Seeing the need not only to fight off Republicans from without but also to halt erosion from within, radical Southerners applauded the movement to re-enslave free blacks in Maryland; many of them proposed reopening the slave trade so that the Gulf states' hunger for slavery could be fed by imported Africans instead of black Virginians; and they strove to gain Kansas in large part to keep Missouri.

When this and much else failed and Lincoln triumphed, lower South disunionists believed they had reached the moment of truth. They could remain in the Union and allow the noose to tighten inexorably around their necks. They would then watch slavery slowly ooze out of the border South and permit their own domain to shrink to a handful of Gulf and lower Atlantic states. Or they could strike for independence while the upper South retained some loyalty to bondage, thereby creating a confrontation and forcing wavering slave states to make their choice. This view of the options helped to inspire the lower South's secession, in part a final convulsive effort to halt the insidious process the Founding Fathers helped begin.[21]

When war came the lower South's confrontation strategy was half successful. Four of the eight upper South states seceded in the wake of Sumter. But four others remained loyal to the North. In the most Northern slave states, Delaware, Maryland, Kentucky, Missouri, and the area to become West Virginia, the slave drain and manumission processes had progressed too far. When the crunch came, loyalty to the Union outweighed loyalty to slavery. Abraham Lincoln is said to have remarked that while he hoped to have God on his side he had to have Kentucky. The remark, however apocryphal, clothes an important truth. In such a long and bitter war border slave states were crucial. If they too had seceded, the Confederacy might have survived. The long-run impact of the Founding Fathers' reforms, then, not only helped lead lower South slavocrats to risk everything in war but also helped doom their desperate gamble to failure.

Any judgment of the founding fathers' record on slavery must rest on whether the long or the short run is emphasized. In their own day the Fathers left intact a strong Southern slave tradition. The American Revolution, however, did not end in 1790. Over several generations, antislavery reforms inspired by the Revolution helped lead to Southern division, desperation, and defeat in war. That was not the most desirable way to abolish slavery, but that was the way abolition came. And given the Deep South's aversion to committing suicide, both in Jefferson's day and in Lincoln's, perhaps abolition could not have come any other way.

This conclusion would have brought tears to the eyes of Thomas Jefferson. Jefferson wrote St. George Tucker in 1797 that "if something is not done, and soon done" about slavery, "we shall be the murderers of our own children."[22] In 1820 he saw with a prophet's eye how that murder would take place. The Missouri crisis, coming upon him like "a Firebell in the Night," almost caused him to shrink from even his own antislavery actions. The "momentous question," he knew, was the "knell of the Union," if not in his own time inevitably soon enough. "I regret that I am now to die in the belief," he wrote John Holmes, "that the useless sacrifice of themselves by the generation of 1776, to acquire self-government and happiness in their country, is to be thrown away by the unwise and unworthy passions of their sons, and that my only consolation is to be, that I live not to weep over it."[23]

No sadder note survives in American literature than this scream of failure from one of the most successful of the Founding Fathers. The irony is that the ambiguous antislavery posture of Jefferson and his contemporaries helped place the nation, unintentionally but perhaps irrevocably, in lockstep toward the blowup. In the late eighteenth century a statesman had two ways to lessen the chance of civil war over slavery. He could ease the racial, sexual, and materialistic fears that made the lower South consider emancipation anathema. Or he could scotch the antislavery idealism the slavocracy found disquieting. Jefferson, mirroring his generation and generations yet unborn, could do neither. Both his antislavery beliefs and his fear of the consequences of those beliefs went too deep. He was caught up too completely in America's most anguishing dilemma. The famed wolf he complained of holding by the ears was his own revolutionary tradition no less than blacks chained in violation of that tradition.

Like reluctant revolutionaries before and since, Jefferson sought to have it both ways. He succeeded, as such men will, in starting something destined to get out of hand. He helped protect slavery where it was explosive and helped demolish it where it was manageable. Meanwhile, he helped give informal sanction to the lower South's worst racial fears at the same time that he helped intensify those fears by unintentionally driving more blacks toward the tropics. Over a seventy-five year period the Founding Fathers' reforms added claustrophobia to a lower South psyche inflamed enough in 1787. When that happened the day of the soldier was at hand.

If in 1820 Jefferson pulled back shuddering from the horror he saw ahead, his imperfect accomplishments had taken on a life of their own. And less than a half century later, though hundreds of thousands lay slain by bullets and slaves were but half free, mournful bells in the night would herald the realization of his most radical dream.

---

[1] Robert McColley, *Slavery and Jeffersonian Virginia* (Urbana, 1964): Staughton Lynd, *Class Conflict, Slavery and the United States Constitution* (Indianapolis, 1968); William Cohen, "Thomas Jefferson and the Problem of Slavery," *Journal of American History,* 56 (1969): 503-26; Winthrop D. Jordan, *White Over Black: American Attitudes Towards the Negro, 1550-1812:* (Williamsburg, 1968). For the fullest summation of the position, see Donald L. Robinson, *Slavery in the Structure of American Politics* (New York, 1971).

[2] Thomas Jefferson to Edward Coles, Aug. 25, 1814, in Paul Leicester Ford, ed., *The Works of Thomas Jefferson* (New York, 1904-05), 11:416.

[3] Jordan, *White Over Black,* 429-81; Merrill D. Peterson, *Thomas Jefferson and the New Nation: A Biography* (New York, 1970), 263.

[4] Jefferson to Coles, Aug. 25, 1814. Jefferson to Jared Sparks, Feb. 4, 1824, in Ford, *Works of Jefferson,* 11: 416, 12: 335-36.

[5] McColley, *Slavery in Jeffersonian Virginia,* 3.

[6] Dumas Malone, *Jefferson the President: First Term, 1801-1805* (Boston, 1970), 498.

[7] See the stimulating comments on the matter in Jordan, *White Over Black,* 468, and Eric McKitrick, "The View from Jefferson's Camp," *New York Review of Books,* Dec. 17, 1970, p. 37.

[8] Jefferson to George Logan, May 11, 1805, in Ford, *Works of Jefferson,* 10: 141-42.

[9] Jay to Granville Sharp [1788], in Henry P. Jackson, ed., *The Correspondence and Public Papers of John Jay* (New York, 1890-93), 3: 342

[10] Arthur Zilversmit, *The First Emancipation: The Abolition of Slavery in the North* (Chicago 1967).

[11] Quoted in Peterson, *Jefferson,* 283.

[12] The Indiana-Illinois story can best be followed in Jacob P. Dunn, Jr., *Indiana: A Redemption from Slavery* (Boston, 1888); Theodore Calvin Pease, *The Story of Illinois* (Chicago, 1949), 72-78; and Adrienne Koch, *Madison's "Advice to My Country"* (Princeton, 1966), 144-51.

[13] James D. Richardson, ed., *A Compilation of the Messages and Papers of the Presidents* (Washington, 1910), 1: 396.

[14] Philip D. Curtin, *The Atlantic Slave Trade: A Census* (Madison, 1969).

[15] See the judicious remarks in C. Vann Woodward, *American Counterpoint: Slavery and Racism in the North-South Dialogue* (Boston, 1971), 97-106.

[16] U.S. Census Bureau, *The Statistics of the Population of the United States: Ninth Census—Volume 1* (Washington, 1872). 3-8.

[17] Helper is too often treated as a lone voice crying in the wilderness when in fact he was the man who summed up in book form an argument heard constantly in the upper South. See, for example, the files of the St. Louis *Democrat,* Baltimore *Patriot,* and Wheeling *Intelligencer* during the 1850s.

[18] See, for example, John C. Rutherfoord, *Speech of John C. Rutherfoord of Goochland, in the House of Delegates of Virginia, on the Removal from the Commonwealth of the Free Colored Population* (Richmond, 1853).

[19] James M. Wright, *The Free Negro in Maryland, 1634-1860* (New York, 1921).

[20] The Wimer-Blair position is best laid out in the St. Louis *Democrat.* See also Albert T. Bledsoe, *An Essay on Liberty and Slavery* (Philadelphia, 1856), and the ambiguities omnipresent in such upper South newspapers as the Baltimore *American* and Louisville *Courier* throughout the fifties.

[21] I hope to demonstrate at length the positions outlined in the last two paragraphs in my forthcoming *History of the South, 1850-61,* to be published by Harper and Row. The best sources on fire-eater positions in the 1850s are the Charleston *Mercury,* New Orleans *Delta,* and *DeBow's Review.* The clearest statements of the connection between lower South secession and upper South wavering are in John Townsend, *The South Alone Should Govern the South* (Charleston, 1860), and Henry L. Benning, *Speech . . . November 6, 1860* (Milledgeville, Ga., 1860). For a preliminary estimate of how the same thinking affected the Virginia Secession Convention, see William W. Freehling, "The Editorial Revolution, Virginia, and the Coming of the Civil War: A Review Essay," *Civil War History,* 16 (1970): 64-72.

[22] Jefferson to St. George Tucker, Aug. 28, 1797, in Ford, *Works of Jefferson,* 8: 335.

[23] Jefferson to John Holmes, Apr. 22, 1820, in *ibid.,* 12: 158-60.

The American World Was Not Made for Me: The Unknown Alexander Hamilton

James Thomas Flexner

James Thomas Flexner, whose multivolume biography of George Washington won a special Pulitzer Prize citation and the National Book Award for biography in 1973, has now written The Young Hamilton, *published by Little, Brown & Company. The article excerpted below is Mr. Flexner's last chapter, the conclusion of his thoughtful psychobiography.*

Alexander Hamilton's contribution to welding the thirteen semi-independent states which had won the Revolution into a unified political entity was greater than that of any other Founding Father, with the possible exception of Washington. But this tells only half the story. The other half is that while Hamilton's genius built national unity, his psychic wounds caused disunion which was also absorbed into the permanent structure of the United States.

Hamilton's lack of balance was such that his greatest contributions were realized only when he was working side by side with another statesman, also brilliant but more stable. He had two major collaborators: James Madison and George Washington.

At the Annapolis Convention of 1786, Madison changed into what was almost a new document the overaggressive and overvisionary summons Hamilton had drafted to call up the Constitutional Convention of 1787. And Madison was a collaborator on the *Federalist Papers* in which Hamilton supported and explicated, with such lasting effect, a Constitution that he had opposed as too mild and in which he was never really to believe. Hamilton's most impressive solo flight took place shortly thereafter when he dominated New York's ratifying convention, persuading that crucial but reluctant state to join the other states in the by then already established union.

Washington's role as what Hamilton called "an aegis essential to me" was divided into two extensive phases. Hamilton's most important contributions to winning the Revolutionary War were carried out as Washington's aide. And the achievements which have given Hamilton his greatest fame came, some years later, when he was Washington's Secretary of the Treasury. Then, he carried to fruition the fiscal reforms he had been advocating in vain for so long: payment of debts to the public creditors; the establishment of long-range federal funds which guaranteed that the government would stay indefinitely financially afloat; the chartering of a private national bank with federal support. He created all the institutions then needed to balance the lopsided agricultural economy, making possible a strong and permanent nation. In his *Report on Manufactures*, which was too far ahead of its time to receive Washington's sanction or pass Congress, Hamilton prophesied much of post-Civil War America. And, by a brilliant report to Washington that eventually won almost universal conviction, he established the doctrine of "implied powers," which unshackled the Constitution from its exact wording, enabling the government that rests upon that Constitution to change with the times, satisfying the needs of new generations as they come and go.

After Hamilton had resigned from Washington's Cabinet, he made his last major contribution, paradoxically in closer collaboration with his long-time chief than he had been since he had served as a youthful military aide. Putting on paper Washington's ideas, with which he had become so familiar through years of association, he drafted another of America's basic documents—*Washington's Farewell Address*.

Hamilton was born, almost certainly in 1757, on a British West Indian island, probably Nevis. His childhood experiences have been viewed by his biographers in a distorting light engendered by their affections and their desire to have their hero's career appear respectable throughout. Around the undeniable fact of his illegitimacy there has been constructed a saga of a warm homelife lived out in affluent surroundings. An impartial reexamination of the evidence turns the accepted story upside down. Not affluence is revealed but scrounging and relative squalor; not warmth within the home but fighting, the expulsion of the father, the betrayal of her illegitimate sons by the sexually wayward mother. Hamilton's position in the world was thus defined in local court documents—"obscene child." Having no true home to go to, standing up to obloquy, to silent sneers and surely open taunts from other children in the street, Hamilton learned to fight and to despise his fellow humans, and nurtured an ambition to prove himself immeasurably superior to them all.

As a shift in the grounding alters a projectile's flight, so the truth about Hamilton's childhood propels the biographer into previously unscanned skies. It becomes manifest that Hamilton appeared from the Leeward Islands to serve the emerging United States as by far the most psychologically troubled of the Founding Fathers.

Hamilton, who had been as a child, through no fault of his own,

Reprinted from *American Heritage*, December 1977, by permission of the author.

considered an outcast, brought with him to America an attitude, fundamental to his thinking, that was not shared by any other of the Founding Fathers: the conviction that the human race was not only unworthy, but to him a personal enemy that must be fought and conquered. This gave rise to his basic pugnacity, the adversary turn of mind that played such a major part in his successes, so major a part in his failures.

Hamilton had no experience of America until he arrived in New York in 1773 at the age of sixteen. Immigrants can fall in love with their new homes, becoming more vociferous patriots than many birthright inhabitants, but this was impossible for a youth already firmly conditioned to scorn and distrust his fellow man. Hamilton hugged to his breast the sensational opportunities offered by the environment where chance had thrown him, but he never appreciated or bothered to understand that environment. Thus, if he wished to be for once discreet and conciliatory, he did not know how to go about it. Much is explained by a statement he made when, as Secretary of the Treasury, he was at the height of his career and influence: "Though our republic has only been in existence some ten years there are already two distinct tendencies—the one democratic, the other aristocratic." The people of the United States, Hamilton continued, "are essentially business men. With us agriculture is of small account. Commerce is everything." How wrong he was in his assessment of the primarily republican and agrarian nation was soon revealed when he and his party were submerged by the Jeffersonian tide.

Had Hamilton cared, he would undoubtedly have learned how to analyze popular opinion. But he did not care. His weapon was the sword. In his romantic dreams it was a physical sword. But neither his body nor his true gifts were martial. The sword he was born to wield was forged in the brain.

Almost all people allow their primitive drives to be suppressed by prudence. Statesmen in particular think thrice before they act. Hamilton inspired wonder and also vicarious satisfaction by the freedom with which he slashed around him. But such a champion is truly valued only on his own side of the battle line. On the far side, sharpshooters squint through their sights to bring him down.

In realizing, during the Revolution, that the difficulties of the emerging United States were increasingly financial and governmental and in seeking apposite solutions, Hamilton was far from alone. In fact, the inexperienced and extremely busy military aide appeared on the scene later than others. But he attracted attention (particularly among historians) by adopting extreme positions and putting on paper what others considered it impolitic to disseminate. Every reform has such outriders, although rarely persons as brilliant as Hamilton. To assess their effect is difficult. They implant presently unpopular ideas in many minds, but at the same time impede the efforts of more practical reformers to proceed step by acceptable step.

Hamilton's pessimism about human nature did not extend to himself or to those who demonstrated what he considered their ability and integrity by agreeing with what he himself considered revealed truth. He could thus share in the Enlightenment doctrine of progress. Where Jefferson believed in the perfectibility of mankind, Hamilton believed in the perfectibility of the few who were the rightful leaders of mankind. Considering himself the leader of leaders, he was reluctant to make his visions impure by compromising with the imperfect ideas that were acceptable at the moment. Progress, he believed, would demonstrate that he was altogether right. Then a new generation of the most brilliant, able at long last to carry Hamilton's inspirations to fruition, would follow the torch Hamilton had lighted and kept unsullied.

The man whose youthful ambition had been for "literary pursuits" published in newspapers and often as pamphlets hundreds of political and polemical essays, almost invariably urging his compatriots to action. These sallies covered a wide range of prophetic possibilities. At their most achievable—as in such fiscal and constitutional ideas as he was in his lifetime able to put over—he was in the vanguard, as he had wished Washington would let him be in battle, of columns already forming which were in need of such leadership. In his practical but visionary phases— as in his *Report on Manufactures*—he was defining the future. But others of his ideas—such as his recommendation at the Constitutional Convention that the President and the senators should be chosen for life by an electorate limited to the prosperous—were too alien to America to have a chance of realization.

Hamilton's prophecies, whether practical or extreme, sounded together through the same eighteenth-century air, the grievously unpopular and wild discrediting the immediately advantageous and sane. His *Report on Manufactures* seemed to the agrarian majority to reveal Hamilton as another Lucifer revolting to create a money-changers' hell. And Hamilton's speech at the Constitutional Convention encouraged his opponents to diagnose monarchical scheming in his financial panacea which, in fact, exemplified middle-class conceptions that were to prove the greatest enemies of kings in all history.

Hamilton enjoyed inciting contention. When Jefferson showed him portraits of Francis Bacon, Isaac Newton, and John Locke, saying that these were the greatest men in history, Hamilton replied that in his opinion the greatest man that ever lived was Caesar. There was no integral reason for his financial recommendations to be coupled with expressions of disdain for the common man. Nor was it necessary for the West Indian from a most dubious background to set up himself and the self-made money-men who were his followers as an American elite in opposition to the traditional aristocracy, as represented by inheritors of land such as Madison and Jefferson. In fact, Hamilton could hardly have sponsored necessary reforms in a manner more divisive.

In order to get his first set of financial plans through Congress, Hamilton was ultimately forced to make a concession to the South by agreeing to the location of the national capital contiguous to Virginia, but from this he learned no lesson. His plan for the Bank of the United States, the measures he proposed for fostering manufactures, flew—without any concessions—straight in the face not only of the Southerners, but of all the farmers who formed the vast majority in the United States. He outraged Jefferson by saying to him that corruption was an essential aspect of effective rule. Jefferson's reiterated accusation that Hamilton was subverting the federal government through a bribed "corrupt squadron" was only a paraphrase of one of Hamilton's often-stated contentions: federal financial institutions would stabilize the nation by cementing to the central power rich men whose prosperity would depend on federal authority.

One of Washington's greatest gifts to the founding of the United States was his perpetual concern with quelling dissension, drawing to the national standard every individual who could thus be drawn. This had been essential to winning the Revolutionary War since, in the long run, the British could only triumph by dividing the patriot cause. His Excellency so controlled his young military aide that Hamilton got into no controversies of any sort, committed no indiscretions, while serving officially at headquarters. But as soon as Hamilton stepped into a private role—whether it was through unguarded statements at a drinking party in Philadelphia, or in his yearning for an army revolt, or his sometimes hysterical leadership in Congress—his fierce aggressions appeared.

As the President, Washington became the head of a government completely untried, supported by only a small majority of the people, with two of the thirteen states still unconvinced and staying outside. An administration that would pull together, that would create ever mounting national unity was the overwhelming need, and this Washington established so effectively that Jefferson wrote, on arriving to become Secretary of State, "The opposition to our new Constitution has almost totally disappeared. . . . If the President can be preserved a few more years, till habits of authority and obedience can be established generally, we have nothing to fear."

Before Congress authorized the Cabinet, Madison, who was in the House of Representatives, was Washington's closest adviser. To the Cabinet, Washington appointed the best men he could find, including Jefferson and Hamilton, who had previously not known each other. Madison, who was close to both, brought them together, eager to encourage what he assumed would be, under Washington's broad wing, a warm and fruitful partnership. Jefferson and Madison rescued Hamilton's first set of financial schemes by arranging the deal concerning the national capital.

Then came Hamilton's utterly unconciliatory recommendation for the Bank of the United States, which seemed to Jefferson's and Madison's Virginia constituency a naked power play in favor of men they saw as foreclosers of mortgages. Jefferson and Madison, still thinking in terms of cooperation, went along until the bill had passed Congress and was on the President's desk for signature. Then Madison, suddenly taking alarm and seeing no other way to prevent the signing, turned about-face on the doctrine of "implied powers," which he had supported in *The Federalist*. He tried vainly to persuade Washington to veto the bank as unconstitutional, since the establishment of such institutions had not been specifically provided for.

Thus began the famous fight, between Jefferson and Madison on one side, Hamilton on the other. Hamilton already had a newspaper, supported by Treasury advertising, that was his personal organ. With Madison's conniving, Jefferson gave Philip Freneau a job in the State Department that left him time to edit an anti-Hamiltonian newspaper. Freneau, also a born fighter, went for Hamilton like an angry hornet. Hamilton retaliated. As the charges and countercharges went back and forth, Washington became not only upset but puzzled. Convinced that there

was no real basis for controversy, he could hardly believe that his two ablest Cabinet ministers were at each other's throats.

Washington wrote both Hamilton and Jefferson in almost identical terms: "Without more charity of the opinions and acts of one another in governmental matters; or some more infallible criterion by which the truth of speculative opinions, before they have undergone the test of experience, are to be forejudged than has yet fallen to the lot of fallibility, I believe it will be difficult if not impracticable to manage the reins of government or keep the parts of it together. . . . My earnest wish and my fondest hope therefore is that, instead of wounding suspicions and irritable charges, there may be liberal allowances, mutual forebearances, and temporizing yieldings on *all sides*. Under the exercise of these, matters will go on smoothly and, if possible, more prosperously."

Then came the wars of the French Revolution. Jefferson, regarding the upheaval as a continuation of the American struggle for liberty, was determined to support France in her conflict with aristocratic England. Stressing not the reforms but the excesses of the French Revolutionaries, and, in any case, led by considerations of national finance to favor cooperation with the greater naval power, Hamilton preferred the British cause. The result was a major controversy within the United States which deeply disturbed Washington. He believed that the correct role for the United States was an even-handed neutrality, and appealed to both Jefferson and Hamilton to keep the nation free from foreign entanglements that might lead to war.

Was Washington right in his belief that, with good will on both sides, the controversies that wracked his administration were unnecessary? There are reasons to think so. Despite daily donnybrooks and opposite brinkmanships, Hamilton and Jefferson were forced by the realities of the situation to agree that keeping out of the Anglo-French wars was greatly to the American advantage. And Jefferson, as President, continued Hamilton's financial measures, including the Bank of the United States.

Why then fight; why did not Washingtonian unity prevail? It is difficult, when the facts concerning Hamilton are in, not to see a trail leading back to the Leeward Islands.

Although Jefferson could be adept, and sometimes devious, in defending himself and what he considered the interests of the people who were his constituents, he was not a dedicated fighter. He had been a failure as wartime governor of Virginia. When he became President, he ran the country not by controversy but by manipulation. And Madison, despite a tendency to vociferous outrage, would rather read a book and think a thought than take part in a row. It was Hamilton who relished hand-to-hand fighting.

A really first-class fight requires, of course, already existing differences that can be incited. The divide along which the Hamilton-Jefferson belligerence developed had long worried Washington, whose election as commander in chief had in part grown out of it. (Since the Revolution was then being fought in New England by an exclusively New England army, Continental rivalry required a Southern, preferably Virginian, commander.) The South and the Northeast were naturally suspicious of each other, in part because of opposing economic interests. Endeavoring to reconcile all differences, Washington had hoped to hand

16. The American World Was Not Made for Me

on to his successor a profoundly united nation. He failed, and surely the major blame for this failure can be attributed to Hamilton, who exacerbated conflicts and suspicions that were, as generation followed generation, to eventuate in the Civil War.

All myths to the contrary, President Washington was not led by his Secretary of the Treasury. Nor was he—at least until the very end of his battered second term—a partisan of the Federalists. Yet his value to Hamilton was immense.

Having suffered through the Revolutionary command (neither Jefferson nor Madison had been with the army), Washington realized how greatly the emerging nation needed, in order to be self-sufficient, a sound, central financial structure. His attitudes toward Hamilton's innovations were thus admiring and supportive. This persuaded Hamilton's opponents that they would have to reduce Washington's prestige in order to overthrow Hamilton. The tactic boomeranged. Hamilton and his supporters were enabled to reassure the American people by claiming identity with the long-time leader who was resolutely loved.

The seven years between Hamilton's appointment as Secretary of the Treasury and Washington's retirement from the Presidency were, indeed, enchantingly fulfilling, the most fulfilling of Hamilton's career. Washington was to him no longer the all-controlling father he had been as commander in chief. Hamilton was now more truly self-confident; the scene was now much larger; Hamilton now possessed his own special field of knowledge.

As when he had been commander in chief, President Washington felt no desire to lead Congress. Although that body was now an integral part of the process over which he presided, he was so devoted to the separation of powers that he believed the President should not interfere with the functions of the legislators. His clear constitutional duty was to point out areas that required action and to decide, at the end of the legislative process, whether he would sign into law the bills that had been passed. Beyond that he was unwilling to go. This left a power vacuum into which Hamilton leaped, setting up, before Jefferson realized the possibility, his own block in Congress. For a while, Hamilton led Congress, and throughout Washington's Presidency, he remained puissant among the legislators.

It made Hamilton's role easier that the President admired his fiscal plans and operations, while his opponents lacked the financial know-how to interfere in more than a bumbling and usually ineffectual manner. Another opening for Hamilton in his pursuit of power was provided by the fact that Washington thought of his Cabinet as a unified body. Each secretary was given for administrative purposes his own specialty, but major decisions were made, under the President's final authority, by the Cabinet as a whole. This allowed Hamilton, who was endlessly energetic, intelligent, hardworking, and full of determination, to move across the board, interfering in particular with foreign policy. When he could not operate openly, he went underground, communicating behind Washington's and Jefferson's backs with the British minister.

Hamilton, however, preferred to move with the maximum of visibility. Part of his satisfaction came from having all eyes upon him while, as an individual champion, he achieved, or seemed to achieve, heroic deeds. Jefferson was at first so far behind in these

lists that it was Hamilton himself who made the Virginian a public figure by selecting him as the most conspicuous target of his resounding attacks.

Those were the years when Hamilton's youthful fantasies came almost altogether into being. Powerful men were his sycophants; women adored him; and if he made a flood of enemies, that was, as long as he could overcome, an integral part of his triumphant dream. Then the music stopped.

After Washington's retirement from the Presidency, Hamilton's life proceeded in directions which he could not traverse with pride or even with personal satisfaction. He had reached an eminence which demanded that he become, if there were not to be a letdown, the next President of the United States. But his warrior approach had made him so unpopular that even his greatest admirers realized he could not hope to achieve a top post in an elective government. To compound his plight, he had, in his determination to shine alone, failed to attract to himself followers of possible presidential stature. Where Jefferson, succeeded by his intimates Madison and Monroe, was to exert power in the Presidency for twenty-four years, Hamilton had no surrogate. When Washington announced his retirement, the Federalists nominated, to run against Jefferson, the archetypical New Englander John Adams, who owed nothing to Hamilton and was repelled by the West Indian's sword-waving flamboyance. After Adams had succeeded to the Presidency, Hamilton was reduced to the mean expedient of plotting behind the President's back with members of the Cabinet.

Then there arose the fascinating possibility that Hamilton might find escape from a "groveling" situation through the phenomenon he had longed for in his first known letter—a war. And from his point of view the right war—against France. The pendulum of foreign policy having swung toward England, the French were threatening to attack the United States. Congress voted to enlist a federal army. By intriguing mightily, Hamilton secured the post of second in command, which was in fact more than that, since Washington, the titular commander in chief, was far beyond his prime. Hamilton, who never achieved any deep satisfaction from his lucrative practice of the law, abandoned everything to live with and preside over the embryo army. He inscribed such masses of "routine and even petty and trivial" orders that the indefatigable editors of the normally exhaustive Hamilton papers decided that to print more than a few samples would be a waste of time, ink, and paper.

Hamilton had visions of leading the army against the Spanish Southwest and perhaps even annexing part of South America to the United States. But Adams had never really wanted the army—he thought a navy a better defense—and had been outraged at being maneuvered into appointing Hamilton, whom he deeply distrusted. The more orders the major general sent out in a mounting frenzy, the fewer soldiers there were to be efficiently organized. And then Adams, without consulting his Cabinet, which he now realized had been infiltrated by Hamilton, made peaceful overtures to France, abolishing the threat of war and exploding forever Hamilton's visions of military glory.

In 1799 the Federalists renominated Adams. In pain and outrage, Hamilton wrote a voluminous attack on Adams—more than fifty printed pages. Yet he preferred his Federalist rival to

109

his ancient enemy Jefferson; he ended by urging his readers to vote for Adams anyway. He was, indeed, so upset by the indications of a Jeffersonian victory that he suggested to John Jay, the governor of New York, a method for stealing that state's electoral votes. Jay indignantly refused.

After Jefferson had won the election, the failure of the Constitution to distinguish between votes in the Electoral College for President and Vice President opened up a possibility for frustrating the will of the people by seating in the Presidency not Jefferson but the vice-presidential candidate, Burr. Of the two, Hamilton despised Burr more; he opposed a Federalist drift toward using this loophole.

After Jefferson was seated, the Northeastern Federalists considered his Presidency so overwhelming a menace to all that was good and decent that they discussed taking their states out of the Union. Now Hamilton fought for the Union, helping to suppress the move toward secession. As part of this campaign, he intervened successfully to prevent Burr from becoming governor of New York.

Hamilton was still powerful in his own party in his own region; he still had his law practice to fill his mind to the extent that things which did not basically interest him could—but how small was the stage compared not only to what he had dreamed of, but to what he had once achieved!

The interaction of Hamilton's temperament with his formative experiences had not prepared him to create or enjoy a satisfactory private life. Although he yearned to escape from his storm-tossed ambitions to a warm and peaceful home, no walls that he could build were long impermeable to outside tempests, nor, even at home, could he keep from engendering troubles. Throughout his life, he continued to write his wife Betsey in the high style of romance and perfect love which had characterized his letters during their courtship. Again and again and again he stated that his one wish was to desert the great world to be forever at her side. Although Betsey insisted that she adored her husband, the evidence hardly points to a contented marriage.

Betsey became an extreme neurasthenic, grasping desperately, like a shipwrecked sailor, at supports that she feared were not steadfast enough to keep her head above the waves. She was often sick from nerves, and she was further separated from her husband's active life by a long succession of pregnancies. Apart from miscarriages, with which she was regularly threatened, she bore eight children.

After her husband's death, Betsey's health seems to have improved: she lived to be ninety-seven, a most redoubtable old lady. During her fifty years of widowhood, her husband was all her own: he could escape her no longer. Summoning various men to be his biographers, she repelled them all by her possessive effort to dictate what they should write. She even engaged in a lawsuit with one of her dead husband's most intimate colleagues to gain possession of papers which she believed would enhance her husband's reputation. Not until Hamilton had been dead for thirty-six years and Betsey was very old was a biography of Hamilton written—by their son, John C. Hamilton. It was reverent in approach and exaggerated in claims.

That the living Hamilton had been a dedicated and accomplished pursuer of women was implied by the documents of

his young manhood and became standard gossip during his years of fame. How much Betsey heard or suspected, the records do not tell, but we know that two situations were forced on her attention. A close friendship went on, for all their relations and friends to see, between her husband and her dashing sister Angelica, who wrote Betsey in 1794, "I love him very much and, if you were as generous as the old Romans, you would lend him to me for a little while." Did Betsey believe Angelica's further statement that the wife need not "be jealous" since all the sister wanted was to "promote his glory" and enjoy "a little chit-chat"? In any case, the wife remained emotionally dependent on the sister.

Hamilton himself made as public as anything could possibly be what he asserted had been his affair with Maria Reynolds. He had engaged in financial dealings with this lady's disreputable husband which came to the knowledge of his political enemies. They concluded that James Reynolds had been serving as the Secretary of the Treasury's agent in buying up, at a low price, certificates which Treasury policy would make valuable, the owners to be swindled having been identified from Treasury records. To demonstrate that he had not been engaged in peculation but had, in fact, been paying blackmail, Hamilton published a pamphlet displaying a liaison with Reynolds' wife. The accepted judgment on his behavior is that expressed by Allan Nevins in the *Dictionary of American Biography:* the revelation "had the merit of a proud bravery, for it showed him willing to endure any personal humiliation rather than a slur on his public integrity."

Assuming only sex and blackmail were involved, Nevins' explanation would be the basic one. But overtones inevitably sound in the ears of someone who has from the start followed Hamilton's dilemmas. All that the situation had required of Hamilton was that he demonstrate enough factual information about the liaison and the resulting blackmail to convince the public. But Hamilton included in his pamphlet, which ran to ninety-five pages, the entirely unnecessary statement that he entertained Maria in his own home, and quoted entire love letters in which his paramour expressed the extremities of passion for him, and an almost suicidal despair when he neglected her. As one reads on and on, a feeling grows that there was a personal need behind all this quoting. Was Hamilton, probably unconsciously, identifying Maria with his mother? Was he trying to overcome unslaked humiliations by putting himself, as publicly in the great world as had been his disgrace in his childhood environment, triumphantly in the role of his mother's lovers who had incited his impotent jealousy and rage when he had been a child?

Not everyone was convinced, then or now, that Hamilton was in fact guilty of infidelity rather than some activity he was hiding. His contemporary tormentor, James Thompson Callender, wrote, "Those letters from Mrs. Reynolds are badly spelt and pointed [punctuated]. Capitals also occur in the midst of words. But waiving such excrescences, the style is pathetic and even elegant. It does not bear the marks of an illiterate writer."

When I myself was making preliminary survey of the Hamilton material, before I realized that any questions had been raised about the Reynolds affair, I was struck by the resemblance between the perfervid style attributed to Maria and that authentically used by Hamilton in his love letters to his fiancée and then wife. The modern historian, Julian Boyd, has pointed out that, despite urgings and expressed doubts, Hamilton kept hidden from all reliable eyes the originals of the letters he was willing to publish so widely. If Hamilton did write these love letters to himself, the implication of childhood fantasy is overwhelming.

There is no reason to believe that whatever love affairs Hamilton did have brought him anything but temporary surcease. And his legitimate family life mounted to a double tragedy. He had brought up his eldest son, Philip, according to his own ideas. And at the age of nineteen, Philip, having himself picked the fight, challenged to a duel a political enemy of his father's. Probably close to the spot on the Jersey Highlands where the father was to be mortally wounded, Philip received a fatal wound. We are assured by Hamilton's grandson, Allan McLane Hamilton, who was in his own lifetime famous as a doctor for the insane, that the shock of Philip's death drove Hamilton's second child—she was named Angelica after her aunt—over the edge into an insanity from which she never recovered, although she lived to be seventy-three.

Hamilton had, of course, his circle of male admirers—politicians and businessmen of ability, wealth, and influence—who accorded him all the esteem that, as a scorned and then disinherited youth, he had so passionately desired. But he could not translate this admiration into what he even more desired: power. Power not for its own sake, not for the license it gave to destroy, but for the opportunity to create order and system, to build. He had a vision of the perfect state, a vision orderly when he could hold onto his passions, and for a time it had seemed that he could turn that vision into reality. He could not foresee that his conceptions, which he believed had been defeated, would rise again, achieving in later generations dimensions in many ways above his most ambitious dreams. Before his living eyes the nation was dissolving into what he considered chaos—and he had lost the power effectively to intervene.

16. The American World Was Not Made for Me

The French statesman Talleyrand became intimate with Hamilton during two years of exile in America and then returned to France to dominate, as Napoleon's foreign minister, European international affairs. He wrote, "I consider Napoleon, [the British statesman, Charles James] Fox, and Hamilton the three greatest men of our epoch, and if I were forced to decide between the three, I would give without hesitation the first place to Hamilton. He divined Europe."

Should Hamilton have settled in the Europe he had divined? Had it been an evil wind that had blown him from the Leeward Islands to a continent where the people, those vicious clods who had been his enemies since childhood, could prevent a man of vision from grasping the power he needed to achieve personal glory and also bring into being what he knew was best for everyone?

In 1802, Hamilton wrote his friend Gouverneur Morris, "Mine is an odd destiny. Perhaps no man in the United States has sacrificed or done more for the present constitution than myself; and contrary to all my anticipations of its fate . . . from the very beginning, I am still laboring to prop the frail and worthless fabric, yet I have the murmurs of its friends no less than the curses of its foes for my reward. What can I do better than withdraw from the scene? Every day proves to me more and more that the American world was not made for me."

A long-envisioned way out was left to him. He had written John Laurens, a friend now dead these twenty-two years, "I have no other wish than as soon as possible to make a brilliant exit." Aaron Burr had sent him a duelist's challenge. Although Hamilton admitted that dueling was the worst way of determining the justice of a quarrel, such encounters were part of the military, the ceremonial, the chivalric world. He would expose his body to Burr's bullet, but himself fire in the air.

On July 11, 1804, a bullet entered Alexander Hamilton's liver. The next day he died in great pain.

111

George Washington and "The Guilty, Dangerous & Vulgar Honor"

In an age of ersatz heroes, a fresh look at the real thing

Garry Wills

Garry Wills is the author of Inventing America, *which won the National Book Critics Circle Award for 1978. He is currently working on* Cincinnatus, *to be published soon by Houghton Mifflin and from which this essay is adapted.*

George Washington, writes Garry Wills, "succeeded so well that he almost succeeds himself out of the hero business. He made his accomplishments look, in retrospect, almost inevitable. Heroism so quietly efficient dwindles to managerial skill."

But if Washington today strikes some as a remote figure who merely had the good fortune to be there when history was ready for him, he was an object of extraordinary reverence to his contemporaries. Their adoration gave rise to a society which, many believed, threatened the very existence of the new republic. In this perceptive essay, Wills shows how Washington's essential greatness allowed him to cope with veneration just as, a few years earlier, it had helped him stave off despair, calumny, and defeat.

Charles Willson Peale's loving portrait of his brother James shows the brother wearing the blue ribbon and gold eagle of the order of the Cincinnati, a medal displayed with great pride by officers of the Revolution. Gilbert Stuart painted veterans by the dozen who wanted to be immortalized with that emblem. In France, Lafayette wore it proudly at court, and Rochambeau petitioned for membership in the society. John Trumbull, the painter who boasted on his tombstone that he was THE FRIEND OF WASHINGTON, had himself sculpted by John Ball Hughes wearing the medal. He was not only Washington's friend; he had fought beside him. The eagle was designed by Pierre L'Enfant, who would later plan the federal city. His striking use of the American eagle's white plumes helped fix the national symbol as, precisely, a *bald* eagle.

But if this was a coveted honor, it was also a resented privilege. Only those who were officers at the end of the Revolution, or had served three years at officer's rank, could join. Hugh Henry Brackenridge, Madison's classmate at Princeton, mocked the society in his 1786 *Hudibrastics*. He said the first Cincinnatus returned to his plow

Without a goose-resembling bauble
Or other bird or beast could gabble
A word of Latin or Greek.

Benjamin Franklin too had questioned the Latinity of the medal's legend (*Omnia Relinquit Servare Rempublicam*). But even with his misgivings about eagles, Franklin knew how to get on both sides of any issue: he joked about the society but accepted honorary membership in it.

Brackenridge makes noncommissioned soldiers grumble in rhyme:

Because we have not at our bosum
That thing of yours, a rosy cruzum;
Are not embellish'd with a broach
At heart, or neck, or breast, or crotch.

The Connecticut Wits, themselves Cincinnati, counterattacked in verse. David Humphreys mocked Aedanus Burke, the pamphleteer against the society:

Scar'd at the shape of Cincinnatus'
  name,
The envious Burke denied that road to
  fame,
Stars, ribbands, mantles crowding on
  his brain.

Since Mirabeau translated Burke into French, to attack Lafayette and others for wearing the order of the society, Humphreys wrote of Burke:

From him shall Gallic scribblers learn
  their lore
And write (like him) as man ne'er
  wrote before.

Beneath all this raillery there was a serious struggle. Some tried to outlaw the Society of the Cincinnati, to prevent its spread, to disfranchise its members. On the other side, members of the society defied their own leader to keep the company alive. Brother served

©1980 American Heritage Publishing Company, Inc. Reprinted by permission from *AMERICAN HERITAGE* (February, 1980)

against brother in Shays' rebellion; and conflict over the Cincinnati almost prevented (with incalculable results) General Washington's attendance at the 1787 Constitutional Convention.

The struggle around the little eagle involved, in time, all the problems of the country's difficult transition from the Revolution to the Constitution. A false step by Washington could have destroyed the moral authority he brought to bear for adoption of the Philadelphia document. Historian Charles Beard, at his most conspiratorial, saw the Cincinnati as (in part) a scheme to redeem bonds held by Revolutionary officers at the expense of rank-and-file veterans.

The Cincinnati were, after the disbanding of the Continental Army, the one organization that could muster support for the Constitution among recognized leaders in all thirteen states. Their enemies made this an argument against adoption of the Constitution. They felt that the society would control any government it brought into being.

The argument strayed into very strange channels. While most people were attacking the society as a nascent aristocracy, Elbridge Gerry feared demagogy. He used the society as an argument against popular election of a President: "The ignorance of the people would put it in the power of some one set of men, dispersed through the Union and acting in concert, to delude them into any appointment." He observed that such a society of men existed in the Order of the Cincinnati. They were respectable, united, and influential. They would in fact elect the chief magistrate in every instance if the election were referred to the people. His respect for the characters composing this society could not blind him to the danger and impropriety of throwing such a power into their hands.

Washington weighed these criticisms carefully. He asked Jefferson to put his objections to the society in writing. He read the Burke pamphlet and a translation of Mirabeau. Since none dared attack Washington directly, they tried to flatter him away from his followers: "Was it possible," wrote Mirabeau, "he

should not feel how much his name was superior to all distinction? The hero of the Revolution which broke the chains of half the world—was it possible that he should not scorn the guilty, dangerous, and vulgar honor of being the hero of a party?" Jefferson struck the same note, hoping that "the character which will be handed to future ages at the head of our Revolution may in no instance be compromitted by subordinate altercations."

Still, veterans were anxious to join the society. Washington had been hailed around the world as the modern Cincinnatus when he resigned his commission at the end of the war. Any tie to him was welcomed. Desmoulins would suggest that French revolutionaries adopt a blue cockade to associate themselves with the first successful revolution of the modern world. The society's medal was the only foreign order that could be worn at the French court. When, at first, French naval officers were not invited to join, they petitioned for admission. When this was granted, they sent Washington an eagle formed of diamonds and emeralds to express their gratitude.

Late in his life, Trumbull pointed at a wounded American sprawled behind the standing Hessian in his painting of Washington at Trenton and said, "But for that he would never have been President." The young lieutenant with the wound was James Monroe. Trumbull exaggerated; but it was certainly no political liability to have served with Washington. There was a special glamor thrown, all the rest of their lives, around the men who rode with him.

Enemies of the Cincinnati had good reason to fear the awesome power Washington exerted over and through the Revolutionary officers—the men who would boast on their tombstones they were friends of Washington. He did forge a high level of military pride in an army endangered by rancorous divisions, interstate rivalries, and demoralizing recruitment procedures. The achievement of this spirit contributed significantly to the acceptance of the federal union. Stanley Elkins and Eric McKitrick point out that the *young* men of the Revolution took

the lead at the Constitutional Convention, men formed by experience in the Continental Army or the Continental Congresses. Edmund Randolph, arguing for Virginia's ratification of the Constitution, said, "I am a child of the Revolution." (Randolph felt a special affection for Washington, since the general had stood warrant for his patriotism when Randolph's Tory father fled to England.)

It is easy to forget how extraordinary was Washington's achievement in creating this solidarity among officers bred to colonial prerogative and to the pride of local militias. When he first arrived at Boston, some camps would not even admit this stranger from the South. He had to win the respect of men who had every regional cause to resent him. So spectacularly did he succeed that service on his staff or in his guard became a highly desired prize.

We mistake the impact of Washington when we think of his peers as fellow "founders" like Franklin or Madison. He stood as clearly above them in the popular regard as he did above fellow officers like Gates or Putnam. His contemporaries very soon ranked him in stature (though not in character, where he was their superior) with the charismatic nation builders, with Alexander, Caesar, Cromwell. He differed from them—and later on, from Napoleon—by not overreaching himself. There would be no doomed romance of failure around him. He accomplished everything he set out to do, went home, and died prosaically in bed. He succeeded so well that he almost succeeds himself out of the hero business. He made his accomplishments look, in retrospect, almost inevitable. Heroism so quietly efficient dwindles to managerial skill.

But there was nothing inevitable about the task when he took it up. Then it looked impossible. His firmness and resolve, which looked stolid at a distance, gave heartening defiance to panic for those around him. Part of his sway over others was precisely the quiet strength that his whole physique conveyed. He was a giant for his day, linked to the legendary size of his French ally, the Comte de Grasse. The doctors who measured him on his deathbed probably made a mistake when they said he was six feet three inches tall; but even at six-two, in military boots he would have towered over most eighteenth-century men. Despite his size, and despite a rather clumsily shaped body, he was extraordinarily graceful in all his movements. Quick reflexes made him a model horseman, dancer, and athlete. At his favorite recreation of throwing weights, no one could equal him. Charles Willson Peale, at Mount Vernon to do his first portrait of the forty-year-old Washington, wrote that the plantation owner came out while the young men were throwing weights in their shirtsleeves and, without removing his coat, threw it far beyond their best mark. Travelers noted that, when water got rough in raft passages, the athletic Washington took the steering pole himself.

Washington had great stamina, and an immunity to smallpox (after a mild case in Barbados) that let him move freely among his men, even the quarantined. In eighteenth-century war, it was the custom for senior officers to go home while the army was in winter camp. But Washington did not see Mount Vernon in six years, and then only because the route to Yorktown took him past his estate. Other generals were constantly going to Philadelphia, dabbling in the politics of command and appointments; Washington went only when summoned. His presence was often the only thing holding the army together. That is why he could not be tempted away from Valley Forge or Morristown toward the milder winters of Virginia.

Though he did not indulge in empty theatrics, Washington knew that armies live on pride as well as on earthier provisions. At the retreat from Harlem Heights, a contemptuous British trumpeter sounded the hunt signal for "defeat" of a fox, not the military recall. Washington, who had hunted on the Fairfax estate, and whose horn still hangs at Mount Vernon, sent a cavalry detachment to strike at those guilty of the insult.

Like most military leaders, Washington was acutely aware of psychological advantage and knew how to use the grand gesture. The Marquis de Chastellux, French academician and generous supporter of the war, was irrevocably won to Washington by the farewell gesture when he left his camp: "The weather being fair on the 26th, I got on horseback after breakfasting with the General. He was so attentive as to give me the horse he rode on the day of my arrival, which I had greatly commended. I found him as good as he is handsome, but above all perfectly well broke and well trained, having a good mouth, easy in hand, and stopping short in a gallop without bearing the bit. I mention these minute particulars because it is the General himself who breaks all his own horses, and he is a very excellent and bold horseman, leaping the highest fences and going extremely quick without standing upon his stirrups, bearing on the bridle, or letting his horse run wild."

The British, practicing their own form of psychological warfare, constantly denigrated Americans, treating only the French officers as belonging to a *real* army. The Americans, it was thought, could be demoralized if they were handled as mere riotous subjects of the king, a rabble on the run. Thus General Howe at first refused Washington any military title, sending his first missive to "George Washington, Esq." Washington, after consultation with his staff, refused to accept the message. The story was later embellished by his staff, in ways that show their feeling for the leader. A newly arrived French officer heard the story this way: "One of the company (if I remember rightly, it was, I think, Colonel Hamilton, who was afterwards so unfortunately and prematurely snatched from the hopes of his country) related the manner in which the General had received a dispatch from Sir Henry Clinton [sic], addressed to 'Mr. Washington.' Seeing the address, 'This letter,' said he, 'is directed to a planter of the state of Virginia. I shall have it delivered to him, after the end of the war; till that time it shall not be opened.' A second dispatch was addressed to His Excellency General Washington."

These were not empty matters of etiquette. Unless the rules of war were established, American captives could not count on proper treatment. Washington had to live like the leader of an outlaw band at times but command respect even from his foes. His well-uniformed guard, chosen (among other things) for height and looks, attended him at the grand linen marquee that can only be displayed half-open at the Smithsonian. These were meant to impress arriving recruits as well as enemy emissaries. What was at stake was illustrated when Charleston fell to the British. General Benjamin Lincoln was denied the honors of war, sent out with veiled colors in humiliation. At the fall of Yorktown, Washington insisted on the same conditions for Cornwallis (he did not know this was the last major battle of the war—no one knew at the time).

Cornwallis, angered at this treatment, sent out a subordinate to surrender, with orders to yield his sword to a French officer. But no Frenchman would accept it; they gestured the man toward Washington—who gestured him toward General Lincoln. The man humiliated at Charleston received the great surrender.

His men were fiercely loyal to Washington. It is easy to see why the sentimental Henry Knox formed the Society of the Cincinnati as an expression of that loyalty. Knox, the genial Boston bookseller who wrestled British guns through forests down from Canada to found the American artillery corps, proposed the society in 1783 as a charitable organization to care for the widows and orphans of fallen officers. But his real aim was emotional, to preserve the camaraderie he had enjoyed. There is, after all, a remarkable fulfillment in the society of Henry V's vision as Shakespeare presents it. Substitute different names for "Bedford and Exeter . . ."—names like Laurens and Hamilton, Monroe and Knox, Lincoln, Lafayette—and the familiar lines become vividly applicable. What Shakespeare only dreamed, Henry Knox accomplished:

He that shall live this day, and see old age,

Will yearly on the vigil feast his
  neighbors,
And say, "Tomorrow is Saint
  Crispian:"
Then will he strip his sleeve and show
  his scars,
And say, "These wounds I had on
  Crispin's day."
Old men forget: yet all shall be forgot,
But he'll remember with advantages
What feats he did that day. Then
  shall our names,
Familiar in his mouth as household
  words,
Harry the King, Bedford and Exeter,
Warwick and Talbot, Salisbury and
  Gloucester,
Be in their flowing cups freshly
  rememb'red.
This story shall the good man teach
  his son;
And Crispin Crispian shall ne'er go
  by,
From this day to the ending of the
  world,
But we in it shall be remembered . . .

Gouverneur Morris, in his speech on Washington, compared Valley Forge to the eve of Agincourt. Once again the drama's words fit history eerily well. The leader's men,

Like sacrifices, by their watchful fires
Sit patiently and inly ruminate
The morning's danger, and their
  gesture sad,
Investing lank-lean cheeks and war-
  worn coats,

Presented them unto the gazing moon
So many horrid ghosts. O now, who
  will behold
The royal captain of this ruin'd band
Walking from watch to watch, from
  tent to tent . . .

Inspiring as this vision might be, and flattering to him, Washington would not let the union of his colleagues work against the larger union of the nation. In the war he had made it a point of honor to show no favoritism to Virginians. In peace· he would not favor his fellow officers in a way that could menace civil order. He urged the Cincinnati to remove the hereditary feature from their membership ("This story shall the good man tell his son"). The national meeting agreed, but the state units—as independent as the states themselves in this era of the Articles—refused. Washington made his Presidency nominal, discharging minimum business without enthusiasm. He did not wear the eagle that so many others display in their portraits. Edward Savage put the medal on one of his portraits of Washington, but it had not been worn at the sitting. In 1787 Washington alleged illness as an excuse for absence from the triennial meeting in Philadelphia (see, he could *too* tell a lie). Then, when plans were made to hold the Constitutional Convention in that city, at the very time when the society was assembling, Washington said he could not go because of his earlier story. Only after repeated

urging by Governor Randolph and James Madison, who said the whole cause of national union might depend on his representing Virginia, did he give in. (He dined with members of the society but did not attend its meetings.)

Washington's cool attitude toward the Cincinnati rescued the society from those excesses its enemies feared. The group survived only as Knox had wished, as a sentimental bond among the heirs of heroes. The ties forged during the Revolution helped along the cause of union rather than hindering it. Washington escaped the accusations of partisanship that might have obstructed passage of the Constitution.

Though Washington could not, in conscience, join Lafayette in the revolutionary stirrings of France, French and American officers, fellow Cincinnati, fought in World Wars I and II and celebrated their solidarity across the centuries—no doubt in "flowing cups" and "with advantages."

Lafayette Park in front of the White House has at each of its four corners the statue of a foreign officer who fought in the Revolution—the Comte de Rochambeau, "Baron" von Steuben, General Kosciusko, and Lafayette himself. All, of course, were Cincinnati. Lafayette is shown pleading with the French to aid America, and four French officers who responded stand at the base of his statue. All five of them wear sculpted eagles of the society.

DO WE CARE IF JOHNNY CAN READ?

Americans first learned to read to save their souls, then to govern themselves. Now the need is not so clear.

Anthony Brandt

Anthony Brandt is a widely published free-lance writer, and author of Reality Police: The Experience of Insanity in America. *This history of literacy is his first contribution to* AMERICAN HERITAGE.

N 1765 JOHN ADAMS WROTE that "A native of America who cannot read or write is as rare an appearance as a Jacobite or a Roman Catholic, that is, as rare as a comet or an earthquake." He went on to say that "all candid foreigners who have passed through this country and conversed freely with all sorts of people here will allow that they have never seen so much knowledge and civility among the common people in any part of the world." It is a broad claim. The question is, was it true? Were the colonists as literate as Adams said they were, or was this merely a piece of pre-Revolutionary propaganda?

If we refer the question to Adams' "candid foreigners," we find that they were indeed often surprised by the fact that most ordinary Americans were literate. Moreau de Saint-Méry, for example, while writing his account of his travels through the United States in the 1790's, remembered that as a boy in Martinique, where he served as a clerk in the record office of the Admiralty, he could offer a pen to American sailors when they had to sign a document in full confidence that they could do so, "while the great part of the French sailors didn't know how to write, which was always humiliating to my national pride." Daniel Boorstin notes that by the early 1800's the American working class was "known the world over for literacy and intelligence," and in 1847 the

Argentinian statesman Domingo Faustino Sarmiento wrote, in envy and admiration, that "United States statistics show a figure for adult males which would indicate a total population of twenty million inhabitants, all of whom are educated, know how to read and write, and enjoy political rights, with exceptions so few that they cannot even be said to qualify the generalization." A year or two later an Englishman named Frank Marryat, describing Gold Rush San Francisco ("that then city of tents"), was amazed to find that even in the primitive conditions of 1848, when "*selfishness*, as is natural, reigned paramount," a public school was founded. "Apparently," he went on to say, "every Californian can read, and judging from the fact that the mails take an average of fifty thousand letters to the United States every fortnight, we may presume that there are few among them that cannot write."

The evidence is indeed impressive; the "candid foreigners" all seem to be in agreement. But were Americans in fact as literate as these men made them out to be? Can this glowing testimony be taken at face value? The question is especially pertinent now, when literacy appears to be on the decline among Americans. Estimates of the number of "functional illiterates" in the adult population range up to 23,000,000. Scores on the verbal section of the Scholastic Aptitude Test are dropping every year, and it has become a familiar complaint among college teachers that incoming freshmen are more often than not unable to write coherent expository prose. A college education does not seem to correct the situation, for teachers at the graduate school level make similar complaints. There is evidence that the teachers themselves, for that matter, are frequently less than expert in the use of language. In one Maryland county half of the applicants for jobs as teachers of English failed a simple test in grammar, punctuation, and spelling. It is not an exaggeration to speak of a literacy crisis.

A crisis mentality has developed, in fact, and one result has been a "back to basics" movement among critics of the school system, which generally is held to be responsible for the crisis. If Americans were once as literate as John Adams and all those

"Do We Care If Johnny Can Read?" by Anthony Brandt, *American Heritage,* August/September 1980. Reprinted by permission.

other witnesses said they were, the argument runs, it must be because they all got a thorough education in reading, writing, and 'rithmetic. The legendary little red schoolhouse of the American past, with its legendary schoolmarm, may not have enjoyed the benefits of the modern school—its broad curriculum, its marvelous physical plant, its enlightened attitudes—but it got the job done; the schoolmarm's graduates knew their ABCs, and they could spell as well as Noah Webster himself. A return to the emphases, if not the actual conditions, of an earlier time could, the critics claim, re-establish earlier levels of literacy.

The trouble with this appeal to the past is that the past was much more complicated and is much less well understood than the critics have imagined. The history of literacy in America, which historians only recently have begun trying to untangle, has turned out to be exceptionally problematic, mostly because reliable data about literacy rates are very hard to develop and even harder to interpret. Eric Havelock writes: "Of all the activities of mankind which we now take to be ordinary, reading is historically the one which is most sparsely recorded." Further complicating the problem is the fact that definitions of literacy differ for different historical periods. The United States government defines "functional literacy" not according to some standardized test, but by levels of schooling; if a child has successfully completed the fifth grade, the government considers him literate, at least for statistical purposes. John Adams probably wouldn't have considered that to be at all adequate as a definition, yet for estimates of literacy rates in Adams' time, and for all other periods before the government began collecting this kind of statistical information, historians have to rely on even less adequate data, usually the proportion of signatures to marks on wills. Neither of these measures, of course, indicates how literate someone is, whether he stands at the bottom end of the scale and can barely read, or at the top, completely at ease with the intricacies of *The Federalist Papers*.

Because of these difficulties, historians have not made a great deal of progress yet in the study of literacy.

From what they have learned so far, indeed only one thing is clear: no blanket claims such as John Adams made about the literacy of the American people are likely to be valid. In some areas, among some classes, at certain times, probably nearly everyone could read and write; but such has never been the case everywhere and at all times. It is not the case now. An appeal to the past based on evidence like the statements of Adams and Sarmiento, then, cannot bear the weight. The past was no lost paradise of literacy.

The critics are right about one thing, nevertheless: a crisis is indeed an appropriate time to look to the past, if only to see where our current problems came from, what their roots are.

AT THE TIME OF THE DIS-covery and settlement of America, European culture was emerging from a long period of domination by the Church, a domination that included a virtual monopoly of the ability to read and write. Of the three estates—warriors, workers, and clergy—only the clergy was literate. Literacy among the nobility was so rare that literate nobles were often nicknamed "the Clerk," and for the first five hundred years of English history, from about the sixth to the eleventh centuries, only three kings were able to sign their names. By the fourteenth century, however, the situation was changing rapidly. Edward III was literate, and so were all English kings after him. In the thirteenth century the wealthy burghers of Ypres founded a lay school for their young; the Church excommu-nicated them for contesting its monopoly of education, but a trend had been established and more such institutions began to come into being. Culture was still oral—Chaucer had to read his poems aloud to his courtly audience—but the gradual development of urban centers and the growing need to keep commercial records wore steadily away at the Church's monopoly. In Genoa, Venice, and other commercial centers, schooling specifically designed for commercial purposes, and thus literacy of a sort, became almost common.

The most influential source of change, however, was not commerce but religion. It was the Protestant Reformation, and the Protestant insistence that every man have free access to the Word, without priestly interference, that finally broke the Church's monopoly on literacy. The invention of printing, which made possible the widespread diffusion of books, was also an important factor, but printed books, although cheaper than manuscripts, were still too expensive for the common people, and it is unlikely that printing would have had the impact it did if the Reformation had died aborning. Another important factor was the triumph of the vernaculars; as long as Latin remained the principal means of written communi-cation, not only among the learned but in government and commerce as well, literacy could not extend very far into the populace. Here again, however, the main source of change was Protestant religious feeling. Free access to the Word meant translation of the Bible into the vernacular, and not until that victory had been won was the triumph of the vernaculars assured.

2. REVOLUTIONARY AMERICA

If the American people were, as Tocqueville said, "that portion of the English people which is commissioned to explore the wilds of the New World," it is the situation of literacy in England during the Reformation that is of most interest to us; and in England, it was the force of Puritan beliefs, not the more conservative Anglican, that was transforming the literacy rates. The social historian Lawrence Stone notes that England experienced an "educational boom" in the period from 1540 to 1640, and he attributes it primarily to "Puritan zeal." A higher proportion of Englishmen was being systematically educated during this period than at any time until the late nineteenth century. The result was a dramatic increase in literacy from Medieval times, with perhaps 60 per cent of the adult males in London and its immediate environs being able to read and sign their names, while the average rate for the country as a whole stood at about 30 per cent.

The Puritans were no doubt literate at rates toward the higher end of this scale; and since it was the Puritans who emigrated to New England, that region was blessed with an especially high rate of literacy during the seventeenth century. Exactly how high is another question. Measurement of literacy rates for periods before the late nineteenth century, as noted earlier, has usually depended on the proportion of signatures to marks on wills; wills are practically the only written records (sometimes marriage registers are used when parish records have survived) covering broad enough segments of the population to be representative. The inference is that if someone could sign a will, he could probably also read. The problem is, however, that a sample derived from wills is inevitably biased. Not everyone makes a will, and those who do tend to be wealthier, more urbanized, and older than the rest of the population; and wealth, "urbanity," and age are all factors known to affect literacy rates.

Some scholars think the bias is so great as to render the evidence useless. Others try to allow for it. Among the latter is Kenneth A. Lockridge, who has made his own analysis of literacy in colonial New England as statistically sophisticated as possible. Lockridge believes that the literacy of the adult male population of New England as a whole stood at about 60 per cent by the end of the seventeenth century. This is the same as the rate Lawrence Stone found for London during the same period, confirmation, says Lockridge, that New England did indeed draw from the most literate portions of the English population. While literacy rates in England, however, stagnated or even declined after the restoration of the monarchy in 1660, in New England literacy increased. Lockridge traces a steady rise in both adult male and adult female literacy in New England during the late seventeenth and the eighteenth centuries. By the 1790s', he says, 90 per cent of New England men were literate; the rate for women was about 50 per cent. On John Adams' home ground, then, his remark about the rarity of illiterate Americans, while an exaggeration, did have some basis in fact. Lockridge agrees

with Stone that the critical factor in this rise in literacy was, once again, Puritan zeal for education.

It was this zeal which led to the well-known Massachusetts school laws, the most important of which, the "old deluder, Satan" law of 1647 ("It being one chief project of that old deluder, Satan, to keep men from the knowledge of the Scriptures . . ."), specified that every town of fifty families or more must appoint a schoolmaster to teach the town's children to read and write, while every town of one hundred families was supposed to establish a grammar school (devoted to Latin and the classics) as well. Connecticut enacted a similar law a few years later. It is not known how many towns actually complied with this law, or how vigorously it was enforced. Literate Puritans generally taught their own children to read and write in any case (servants' indentures often specified that one of the master's duties was to teach his servants to read and write, and to catechize them as well), and teaching methods were the same whether in the school or at home.

The child's first "book" was usually a hornbook, a piece of wood shaped like a paddle with a sheet of paper tacked to one side; on the paper were printed the alphabet, a short syllabary, and perhaps the Lord's Prayer—covered with a transparent sheet of horn to protect it. The child was expected to memorize the alphabet until he could repeat it backward and forward. The process was inevitably somewhat tedious; the alphabet and syllabary were not taught as the components of meaningful words but as lists that simply had to be memorized, come what may. Some attempts were made to ease the burden of memorization; there are surviving examples of hornbooks which doubled as battledores—a kind of paddle, used in the game of battledore and shuttlecock— and of cookie molds from which an edible hornbook might be made. Presumably the child was allowed to eat those portions of the alphabet he had gotten by heart. But these examples are rare. Making it worse for the child was the fact that teaching of the alphabet started very early; Samuel Sewall recorded in his diary sending his son Joseph to school, an older cousin accompanying him to carry his hornbook, at the age of two years and nine months.

If a child did learn to read at school rather than at home, it was normally at what was called a "dame school" or "petty school," the sole function of which was to teach basic literacy in one's native tongue, with perhaps a little arithmetic thrown in. The schoolmaster or, much more commonly, schoolmistress used a hornbook or primer, just as the child's parents might, and taught pupils not collectively but one by one, the rest of the class being required to sit quietly and wait their turn. This method of teaching, by rote memorization, was very old; children in classical Greece were taught to read in precisely the same way, and the job required so little imagination and was so despised that it was usually assigned to a slave. In colonial America the job often fell to widows or spinsters, who taught to supplement a meager income.

118

ORNBOOKS WERE IN USE in America until well into the nineteenth century, but so were the early primers, especially the *New England Primer*, of which one scholar estimates some three million copies were eventually printed. Very few survive; these books were used to death. Of thirty-seven thousand copies of the *New England Primer* printed by Franklin and Hall over a seventeen-year period, only one is known to exist. The primers contained an alphabet, a much more extensive syllabary than the hornbooks, the Lord's Prayer, and any number of other things. The earliest known copy of the *New England Primer*, for example, prints the entire "Shorter Catechism" used in New England churches; it consisted of 107 questions, the answers to which—some of them ran to a hundred words—had to be learned by heart. To help memorize the alphabet, the *Primer* contained a series of rhymes for each letter; for *A* the verse ran, "In *Adam's* Fall / We sinned all." Some of the others were equally severe: "As runs the *Glass* / Man's life doth pass"; "The idle *Fool* / Is whipt at School." There was "An Alphabet of Lessons for Youth," consisting of sentences such as "*Except* a Man be born again, he cannot see the Kingdom of God"; "*Foolishness* is bound up in the heart of a Child, but the rod of correction shall drive it far from him"; "*Liars* shall have their part in the lake which burns with fire and brimstone." The book also contained lists of words; the whole numbers from one to one hundred; and the names and order of the books of the Bible. This was the standard first reading fare of young children in the American colonies. Indeed, it was frequently their only reading outside the Bible and the ubiquitous almanacs. Most households were innocent of other books, while newspapers were not widely distributed in America before the middle of the eighteenth century.

Statistics on the literacy of populations in other colonies are scarcer than those for New England. Puritan zeal, of course, was not a factor in the Middle Colonies or the South (it also failed to operate in Rhode Island), and what evidence is available indicates that literacy rates varied fairly widely, depending on the availability of schools, the wealth and density of the population, prevailing religious beliefs, and so on. Along the frontier, and in areas like Virginia where there were no towns to speak of and people lived on widely scattered plantations, schools were rare. In 1689, for example, Virginia had just six, serving a much larger population than Massachusetts, which had twenty-three. (These figures may not be entirely accurate, but they are indicative.) Virginia made no attempt to organize an educational *system*, as Massachusetts did. The literacy of Virginians was therefore appreciably lower than that of the Massachusetts Puritans.

Some sense of what literacy entailed in a colony with few schools can be gathered from the autobiography of Devereaux Jarratt, who was born in the county of New Kent, Virginia, in 1733. The son of poor but pious farmers whose highest ambition, he says, "was to teach their children to read, write, and understand the fundamental rules of arithmetic," Jarratt had the good fortune to be born with a remarkable memory; "Before I knew the letters of the alphabet, I could repeat a whole chapter in the Bible, at a few times hearing it read, especially if the subject of it struck my fancy." This memory no doubt stood him in good stead when, at the age of eight or nine, he was sent to an "English" (i.e., petty) school in his neighborhood. Schooling for Jarratt, however, and probably for most of his contemporaries, was a hit or miss affair; he attended one master or another until he was twelve or thirteen, "though not without great interruptions," probably for work on the farm. By the time he left school he had learned to "read in the Bible (though but indifferently), and to write a sorry scrawl, and acquired some knowledge of Arithmetic." At this time his mother died and he went to live with his older brother, whose chief occupation, he says, was horse racing, cockfighting, card playing, and general rowdyism. Because Jarratt had been to school at all, he had the reputation of being a scholar.

UT JARRATT HIMSELF KNEW better about his scholarly abilities, and on his own, during noontime breaks in plowing or harvesting, he undertook to study arithmetic more thoroughly and soon became fairly expert at it. On the strength of this expertise he was asked, at the age of nineteen, to become a schoolmaster on a plantation near the frontier. He accepted the job, having little taste for manual labor, bought himself a wig and two new shirts—aside from his everyday clothes, these items constituted his entire personal property—and moved west. There he happened to come upon a book of sermons by the New-Light preacher George Whitefield, and, wanting to understand better the things he read in the Bible, he took it up and tried to read it.

2. REVOLUTIONARY AMERICA

But he had to confess that "I was but a poor reader, and understood little of what I did read." (At this time he was teaching other people to read.) Conscious of his inadequacy and wanting to improve, he cast about for ways to develop his reading ability, but, he says, "I had not a single book in the world, nor was I able to buy any books, had I known of any for sale." When he was finally able to borrow a book, he had no candle to read by at night and was forced to read by firelight. Nevertheless his efforts bore fruit: "It pleased God mightily to improve my understanding, by these means—and I soon became, what was called a good reader, and my relish for books and reading greatly increased." In his mid-twenties Jarratt learned Latin; eventually he became a minister.

It would be a mistake to generalize too broadly from this particular account, but we do get a sense from Jarratt of how tenuous an acquisition literacy could be in the American colonies, particularly among the poor and those isolated on the frontier. Jarratt had to make what amounted to heroic efforts to improve his reading abilities; for those not willing to make such efforts, literacy probably extended no further than the ability to read, without much understanding, portions of the Bible, and to sign one's name. People in towns, and the wealthier sort generally, had a much better chance than someone like Jarratt to become fully literate, but even wealth did not guarantee it. Lockridge estimates that by 1800 male literacy in Virginia among those with personal estates of £200 or more was no higher than 80 per cent, while for those with estates under that amount it was only 50 per cent. The situation in Pennsylvania was not materially better; in states like South Carolina, which made no efforts whatsoever to provide schools for any but the rich, it was probably worse. Only in New England, then, were the literacy rates in colonial times high, and they were high there only because the Puritans believed so strongly that everyone should read the Word for himself.

By the Revolution, of course, the strength of Puritan beliefs had greatly waned. The heritage of public schooling in New England was as honored in the breach as in the practice, and elsewhere in the colonies it hardly existed at all. Revolutionary leaders saw clearly the need for a new educational ideology. They found it in the need to secure the Revolution; if the people were to govern themselves, they had to be educated well enough to be able to understand and avoid the dangers attendant on the exercise of power. This was a particular concern of Jefferson's, who wrote to Washington that "It is an axiom in my mind that our liberty can never be safe but in the hands of the people themselves, and that too of the people with a certain degree of instruction." An illiterate electorate, Jefferson felt, obviously could not protect itself from demagoguery, or from the designs of a would-be aristocracy. The only solution was to make sure the people were literate. His famous Bill for the More General Diffusion of Knowledge, proposed to the Virginia legislature in 1779, envisioned, among other things, a system of free elementary schools, to be established in every ward of every county, to meet the need. A similar interest in education was evident in Congress, which, in the Ordinance of 1785, set aside one out of the thirty-six lots

in every township in the Western Territory for the maintenance of free public schools.

Universal schooling was not to be obtained so easily, however. Neither in Virginia nor elsewhere was the idea of free, tax-supported public schooling quickly accepted; Jefferson's bill never passed the Virginia legislature, and the school lands in the Western Territory were used as often for land speculation as for the establishment of public shcools.

Indeed, it took a good part of the nineteenth century, and an enormous amount of acrimonious debate, to establish free public school systems across the United States. There were plenty of schools, to be sure, some of them private, some supported by tax revenues; still others charged tuition to those parents who could afford it and provided the rudiments of an education free to those who could not. Owners of large plantations in the South continued to hire private tutors for their children. But in spite of these many systems of education, the education of children could not be called systematic in any general sense. The idea of compulsory education had yet to be conceived; not every child, therefore, attended school. Even if a child did attend, he might be taken out at his parents' will, to help plow or harvest, to work in the mills, perhaps to move farther west. School enrollment in 1860 for children from five to nineteen years of age stood at 66 per cent in the North, 44 per cent in the South. More than a third of the school-age children in the United States, in other words, were not attending school.

Universal literacy, however, was practically a reality by 1860, in spite of the spotty school attendance. By the census of 1850, in fact, the adult literacy rate for both males and females had reached 90 per cent, which was far ahead of every European country except Sweden. There were regional variations, of course; in the South, where fewer than half the white children attended school (blacks were denied any sort of education), literacy rates were lower than the national average; in North Carolina, for example, the rate for adult males in 1850 was 80 per cent, for females 67 per cent. Here again, however, the rates are higher than the school attendance rates. Apparently children were attending school long enough to acquire basic literacy, then dropping out, or else they were learning to read and write outside school, perhaps from a parent or other relative. Such was the case, for example, with Abraham Lincoln, of whom it was reported: "While living in Ind. his cousin D. F. Hanks learned him to spell, Read & write." Hanks himself, however, said it was Lincoln's mother who taught Lincoln his ABCs, even though, as still another source reported, she was "absolutely illiterate." Whoever taught him, evidently Lincoln knew how to read before he went to school.

The method of teaching children to read and write remained the same throughout most of the nineteenth century, and the occupation remained the province of young men and women unable to find anything better paid to do, or of older women, usually poor, sometimes not too well educated themselves. S. G. Goodrich, better known as Peter Parley, author of innumerable children's books, gives us what is probably a fairly accurate picture of the typical dame school as it was run in the early 1800's. Goodrich grew up in Ridgefield, Connecticut, and his particular "dame" was a spinster of fifty named Aunt Delight. Her school consisted of a rough, unpainted clapboard building of one large room and a small anteroom or foyer; the building was located on land owned by the town. Money was seldom wasted on amenities in these schools, inside or out. The traditional little red schoolhouse was red only because red paint was the cheapest available; no paint at all, of course, was cheaper still. The benches in Aunt Delight's school were made with what were called slabs, boards with the rounded part of the log on the bottom side; they were useless for other purposes. The benches, of course, had no backs. The only source of heat was a large fireplace; in the winter those close to the fire roasted, those far away froze. When the school ran out of firewood—providing the wood was usually the responsibility of the parents—it closed.

UNT DELIGHT'S METHOD OF teaching, as Goodrich recounts, remembering his first day at school, was wholly traditional; she called her pupils up one by one, waited until each made "his manners," then asked each child to identify the letters of the alphabet as she pointed to them. Goodrich's own reaction to the procedure is worth recording: "I looked upon these operations with intense curiosity and no small respect, until my own turn came. I went up to the school-mistress with some emotion, and when she said, rather spitefully, as I thought, 'Make your obeisance!' my little intellects all fled away, and I did nothing. Having waited a second, gazing at me with indignation, she laid her hand on the top of my head, and gave it a jerk which made my teeth clash. I believe I bit my tongue a little; at all events, my sense of dignity was offended, and when she pointed to A, and asked what it was, it swam before me dim and hazy, and as big as a full moon. She repeated the question, but I was doggedly silent. Again, a third time, she said, 'What's that?' I replied: 'Why don't you tell me what it is? I didn't come here to learn you your letters!' "

Aunt Delight visited the little boy's parents that evening and he was properly rebuked for his impudence. Goodrich says that he "achieved the alphabet" that summer and attended the school for the next few years, learning to write and making "a little progress" in arithmetic. His teacher

in those years was a man, and he adds, "There was not a grammar, a geography, or a history of any kind in the school. Reading, writing, and arithmetic were the only things taught, and these very indifferently—not wholly from the stupidity of the teacher, but because he had forty scholars, and the standards of the age required no more than he performed." This, by the way, was the only formal education Goodrich received.

The deficiencies of such schools as Aunt Delight's became increasingly troubling to educators as the nineteenth century progressed. Education itself was gradually becoming professionalized as state governments began to exert more control over local educational systems, as state "normal" schools were established to train teachers, and as the graded school, in which children were divided into grades according to their age, became standard. These changes were largely the work of educational reformers such as Horace Mann; the irony is that their reforms eventually solidified in highly bureaucratic school systems, which in turn inspired new waves of reform, creating a cycle of bureaucratization and reform that is still with us.

The teaching of reading was an early target of the reformers, who were appalled by the deadening effects of long hours of rote memorization on a child's enthusiasm for learning. The influential reformer Thomas Palmer described the problem well in his *Teacher's Manual*, published in 1840:

"The first branch of knowledge, to which the attention of the child is directed on entering school, is *Reading*. Hitherto his studies have been altogether delightful. His progress has been constant and rapid; for, as yet, he has dealt with nothing but real knowledge. No barren sounds, no unintelligible words have occurred, to embarrass and impede him. But now, very different becomes his situation. A *book* is placed in his hands, which he is told he must learn to *read*, that he may know how to become wise and good, and he is delighted with the prospect. But, alas! how grievous the disappointment! For months, nay, sometimes for years, his studies consist of nothing but mere *sounds*, to which it is impossible he can annex any idea whatever. His school-hours are solely occupied with As and Bs, abs, ebs, and ibs. Now, what must be the effect of all this, upon an intelligent child?"

The answer, said Palmer, was woolgathering. All this memorization led to "the habit of mental wandering." Horace Mann pointed out that not only was rote memorization stultifying, it was irrational as well, for the sounds of the letters—that is, the sounds of their names—did not correspond to the way they actually sounded when combined into words: "When a child is taught the three alphabetic sounds *l e g*, and then is told that these three sounds, when combined, make the sound *leg*, he is untaught in the latter case what he was mistaught in the former. *L e g* does not spell *leg*, but if pronounced quickly, it spells *elegy*." As a solution to the problem, Palmer, Mann, and other reformers advocated a method derived from French and German educators—the Prussians were especially inventive in the field of primary education—in which the student was first taught whole words, learning the alphabet only after he had mastered a small vocabulary. The idea was to arouse the child's interest by letting him see how letters were arranged in meaningful combinations before requiring him to learn the letters.

This method, however, called the words-to-letters method, was really just a modification of the traditional method of teaching children to read; only about fifty words were taught before the child's attention was directed to the alphabet, which still had to be memorized. Radical change had to wait for the development of the words-to-reading method, most forcefully advocated by the controversial Francis Wayland Parker, who was superintendent of schools in the town of Quincy, Massachusetts, in the 1870's. Parker abandoned the teaching of the alphabet altogether; children were "learning how to read," wrote Charles Francis Adams, Jr., ". . . exactly as they had before learned how to speak, not by rule and rote and by piecemeal, but altogether and by practice. . . ." Parker was never entirely clear about exactly how this was done, but apparently it involved sounding out words and sentences as the child read them, a method which is now called the "look-and-say" method. Parker moved to Chicago after his stay in Quincy and there founded the Chicago Institute, which eventually became part of the School of Education at the University of Chicago. John Dewey came under the influence of his ideas there; Dewey called Parker the father of progressive education. The subsequent triumph of progressive education in twentieth-century America also meant the triumph of the look-and-say method of teaching children to read.

T WAS BY NO MEANS AN easy victory; the old method of teaching children to read died very hard. Webster's elementary spelling book (Ole Blueback, as it was called), the principal "text" of the traditional ABC method, sold throughout the nineteenth century in numbers which one scholar claims "must have approached the hundred million mark." Even more popular were the McGuffey readers, also based on the old method; sales of those reached 122,000,000. The public had been raised on this standard fare and was familiar with it, so reformers had to contend with this public conservatism as well as the entrenched skepticism of teachers who had been using the old method all their lives. Even the relatively modest reform

involved in the words-to-letters method was stoutly resisted; Horace Mann, who campaigned for it throughout his tenure as secretary of the Massachusetts Board of Education in the 1840's, was never able to get it adopted in the Massachusetts school system. One critic said of the words-to-letters method, "The letters . . . have to be learned eventually. If any success attends the child's learning of words, the teacher may be sure of encountering added resistance when she endeavors to teach letters to a child who is succeeding already without knowing them."

The critic also complained that the new method, by, in effect, eliminating the alphabet, reduced English to the status of Chinese, and, most important, that it made "spelling, a grievous burden at best, still more difficult." The same complaints were made later about the words-to-reading or look-and-say method, and in the 1870's the state administered a statewide spelling test to compare the spelling abilities of Francis Parker's Quincy students with those of other Massachusetts students. The results were not very encouraging to the proponents of either method: "In their written work, pupils in the primary grades spelled *whose* in 108 different ways; *which* in 58; *depot* in 52, and *scholar* in a grand total of 221." Parker's Quincy students performed better, on the average, than those in the rest of the state, but evidently few students anywhere performed very well.

It has yet to be conclusively demonstrated that look-and-say is a real improvement on the old ABC method, for spelling or for anything else. By about the 1940's look-and-say had become the standard method of teaching children to read in American schools, but many critics claim that it is precisely look-and-say that is responsible for the current literacy problem. The criticisms are much the same as those voiced in the nineteenth century: look-and-say makes English an ideographic language, like Chinese; children emerge from it not knowing how to spell or to "sound out" new words; their vocabulary grows much more slowly than that of children taught from the beginning by the phonics method, which is essentially an updating of the ABC method. One critic, Selma Fraiberg, notes that by the fourth grade an American child is expected to have built a vocabulary of between eighteen and twenty-five hundred words, while a Soviet child of the same age, taught by the phonics method, will have a vocabulary of ten thousand words and already will have been reading complete, uncut stories by Tolstoy, Chekhov, and Gorky, and poems by Nekrasov and Pushkin. The American child will still be reading about Dick and Jane. Fraiberg thinks that the American reliance on look-and-say is a major cause of this large "reading gap."

The battle of methods has gone on for well over one hundred years now, and it may go on for another hundred. It is a real question, however, whether pedagogical methods are the most serious aspect of the problem. One hundred years ago the literacy rate was considerably higher than the percentage of children attending school; now everyone attends school, and levels of literacy are dropping steadily. A cynic might say that this only proves the incompetence of the schools, but it may be that schools and their teaching methods are not the whole story, that declining literacy is, in fact, a much larger problem which is not simply the result of incompetent schools, but includes them.

THE LARGER PROBLEM, THE historian Carlo Cipolla suggests, is the problem of values. What the history of literacy in America seems to demonstrate is that a highly literate society evolves out of deeply held values, not out of teaching methods, and where such values are missing, literacy will decline no matter what the teaching methods. Puritan New England became highly literate because the Puritans believed so strongly in the value of access to the Word, not thanks to any teaching method; a Puritan *had* to learn to read in order to save his unregenerate soul from the vividly imagined fires of Hell. Later, literacy became a way up and out of one's economic or social circumstances; Devereux Jarratt *had* to learn to read if he wanted to escape the farm. If one wanted to rise, or become involved in the country's political life, or master the complexities of an increasingly industrialized environment, literacy was a necessity. In the eighteenth and nineteenth centuries, then, America was full of self-made readers, men who had had to struggle to become literate, ambitious men like Abraham Lincoln who were unwilling to spend the rest of their lives splitting rails. Books were scarce, teachers were few and often incompetent, but the desire was there; consequently literacy did not depend simply and solely on the schools.

Now the desire seems to be on the point of disappearing. For whatever reason—television, widespread anomie, the anti-intellectualism that is also part of our history—we no longer value literacy as we once did. The public worries about the high rates of functional illiteracy and talks nostalgically about a return to the three Rs, but that same public would just as soon watch television as read a book. The problem is not just a technical problem of teaching methods, of "language skills"; it is based on a profound public indifference to the blessings which only the printed word can bestow.

"We shall some day accept the thought that it is just as illogical to assume that every boy must be able to read as it is that each one must be able to perform on a violin, that it is no more reasonable to require that each girl shall spell well than it is that each one shall bake a cherry pie." The speaker was a junior high school principal, but he can be taken to represent more than an obtuse educational establishment; educators do not exist entirely isolated from the public, or opposed to it, but must be understood as in some degree reflecting public attitudes. And a public that would tolerate such a remark from an educator is a public that has lost, or forsaken, its belief in the value of literacy.

Yet we must remember that this is a value that, from the long perspective of history, we have acquired very recently. "It is only during the present century that the goal of reading for the purpose of gaining information has been applied in ordinary elementary schools to the entire population of students," write Laura and Daniel Resnick. As these writers also point out, the standard of skill required to make one functionally literate is rising; literacy skills which were sufficient one hundred or even fifty years ago will no longer suffice. This is especially true in technology. The U.S. Navy's most advanced weapons system in 1939 came with a technical manual of five hundred pages. Its most advanced system in 1978 came with three hundred thousand pages of documentation. Many other technical systems require more reading, at a higher level, than those of the past; computers are especially prolific, printing out enormous quantities of information and analysis, which someone has to read. Literacy is declining, then, even as the demand for higher and higher levels of literacy grows.

What the outcome of these trends will be is anybody's guess. Perhaps we will return once more to conditions similar to the "craft literacy" that prevailed in the Middle Ages, when the clergy monopolized the instruments and organization of knowledge. Or perhaps public attitudes will shift and people will again demand access to the word. Literate persons can only hope that a hundred years from now we will have a public in which, fulfilling John Adams' claim, someone who cannot read and write will indeed be as rare as a comet or an earthquake.

National Consolidation and Expansion

3

Because the government our founding fathers created has endured for almost two hundred years, most Americans do not realize how fragile it was during its infancy. Some scholars believe that were it not for President George Washington's enormous prestige, Secretary of the Treasury Alexander Hamilton's various economic programs, and adroit diplomacy the fledgling government may well have gone under. Hugh B. Hammett's essay on the Jay Treaty with Great Britain provides some insights to how perilous things really were at the time.

The sixty-year period between the election of Thomas Jefferson in 1800 and the onset of the Civil War was one of bewildering changes. Through diplomacy and through conquest, this nation had more than doubled its size. One by one the territorial claims of the major European powers were eliminated until the United States stretched from the Atlantic to the Pacific. And the expansion was not confined to territory. Population, agricultural and industrial production, and virtually everything else measurable grew apace. Railroads now spanned the continent and, together with other improvements in transportation, helped to generate economic growth. There was an underside to all this, however. Periods of prosperity alternated with depressions during which businesses

went bankrupt and many workers lost their jobs. Laboring conditions in general were deplorable, with long hours and low pay the norm. And worst of all, a significant part of the nation's economy rested upon the deplorable institution of slavery.

Aside from the slavery question, which was fought over with increasing frequency and venom as the years wore on, this was a period of widespread social ferment. Essays in this section on communal movements, prohibition, women's rights, and the treatment of Indians help to convey a sense of this ferment. No era in history is ever completely static, but this was a time when many people thought they could create a truly just and equitable society through reform.

The readings included in this unit raise a number of large questions you might consider. Just how "democratic" was our society before—and after—the Jacksonian period? Which groups were excluded from participation throughout the period? Did the agitation over slavery encourage or inhibit reform movements in other areas? Did the acquisition of new territories, in the end, help tear the nation apart in civil war? And finally, to what extent did the vastness of our land, with its apparently inexhaustible resources, help shape a national consciousness to which the notion of social responsibility is alien?

The Jay Treaty: Crisis Diplomacy in the New Nation

Hugh B. Hammett

Gently down the Hudson, past the Battery and Governors Island, slipped the *Ohio*. Although small crowds clustered at two places along the route to wave and cheer, nothing about the ship or its passengers appeared remarkable; indeed, the casual observer on shore would likely have overlooked the vessel entirely. In a real sense, however, the destiny of the American republic tossed on board the unremarkable ship on that unpretentious May morning in 1794.

On deck stood a solitary erect figure, gazing pensively over the receding shoreline. Tall and spare with sharp, almost severe, angular features, John Jay was not a magnetic or charismatic figure. In self-possessed, formal demeanor he resembled his chief, George Washington. In spite of his austere manner Jay was capable and intelligent, of indisputable integrity, and above all was experienced in diplomacy. That he was on the *Ohio* bound for England shows the measure of President Washington's confidence in the New Yorker. John Jay was on a peace mission of crucial import. Relations between the United States and Great Britain had become so strained that press and public no longer only hinted darkly at war. In America, Jeffersonian politicians openly demanded immediate commercial warfare while Federalist leaders grimly voted military appropriations for an even larger and undoubtedly bloody potential conflict. John Jay's mission represented an eleventh hour attempt on the part of the Washington administration to head off war.

The events leading to this perilous state of affairs dated as far back as the end of the American Revolution. By the treaty of 1783 (incidentally, negotiated in part by John Jay), Great Britain had recognized American independence and had granted ample borders that bounded on the Mississippi in the West and on the present Canadian border in the North. United States sovereignty was assured only on paper, however, because the British, anxious to retain the northern fur trade, steadfastly refused to vacate a string of seven frontier forts on the American side of the boundary line. American leaders were galled at such flagrant abuse of national sovereignty, but the weakness of the United States in the decade immediately after the Revolution allowed no challenge to the British occupation. Early in 1794 the disgraceful situation worsened when inept British officials in Canada began openly to stir up the Indians along the border; and to support their Indian allies the Brtish then brazenly occupied a new fort on American soil.

The frontier situation, however, was only the beginning of troubles for the new nation. In 1792 Europe had erupted into war; and when England, the leading seapower, joined with several other powers in a coalition against France the following year, maritime disputes arose to plague further the relations between America and Britain. As the war spread over Europe, the French (unable themselves to challenge the peaceful British fleet) opened to neutrals the lucrative trade of their West Indian island colonies, Santo

Reprinted by permission from *The Social Studies*, Vol. LXV, No. 1, January 1974. Published by Heldref Publications, Washington, D. C.

Domingo, Martinique, and Guadeloupe. Joyful American captains, having been denied access to British Caribbean possessions since the Revolution, rushed to claim the rich fruits of the neutral carrying trade.

England, however, had no intention of allowing France to compensate for her lack of seapower by using vessels under neutral flags to maintain contact with her islands. Beginning in June, 1793, the British issued a series of strict Orders in Council designed to halt the traffic. In London the Admiralty neglected to inform the American Minister Thomas Pinckney of the new restrictions against the trade in time for him to alert American captains. Heavyhanded British naval commanders were informed, however, and they eagerly began collecting American ships and crews, at times employing brutal and humiliating tactics. Many United States seamen were imprisoned; some even were naked, their captors having stolen their clothes. In March, 1794, news reached the United States that roughly three hundred ships had been captured by the British. Although records today show that the British Government did not want war with the United States, whether wittingly or not, British actions had caused to be assembled the combustible materials from which war might be easily ignited.

Although a feeling of outrage and resentment at British policies was nearly unanimous in the United States, there was by no means uniformity of agreement as to the way the nation should respond. Indeed, rather than uniting Americans the crisis in foreign policy only intensified a growing partisan division. Opinion tended to polarize around two men: Thomas Jefferson, recently Secretary of State, and Alexander Hamilton, the Secretary of the Treasury. Difference over foreign policy was only one manifestation of a far deeper philosophical rift between these two leading lights of Washington's first administration. Jefferson, a brilliant and accomplished Virginia aristocrat, was representative of southern and western agrarian attitudes. Fearful of large cities, excessive government, and ponderous military establishments, Jefferson reflected the aspirations and prejudices of the common man. In viewing Europe, the Virginian had especially strong preferences. The English he considered to be "proud, hectoring, swearing, squibbling, carnivorous animals" as contrasted to the "polite, self-denying, feeling, hospitable, good humoured" French people. The Virginian, while a nationalist first, favored close ties with France and maintenance as far as was reasonable of the political and military obligations of the French Alliance dating from the American Revolution.

Alexander Hamilton, an urbane and equally brilliant New Yorker, was field commander of the Federalist opposition to Jefferson's Democratic-Republicans. Mistrustful of the common rabble and devoted to northeastern commercial interests, Hamilton favored strong central government that might unify a weak, divided collection of states. Only a dynamic, powerful federal government could protect commerce and command respect in the international community. Emerging as the dominant force in the Washington administration, Hamilton skillfully drafted an elaborate financial structure designed to insure the credit and stability of the new government under the Constitution. Most of the revenue for operating the federal structure came from tariffs on British imports to the United States; and after 1789 English goods accounted for a phenomental ninety per cent of America's import trade! The Jeffersonians lamented such dependence on another nation as an indication of appalling national weakness. Hamilton and his Federalist followers were not disturbed, however, since most of them were as ardently pro-British as Thomas Jefferson was pro-French.

Both factions claimed that they did not want war with Great Britain. The heart of the dispute, then, between the Jeffersonians and the Federalists was a matter of tactics. How far could the United States go in opposing the deplorable British frontier and maritime policies? Advancing a theme that was to be a major component of their policy for the next twenty years, the Jeffersonians called for swift commercial retaliation against England. Holding as ideal the self-sufficient agrarian state, Jefferson and his chief collaborator James Madison were not averse to sacrificing American commercial interests by using them as a retaliatory tool for "peaceable coercion." Of such little domestic consequence did Jefferson consider foreign trade that he had even suggested on one occasion that the United States sever all economic ties and "stand with respect to Europe precisely on the footing of China."

When news of British maritime depredations reached the United States in March, 1794, James Madison seized the initiative to press through the Congress a month's embargo. Disillusioned by the frontier and maritime crises, many Federalists in both the House and Senate reluctantly went along. The Jeffersonians then began to clamor for more severe strictures aimed specifically at Great Britain. Nevertheless, the Federalists, led by Alexander Hamilton, were already moving to advance their own conception of the national interest. To Hamilton the Jeffersonian policies were an invitation to national suicide. With ninety per cent of America's imports and almost fifty per cent of her exports tied to Britain, it was clear to the Federalists that American prosperity in general and the success of the constitutional experiment in particular were irretrievably linked to the maintenance of the commercial relationship. Although the trade may have been essential to continued British prosperity in 1794, it appeared to be vital to the very survival of the United States.

Hamilton and other Federalist tacticians like Rufus King and Oliver Ellsworth then developed a scheme to counter the Republican initiatives. While Federalist orators attempted to fend off other bills for economic retaliation in the Congress, the party leaders implored President Washington to dispatch a special emissary to make a final attempt to negotiate a peaceful resolution of the crisis. In the meantime to preserve credibility and also to prepare for the possibility that the peace mission might fail, Federalist congressmen grimly pushed for increased military and naval appropriations, much to the discomfiture of the Republicans, who liked to talk belligerently but who never liked to vote money for military preparedness.

Although President Washington personally believed that war was inevitable, he agreed to send an envoy extraordinary in one last effort to save the peace. After lengthy deliberations within the administration, John Jay was selected. Republicans were none too pleased with Jay's nomination, and in the Senate eight of them fruitlessly voted against confirmation. As Professor Alexander De Conde has observed in his book on the politics and diplomacy of the period, "No one but a Jeffersonian would have pleased the Republicans. . . ." Indeed, many Jeffersonian partisans opposed the idea of the peace mission altogether. In the West especially, where John Jay had never been popular, bitter protests against the selection arose. Fanatics in Lexington, Kentucky, held a dramatic public demonstration in which an effigy of the Chief Justice was guillotined and burned. It is clear, therefore, that the Jay mission began under a severe handicap; so adamant were his opponents that it is difficult to imagine any conceivable way that Jay might have won their approval, however well he did his work.

In retrospect, nevertheless, it is hard to fault President Washington's choice. Perhaps John Jay might rightly be characterized as a "high priest of Federalism" (as his adversaries frequently did). It is understandable, however, that having rejected the harsh Republican approach, President Washington could hardly have delegated one of their number to execute his alternate plans. In a time of excessive foreign prejudices, Jay was a moderate. Of Huguenot descent, he was one of the few Founding Fathers not of

English heritage. He was never as pro-British as Hamilton; nor did he favor England with as much devotion as Jefferson embraced France. Moreover, in sending John Jay to London, Washington had chosen one of the republic's most experienced diplomats. Jay had been the nation's first minister to Spain, had been a principal negotiator of the Treaty of Paris of 1783, and had then served for six years as Secretary for Foreign Affairs under the Confederation. Jay knew from intimate experience the devious workings of the European balance of power. Additionally, he knew from firsthand frustrations the weakness and limitations of his own country. John Jay would give nothing away free, but neither would he ask too much.

Not surprisingly, although Secretary of State Edmond Randolph transmitted the documents, Jay's instructions clearly mirrored the advice of Alexander Hamilton to President Washington. Basically, Jay was to try to settle the boundary dispute and other minor differences arising from the Treaty of 1783, to gain compensation for maritime losses along with recognition of American neutral rights if possible, and to attempt to secure a commercial agreement that would allow American trade to the British West Indies. The envoy, of course, was to do nothing to abridge the French Alliance.

Having thankfully left far behind the complaints of Republican orators, John Jay arrived in London on the morning of June 15, 1794. The voyage from New York lasted just under one month; and, as was his custom, Jay had been seasick most of the time. The hardship of the journey was quickly forgotten, however, in the warm glow of the gracious reception that the British gave to the American envoy. Lord Grenville, the perceptive Foreign Minister, realized that if John Jay had any fault it was a lack of modesty rather than of ability or integrity. Consequently, Jay was wined and dined through five months of negotiations. Jay came to like his English hosts immensely. He enjoyed the company of the high-born and well-educated of English society, and they in turn evidently came to appreciate Jay. Although English foreign policy was never motivated by sentiment or expressions of cordiality, Jay's magnanimous reception was important symbolically at least of the British government's desire to avoid war.

Day-to-day deliberations were long and complex. Like any good negotiator, Jay took the offensive from the start. He was aware that pressing military obligations on the Continent had dangerously drained British military manpower in Canada. Also, General "Mad Anthony" Wayne's expedition in northwest Ohio (launched the previous fall) might still severely strike at the power of the Indian allies.

The imperturbable Grenville allowed Jay the luxury of a small summer offensive before aggressively undertaking an extensive autumn foray of his own. Grenville rightly reminded the American that the Crown had already repealed the most objectionable of the maritime regulations. In spite of Canadian weakness, there was still the awesome British fleet that could lay waste at will America's shipping and coastal cities. The strongest trump card, however, that the Foreign Secretary held was his knowledge of American weakness. Professor Jerald A. Combs has pointed out in his new book *The Jay Treaty* that English representatives in America had frequently reported the financial dependence of the American government on revenue from British trade. Although Lord Grenville was willing to make some concessions, his was the stronger position; and it was clear that Jay would have to modify his earlier ambitions.

After arduous negotiations, mostly confidential from which even private secretaries were banished, the two men reached an accord. The final draft, a document of twenty-eight separate articles, was signed on November 19, 1794. Jay's great victory was Grenville's promise to withdraw the offending British troops from American soil in the Northwest by June 1, 1796, thus restoring

United States territorial integrity. Otherwise, the New Yorker's gains were uncertain. Lord Grenville rejected the American definition of neutral rights but did agree that claims arising from British maritime seizures would be settled later by joint abitration. Jay was able to secure entry into the British West Indies for limited trade only by very small American vessels. The strength of the British position was revealed also by other omissions from the pact. The agreement said nothing about Canadian machinations with the Indians on the frontier or the growing problem of impressment.

Although he had been forced to compromise his original ambitions on a number of points, John Jay was satisfied with the treaty. He wrote Secretary of State Randolph, "I have no reason to believe that one more favorable is attainable." To his personal gratification at least, the New Yorker believed that he had preserved the peace and thus gained the ultimate goal of his mission at a reasonable cost. Remaining behind in England to avoid a bitter winter ocean voyage, Jay dispatched copies of the new agreement to the United States. After numerous delays and perils (not the least of which was near capture by a French cruiser), a copy of the treaty arrived in Philadelphia on March 7, 1795.

Perhaps the most interesting aspect of the entire diplomatic episode was the angry public furor that greeted the treaty at home. The bitterness and vindictiveness of Republican partisans was so great as almost to exceed the bounds of imagination for one not familiar with the political mores of the time. President Washington, fearing an intemperate public outcry and discouraged with some parts of the treaty himself, kept the document secret until June, 1795, when he finally submitted the treaty—in confidence—to a special session of the Senate. Washington's decision for temporary secrecy only whetted the sharp suspicions and rumors that circulated among Republican partisans. After a two-week debate the Senate approved the

agreement by the proper two-thirds majority with not a single vote to spare—not however, before angry (and perhaps ambitious) Senators filched copies of the treaty and leaked them to Republican leaders and press.

Having failed to stop the pact in the Senate, James Madison and Republican chieftains in the House of Representatives then hoped to prevent the appropriation of funds necessary to implement the treaty. Failing there, it might be possible as a last resort to exert enough public pressure on President Washington to cause him to refuse to ratify the pact. In objecting to the agreement, the Republicans derided the commercial provisions of the treaty as worthless; indeed, so restrictive was the article providing for West Indian trade that the Federalist Senate had already deleted it. The Jeffersonians were even more angered that Jay had failed to gain acceptance of a liberal interpretation of neutral rights.

As the specifific terms of the treaty gradually spread from one newspaper to another, Jeffersonian partisans across the Union raised calamitous howls. Jefferson himself was far more restrained than many of his adherents when he wrote to Edward Rutledge of South Carolina to brand the treaty an "execrable thing." A bit of anonymous Republican graffiti on a fence summed up the sentiments of many common men: "Damn John Jay! Damn every one that won't damn John Jay!! Damn every one that won't put lights in his windows and sit up all night damning John Jay!!!" When Alexander Hamilton took the stump in New York to defend the treaty, he was stoned by a hostile mob; reportedly, he cried to his attackers as he fled bleeding from the platform, "If you can use such knockdown arguments I must retire." (Federalist wags later said that the Republicans were trying to knock out Hamilton's brains so they would at last be equal with him.) In Boston an irate mob descended on a hapless British vessel that had wandered into the harbor and put it to the torch. Effigies of John Jay were burned in numerous demonstrations throughout the country.

In the South the frenzy resumed intermittently over a period of several months. The Franklin Society of Pendelton, South Carolina, held impassioned rallies to denounce the treaty as a work of "treachery," "detestable in its origins" and "contemptible in its event." "Liberty lies prostrate!" went up the cry in Pendelton. Not content with oral denunciations alone, the citizens passed twenty-seven separate resolutions condemning the treaty. One gentleman who attended the festivities wrote to a nearby newspaper: "I know the public curiosity has been on tiptoe to learn the manner in which the frontier district of South Carolina would receive the *celebrated* treaty of the *celebrated* Jay—We did not burn him in effigy—we are too dignified for such business—but were the *original* among us, I would not insure him but at a very high premium." *The South Carolina State Gazette* published its own bawdy "Dialogue on the Treaty":

J-Y
May't please your highness, I John Jay
Have travell'd all this mighty way
To inquire if you good Lord, will please
To suffer me while on my knees
To show all others I surpass
In love-ly kissing of your a-se:
As by my 'xtraordinary station,
I represent a certain nation;
I thence conclude and so may you,
They all would wish to kiss it too.
So please your highness suffer me
To kiss, I wait on bended knee.

KING
What you, a rebel, scoundrel dog!
You villain, rascal, knave and rogue!
Think you my honor I'll disgrace,
And suffer you to kiss my a-se?
No, No, I'm no such arrant fool,
There's Grenville, who's my humble tool;
If he'll vouch safe you such a bliss,
He may, but mine you cannot kiss. . . .

The Federalists were shocked and dismayed at the vigor of their opponents. President Washington wrote that the "cry against the treaty was like that against a mad dog." John Quincy Adams, writing later, said that the pact "brought on the severest trial which

the character of Washington and the fortunes of the country have ever passed through."

Recovering their composure at last, the Federalists counter-attacked. Jay, Rufus King, and Hamilton took up pens to vindicate the administration's policy. The latter was especially devastating in his famous "Camillus" letters, writing so persuasively that Jefferson lamented him as a "host within himself." Bucking the public outcry the Federalists won the appropriations battle in the House in late April, 1796. President Washington stoically ignored the personal abuse and the torrent of petitions that rained down on him. Convinced that the good of the country was at stake, he ratified the agreement on August 14, 1795. With Washington's firm decision and the failure of the sky to fall or the Union Jack to appear over Independence Hall, the most ardent Jeffersonians ceased to fulminate once the press lost interest in their activities. Charles Frazer, a citizen of Charleston, South Carolina, who witnessed some of the most violent demonstrations, tersely summed up the situation, "The treaty became law—the nation acquiesced in it, and went on prospering."

The decline of immediate agitation, however, did not mean that the Jay Treaty was without profound import and lasting significance to the early history of the nation. From the time of the treaty debate until the demise of the Federalists after the War of 1812, there was to be no party peace. One scholar, Joseph Charles, has argued persuasively that this diplomatic episode was the paramount event in the crystallization of a clear two-party system. Ironically, the definite party division was the beginning of the decline of the Federalists. Foreign policy issues in general and the Jay Treaty in particular were hotly debated in the elections of 1796; and although the Federalists managed one last presidential victory, the party had lost favor with the masses. The Federalists might still be the party of the best, but the Republicans were the party of the most. In only four years the tides of participatory democracy would wash the Federalists from dominance forever.

John Jay's own career suffered decline as a result of his diplomatic service. On his return to America in May, 1796, he learned the surprising news that *in absentia* he had been elected Governor of New York. His administration was conservative and uneventful. Except for assisting Hamilton on drafts of the "Camillus" papers, Jay stolidly refused to become involved in the public acrimony over the treaty that bore his name. Discredited among much of the populace by that document, Jay was never again a national political figure.

The most obvious liability of the Jay Treaty was increased friction with France. Pained Jeffersonians lamented that the agreement was an affront to the French Alliance. To be sure, the French government interpreted Jay's maritime concessions as favorable to its archenemy, and it ordered the confiscation of American ships in retaliation. Professor Alexander DeConde has argued that, although the treaty preserved peace with England, it made more likely a disastrous war with France. It seems useful in retrospect to observe, however, that wars with England and France were qualitatively quite different. Had the United States been on the European continent, France would have indeed been a severe threat. In the middle 1790's, because of America's pitiful vulnerability on her coasts and in the Atlantic, it was imperative to avoid conflict with England, the leading seapower. An undeclared naval war with France did erupt in only three years, but it was hardly disastrous. The French, in fact, had no stomach to continue the fighting once they saw that Americans were serious about defending the national interest.

For a good many years it was the custom of historians to accept the opinion of Henry Adams that the Jay Treaty was an unnecessary debasement of the national honor. Since 1923, however, with the publication of Samuel Flagg Bemis's epochal *Jay's Treaty*, most scholars have been inclined to accept the Federalist policy as somewhat unpalatable but eminently realistic. The argument is still offered by some authorities that Jeffersonian "peaceable coercion" through economic retaliation was never given a chance in the middle 1790's and that it might have won further concessions without war. In historical retrospect, nevertheless, the Jeffersonian viewpoint seems rather dubious. In less than ten years the Jeffersonians did have the occasion to implement such policies against England with the well-known result of the perilous War of 1812. One is moved to ask, if Republican policies were so nearly disastrous in 1812, how could a United States far more weak and divided in 1795 have survived?

Indeed, the most recent researches by Professors Jerald Combs and Charles Ritcheson in British sources have confirmed the probability of war. Ritcheson in *Aftermath of Revolution* puts it bluntly: "There is not the slightest doubt that Britain would have gone to war with the United States rather than acquiesce in the Jeffersonian view of neutral rights. Can it be seriously maintained that American welfare would have been served in 1794 by a war fought to defend a shadowy and insubstantial 'consensus' about neutral rights, when the country's most important interests and even its existence would have been at stake? John Jay and the Federalists did not think so; and they were right."

In summary, it is hard to fault the realism and skill of Federalist diplomacy in this most serious diplomatic crisis to face the new nation since independence. If they lacked the elegance and aplomb that characterized the European style of foreign relations, it is enough to say that the Federalist diplomats achieved the ultimate goal of all good foreign policy: they defended the national interest and preserved the nation to play another hand in the international game. It has often been debated whether the treaty that resulted should be called Jay's or Hamilton's or Washington's. It did not belong to any of the three. It was America's.

EXPERIMENT AT NASHOBA PLANTATION

Peggy Robbins

In researching the story of Frances Wright and her Nashoba experiment Peggy Robbins found the following two books particularly helpful: Frances Wright: Free Enquirer (1939), by A.J.G. Perkins and Theresa Wolfson, and William Randall Waterman's Frances Wright (1924).

The first half of the 19th century has been called "the age of utopian communities" in the United States because during that time and a few preceding years over 170 "social experiments" enlivened the American scene. None was stranger than the Nashoba experiment of Frances Wright, a wealthy Scotswoman who planned to "remodel Southern society" by freeing the slaves in a program of "self-emancipation" through a system of cooperative labor. This "great humanitarian experiment" represented the first serious attempt to end slavery peacefully in America, and it pioneered several equal-rights movements that were to realize success long afterward. It might have succeeded if it had not turned into a "free love colony" in an era when such a community was overwhelmingly considered to be "one great brothel."

In early October 1825, 30-year-old Fanny Wright, a tall, somewhat mannish, but handsome woman, created a stir in Memphis when she arrived on horseback from Nashville and announced her intention to launch her experiment in the vicinity. Miss Wright's pamphlet, *A Plan for the Gradual Abolition of Slavery in the United States without Danger of Loss to Citizens of the South*, had been published in Baltimore in September 1825, but it had provided no information as to where she would demonstrate its practicability.

Her plan involved buying slaves, with no loss to their owners, and establishing them in a colony where they would be taught a trade to make them self-supporting and otherwise prepared for freedom. She was sure that the colony, once well established, would be self-sustaining and would provide funds for purchasing and training more slaves as numbers were freed. It was a plan in which such prominent slave-owners as Thomas Jefferson and Andrew Jackson saw merit.

The young woman had been denouncing social evils since she was a child and dreaming of a utopia in which inequalities of race, birth, wealth, and sex would be eliminated. She was confident that the success of her colony would encourage the establishment of other such communities throughout the South, so that in time all the slaves would "work themselves free." It was quite a dream, considering that at the time, according to Thomas Jefferson, there were approximately four million slaves in the United States.

Fanny, accompanied by her younger sister Camilla, had first visited the United States in 1818; she had stayed nearly two years, and then, back in Europe, had published her *Views of Society and Manners in America,* which included a discussion of Negro slavery in "a land devoted to liberty": "The sight of slavery is revolting everywhere, but to inhale the impure breath of its pestilence in the free winds of America is odious beyond all the imagination can conceive. . . ."

By the time four more years had passed, Frances Wright had decided that it was up to *her* to solve "dear America's terrible social problem," and she and Camilla returned to the United States. Camilla would assist her in whatever manner she wished; Camilla always did.

From *American History Illustrated,* April 1980. Reproduced through the courtesy of The National Historical Society, publishers of *American History Illustrated,* P.O. Box 1831, Harrisburg, PA 17105.

3. NATIONAL CONSOLIDATION AND EXPANSION

Through the sisters' friendship with General Lafayette, who was visiting in America at the time [see "Return of a Hero," October 1979 *AHI*], Fanny was able to visit such noted Americans as ex-Presidents Thomas Jefferson and James Madison, and President Monroe, to discuss the whole question of slavery with them. While at Monticello, she tried to get Jefferson actively involved in the proposed experiment. He declined but "heartily approved" of her efforts.

By the time Fanny's *Plan for the Gradual Abolition of Slavery* was published, she and her advisers believed that they had worked out the major problems associated with the scheme. As an incentive for full cooperation of the slaves, they would be promised, in addition to freedom, the education of their children. Discipline would be maintained by lengthening the term of service for misconduct. The required service term would depend largely on a slave's purchase price and how diligently he worked off that debt; it was roughly estimated at from one to five years. The plan provided for the colonization of the freed Negroes as independent farmers.

Fanny estimated that it would cost about $41,000 to establish a colony of 100 slaves; she optimistically predicted that such a cooperative venture as she proposed would boast a net profit of some $10,000 at the end of its first year. All she needed to get started, she declared, was land and slaves.

In September 1825, after Fanny had spent some time in cooperative communities in Illinois studying their operation, she started south to find a location for her great experiment. With her was George Flower, a friend of General Lafayette, an ardent abolitionist, and a man with experience in cooperative living and extensive knowledge of farming.

Flower, who had been one of the founders of the English community at Albion, Illinois, had enthusiastically volunteered as a partner in the lady reformer's venture. Flower's wife and three children and Camilla Wright were left in Albion, and the new partners set forth.

They first journeyed to Nashville for a visit with Andrew Jackson which had been arranged by Lafayette when he had been in the city on his tour. Fanny found General Jackson ready to give assistance in her quest for land and slaves. When she and Flower rode into Memphis in October 1825 she owned eight slaves—five males and three females—whom she had bought in Nashville and who were waiting there to be sent for. And the pair of reformers knew where the experimental community would be located: Jackson had suggested land near Memphis, on the Wolf River in the Chickasaw Purchase, and had directed Flower in purchasing procedure.

In a letter written in December from Memphis, Fanny told a friend in France, "Here I am at last, property-owner in the forests of this new territory, bought from the Indians by the United States about five years ago and still inhabited by bears, wolves and panthers. . . . If your map is good you will find a little river called the Wolf, which flows into the Mississippi at this place. It is on the borders of this stream and about fifteen miles from here that I have actually bought 320 acres, am in negotiation for 320 more, and shall also take possession of 600 acres which surround my plot, when they come up for sale a few months from now, at nine cents the acre. . . ."

The writer said that her "excellent fellow-countryman, Mr. Flower" had returned to Illinois to bring back his family and Camilla, as well as "all the necessary farm material." "In the meantime," she continued "I am over-seeing the construction of houses on my land with a well which furnishes very good water. All these small matters keep me very busy, for there is nothing more difficult than to make men work in these forests. But with the help of the legs of a perfect horse . . . I do forty miles a day going and coming. . . . I am beginning to find an unaccustomed joy in life. . . ."

Before long, Frances Wright owned about 2,000 acres on the Wolf River. She had named the site of her settlement "Nashoba," the Chickasaw word for "wolf."

During Flower's absence, Nashoba gained a new friend in Memphis, a man who was to help the struggling settlement in many ways. He was Marcus Winchester, son of Revolutionary War General James Winchester, one of the three original owners of the town of Memphis and much of the surrounding territory. Marcus, the town's leading lawyer and a little later its first mayor, was a brilliant man. He was considered radical in his attitude toward slavery because he kept a strict account in his dealings with his own slaves and had the idea of eventually emancipating them; he had married a woman of mixed blood, a beautiful, accomplished French quadroon who was excluded from "respectable white society" in Memphis, and he undoubtedly felt that he and Frances Wright were kindred spirits. He helped get supplies to the new settlement, and he and his wife Lucy Lenora opened their home and their hearts to Wright.

In early February 1826 the Nashoba experiment got started in earnest. Robert Wilson, a gentleman from South Carolina, arrived in Memphis with a family of slaves, all female—pregnant mother and five young daughters—whom he wished to "place with Miss Wright as a gift." Fanny accepted them, and after the execution of a contract covering their participation in the experiment and their eventual colonization as free Negroes—a contract drawn up and witnessed by Marcus Winchester—Mr. Wilson went home with $446.76 received in payment for his expenses in transporting the family the 600 miles from South Carolina.

On February 27, George Flower and his family and Camilla, comprising "a small caravan laden with supplies," arrived. Two days later Fanny's eight slaves purchased in Nashville appeared. By this time two double log cabins had been built at Nashoba and a small acreage of land had been cleared. All hands set out for the place, where the white people were quartered in one log house and the Negroes, including more slaves as they arrived, in the other. Not long thereafter the community was joined by James Richardson, an eccentric Scots physician Fanny had met in Memphis, a man described by an acquaintance as "upright, impracticable, and an acute metaphysician."

The next white newcomer to the group at Nashoba was Richeson Whitby, a timid, unpretentious young Quaker who had had experience in communal living at New Harmony, Indiana, as a disciple of the English philanthropist and utopian socialist Robert Owen. One early account called Whitby "a mild Quaker nincompoop," and said that "Miss Wright's assemblage" at Nashoba was "a strange lot of relatives, crackpots, and slaves."

From the beginning the white leaders of the community had trouble getting the Negro laborers to work and not to fight. Richardson pointed out that quarrels among the field hands had to be squelched, and soon the Wright sisters found themselves condoning and actually watching floggings for gross breaches of discipline.

As work proceeded—planting a vegetable garden, clearing more land, building more cabins, planting cotton, corn, and fruit trees—the Wright sisters labored along with the others. The sisters were not accustomed to such grueling work, and Camilla soon became ill. She and the Flower children, also sick, were sent back to Albion. In May, Fanny was forced to go north for a few weeks' rest. After a short period at Albion, she spent most of her time at Robert Owen's New Harmony "Heaven."

The sisters returned to Nashoba at the end of June, and during July and August Fanny again rode horseback all over the settlement in the blistering sunshine. She ignored warnings about the malarial climate of the area, sometimes even sleeping in the woods at night. She came down with "brain fever" and lay near death for weeks. Only the medical knowledge of James Richardson pulled her through. He convinced her to seek another climate and stay there until she regained her health. The development of Nashoba Plantation was proceeding, if slowly, and she felt sure it would continue to do so in her absence.

By this time considerable progress had been made in establishing supply lines to Nashoba, and the slaves, being better provided for, were turning out more work. Purchases Fanny had made with the help of Marcus Winchester, through agents in New Orleans, and through Jeremiah Thompson, an acquaintance in New York, had arrived. Fanny had written Thompson, a Quaker merchant and cotton exporter, of her need to buy certain articles "for home consumption at a cheap rate until we can manufacture them ourselves": merchandise

to be used as stock in trade at the newly established plantation store. Fanny received a letter from him saying that the $580.02 he had spent in purchasing the articles was his mite "in aid of thy good efforts," and required no repayment.

On December 17, 1826, Frances Wright by a deed of trust conveyed the lands of Nashoba and all her personal property in the settlement, which included the slaves, to ten trustees—George Flower, James Richardson, Richeson Whitby, Camilla Wright, General Lafayette, Robert Owen, Robert Dale Owen, William Maclure, Robert Jennings, and Cadwallader Colden—to be held during her absence "in trust for the benefit of the Negro race." The majority of the trustees had no idea that they had been so named. The aging Lafayette, in France, could hardly be active in the matter, and the Owens, father and son, and Maclure, were busy at the time with their own problems at New Harmony.

Jennings, an ex-Unitarian minister, was a controversial character Fanny had met on her first visit to New Harmony; he had attracted Fanny's attention as a possible schoolmaster at Nashoba, but he had been so involved in trying to raise money to support his family somewhere back in the East that nothing had come of that idea. Cadwallader Colden, ex-mayor of New York and a most conservative old gentleman, had once as a lawyer given Fanny some legal help. He did not know until long after the fact that he had been named one of the "board members" of Nashoba Plantation; he was furious, as by that time the "social experiment" was engulfed in scandal. If Colden had, as Fanny once claimed, "secret liberality of opinions," he never admitted it, and he resented the liberty she had taken with his name.

The actual control of Nashoba was placed in the hands of the trustees in residence. They, unfortunately, turned out to be only Richardson, Whitby, and Camilla, because Flower, who had more common sense and sound judgment than all the others, soon withdrew from the undertaking and returned with his wife to Illinois.

Certain provisions of the deed of trust, effecting changes in the character of the Nashoba experiment, reflected the extent to which Robert Owen's ideas had begun to influence Frances Wright. No longer devoted solely to the self-emancipation of slaves, Nashoba would operate as a cooperative community pledged to the social reform of all mankind, somewhat after the manner of New Harmony, but with the Negroes doing the heavier work as they "labored themselves into freedom and colonization." The community would foster Owen's theory that in the "mental liberty" attainable when the fetters of convention and prejudice were broken lay the panacea for all human ills. Like New Harmony, Nashoba would promote radical discussion of every kind, with no social institution free from attack.

Fanny was at New Harmony in the spring of 1827

when the experiment there came to an end and Robert Owen and his son were preparing to leave for England. The 31-year-old "dynamic Miss Wright" had no difficulty in persuading the 25-year-old Robert Dale Owen to change his plans and visit Nashoba with her. After a few days at the settlement, during which Richardson prescribed a sea voyage for Fanny's health, Miss Wright and Mr. Owen departed for New Orleans. There they took passage for Europe, confident that in Paris and London they would "find congenial associates for membership in the Nashoba community."

While in New Orleans, Fanny hired "a certain Mam'selle Lolotte, a free colored woman of mixed blood with a family of nearly white children," to go to Nashoba to teach school (although no school had been established there).

Fanny's confidence that the policies she and Flower had established for the operation of the plantation would continue in her absence was unwarranted. Whitby and Camilla lacked the force and decision necessary to handle the operation and both fell completely under the influence of James Richardson, who was soon in sole control. For some unexplained reason Whitby, whom Fanny had named "overseer," simply left the plantation for a two-months' visit in Ohio.

Richardson as doctor and storekeeper had been invaluable in both routine procedures and emergencies. He and Fanny had been drawn together by their mutual passion for metaphysical discussion and their revolt against various popular prejudices. What one observer called the "streak of cruelty in the depth of James Richardson's nature . . . his capacity for doing harm even to those persons to whom he was most pledged to do good" had not surfaced. It did so after his position as master at Nashoba furnished opportunity for him to verbally release his "hatred of sham."

He spoke out, both to curious visitors and to the customary weekly gatherings of all who were in residence at Nashoba, against the "absurd custom of marriage"; he decried the Christian religion, with its "ridiculous taboos," and he praised atheism as the solution to social problems. "I am an Atheist," he wrote, "and on the diffusion of Atheism rests my only hope of the progress of Universal Emancipation."

It has been pointed out by social historians that Richardson's feelings were not very different from those of the founder of Nashoba. One of Frances Wright's contemporaries wrote about hearing her "lecture against the Bible. She was quite fluent and eloquent, as if it came from the bottom of her heart." But Fanny delivered her opinions publicly only after the failure of Nashoba. She would never have done so at a time when it would have endangered the progress of the community.

Not so James Richardson. As recorder of the *Journal of Nashoba Plantation* after Fanny's departure, he wrote down not only the daily occurrences but the beliefs of the community's operators. Benjamin Lundy, the Baltimore publisher of the lively newspaper *The Genius of Universal Emancipation*, had requested from time to time that Frances Wright send him information about the proceedings at Nashoba, but she had sent him only what she wished published. As soon as she and Owen had left for Europe, Richardson sent Lundy an article covering the experiment's "aims and beliefs," which included excerpts from the *Journal*, with "permission to give every degree of publicity to them." The material arrived during Lundy's absence and was published *in toto*.

The excerpts were similar to this one, dated June 1, 1827:

> Met the slaves at dinner time—Isabel had laid a complaint against Redrick, for coming during the night to her bedroom, uninvited, and endeavoring, without her consent, to take liberties with her person. Our views of the sexual relation had been repeatedly given to the slaves . . . that we consider the proper basis of the sexual intercourse to be the unconstrained and unrestrained choice of *both* parties. Nelly having requested a lock for a door of the room in which she and Isabel sleep, with the view of preventing the future uninvited entrance of *any* man, the lock was refused, as being inconsistent with the doctrine just explained. . . .

Another published entry, dated June 17, 1827, stated:

> Met the slaves—James Richardson informed them that, last night, Mamselle Josephine and he began to live together; and he took this occasion of repeating to them our views on color, and on the sexual relation.

Richardson's article caused a furor in the United States. Even Lundy, in whose newspaper it was first published, protested against certain practices at Nashoba, and one *Genius* correspondent went so far as to label the community "one great brothel." Fanny and Robert Dale Owen were visiting Lafayette at La Grange, his estate in France, when they received the news that "free love, racial equality, and amalgamation of the races are being preached and practiced at Nashoba." Mail poured in, some letters expressing disbelief and requesting explanation, some condemning the Nashoba experiment, and several forwarding newspaper reports which had picked up the "one great brothel" label and were gleefully headlining Frances Wright as "The Priestess of Beelzebub."

Ex-President Madison wrote a prim note to Lafayette, asking the general's opinion of the "late developments" at Nashoba. Lafayette responded with praise of the "intentions and exalted character" of those who were devoting themselves "to the benefit of the human and particularly the coloured race" in the Nashoba experiment, but he skirted the issue of the "late developments."

One result to Nashoba of the bad publicity was the adverse effect it had on the recruiting efforts of Fanny and Owen. Several prominent figures in Paris and London suddenly lost all interest in joining, or even visiting, the "social experiment in the wilds of Tennessee."

Fanny, however, in her letters to Richardson did not question the views he had expressed. She did question his judgment in publishing material "not originally prepared for publication. . . ."

By the time Fanny got back to Nashoba, early in 1828, Richardson and his Josephine had left the settlement for good, and Camilla Wright and Richeson Whitby had been married by a Justice of the Peace! Camilla had started keeping the *Journal* after Richardson's departure and, judging from her long, elaborate, recorded apology for "engaging in a marriage ceremony," which was a "dereliction from one of the fundamental principles frequently advocated in these records," there is little wonder that her marriage was short-lived and unhappy. She went north in bad health and died three years later in Paris.

Frances brought with her to Nashoba an English friend, Mrs. Frances Milton Trollope, whom she had almost convinced that the community was just the place where some of her family should settle. With them were a son (Anthony, later a well-known author) and two daughters of Mrs. Trollope, and Monsieur A. Hervieu, a drawing master Fanny had interested in taking over the operation of the Nashoba school. Frances Trollope was shocked to find "desolation" at Nashoba, and no white people except Whitby and the sick Camilla.

As for Hervieu, according to Mrs. Trollope, "He asked, 'Where is the school?' and was answered, 'It is not yet formed.' I never saw a man in such a rage. He wept with passion and grief," hurriedly drew a sketch of Nashoba at Mrs. Trollope's request, and then departed.

Robert Dale Owen arrived at Nashoba shortly after Fanny. Together they did all they could to bring order and productivity out of the chaos of mismanagement and neglect, but it was a losing battle. One problem was the hostility of the people of Memphis. Only the Winchesters remained friendly.

Owen inserted in the *Journal* a record of Nashoba's production during the entire year of 1827:

```
75 pounds of corn at $2 . . . . . . . . . . . . . . . . . . . .$150.00
Fodder . . . . . . . . . . . . . . . . . . . . . . . . . . . . . . .  25.00
2,964 pounds of cotton at .02 . . . . . . . . . . . . . .  59.28
8 dozen eggs
68 pounds of butter
73 chickens
```

At the end of the year the slaves owed the community $159.79, but Fanny and Owen decided that balance against them should be canceled.

Fanny even tried a "new experiment," which involved openly operating the settlement under the "true freedom advocated by liberal thinkers." This largely followed the principles Richardson had publicized and included frank advocacy of the amalgamation of the races, which Fanny boldly defended in a long letter to the Memphis *Advocate*. Hostility toward Nashoba rose to fever pitch; one Southern gentleman wrote that he "would not be surprised if Miss Wright should, one of these mornings, find her throat cut!" Before that happened, the struggle at Nashoba ended, with Fanny admitting that her great experiment had failed. But, she declared, it had been "good experience" which would help her in the reform work she would continue.

Robert Dale Owen had gone to New Harmony, and from there he wrote Fanny, "I think that for a short time Nashoba can take care of itself." In June 1828 she joined him and together they published the *New Harmony Gazette*, a weekly filled with radical propaganda.

Nashoba was left under the sole management of an overseer, John M. Gilliam, who had Fanny's promise that the failure of her self-emancipation experiment would not keep her from freeing the slaves as soon as a plan for their "convenient removal" could be worked out. Gilliam required little of the slaves and the plantation ran down rapidly.

Fanny returned to Nashoba late in 1829 with the decision to place "the 30-odd former slaves" on the island of Haiti under the protection of President Jean Pierre Boyer, who had agreed to put them first on one of his estates as tenants, and then, if they chose to become land-owners, give them grants of government land. It was a long and difficult undertaking, and it used up much of what remained of Fanny's fortune, but, she said, she would not have considered doing otherwise.

Frances Wright continued to expound her radical ideas until her death at the age of 57 in Cincinnati in 1852, except for a brief period during which she tried marriage and motherhood.

The Nashoba land stood idle for decades, and then was sold by Frances Sylva d'Arusmont, Frances Wright's daughter, who had inherited it; it was finally subdivided. Today, on a highway outside Memphis, a Tennessee Historical Commission marker tells passers-by: "Here in 1827, a Scottish spinster heiress named Frances Wright set up a colony whose aims were the enforcement of cooperative living and other advanced sociological experiments. It failed."

Somehow, those few words about a remarkable and dramatic episode in American history—even though it was a social experiment that did, indeed, fail—do not seem adequate.

*On the night of August 30, 1800, Virginia slaves
crept from cabin and cookhouse
to join an ingenious plot
to take Richmond from
their white
masters.*

Gabriel's Insurrection

Virginius Dabney

This article is edited from a chapter in Virginius Dabney's book, Richmond, *published by Doubleday. Mr. Dabney edited the Richmond* Times-Dispatch *for thirty years and has won a Pulitzer Prize for editorial writing. General accounts of Gabriel's Insurrection appear in* Slavery and Jeffersonian Virginia (1964), *by Robert McColley;* Slave Insurrections in the United States (1938), *by J.C. Carroll; and* Black Resistance before the Civil War (1970), *by William F. Cheek.*

Nat Turner's Insurrection of 1831 in Southampton County, Virginia is widely believed to have been the greatest and most significant slave conspiracy in the history of the United States. Yet a slave plot that occurred nearly a third of a century earlier, centering in the Richmond area and extending throughout much of the commonwealth, was even more alarming. Led by a slave named Gabriel Prosser, it was known as Gabriel's Insurrection. Most Americans have never heard of it.

Thousands of blacks were involved in the Gabriel affair—which took place in 1800—and in the events that followed during the ensuing two years. The large number of participants contrasts with the small band of about sixty slaves who followed Nat Turner. The attempted rebellion under Gabriel was designed to bring about a wholesale massacre of the whites, not only in Richmond but throughout the slave-holding areas of Virginia and beyond. In 1801 and 1802 there were other planned insurrections and intended massacres in half a dozen Virginia counties and several cities, as well as in a comparable number of counties just over the border in North Carolina.

The significance of Gabriel's planned uprising lies not so much in the failure of these efforts to butcher the slave owners as in the fact that so much deep-seated hostility toward them was revealed.

The slaves did not hesitate to risk their lives in these desperate adventures. Even after Gabriel and some thirty-five of his followers had been hanged,

further plots were hatched in both Virginia and North Carolina. All these schemes were thwarted, several of them as a result of timely information furnished by bondsmen loyal to their owners—evidence that there were slaves who felt genuine affection for their masters and mistresses. At the same time, antagonism toward many slaveowners was shown to be great.

Rumors of impending insurrection had been heard off and on since the American Revolution, during which much emphasis had been placed on the "rights of man." Dr. William P. Palmer, a scholarly Richmond physician who was vice president of the Virginia Historical Society noted in a series of articles for the Richmond *Times* in the late 19th century that after the Revolution "a vague idea of future freedom seemed to permeate the entire slave community" of Virginia. He added that "at one time there was scarcely a quarter of the state in which there was not a feeling of insecurity . . . Richmond itself seemed to be quaking with apprehension." Appeals to the governor for arms as protection against possible uprisings were received by the executive from various directions.

The frightful massacres by the slaves of their often cruel French masters in Santo Domingo (now Haiti) beginning in 1791 caused rumblings of revolt in various parts of Virginia and as far south as Louisiana. In July 1793 one hundred thirty-seven square-rigged vessels, loaded with terrified and destitute French refugees and escorted by French warships, arrived at Norfolk. A considerable number moved on to Richmond and other cities.

The manner in which the blacks had taken over in Santo Domingo by liquidating the whites caused apprehension in Virginia and other slave states. As one historian put it: "The fame of Toussaint L'Ouverture had spread to every corner of the Old Dominion. Around the cabin fires of slave-quarters excited Negro voices repeated again the saga of the black hero who had defied Napoleon himself to free his people."

 From *American History Illustrated*, July 1976. From RICHMOND, copyright © 1976 by Virginius Dabney, published by Doubleday & Co., Inc.

Richmonders asked themselves: If the blacks had managed this coup in a Caribbean island, what was to prevent their attempting to do the same in Virginia or elsewhere?

A prominent Richmond citizen wrote Governor "Light Horse Harry" Lee on July 21, 1793 that he had heard two Negroes talking of insurrection. He had gone quietly to a window in the darkness and had listened as one black told another of a plot "to kill the white people . . . between this and the fifteenth of October." The Negro called attention to the manner in which the blacks had slain the whites "in the French island and took it a little while ago."

John Marshall, the future chief justice, wrote Governor Lee in September and enclosed a communication concerning the situation in nearby Powhatan County. The letter stated that about 300 slaves had met shortly before in the county, several Negro foremen "had run away," and the writer believed "the intended rising is true." As for Richmond, Mr. New, captain of the guard, had "a few men and guns" but not a "pound of shot," in case of trouble.

Other reports of a like nature came from the Eastern Shore, from Cumberland, Mathews, Elizabeth City, and Warwick counties, and from Yorktown, Petersburg, and Portsmouth. In the last-named place, four Negroes were found hanging from a cedar tree in the center of town. The Portsmouth citizen who communicated this news to the governor said the men had been executed by other Negroes, which may or may not have been correct.

The authorities were largely indifferent to these reports until an awareness of the realities roused them to action. In many areas the militia were armed and held in readiness, other whites were supplied with weapons, and volunteer guards and patrols watched the movements of the slaves. The presence in Virginia of some 5,000 veterans of the Revolution also had its effect.

"The summer and autumn of 1793 was long remembered as one of the most trying periods of the state's history," Dr. Palmer wrote a century later. The unrest among the slaves occurred despite the fact that after the Revolution their treatment had been markedly better. They were given more freedom to move about, and punishments inflicted on them were less severe.

After the rumblings of 1792 and 1793 were quelled, the slave population in Virginia was almost entirely quiet for seven years. Then, in the midst of this treacherous calm, pent-up resentments exploded in the most far-reaching plot for massacre that has ever occurred within the borders of the United States.

Although hundreds, if not thousands, of blacks were scheming for months to kill the whites, hardly a hint reached the ears of the latter until a few hours before the murders were to begin. The plans were laid in the Richmond area by slaves who were allowed to attend religious gatherings and barbecues, and were free to roam after nightfall.

The leader of this widely ramified plot was a powerfully built, 24-year-old slave named Gabriel Prosser, the property of Thomas H. Prosser, who had a large plantation a few miles north of Richmond in a well-cultivated section of Henrico County. There were various other extensive plantations in this attractive region, owned by such families as the Winstons, Prices, Seldens, Mosbys, Sheppards, Youngs, and Williamsons. Prosser's house, Brookfield, was less than a quarter of a mile from, and on the eastern side of, what was later called Brook Turnpike. It was just beyond the bridge over the Brook, or Brook Run.

Brookfield has vanished and only two residences from that period are standing today in the area. One is Meadow Farm, the Sheppard home near Glen Allen, owned in 1800 by Mosby Sheppard who had an important role in thwarting the uprising. A century and a half later it was occupied by his descendant, Major General Sheppard Crump, Adjutant General of Virginia. The other dwelling surviving from that era is Brook Hill, home at that time of the Williamsons, and situated just across the Brook from the Prosser plantation where Gabriel planned the rebellion. It was lived in for generations by the Stewart family, descendants of the Williamsons. On the death of the last of the Stewart ladies it became the home of their great-nephew, Joseph Bryan III, a current author.

Gabriel was Prosser's most trusted slave. His brothers, Solomon and Martin, also were on the Prosser plantation. The killing was to begin with the Prosser family and spread to nearby plantations, and then to much of the state.

Preparations had been careful and extensive throughout the whole Richmond-Petersburg region, and in Louisa and Caroline counties, the Charlottesville area, and portions of the lower Tidewater. James River watermen spread the word up and down that stream. A post rider whose route extended from Richmond to Amherst County enlisted recruits along the way. He also was active in the vicinity of the state arsenal at Point of Fork. A preacher in Gloucester County was a part of the plot.

All the foregoing participants were black, but there are excellent reasons for believing that at least one Frenchman—and probably two—were important to the enterprise. The slaves steadfastly refused to give the names of these men. However, Gabriel was known to have declared that a Frenchman "who was at the siege of Yorktown" would meet him at the Brook and serve as commander on the first day of the revolt, after which he himself would take over. This Frenchman may well have been Charles Quersey, who had lived at the home of Francis Corbin in Caroline County a few years prior to the Gabriel plot. Gilbert, another slave who was a leader in the intended rebellion, was quoted as stating that Quersey frequently urged him and other blacks to rise and murder the whites. Quersey said he would help them and show them how to fight. Gilbert was informed that Quersey had been active in fomenting the Gabriel uprising.

The feeling was widespread that certain refugees from the island of Santo Domingo, both white and black, had important roles in planting the idea of insurrection in the minds of Virginia slaves. A number of free Negroes also are said to have been active in aiding with the plans.

Gabriel's right-hand man was a huge slave named Jack Bowler, 6 feet 5 inches tall, "straight made and perhaps as strong a man as any in the state." He had long hair, worn in a queue and twisted at the sides. The 28-year-old Bowler sought to lead the rebellion, but when a vote was called for, Gabriel was elected "general" by a large majority.

The slave, Gilbert, a thoughtful man, was determined to go through with the plot, but said he could not bring himself to kill his master and mistress, William Young and his wife, since they had "raised him." He agreed, however, that they should be put to death.

Principal places of rendezvous for the plotters in those hot summer months of 1800 were at Young's Spring in the vicinity of Westbrook, at Prosser's blacksmith shop, and at Half Sink, the Winston plantation on the Chickahominy River.

Antagonism, even hatred, toward the whites was revealed at various parlays. Several slaves said they would have no hesitation in killing white people. One was quoted as saying that he could kill them "as free as eat."

Nothing less than revolution was envisioned. The first blow would fall on Saturday night, August 30. Martin, Gabriel's brother, pointed out that the country was at peace, the soldiers discharged, their "arms all put away," and "there are no patrols in the county." It seemed an ideal time to strike. "I can no longer bear what I have borne," Martin declared.

The number of slaves who had enrolled for the massacre cannot be determined with any exactitude. Gabriel claimed "nearly ten thousand" at one point, but this extravagant figure was apparently used to impress the slaves to whom he was speaking. That number, and many more, were expected to join him when the plot succeeded, but it seems certain that nothing like so many had enlisted at the outset. The secret nature of the plans, the absence of written records, the wide area over which the participating slaves were scattered, all combined to preclude accurate estimates of the number involved. Dr. Palmer held it to be "abundantly proved" that the plot's "ramifications extended over most of the slave-holding parts of the state."

Weapons were fashioned by the slaves in anticipation of the coup. There were frighteningly lethal swords made from scythes, as well as pikes, spears, knives, cross-bows, clubs and bullets, plus stolen muskets and powder. The plan was to seize many additional arms at the capitol in Richmond and others at the magazine, to release the convicts from the penitentiary, commandeer the treasury, and gain control of the city. Gabriel or one of his agents had somehow managed to enter the capitol on Sunday, when it was supposedly closed, and had found where the arms were stored.

Crucial to the success of the conspirators was the ingenious plan to move in the middle of the night and set fire to the wooden buildings along Richmond's waterfront at Rocketts. The whites would rush en masse from Shockoe Hill and Church Hill down to the river to put out the flames. Once they were fully occupied, slaves numbering perhaps a thousand would enter the city from the north. When the whites returned exhausted from fighting the conflagration, the blacks would engage them and wipe them out if possible. The insurrectionists also planned to kidnap Governor James Monroe.

Vague rumors of impending trouble were heard in Richmond during August, but nobody was able to pinpoint them. Dr. James McClurg, Richmond's mayor, ordered temporary patrols, but the whites by and large remained in blissful ignorance of what was impending.

On Saturday, August 30 a strange phenomenon was noted. Whereas on Saturdays the slaves were accustomed to leave the surrounding areas for diversion in Richmond, it was observed that nearly all of them seemed to be going in the opposite direction. They were heading for Gabriel's prearranged meeting place just north of the Brook.

Mosby Sheppard, one of the leading Henrico County planters, was sitting in his counting room on that day when two slaves, Pharoah and Tom, came in and nervously shut the door. They told him that the blacks planned to rise that night and kill him and all the other white people in the area. They would then proceed to Richmond and attempt to seize the city and murder its white population.

Sheppard got this alarming word to Governor Monroe at once. The latter called out all the militiamen who could be reached. He ordered them to guard the capitol, the magazine, and the penitentiary, and to patrol the roads leading into Richmond.

That afternoon dark clouds gathered in the west, thunder rolled, and jagged lightning stabbed the sky. Rain fell in sheets. It was a storm such as Virginia had seldom experienced. Roads were turned into quagmires, streams into roaring cataracts. The brook rose far out of its banks and became a foaming torrent. If the blacks had tried to cross it in either direction, they could not have done so. Disheartened by the rushing water and bottomless mud, and viewing the storm as a heavenly portent, Gabriel postponed the uprising until the next night. By then, the governor's patrols were covering the city and its environs so thoroughly that there was no chance for a successful uprising. The entire plan was abandoned and the leaders fled.

Most of them were rounded up promptly. No efforts were made by the whites to take the law into their own hands, and though some accounts claim the opposite, the men were apparently tried in strict accordance with legal procedures. The Henrico defendants, who constituted the great majority, were furnished with counsel. There was no disorder in any of the counties or cities where the hearings were held.

The dimensions of the plot unfolded as various slaves turned state's evidence against their fellows. There were some conflicts as to details, but the general outlines of the conspiracy were clear. All agreed that the whites in a large area of Henrico were to be massacred, after which the slaves would march on Richmond and carry out their plan for wholesale arson and slaughter. There was some disagreement as to exactly what would happen once Richmond was in the hands of the black insurgents. Gabriel was aware that unless his plan achieved almost instant success, with the whites defeated and the city seized, there would be no mass uprising of the slaves. But if the city surrendered and the whites agreed to free their chattels, Gabriel planned to raise a white flag as a signal to blacks in the countryside to rise and join him. He would also "dine and drink with the merchants of the city." Whites whose lives were spared would "lose an arm," according to one version. Methodists, Quakers, and Frenchmen would not be harmed, according to another. The prominent Mrs. David Meade Randolph, it was further reported, would be made Gabriel's "queen" because of her virtuosity as a cook.

Whatever the precise details of the plot, those who studied the evidence had no doubt as to its main outlines. Governor Monroe spoke positively to the General Assembly on December 5, 1800, four months after the scheme had been smashed:

> It was distinctly seen that it [the conspiracy] embraced most of the slaves in this city and neighborhood, and that the combination extended to several of the adjacent counties, Hanover, Caroline, Louisa, Chesterfield, and to the neighborhood of Point of Fork; and there was good cause to believe that the knowledge of such a project pervaded other parts, if not the whole, of the state.
>
> The probability was if their first effort succeeded, we should see the town in flames, its inhabitants butchered and a scene of horror extending through the country.

The governor also believed that someone other than the slaves had instigated the plot. He deemed it "strange that the slaves should embark in this novel and unexampled enterprise of their own accord." He suspected that they were "prompted to it by others who were invisible."

Most of the slaves who had been active in the plot were arrested within a few days of the conspiracy's collapse, but the two principal leaders, Gabriel and Jack Bowler, remained at large for weeks. Bowler was the first to be apprehended, but Gabriel managed to elude his pursuers until September 24. He hid in the swamps along the James below Richmond until the three-masted schooner *Mary* came down the river. Gabriel hailed the ship and was taken aboard by Captain Richardson Taylor. Isham and Billy, two slaves who were serving in the crew, told Captain Taylor that they believed this was the man for whose capture a $300 reward had been offered. But Taylor, an antislavery Methodist, made no move to arrest his newly acquired passenger. When the ship arrived at Norfolk, Billy managed to get word of his suspicions to an acquaintance, and Gabriel was taken into custody by constables. Captain Taylor evidently had realized the slave's identity, but had been unwilling to turn him in.

Gabriel remained almost totally silent after his capture. He refused to tell Governor Monroe or anyone else details of the plot. He was tried and condemned to death.

While about thirty-five slaves were executed, this was a relatively small number, considering the hundreds if not thousands, who were involved in the conspiracy. Not only so, but at least twelve were acquitted and several more were pardoned. Several pardons were granted on the petition of persons whom the condemned men admitted they had planned to kill. The clemency was on condition that those who received it be sold into slavery in the far South or the West Indies. Owners of executed slaves had to be compensated financially by the state for their loss. This may have tended to hold down the number of convictions.

John Randolph of Roanoke, who witnessed some of the trials, wrote a friend that "the executions have not been so numerous as might under such circumstances have been expected," but added these pregnant words: "The accused have exhibited a spirit which, if it becomes general, must deluge the Southern country in blood. They manifested a sense of their rights and contempt of danger, and a thirst for revenge which portend the most unhappy consequences." A Richmond resident wrote one of the local newspapers that the condemned men "uniformly met death with fortitude."

The hangings were carried out at various points in Henrico, and also in Caroline and elsewhere, but the great majority were held in Richmond at the usual place of execution. This was a small clearing, surrounded by pines and undergrowth, just north of the intersection of today's Fifteenth and Broad streets. Crowds attended the hangings, and the doomed men went to their deaths "amid the singing of hymns and the wails of their fellow-slaves and friends."

Richmonders were profoundly affected by these tragic events, and for years thereafter they avoided passing by the place where the gibbets stood.

Governor Monroe's conduct throughout the crisis was exemplary. He leaned over backward to be fair, and was careful not to issue inflammatory statements. He resisted the appeals of citizens who were inclined to take the law into their own hands among whom Joseph Jones of Petersburg was conspicuous. Jones, one of the leading citizens of Virginia, wrote the governor that "where there is any reason to believe that any person is concerned, they ought immediately to be hanged, quartered and hung upon trees on every road as a terror to the rest." He urged that trials be under martial law, since "if they are tryed by the Civil Law, perhaps there will not be one condemned; it will not do to be too scrupulous now." Monroe paid no attention to such hysterical appeals.

His friend, Thomas Jefferson, was a calming influence throughout. Like Monroe, Jefferson was opposed to slavery. He replied to Monroe's request for advice as follows: "The other states & the world at large will forever condemn us if we indulge a principle of revenge, or go one step beyond absolute necessity. They cannot lose sight of the rights of the two parties, & the object of the unsuccessful one."

Governor Monroe was determined to prevent Gabriel's desperate design from being revived. He ordered a "respectable force" to parade "Daily on the Capitol Square . . . that our strength might be known to the conspirators." The move was temporarily successful, but in his message to the General Assembly four months later the governor said: "What has happened may occur again at any time, with more fatal consequences, unless suitable measures are taken to prevent it."

George Tucker, youthful cousin of the famous St. George Tucker, was so concerned that he published a pamphlet. "The late extraordinary conspiracy . . . has waked those who were asleep," he wrote, and he went on to describe the situation in Virginia as "an eating sore" that was rapidly becoming worse.

The alarm was so general that a permanent guard was stationed at the capitol. It remained there until the Civil War.

Governor Monroe's forebodings of further trouble were soon borne out. Despite the execution of Gabriel and his fellow-conspirators, the fires of revolt had by no means been quenched.

There were definite evidences in late 1801 that all was far from serene in the cities and on the plantations. Monroe described some of the happenings in a message to the General Assembly in January 1802. He stated that "an alarm of a threatened insurrection among the slaves took place lately in Nottoway County which soon reached Petersburg . . . . the publick danger proceeding from this . . . is daily increasing." Monroe expressed the view that "a variety of causes" were responsible, including "the contrast in the condition of the free Negroes and slaves, the growing sentiment of liberty existing in the minds of the latter, and the inadequacy of existing patrol laws."

The interception of a letter from a Negro named Frank Goode to a man named Roling Pointer in Powhatan County caused further apprehension. "We have agreed to begin at Jude's Ferry and put to death every man on both sides of the river to Richmond," said this missive. It declared further that "our traveling friend has got ten thousand in readiness to the night." Nothing of this magnitude developed, but there was decided slave unrest in that area, as well as in much of lower Tidewater and especially in the Southside.

Two slaves were executed in Brunswick County and another in Halifax for involvement in plots to murder the whites. A third was hanged in Hanover County on a similar charge. Two slaves were sentenced to die in Norfolk when a plot to burn the city and massacre the white population was discovered. Governor Monroe granted the men a temporary reprieve, which brought a remonstrance from the mayor and 227 citizens of Norfolk, who signed a petition urging no further clemency. One of the men was hanged soon thereafter, but the other was transported out of the state.

In Williamsburg and Suffolk there was much unrest among the slaves. Across the border in North Carolina there were threats of an uprising. From Hertford County came a letter "to the citizens of Nansemond County," Virginia that "a horrid plot has been discovered amongst the Negroes of this county and the county of Bertie, which has for its object the total destruction of the whites . . . there is not a doubt remaining that such a plan does exist." A letter giving details had been found "in a cotton barrel in one of their cabins."

There were repercussions from these events in the Carolina counties of Camden, Currituck, Martin, Halifax, and Pasquotank. Historians have estimated, on the basis of incomplete newspaper accounts, that at least five slaves were executed in North Carolina, with others lashed, branded, and cropped. This last refers to the cropping of ears. It appears probable that the total number hanged was nearer fifteen than five.

Participation of white men in some of the Virginia slave plots of 1802 is apparently established. Documents from Halifax, Nottoway, and Henrico counties seem to bear out this suspicion. Arthur, a slave on the plantation of William Farrar of Henrico, is supposed

142

to have referred to "eight or ten white men" who were cooperating with him.

A certain amount of hysteria was involved in several of the above-mentioned alarms over the years in both Virginia and North Carolina, and some of the reports of planned insurrections were undoubtedly exaggerated. On the other hand, there was enough evidence of genuine conspiracy in both states, especially Virginia, to cause widespread and justifiable uneasiness.

This uneasiness was aroused only spasmodically in the years after 1802, until the Nat Turner outbreak of 1831. There were specific developments in 1808 and 1809, and Richmond seems to have been the center of these. Lieutenant Governor Alexander McRae informed the military on December 19 of the former year that he had satisfactory evidence, verbal and written, of an impending uprising to take place during the following week. Samuel Pleasants Jr. of Richmond published a circular "respecting insurrection of Negroes." The military was called out in the capital and remained on the alert until January 1. There were other similar warnings in Chesterfield County, as well as in Norfolk and the counties of Nelson and Albemarle.

Richmond was the center of further alarms in 1813. Mayor Robert Greenhow wrote that there were insurrectionary movements among the blacks, at the instigation of the British, with whom we were fighting the War of 1812. The mayor called out patrols and urged removal of the powder magazine to a safer place.

A conspiracy with greater potentialities was formed in 1815 and 1816 in Spotsylvania, Louisa, and Orange counties. It was the work of a weird character named George Boxley, a white man who kept a country store.

Boxley declared that a little white bird had brought him a holy message, directing him to deliver his fellow man from bondage. He persuaded many slaves to join him in a planned revolt, which was to involve an attack on Fredericksburg and then a march on Richmond. As had happened with several previous attempts at insurrection, a loyal slave informed her master of the plot. Many were arrested, including Boxley. He escaped and was never recaptured, but six slaves were hanged. Six others were sentenced to the same fate, but many whites appealed for clemency, and the blacks were reprieved and banished.

All this unrest among the slaves, especially that evidenced in Gabriel's attempted insurrection, caused a marked lessening of efforts by the whites to abolish chattel servitude. Such efforts had been actively pursued in the years following the Revolution, albeit without tangible results. But after 1800 the trend was the other way, and the Virginia Abolition Society ceased to function, as did all other such societies in the South. Not only so, but Virginia passed a law in 1806 providing that any slave who was freed had to leave the state within twelve months. This law was later modified to permit local courts to give certain manumitted slaves permission to remain, but passage of the harsh statute showed the tenor of the time.

A melancholy ballad, set to music, entitled "Gabriel's Defeat," is said to have been composed by a black, following the collapse of Gabriel's epochal rebellion. A reporter claimed to have heard it "at the dances of the whites and in the huts of the slaves." The song soon faded away and has not been heard for many years. Its mournful notes may well have provided an appropriate requiem for the revolt that failed.

The War Against Demon Rum

With alcohol consumption on the rise in 19th-century America, the temperance cause took root.

Robert Maddox

Robert Maddox, of Pennsylvania State University, is a distinguished historian whose article "War In Korea: The Desperate Times" appeared in the July 1978 issue of AHI. For those interested in reading further on the subject of temperance he suggests The Origins of Prohibition *(1925), by John Allen Krout and* Ardent Spirits *(1973), by John Kobler.*

"Good-bye, John Barleycorn," cried the Reverend Billy Sunday to an approving crowd, "You were God's worst enemy. You were Hell's best friend. I hate you with a perfect hatred. I love to hate you." The date was January 16, 1920, the day when the Eighteenth Amendment to the Constitution went into effect. Drys across the nation celebrated happily, while drinkers cursed and contemplated a future without alcohol. Both were premature. John Barleycorn was by no means dead, though he did go underground for more than a decade. But on that first day, those who had worked on behalf of prohibition could congratulate themselves on a victory over what at times had seemed insurmountable odds.

From the first settlements at Jamestown and Plymouth Rock, Americans have brewed, fermented, and distilled everything they could. Though their drinking customs were from Europe, the colonists displayed remarkable ingenuity in devising additional reasons for having a cup of this or a mug of that. Writers of early travel accounts express surprise as to the amount of alcohol the colonists consumed. Everything from the crudest beers and ciders to the most elegant wines ran down American throats in amazing quantities.

During the colonial period there were few attempts to restrict the availability of alcohol, much less to prohibit it entirely. Public houses and taverns abounded. Even in Puritan New England, contrary to popular legend, the people had virtually unrestricted access to spirits of all kinds. Indeed, alcohol was seen as one of God's blessings, to be enjoyed as He intended. When taken in moderation, it was believed to be beneficial for both the mind and the body.

Drunkenness was another matter. Defined in one colony as "drinking with excess to the notable perturbation of any organ of sense or motion," public inebriation was dealt with harshly. The penalties varied from place to place but ranged from fines for first offenders to hard labor or whippings for chronic indulgers. Still, drunkenness was seen as a personal weakness or sin, and the guilty party had no one save himself to blame. Alcohol bore the repsonsibility scarcely more than did the fire which burned down a careless person's home.

A number of people, principally clergymen, spoke out or wrote locally distributed tracts denouncing the intemperate use of intoxicants. This was particularly true after the middle of the 17th century when rum and whiskey replaced the milder ciders and wines. To some it appeared their communities were in danger of drowning in alcohol. It was not until 1784 that any single temperance tract received wide attention. In that year the eminent Philadelphia physician, Dr. Benjamin Rush, published his "An Inquiry into the Effects of Spiritous Liquors on the Human Body and Mind." This pamphlet went through many editions and portions of the work were widely reprinted in newspapers and almanacs across the entire country.

The reception accorded Rush's tract undoubtedly reflected a growing concern about the problems concerning alcoholic consumption. Aside from its popularity, the pamphlet differed from earlier ones in several ways. First of all, as a physician-general in the Continental Army during the Revolution, Rush had had ample opportunity to observe the effects of drinking on soldiers. Thus his words had the backing of what appeared to be scientific examination, rather than mere moral exhortation. Rush denied the popular notions that drinking helped prevent fatigue, protected one against cold, and many other popular myths of the day. Quite the contrary, he argued, in general the consumption of alcohol helped *bring on* diseases of both the mind and of the body. Second, his pamphlet differed from previous ones in that he not only warned against excessive amounts of drink, but claimed that even moderate use over an extended period of time would have harmful effects. It is interesting to note, however, that Rush's

From *American History Illustrated*, May 1979. Reproduced through the courtesy of the National Historical Society, publishers of *American History Illustrated*, P.O. Box 1831, Harrisburg, PA 17105.

broadside was directed against distilled spirits only. Beers and light wines, he thought, *were* beneficial if taken in moderation.

How much effect, if any, Rush's pamphlet had on the consumption of alcohol at the time is uncertain. But it did inspire a number of reformers who took up the temperance cause in the years following. Perhaps the most important, and colorful, of these was the Reverend Lyman Beecher of East Hampton, Long Island. Father of thirteen children (including the famous Henry Ward Beecher and the even more famous Harriet Beecher Stowe), Beecher had been appalled by the drinking habits of his fellow students while at Yale and little he saw thereafter reassured him. Indeed, he came to believe, alcohol posed the greatest threat to the society's physical and spiritual well-being. Though males were the worst offenders, even women consumed impressive amounts. Nor were the clergy immune.

Beecher spoke of attending one convocation where, after a time, the room came to look and smell "like a very active grog shop." Worse yet were the amounts of alcohol given to children of all ages. Fairfax Downey, in a recent article about Beecher, tells the story of a 7-year-old girl who visited her grandmother in Boston. When she learned she would be given no spirits, she angrily notified her parents. "Missy," the grandmother learned, "had been brought up as a lady and must have wine and beer with every meal." Beecher was so concerned about the situation that he claimed he never gave a child even the smallest amount of money without adding the warning "not to drink ardent spirits or any inebriating liquor."

Beecher frequently lectured his congregation on the dangers of drink, and became even more active in the cause after taking the pastorate at Litchfield, Connecticut, in 1811. He was instrumental in forming one of the first temperance groups, the Connecticut Society for the Reformation of Morals. Among other things, the Society printed and distributed large numbers of Dr. Rush's pamphlet. In 1825 Beecher delivered six sermons on the temperance issue which later were published in pamphlet form. Widely reprinted in the years following, the "Six Sermons" according to one scholar, "were as widely read and exerted as great an influence as any other contribution to the literature of the reform."

The Reverend Beecher went beyond earlier temperance leaders in several respects. Like Dr. Rush, he believed that the sustained use of liquor was harmful even if one never actually got drunk. "Let it therefore be engraven upon the heart of every man," he wrote, "that the daily use of ardent spirits, in any form, or in any degree, is intemperance." Beecher's prescription was radical; he called for nothing less than total abstinence from distilled beverages. He differed from Rush on the question of drinking wine as well. Rush had recommended it; Beecher thought it a treacherous way station on the road to stronger potions. Under the influence of Beecher, and others like him, the temperance movement had come a long way from mere denunciations of drunkenness.

The 1830's witnessed a remarkable growth of temperance societies. The United States Temperance Union (later renamed the American Temperance Union) was founded in 1833, though four years passed before it held its first national convention. Despite its increasing popularity, the cause suffered grievously from internal disunity. For some, temperance meant what the word itself meant: moderation. For others, such as Beecher, it had come to mean abstinence. And what was to be included in the list of harmful beverages: distilled spirits only, or wines and beers too? Finally, should temperance (however defined) be promoted exclusively by moral suasion, or should the societies enter the realm of politics? Members of the various groups wrangled over these questions in seemingly endless debates which did little to achieve effectiveness.

A new development took place after 1840. Until this time, the most visible leaders of the cause were opinion leaders such as clergymen, newspaper publishers, and college presidents. Beginning with a group which called itself the Washington Temperance Society, however, a new element came to the fore: reformed drinkers. These were men who, some way or another, had seen the light and who wanted to help save others. Who knew better the evils of drink than those who once had been in its clutches themselves? This "Washington revival," as it became known, spread throughout the country and produced a number of eloquent spokesmen for the temperance cause.

One of the most popular of the reformed drunkards was John H.W. Hawkins. Hawkins began drinking as a young lad while serving as an apprentice to a hatmaker. For more than twenty years he alternated between periods of excessive drinking and relative sobriety. Finally, as his bouts with alcohol became longer and more debilitating he was no longer able to provide for his family and became a public ward. According to his own account, Hawkins was redeemed when members of the Washington Temperance Society in Baltimore convinced him to sign a pledge of total abstinence. Possessing impressive oratorical talents, Hawkins went on to become one of the cause's most sought-after speakers. He later estimated that during his first ten years as a reformer he traveled more than 100,000 miles and delivered some 2,500 lectures.

John Bartholomew Gough was equally in demand. Gough too had begun drinking as a youngster, and his habit cost him job after job and several physical breakdowns. During one, when his seriously ill wife tried to nurse him through, the strain proved too much for her and she died. For some time after her death he rarely drew a sober breath. When finally converted by a friend, Gough pitched himself wholeheartedly into the cause. By several accounts he was a masterful speaker, able to manipulate the emotions of his audience as he wished. He boasted in his autobiography that singlehandedly he accounted for more than 15,000 converts to abstinence.

Things did not always go smoothly for Gough. Early in his career as a reformer he "fell off the wagon" and did so again at the height of his popularity in 1845. The latter occasion touched off quite a furor. While visiting New York City Gough disappeared for almost a week. After a desperate search, friends located him in a bawdy house in one of the seedier sections of the city. He was, it was obvious, recovering from a monumental drinking spree. The incident received wide publicity as the anti-temperance press had a field day at Gough's expense. He claimed innocence. An acquaintance, whose name he could not remember, had treated him to a glass supposedly containing only a soft drink. Having consumed the beverage, Gough claimed, he blanked out and did not know how he ended up where he did. How many people believed Gough's explanation—implying as it did that the liquor interests had conspired to do him in—is unknown, but he remained a popular speaker on the temperance circuit for another five years.

The temperance movement evolved one step more during the pre-Civil War years. It was becoming painfully evident to some that, despite the thousands of pamphlets issued, meetings held, and speeches delivered, the drinking habits of most Americans had not changed. Taverns and saloons prospered, men and women reeled about in the streets, and the gallons of drink consumed rose with each passing year. But what of all the converts? The usual evidence of success consisted of the number of signed pledges individuals or societies collected from "redeemed" individuals, who promised either moderation or total abstinence. There were two problems with this approach. First, even in the most rewarding years no more than a tiny percentage of the adult population signed such promises. Second, how valid were they? To be sure, an effective speaker such as Hawkins or Gough could cause people to struggle in the aisles to sign up. But when emotions cooled, it was obvious, many resumed their old habits. Indeed, as one anti-temperance joke had it, some individuals became so elated by taking the pledge that they could scarcely wait to celebrate by having a few drinks. Increasingly, therefore, temperance advocates sought to strengthen moral persuasion with legal enforcement.

Some reformers had advocated legal controls in the 1830's and 1840's, but they were always in the minority. True conversion could only come through education, the majority had argued, and there was great fear that the purity of the cause would become sullied by entangling it in partisan politics. But this position became increasingly untenable as time wore on; unaided moral suasion simply had not achieved the desired effects. Nor was local-option legislation sufficient. This tactic had been tried in many communities, but serious drinkers could always lay in a

supply from nearby towns or cities. Some reformers, therefore, came to believe that nothing less than statewide prohibition could get the job done. A formidable undertaking to be sure, but the prospects were dazzling.

Neal Dow was a successful businessman who looked the part. He wore expensive clothes, a lace-trimmed vest, and kept the time by a fat gold watch reportedly costing more than $200. He was dynamic, aggressive, and exuded vitality. Although slight of stature, Dow feared no man and used his fists effectively when the occasion demanded it. He was also a devout reformer. Dow devoted his life to the temperance cause and, as early as the 1830's, had become convinced that state prohibition was the only answer.

Born and raised in Portland, Maine, Dow practiced the teachings of his temperance-minded parents with a vengeance. At the age of 18 he joined the volunteer fire department of Portland and before very long somehow convinced the group to stop serving alcohol at its social get-togethers. Later, as captain, he enraged many drinkers by allowing a liquor store to burn to the ground without turning a hose on it. Called before the city's board of alderman to account for his behavior, Dow claimed he had acted as he did to "save" adjacent buildings. On another occasion, when the casks of a wholesale dealer were erupting into fireballs, Dow remarked to an aide that it was a "magnificent sight." Small wonder that the liquor interests in Portland would have preferred another fire chief.

But Dow was after bigger game. Throughout the 1840's he worked tirelessly to bring the temperance issue into the political arena. At first he concentrated on turning Portland dry, but statewide legislation was his real goal. He was careful not to allow prohibition to become a partisan issue; he and his allies (he often used his own employees to do temperance work) supported all those who were "right" on the good cause. At last, in 1851, Dow won what had seemed an impossible victory. With many members of both houses indebted to him politically, he shepherded through the Maine legislature the first general prohibition law in American history. Dow, who was by this time mayor of Portland, prosecuted the new law to the best of his considerable abilities.

The Maine Law of 1851 served as rallying point for prohibitionists in other states. Dubbed "The Napoleon of Temperance," Dow became a hero to drys everywhere as the following song attests:

> Come all ye friends of temperance, and listen to my strain,
> I'll tell you how Old Alchy fares down in the State of Maine.
> There's one Neal Dow, a Portland man, with great and noble soul,
> He framed a law, without a flaw, to banish alcohol.

Unfortunately, as Dow himself admitted privately, alcohol was not "banished" from Maine, but flowed rather freely through illegal channels. Still, it was a step forward, and in the next four years two territories and eleven states enacted similar laws. Many people deserved the credit, if such it be, but no one more than Dow who advised and counseled his fellow reformers across the nation.

The hope that prohibition would become an irresistible tide proved illusory after the mid-1850's. The most important reason was the growing sectional struggle which culminated in the Civil War. As compared to the great issues of slavery and secession, prohibition seemed almost trivial except to the faithful. More than twenty-five years were to pass before another state would adopt prohibition. Equally ominous, though less obvious, was a simple statistic. During those years of temperance victories the per capita consumption of wine, whiskey, and beer *rose* from slightly over four gallons to almost six and one-half. Later prohibitionists ignored or downplayed the grim truth that laws in the books were ineffective so long as a sufficient number of people were willing to disobey them.

By the early 1870's, the temperance movement began stirring again. One of the most significant developments of this era was the role women played. Women always had constituted the backbone of the movement in terms of numbers, but men invariably held the positions of leadership. The first sign of change occurred in what became known as the "Women's Crusade." In communities across the nation groups of women assembled in front of saloons and taverns, vowing to remain until owners agreed to close. For hours, days, and even longer the women sang and prayed, and tried to discourage men from entering. Some places indeed did close, but usually only temporarily and the Crusade dwindled after a few years. Veterans of the Crusade were not about to quit, however, and in 1874 formed the Woman's Christian Temperance Union. This organization would play an important part in the drive for national prohibition.

The dominant force of the WCTU until her death in 1898 was Frances Willard. Born into a family dedicated to reform (her father was a member of the Washington Society), Willard was a zealous temperance advocate from youth. Endowed with a formidable intelligence and incredible energy, she received a good education and was a college faculty member at age 23. In 1871 Willard was named president of Northwestern Female College and, when that institution merged with Northwestern University, became dean of women. She subsequently resigned from this post, however, and thereafter dedicated herself to the temperance movement.

Under Willard the WCTU became the largest, best organized, and most powerful temperance organization in the country. It published tons of pamphlets, provided speakers, lobbied legislators. There were few aspects of society the organization failed to penetrate. Willard herself was a dynamo who, when not giving a speech or chairing a meeting, wrote letters and articles in behalf of the cause. Described by one individual as "organized mother love," the WCTU under Willard reached into every community.

Less important than Willard, though far more colorful, was Carry A. Nation ("carry a nation for temperance," she liked to say). A member of the WCTU, Nation circled in her own orbit and in fact was an embarrassment to some of the members. Having grown up in a family where eccentricity was the norm, Carry at age 19 married a man who drank himself to death very quickly. When the daughter of that union developed chronic illnesses of the cruelest sort, Carry concluded they were the results of her husband's addiction to alcohol and tobacco. These two substances became her lifelong enemies. Though she became involved in temperance work earlier, Carry made the full commitment after claiming to have received a direct communication from God during the summer of 1900.

Nation's methods were similar to the Women Crusaders—with a difference. She too prayed and sang that saloon keepers and their customers would repent. But in addition to her words she hurled bricks and bottles. Her favorite weapon came to be a hatchet which she wielded with remarkable verve for a middle-aged woman. "Smash! Smash! For Jesus' sake, Smash!" was her battle cry as she broke up saloons from Kansas to New York. Though she garnered a great deal of publicity, and caused some other women to take up their own hatchets, Carry's impact was not lasting. Indeed, in later years she became a curiosity, touring county fairs and carnivals. At age 64 she collapsed after a lecture and died a few months later in the summer of 1911.

The temperance movement took on new life with the founding of the Anti-Saloon League of America in 1895.

This temperance cartoon was captioned "Commit him for manslaughter in the greatest degree." ("Harper's Weekly," March 21, 1874)

As was the WCTU, it was misnamed. Just as "temperance" really meant abstinence, the Anti-Saloon League was dedicated to banning all alcohol rather than just that dispensed by saloons. It was an effective ploy because the term "saloon" conjured up all sorts of negative images: drunken fistfights, scarlet women, and husbands drinking away their wages. The word "League" was accurate, however, because the organization was nonsectarian and accepted any individuals or groups dedicated to prohibition.

The League's dedication to a single goal made it more effective than its predecessors. It took on no other reforms, rarely got bogged down in internal disputes, and appealed to everyone interested in the cause. The organization was pragmatic to say the least, and subordinated everything to its goal. "Ethics be hanged," as one of the leaders put it, and they very often were. The League regularly supported politicians who were known drinkers, for instance, provided they could be depended upon to vote dry. In the South, League speakers and pamphlets often played upon racial prejudices by describing in lurid terms how alcohol heightened the lust black males had for white women. Dedicated, unscrupulous as to means, the League was able to bring great pressure to bear upon politicians across the country.

During the first decade of the 20th century, the League, the WCTU, and other organizations, succeeded in getting a number of state legislatures to pass prohibitory laws of various kinds. By 1913 the League went on record as favoring a constitutional amendment to make prohibition nationwide. Bills were introduced in Congress and the issue aroused considerable debate, which spurred the drys on to greater efforts. When the 1914 elections were over, men committed to voting dry had gained in both houses of Congress. During the next session a prohibition bill introduced in the House won by a 197-190 majority. This was a good deal short of the two-thirds necessary to start the amendment process (three-fourths of the states

have to concur), but still constituted a victory of which earlier temperance advocates could not have dreamed.

Would the prohibitionists ultimately have prevailed because of their own efforts? Or would the movement have peaked short of its goal, and then perhaps waned as had earlier temperance crusades? The answer is speculative. For it was the onset of World War I—and more particularly, American entry into the conflict—which assured a prohibitionist victory.

American participation in the war gave the drys two additional weapons which they employed with deadly effect. The first stemmed from the simple fact that various grains and sugar are the main ingredients of beer and liquor. At a time when Americans were being called upon to conserve food for the war effort, how could one defend the diversion of these materials into alcohol? Few politicians were prepared to defend themselves against charges that they were willing to see drunks get their liquor while boys in the trenches went hungry. That most breweries and many distilleries bore Germanic names provided a second boon to the drys. They were able to concoct all sorts of horror stories about German plots to undermine the war effort by encouraging soldiers and civilians to drink their vile products. Such allegations may seem absurd today, but they carried weight during a period when sauerkraut was renamed "victory cabbage."

Under these circumstances the prohibition movement was unstoppable. What was to become the Eighteenth Amendment was adopted by the Senate in August 1917 and by the House in December. The wets thought they had outmaneuvered their opponents when they worked in a seven-year time limit on the ratification process, but they were badly mistaken. The required number of states ratified within thirteen months of submission and the Eighteenth Amendment became law on January 16, 1919, (though it was not to take effect until one year from that date). The "Noble Experiment" would soon begin.

The Trail of Tears

DEE BROWN

Dee Brown, long-time contributor to AHI, *is the author of* Bury My Heart at Wounded Knee. *For more reading on the Trail of Tears, he suggests Grant Forman,* Indians and Pioneers, *and John P. Brown,* Old Frontiers.

In the spring of 1838, Brigadier General Winfield Scott with a regiment of artillery, a regiment of infantry, and six companies of dragoons marched unopposed into the Cherokee country of northern Georgia. On May 10 at New Echota, the capital of what had been one of the greatest Indian nations in eastern America, Scott issued a proclamation:

> The President of the United States sent me with a powerful army to cause you, in obedience to the treaty of 1835, to join that part of your people who are already established in prosperity on the other side of the Mississippi. . . . The emigration must be commenced in haste. . . . The full moon of May is already on the wane, and before another shall have passed away every Cherokee man, woman and child . . . must be in motion to join their brethren in the west. . . . My troops already occupy many positions . . . and thousands and thousands are approaching from every quarter to render resistance and escape alike hopeless. . . . Will you then by resistance compel us to resort to arms? Or will you by flight seek to hide yourselves in mountains and forests and thus oblige us to hunt you down? Remember that in pursuit it may be impossible to avoid conflicts. The blood of the white man or the blood of the red man may be spilt, and if spilt, however accidentally, it may be impossible for the discreet and humane among you, or among us, to prevent a general war and carnage.

For more than a century the Cherokees had been ceding their land, thousands of acres by thousands of acres. They had lost all of Kentucky and much of Tennessee, but after the last treaty of 1819 they still had remaining about 35,000 square miles of forested mountains, clean, swift-running rivers, and fine meadows. In this country which lay across parts of Georgia, North Carolina, and Tennessee they cultivated fields, planted orchards, fenced pastures, and built roads, houses, and towns. Sequoya had invented a syllabary for the Cherokee language so that thousands of his tribesmen quickly learned to read and write. The Cherokees had adopted the white man's way—his clothing, his constitutional form of government, even his religion. But it had all been for nothing. Now these men who had come across the great ocean many years ago wanted all of the Cherokees' land. In exchange for their 35,000 square miles the tribe was to receive five million dollars and another tract of land somewhere in the wilderness beyond the Mississippi River.

This was a crushing blow to a proud people. "They are extremely proud, despising the lower class of Europeans," said Henry Timberlake, who visited them before the Revolutionary War. William Bartram, the botanist, said the Cherokees were not only a handsome people, tall, graceful, and olive-skinned, but "their countenance and actions exhibit an air of magnanimity, superiority and independence."

Ever since the signing of the treaties of 1819, Major General Andrew Jackson, a man they once believed to be their friend, had been urging Cherokees to move beyond the Mississippi. Indians and white settlers, Jackson told them, could never get along together. Even if the government wanted to protect the Cherokees from harassment, he added, it would be unable to do so. "If you cannot protect us in Georgia," a chief retorted, "how can you protect us from similar evils in the West?"

During that period of polite urging, a few hundred Cherokee families did move west, but the tribe remained united and refused to give up any more territory. In fact, the council leaders passed a law forbidding any chief to sell or trade a single acre of Cherokee land on penalty of death.

In 1828, when Andrew Jackson was running for President, he knew that in order to win he must sweep the frontier states. Free land for the land-hungry settlers became Jackson's major policy. He

From AMERICAN HISTORY ILLUSTRATED, June 1972. Reproduced through the courtesy of The National Historical Society, publishers of AMERICAN HISTORY ILLUSTRATED, P. O. Box 1831, Harrisburg, Pa. 17105.

3. NATIONAL CONSOLIDATION AND EXPANSION

President Andrew Jackson dispossessed the Cherokees to gain votes from the land-hungry. By this act he broke faith with the Indians who had been his allies. (Kean Archives)

hammered away at this theme especially hard in Georgia, where waves of settlers from the coastal lowlands were pushing into the highly desirable Cherokee country. He promised the Georgians that if they would help elect him President, he would lend his support to opening up the Cherokee lands for settlement. The Cherokees, of course, were not citizens and could not vote in opposition. To the Cherokees and their friends who protested this promise, Jackson justified his position by saying that the Cherokees had fought on the side of the British during the Revolutionary War. He conveniently forgot that the Cherokees had been his allies during the desperate War of 1812, and had saved the day for him in his decisive victory over the British-backed Creeks at Horseshoe Bend. (One of the Cherokee chiefs who aided Jackson was Junaluska. Said he afterward: "If I had known that Jackson would drive us from our homes I would have killed him that day at the Horseshoe.")

Three weeks after Jackson was elected President, the Georgia legislature passed a law annexing all the Cherokee country within that state's borders. As most of the Cherokee land was in Georgia and three-fourths of the tribe lived there, this meant an end to their independence as a nation. The Georgia legislature also abolished all Cherokee laws and customs and sent surveyors to map out land lots of 160 acres each. The 160-acre lots were to be distributed to white citizens of Georgia through public lotteries.

To add to the pressures on the Cherokees, gold was discovered near Dahlonega in the heart of their country. For many years the Cherokees had concealed the gold deposits, but now the secret was out and a rabble of gold-hungry prospectors descended upon them.

John Ross, the Cherokees' leader, hurried to Washington to protest the Georgia legislature's actions and to plead for justice. In that year Ross was 38 years old; he was well-educated and had been active in Cherokee government matters since he was 19. He was adjutant of the Cherokee regiment that served with Jackson at Horseshoe Bend. His father had been one of a group of Scottish emigrants who settled near the Cherokees and married into the tribe.

In Washington, Ross found sympathizers in Congress, but most of them were anti-Jackson men and the Cherokee case was thus drawn into the whirlpool of politics. When Ross called upon Andrew Jackson to request his aid, the President bluntly told him that "no protection could be afforded the Cherokees" unless they were willing to move west of the Mississippi.

While Ross was vainly seeking help in Washington, alarming messages reached him from Georgia. White citizens of that state were claiming the homes of Cherokees through the land lottery, seizing some of them by force. Joseph Vann, a hard-working half-breed, had carved out an 800-acre plantation at Spring Place and built a fine brick house for his residence. Two men arrived to claim it, dueled for it, and the winner drove Vann and his family into the hills. When John Ross rushed home he found that the same thing had happened to his family. A lottery claimant was living in his beautiful home on the Coosa River, and Ross had to turn north toward Tennessee to find his fleeing wife and children.

During all this turmoil, President Jackson and the governor of Georgia pressed the Cherokee leaders hard in attempts to persuade them to cede all their territory and move to the West. But the chiefs stood firm. Somehow they managed to hold the tribe together, and helped dispossessed families find new homes back in the wilderness areas. John Ross and his family lived in a one-room log cabin across the Tennessee line.

In 1834, the chiefs appealed to Congress with a memorial in which they stated that they would never voluntarily abandon their homeland, but proposed a compromise in which they agreed to cede the state of Georgia a part of their territory provided that they would be protected from invasion in the remainder. Furthermore, at the end of a definite period of years to be fixed by the United States they would be willing to become citizens of the various states in which they resided.

"Cupidity has fastened its eye upon our lands and

150

our homes," they said, "and is seeking by force and by every variety of oppression and wrong to expel us from our lands and our homes and to tear from us all that has become endeared to us. In our distress we have appealed to the judiciary of the United States, where our rights have been solemnly established. We have appealed to the Executive of the United States to protect those rights according to the obligation of treaties and the injunctions of the laws. But this appeal to the Executive has been made in vain."

This new petition to Congress was no more effectual than their appeals to President Jackson. Again they were told that their difficulties could be remedied only by their removal to the west of the Mississippi.

For the first time now, a serious split occurred among the Cherokees. A small group of subchiefs decided that further resistance to the demands of the Georgia and United States governments was futile. It would be better, they believed, to exchange their land and go west rather than risk bloodshed and the possible loss of everything. Leaders of this group were Major Ridge and Elias Boudinot. Ridge had adopted his first name after Andrew Jackson gave him that rank during the War of 1812. Boudinot was Ridge's nephew. Originally known as Buck Watie, he had taken the name of a New England philanthropist who sent him through a mission school in Connecticut. Stand Watie, who later became a Confederate general, was his brother. Upon Boudinot's return from school to Georgia he founded the first tribal newspaper, the *Cherokee Phoenix,* in 1827, but during the turbulence following the Georgia land lotteries he was forced to suspend publication.

And so in February 1835 when John Ross journeyed to Washington to resume his campaign to save the Cherokee nation, a rival delegation headed by Ridge and Boudinot arrived there to seek terms for removal to the West. The pro-removal forces in the government leaped at this opportunity to bypass Ross's authority, and within a few days drafted a preliminary treaty for the Ridge delegation. It was then announced that a council would be held later in the year at New Echota, Georgia, for the purpose of negotiating and agreeing upon final terms.

During the months that followed, bitterness increased between the two Cherokee factions. Ridge's group was a very small minority, but they had the full weight of the United States Government behind them, and threats and inducements were used to force a full attendance at the council which was set for December 22, 1835. Handbills were printed in Cherokee and distributed throughout the nation, informing the Indians that those who did not attend would be counted as assenting to any treaty that might be made.

Cherokee chief Major Ridge led the minority group who came to terms with the government in giving up their land. From painting by unknown artist. (Smithsonian Institution)

During the seven days which followed the opening of the treaty council, fewer than five hundred Cherokees, or about 2 percent of the tribe, came to New Echota to participate in the discussions. Most of the other Cherokees were busy endorsing a petition to be sent to Congress stating their opposition to the treaty. But on December 29, Ridge, Boudinot and their followers signed away all the lands of the great Cherokee nation. Ironically, thirty years earlier Major Ridge had personally executed a Cherokee chief named Doublehead for committing one of the few capital crimes of the tribe. That crime was the signing of a treaty which gave away Cherokee lands.

Charges of bribery by the Ross forces were denied by government officials, but some years afterward it was discovered that the Secretary of War had sent secret agents into the Cherokee country with authority to expend money to bribe chiefs to support the treaty of cession and removal. And certainly the treaty signers were handsomely rewarded. In an era when a dollar would buy many times its worth today, Major Ridge was paid $30,000 and his followers received several thousand dollars each. Ostensibly they were being paid for their improved farmlands, but the amounts were far in excess of contemporary land values.

John Ross meanwhile completed gathering signa-

David Vann, Cherokee chief. (Courtesy Smithsonian Institution)

tures of Cherokees who were opposed to the treaty. Early in the following spring, 1836, he took the petition to Washington. More than three-fourths of the tribe, 15,964, had signed in protest against the treaty.

When the governor of Georgia was informed of the overwhelming vote against the treaty, he replied: "Nineteen-twentieths of the Cherokees are too ignorant and depraved to entitle their opinions to any weight or consideration in such matters."

The Cherokees, however, did have friends in Congress. Representative Davy Crockett of Tennessee denounced the treatment of the Cherokees as unjust, dishonest, and cruel. He admitted that he represented a body of frontier constituents who would like to have the Cherokee lands opened for settlement, and he doubted if a single one of them would second what he was saying. Even though his support of the Cherokees might remove him from public life, he added, he could not do otherwise except at the expense of his honor and conscience. Daniel Webster, Henry Clay, Edward Everett, and other great orators of the Congress also spoke for the Cherokees.

When the treaty came to a final decision in the Senate, it passed by only one vote. On May 23, 1836, President Jackson signed the document. According to its terms, the Cherokees were allowed two years from that day in which to leave their homeland forever.

The few Cherokees who had favored the treaty now began making their final preparations for departure. About three hundred left during that year and then early in 1837 Major Ridge and 465 followers departed by boats for the new land in the West. About 17,000 others, ignoring the treaty, remained steadfast in their homeland with John Ross.

For a while it seemed that Ross might win his long fight, that perhaps the treaty might be declared void. After the Secretary of War, acting under instructions from President Jackson, sent Major William M. Davis to the Cherokee country to expedite removal to the West, Davis submitted a frank report: "That paper called a treaty is no treaty at all," he wrote, "because it is not sanctioned by the great body of the Cherokees and was made without their participation or assent. . . . The Cherokees are a peaceable, harmless people, but you may drive them to desperation, and this treaty cannot be carried into effect except by the strong arm of force."

In September 1836, Brigadier General Dunlap, who had been sent with a brigade of Tennessee volunteers to force the removal, indignantly disbanded his troops after making a strong speech in favor of the Indians: "I would never dishonor the Tennessee arms in a

Inspector General John E. Wool. (KA)

servile service by aiding to carry into execution at the point of the bayonet a treaty made by a lean minority against the will and authority of the Cherokee people."

Even Inspector General John E. Wool, commanding United States troops in the area, was impressed by the united Cherokee resistance, and warned the Secretary of War not to send any civilians who had any part in the making of the treaty back into the Cherokee country. During the summer of 1837, the Secretary of War sent a confidential agent, John Mason, Jr., to observe and report. "Opposition to the treaty is unanimous and irreconcilable," Mason wrote. "They say it cannot bind them because they did not make it; that it was made by a few unauthorized individuals; that the nation is not party to it."

The inexorable machinery of government was already in motion, however, and when the expiration date of the waiting period, May 23, 1838, came near, Winfield Scott was ordered in with his army to force compliance. As already stated, Scott issued his proclamation on May 10. His soldiers were already building thirteen stockaded forts—six in North Carolina, five in Georgia, one in Tennessee, and one in Alabama. At these points the Cherokees would be concentrated to await transportation to the West. Scott then ordered the roundup started, instructing his officers not to fire on the Cherokees except in case of resistance. "If we get possession of the women and children first," he said, "or first capture the men, the other members of the same family will readily come in."

James Mooney, an ethnologist who afterwards talked with Cherokees who endured this ordeal, said that squads of troops moved into the forested mountains to search out every small cabin and make prisoners of all the occupants however or wherever they might be found. "Families at dinner were startled by the sudden gleam of bayonets in the doorway and rose up to be driven with blows and oaths along the weary miles of trail that led to the stockades. Men were seized in their fields or going along the road, women were taken from their spinning wheels and children from their play. In many cases, on turning for one last look as they crossed a ridge, they saw their homes in flames, fired by the lawless rabble that followed on the heels of the soldiers to loot and pillage. So keen were these outlaws on the scent that in some instances they were driving off the cattle and other stock of the Indians almost before the soldiers had fairly started their owners in the other direction."

Long afterward one of the Georgia militiamen who participated in the roundup said: "I fought through the Civil War and have seen men shot to pieces and slaughtered by thousands, but the Cherokee removal was the cruelest work I ever knew."

Knowing that resistance was futile, most of the Cherokees surrendered quietly. Within a month, thousands were enclosed in the stockades. On June 6 at Ross's Landing near the site of present-day Chattanooga, the first of many departures began. Eight hundred Cherokees were forcibly crowded onto a flotilla of six flatboats lashed to the side of a steamboat. After surviving a passage over rough rapids which smashed the sides of the flatboats, they landed at Decatur, Alabama, boarded a railroad train (which was a new and terrifying experience for most of them), and after reaching Tuscumbia were crowded upon a Tennessee River steamboat again.

Throughout June and July similar shipments of several hundred Cherokees were transported by this long water route—north on the Tennessee River to the Ohio and then down the Mississippi and up the Arkansas to their new homeland. A few managed to escape and make their way back to the Cherokee country, but most of them were eventually recaptured. Along the route of travel of this forced migration, the summer was hot and dry. Drinking water and food were often contaminated. First the young children would die, then the older people, and sometimes as many as half the adults were stricken with dysentery and other ailments. On each boat deaths ran as high as five per day. On one of the first boats to reach Little Rock, Arkansas, at least a hundred had died. A compassionate lieutenant who was with the military escort recorded in his diary for August 1: "My blood chills as I write at the remembrance of the scenes I have gone through."

When John Ross and other Cherokee leaders back in the concentration camps learned of the high mortality among those who had gone ahead, they petitioned General Scott to postpone further departures until autumn. Although only three thousand Cherokees had been removed, Scott agreed to wait until the summer drought was broken, or no later than October. The Cherokees in turn agreed to organize and manage the migration themselves. After a lengthy council, they asked and received permission to travel overland in wagons, hoping that by camping along the way they would not suffer as many deaths as occurred among those who had gone on the river boats.

During this waiting period, Scott's soldiers continued their searches for more than a thousand Cherokees known to be still hiding out in the deep wildernesses of the Great Smoky Mountains. These Cherokees had organized themselves under the leadership of a chief named Utsala, and had developed warning systems to prevent captures by the bands of soldiers. Occasionally, however, some of the fugitives were caught and herded back to the nearest stockade.

One of the fugitive families was that of Tsali, an

3. NATIONAL CONSOLIDATION AND EXPANSION

aging Cherokee. With his wife, his brother, three sons and their families, Tsali had built a hideout somewhere on the border between North Carolina and Tennessee. Soldiers surrounded their shelters one day, and the Cherokees surrendered without resistance. As they were being taken back toward Fort Cass (Calhoun, Tennessee) a soldier prodded Tsali's wife sharply with a bayonet, ordering her to walk faster. Angered by the brutality, Tsali grappled with the soldier, tore away his rifle, and bayoneted him to the ground. At the same time, Tsali's brother leaped upon another soldier and bayoneted him. Before the remainder of the military detachment could act, the Cherokees fled, vanishing back into the Smokies where they sought refuge with Chief Utsala. Both bayoneted soldiers died.

Upon learning of the incident, Scott immediately ordered that Tsali must be brought in and punished. Because some of his regiments were being transferred elsewhere for other duties, however, the general realized that his reduced force might be occupied for months in hunting down and capturing the escaped Cherokee. He would have to use guile to accomplish the capture of Tsali.

Scott therefore dispatched a messenger—a white man who had been adopted as a child by the Cherokees —to find Chief Utsala. The messenger was instructed to inform Utsala that if he would surrender Tsali to General Scott, the Army would withdraw from the Smokies and leave the remaining fugitives alone.

When Chief Utsala received the message, he was suspicious of Scott's sincerity, but he considered the general's offer as an opportunity to gain time. Perhaps with the passage of time, the few Cherokees remaining in the Smokies might be forgotten and left alone forever. Utsala put the proposition to Tsali: If he went in and surrendered, he would probably be put to death, but his death might insure the freedom of a thousand fugitive Cherokees.

Tsali did not hesitate. He announced that he would go and surrender to General Scott. To make certain that he was treated well, several members of Tsali's band went with him.

When the Cherokees reached Scott's headquarters, the general ordered Tsali, his brother, and three sons arrested, and then condemned them all to be shot to death. To impress upon the tribe their utter helplessness before the might of the government, Scott selected the firing squad from Cherokee prisoners in one of the stockades. At the last moment, the general spared Tsali's youngest son because he was only a child.

(By this sacrifice, however, Tsali and his family gave the Smoky Mountain Cherokees a chance at survival in their homeland. Time was on their side, as Chief

General Winfield Scott had the unpleasant task of superintending the eviction of the Cherokees from their ancestral homes. (Kean Archives)

Utsala had hoped, and that is why today there is a small Cherokee reservation on the North Carolina slope of the Great Smoky Mountains.)

With the ending of the drought of 1838, John Ross and the 13,000 stockaded Cherokees began preparing for their long overland journey to the West. They assembled several hundred wagons, filled them with blankets, cooking pots, their old people and small children, and moved out in separate contingents along a trail that followed the Hiwassee River. The first party of 1,103 started on October 1.

"At noon all was in readiness for moving," said an observer of the departure. "The teams were stretched out in a line along the road through a heavy forest, groups of persons formed about each wagon. The day was bright and beautiful, but a gloomy thoughtfulness was depicted in the lineaments of every face. In all the bustle of preparation there was a silence and stillness of the voice that betrayed the sadness of the heart. At length the word was given to move on. Going Snake, an aged and respected chief whose head eighty summers had whitened, mounted on his favorite pony and led the way in silence, followed by a number of younger men on horseback. At this very moment a low sound of distant thunder fell upon my ear . . . a voice of divine indignation for the wrong of my poor and unhappy countrymen, driven

154

by brutal power from all they loved and cherished in the land of their fathers to gratify the cravings of avarice. The sun was unclouded—no rain fell—the thunder rolled away and seemed hushed in the distance."

Throughout October, eleven wagon trains departed and then on November 4, the last Cherokee exiles moved out for the West. The overland route for these endless lines of wagons, horsemen, and people on foot ran from the mouth of the Hiwassee in Tennessee across the Cumberland plateau to McMinnville and then north to Nashville where they crossed the Cumberland River. From there they followed an old trail to Hopkinsville, Kentucky, and continued northwestward to the Ohio River, crossing into southern Illinois near the mouth of the Cumberland. Moving straight westward they passed through Jonesboro and crossed the Mississippi at Cape Girardeau, Missouri. Some of the first parties turned southward through Arkansas; the later ones continued westward through Springfield, Missouri, and on to Indian Territory.

A New Englander traveling eastward across Kentucky in November and December met several contingents, each a day apart from the others. "Many of the aged Indians were suffering extremely from the fatigue of the journey," he said, "and several were quite ill. Even aged females, apparently nearly ready to drop into the grave, were traveling with heavy burdens attached to their backs—on the sometimes frozen ground, and sometimes muddy streets, with no covering for the feet except what nature had given them. . . . We learned from the inhabitants on the road where the Indians passed, that they buried fourteen or fifteen at every stopping place, and they make a journey of ten miles per day only on an average. They will not travel on the Sabbath . . . they must stop, and not merely stop—they must worship the Great Spirit, too; for they had divine service on the Sabbath—a camp meeting in truth."

Autumn rains softened the roads, and the hundreds of wagons and horses cut them into morasses, slowing movement to a crawl. To add to their difficulties, tollgate operators overcharged them for passage. Their horses were stolen or seized on pretext of unpaid debts, and they had no recourse to the law. With the coming of cold damp weather, measles and whooping cough became epidemic. Supplies had to be dumped to make room for the sick in the jolting wagons.

By the time the last detachments reached the Mississippi at Cape Girardeau it was January, with the river running full of ice so that several thousand had to wait on the east bank almost a month before the channel cleared. James Mooney, who later heard the story from survivors, said that "the lapse of over half

The Cherokee alphabet, a syllabary invented by Sequoyah. From lithograph prepared for American Board of Foreign Missions. (Reproduced courtesy of Smithsonian Institution)

a century had not sufficed to wipe out the memory of the miseries of that halt beside the frozen river, with hundreds of sick and dying penned up in wagons or stretched upon the ground, with only a blanket overhead to keep out the January blast."

Meanwhile the parties that left early in October were beginning to reach Indian Territory. (The first arrived on January 4, 1839.) Each group had lost from thirty to forty members by death. The later detachments suffered much heavier losses, especially toward the end of their journey. Among the victims was the wife of John Ross.

Not until March 1839 did the last of the Cherokees reach their new home in the West. Counts were made of the survivors and balanced against the counts made at the beginning of the removal. As well as could be estimated, the Cherokees had lost about four thousand by deaths—or one out of every four members of the tribe—most of the deaths brought about as the direct result of the enforced removal. From that day to this the Cherokees remember it as "the trail where they cried," or the Trail of Tears.

Our Forefathers in Hot Pursuit of the Good Life

They built their own communes, only to learn that
transcendental ideals and prayer and even
group sex do not suffice to weld a community together

E. M. HALLIDAY

Looking back on his sojourn at Brook Farm, the famous but short-lived transcendentalist community near Boston, Nathaniel Hawthorne felt nostalgia. "More and more," he said, "I feel we struck upon what ought to be a truth. Posterity may dig it up and profit by it."

Posterity has been digging, lately, for whatever truth was buried at Brook Farm and at the scores of other intentionally different communities, set apart from the ordinary culture, that our ancestors hopefully began. One general truth is easily apparent: the democratic society established by the Declaration of Independence and the Constitution was the most open in history, the most hospitable to social innovation running against or across the common grain. What profit, in the present climate of energetic social experiment, can be derived from a look at a few of the more notable efforts of the past?

One thing that quickly attracts notice is that most of the earlier communal experiments were of pitifully short duration, despite the ardor with which they were launched. It is an astonishing fact that the hands-down winner, as far as longevity goes, is a society of dedicated celibates. The Shakers were established in America almost simultaneously with the Declaration of Independence; they throve mightily through the middle of the nineteenth century, and endured into the twentieth. There are very few Shakers left today, total celibacy not appearing to have a strong appeal for modern youth, but their bicentennial, however feeble, is upon them.

Like most communal groups among our forefathers, the Shakers began as a dissenting religious sect. Officially called the United Society of Believers in Christ's Second Appearing, they had an unusual view of that great event, viz., that Christ had *already* appeared a second time, not as a man, but (Gloria Steinem please note) as a woman. Her earthly name was Ann Lee, and she had been born and brought up in the dismal slums of Manchester, England, in the 1730's. She married young and hated it; her aversion was reinforced by a vision in which the Lord, she said, revealed to her the exact identity of Adam and Eve's sin (it was, naturally, sexual intercourse), and furthermore explained that God was bisexual and that she, Ann, was the female incarnation as Jesus had been the male. A small but growing number of disciples believed her, and in 1774, as Mother Ann, she led them to America. Since they were given, in their devotions, to a great deal of writhing, quivering, and general jumping about, they were known to outsiders as Shakers; they didn't seem to mind.

Mother Ann died in 1784, but her truth went marching on. Under the adroit management of one Joseph Meacham, Shaker settlements, or "families," were planted in various fertile spots in upper New York State and in New England. They were communistic, all property being ceded to the society when new members were taken in; and despite God's bisexuality, they were elaborately celibate. Men and women not only slept separately but ate separately and worked separately. They carefully avoided chance physical contact: it was forbidden, for example, for "brothers" and "sisters" to pass each other on a staircase. And they were constantly under surveillance: the family was run by appointed elders who made it their business to know exactly where each individual was at all times.

This sexual austerity projected itself onto their whole life style, which was almost ostentatiously spare in dress, furniture, and décor. Caring nothing for beauty, they produced chairs, tables, and utensils so absolutely functional as to achieve beauty in what now seems a very contemporary mode. And since they had to support themselves, they learned to manufacture things like furniture, brooms, mops, and pails with such honest quality that they were never in want of a market. On top of this the Shakers were produce farmers par excellence: their fruits, vegetables, and seeds were usually the best obtainable for miles around.

 Copyright© 1973. American Heritage Publishing Company, Inc. Reprinted by permission from *Horizon*, Autumn 1973.

For amusement, somewhat surprisingly, the Shakers went in for dancing. The music, to be sure, consisted entirely of hymns celebrating the Shaker way and, sometimes, disparaging the rest of the world, as in this rather vitriolic ex-

ing. The Shakers were also indefatigable spiritualists, and many of them received remarkable and cheering messages from the other world, as, for instance, that George Washington and most of the other Founding Fathers

their integrity. It was these attributes, as well as the assurance of plain but ample fare and a peaceful if somewhat placid existence, that attracted some six thousand adherents to Shakerism when it was at its height in mid-century.

George Ripley

THE TRANSCENDENTAL FARM: Hoping to combine intellectual pursuits with simple living in a classless society, George Ripley and a group of friends set up housekeeping at Brook Farm in 1841. But his ideal community, where all would share the joys of learning and honest toil, floundered after 1846, destroyed by a disastrous fire and a loss of faith among the participants.

Houses at Brook Farm in an early heliotype print

BETTMANN ARCHIVE

ample designed to scotch any lingering fondness for normal family life:

Of all the relations that ever I see
My old fleshly kindred are furthest from me.
So bad and so ugly, so hateful they feel,
To see them and hate them increases my zeal.

Musical instruments were frowned upon, but the Shakers became adept at rhythmical singing and chanting, and on occasion they would amuse themselves by pretending to be a large brass band, each person imitating, with appropriate gestures, the playing of a trombone, trumpet, French horn, or whatever instrument struck the fancy.

Shaker dancing was highly ritualized, and it need hardly be said that there was no body contact, and no conventionalized flirting as in square dancing, reels, or minuets. The company would form concentric circles or squares, the men together and the women together, and perform various gyrations with a quick kind of shuffling step, the rhythm being kept by hand clapping and sing-

had, after thinking it over, taken up Shakerism; or that an entire tribe of Indians, long since deceased, had applied for admission to the Shaker fold.

It was and is easy to make fun of the Shakers, and some critics found their *modus vivendi* dismally unattractive besides. Charles Dickens came, saw, and reported, in 1842: "We walked into a grim room where several grim hats were hanging on grim pegs, and the time was grimly told by a grim clock. . . . Ranged against the wall were six or eight stiff highbacked chairs, and they partook so strongly of the general grimness, that one would much rather have sat on the floor than incurred the slightest obligation to any of them." Yet, on the whole, Mother Ann's heaven on earth earned respect and even admiration from nineteenth-century intellectuals and reformers. They were impressed with the Shakers' pacifism, their relatively equal treatment of men and women, their opposition to slavery, their industry, their steadfast orderliness and cleanliness,

The Shakers were of lowly origin; the Owenites started at the opposite end of the social and economic spectrum. A British prototype of the self-made industrial tycoon, Robert Owen was the proprietor of huge cotton mills in New Lanark, Scotland, before he was thirty. Rich but kindly, he introduced sensational reforms for his workers, refusing to hire children under ten years old and cutting the workday back to ten and three-quarters hours. But he dreamed of better things—a paradise where private property and greed would be abolished, where nobody would work more than three hours a day, and where everyone would be healthy, well-educated, and blissfully happy. Since he was, however, a professed agnostic as well as a socialist, he had difficulty getting philanthropists and statesmen to support his schemes, and in the end he had to finance them himself.

A wonderful chance came in 1825. George Rapp, the spiritual and temporal führer of a group of several hundred German separatists, offered for sale the extremely neat and well-developed communal village that he and his sect had built at Harmonie, Indiana. One reason evidently—and Owen might well have looked into this —was success rather than failure: Rapp felt that his people were getting too fat and prosperous on the Wabash and that a move back to the wilds of Pennsylvania (where they had originally settled) might revive the Rappites' pioneer hardihood. Owen was thus able to purchase, for what even then seemed a bargain price—$135,000—an entire town, complete with twenty thousand acres of good land, large orchards, houses, mills, craft shops, community centers, and a hospital.

Not that Owen was satisfied with the physical layout at Harmonie, or New Harmony, as he soon renamed it. He was one of those visionaries who loved to draw up precise diagrams for future establishments; in fact, after his much-trumpeted arrival in America he traveled around with a six-foot model of the community as he planned to rebuild it. Everything was to be perfectly arranged inside a 1,000-foot hollow square: living quarters for the married, unmarried, and children; a school system complete from nursery to university; lecture halls and a library; scientific laboratories and machine shops; ballrooms and a gymnasium. All was balance and enlightened symmetry.

In the meantime, Owen thought, the actual as opposed to the potential New Harmony was a decent "half-way house," and he invited anyone interested to come and take part. They arrived in large numbers—about a thousand by the end of 1825—and although a high percentage of them were people of refinement, capable of brilliant conversation, elegant entertainments, and endless theorizing, few seemed to have any notion of how (for instance) to plough a field, repair an outhouse, or mix concrete. Owen sanguinely agreed to pay them each $1.50 a week out of his own pocket, no matter what they did,

while he went off to Europe to try to interest more intellectuals in his great project.

He returned early in 1826, followed by a collection of savants so brilliant that it was ever afterward known as "the Boatload of Knowledge." Owen then proposed a new constitution that would put New Harmony, economically, on a true communistic basis. "It found favour," wrote his son Robert Dale Owen subsequently and bitterly, "with that heterogeneous collection of radicals, enthusiastic devotees to principle, honest latitudinarians and lazy theorists, with a sprinkling of unprincipled sharpers thrown in." Nevertheless, there were some dissenters, and with characteristic generosity Owen gave them land a couple of miles out of town where they could set up their own version of the new world order. Only a few weeks later there was another split: this time the separatists objected not to Owen's agnosticism, as the first group had, but to his teetotalism, for there was not a single tavern in New Harmony. Again the founder was agreeable, and the drinking crowd set up housekeeping in a little settlement christened Feiba Peveli. (This was in accordance with a system devised by an Englishman named Stedman Whitwell, who assigned letters of the alphabet to degrees of longitude and latitude so that the name of a town would indicate its geographic location. The results were somewhat Gulliverian: New York, for instance, was to be renamed Otke Notive and London would be called Lafa Vovutu.)

On the Fourth of July, 1826, with New Harmony sliding further and further off key, Owen stubbornly proclaimed the Declaration of Mental Independence, the gist of which was that the new era was still dawning. Less than a year later he was beginning to sell off land in New Harmony to private parties who wished to remain, and the experiment was finished. Owen, however, never abandoned the socialist struggle: he died not only with his boots on, at

the age of eighty-seven (in 1858), but in the middle of a lecture he was giving on "The Human Race Governed Without Punishment."

Notwithstanding the failure of New Harmony, the venture excited enormous interest among America's idealists, including the Boston intellectuals who, following Emerson's lead, called themselves transcendentalists. George Ripley was one of these, a Unitarian minister grown impatient with even that liberal church. He resigned his pulpit early in 1841, made a down payment on an isolated farm a few miles outside of Boston, and managed to lure a handful of friends and acquaintances to join him and his wife in a try at cooperative living.

Brook Farm, as it soon became known, was founded on less radical principles than New Harmony or the Shaker communities. It was not communistic but gently capitalistic, a stock company in which any interested person could buy shares. Its aims, however, were no less idealistic. As Ripley wrote Emerson:

Our objects . . . are to insure a more natural union between intellectual and manual labor than now exists; to combine the thinker and the worker, as far as possible, in the same individual ; . . . to do away the necessity of menial services, by opening the benefits of education and the profits of labor to all; and thus to prepare a society of liberal, intelligent, and cultivated persons, whose relations with each other would permit a more simple and wholesome life, than can be led amidst the pressure of our competitive institutions.

Emerson was too much the individualist to do more than wish the Brook Farmers well, but Hawthorne enthusiastically joined the company in the spring of 1841 and at first enjoyed such bizarre experiences as milking cows—one of them, he wrote his fiancée, was "a transcendental heifer, belonging to Miss Margaret Fuller. . . . very fractious . . . apt to kick over the milk pail. Thou knowest best, whether, in these traits of character, she resembles her

CULVER

John Humphrey Noyes

mistress." Five months later he was writing in a less facetious mood: "Oh, belovedest [sic], labor is the curse of this world, and nobody can meddle with it, without becoming proportionably brutified." He had discovered that after pitching hay or hoeing potatoes all day he was far too tired to think or write, and he left Brook Farm in the fall. It was the epitome of one problem that the community was never quite able to overcome.

Still, things went well for a while. The population gradually rose to several score, and since almost everybody was well educated and of genteel and liberal background, the atmosphere most of the time was like that of a pleasant church supper. There were few shirkers: everybody worked hard and tried to make up for lack of farming skills by persistence and energy. If the diet was somewhat wanting in richness and variety—there was heavy reliance on milk and homemade brown bread—it was certainly healthful, and conversation at meals was often sparkling. There was entertainment as well: musicals and charades and spelling bees; and there were frequent talks by eminent figures from Boston and New York who came to visit. Margaret Fuller declined to follow her heifer and take up residence, but she did offer the members the benefit of her insights into such subjects as "Education, in its largest sense" (she

was annoyed by what she called "a good deal of the *sans-culotte* tendency" in her audience, "throwing themselves on the floor, yawning, and going out when they had heard enough"). The children of Brook Farm liked the place: there were lots of hikes and picnics in the surrounding woods; there was a first-rate toboggan slide in the winter; their parents left them alone for a good part of the day—if, indeed, their parents were there at all, for many sent their offspring to Brook Farm to attend the Ripleys' school, which soon worked up a reputation as the most progressive one anywhere near Boston.

But trouble was brewing. Despite the outstanding success of the school, and the moderate success of the farm itself, the financial status of the community was weak. It was felt that some sort of light industry might save matters, especially if combined with the principles of Charles Fourier—a somewhat mad Frenchman who had died in 1837 without ever seeing the fulfillment of his wildly imaginative schemes.

Fourier believed in social physics, of which the laws of attraction and repulsion were the universal clue. This led him to some interesting views on social organization. Though a bachelor, he had noticed that children seem to enjoy getting dirty, and this suggested a marvelous solution to the problem of unpleasant work like garbage collection: let the kids do it. This was supposed to be an example of the principle of "attractive industry," the essence of which was that people ought to work at what they enjoy most.

"Attractive industry" so enchanted an American named Albert Brisbane that after studying at the feet of the master, he came home and wrote a book called *The Social Destiny of Man* (1840), which in turn enchanted Horace Greeley, the famous editor of the New York *Tribune*. Brisbane and Greeley persuaded George Ripley that Brook Farm should become a Fourierist phalanx (as the Frenchman's basic social unit was called). The pleasant life of the

farm began to wilt under a storm of lectures and demonstrations of Fourierist principles, and when, in 1846, a brand-new central building, intended to allow a great expansion of the community, burned to the ground, it meant, in effect, the end of Brook Farm. There were many broken hearts. "It was like the apple blossoms dropping from the trees," wrote an old man, many years later, who had spent his boyhood there.

John Humphrey Noyes, the founding father of Oneida Community, always acknowledged that it "received a great impulse from Brook Farm. . . . In the fall of 1847, when Brook Farm was breaking up, the Putney Community was also breaking up, but in the agonies not of death, but of birth."

The Putney Community was Noyes's first attempt at an alternative way of living and was the forerunner of Oneida. The son of a Vermont congressman, Noyes had a respectable New England education: Dartmouth, followed by the Andover and Yale divinity schools. But he had more. He had a searching mind, a wonderful sense of pragmatism, and truly amazing nerve. His conversion to fundamentalist Christianity was common enough for his time, but his independent interpretation of the Bible was enough to make any ordinary fundamentalist hysterical. Pondering the Gospel according to St. John one day in 1833, he received an epiphany: the Second Coming of Christ had *already taken place*—and not in the shape of Mother Ann Lee, either. It had occurred in the year A.D. 70; the Kingdom of Heaven was at hand, and the perfection of man was possible here and now. Noyes set out to achieve it.

He was given a boost along the way by the Yale Divinity School, which revoked his preaching license. Undismayed, he started a little periodical called *The Witness* in 1837, and in one of the first issues published his views on love and marriage. It was a breathtaking statement. Queen Victoria had barely ascended her throne, and here was Noyes explaining to the world:

3. NATIONAL CONSOLIDATION AND EXPANSION

When the will of God is done on earth as it is in heaven, *there will be no marriage.* The marriage supper of the Lamb is a feast at which *every dish is free to every guest.* Exclusiveness, jealousy, quarreling, have no place there, for the same reason as that which forbids the guests at a thanksgiving dinner to claim each his separate dish, and quarrel with the rest for his rights. In a holy community, there is no more reason why sexual intercourse should be restrained by law, than why eating and drinking should be—and there is as little occasion for shame in the one case as in the other. . . .

This stunned most readers at the time, but it favorably impressed a dish named Harriet Holton, a granddaughter of a former lieutenant governor of Vermont, and she sent Noyes eighty dollars to carry on his work. He looked her up, fell in love, and married her in 1838 with the understanding that "We can enter into no engagement with each other which shall limit the range of our affections. . ."

The every-dish-is-free-to-every-guest theory remained a theory for eight years, but during that time Noyes learned something else that made the whole thing a lot more practicable. Harriet had four miscarriages out of five pregnancies, and suffered miserably each time. Determined not to inflict this upon her again, Noyes practiced and mastered a technique of intercourse that he called male continence. What it amounted to was the development of tremendous control, so that he could make love indefinitely without ever reaching orgasm. Not only, he wrote later, did his wife find this "very satisfactory," but his own enjoyment was greatly increased. The method allowed "all and more than all the ordinary freedom of love (since the crisis always interrupts the romance)," and it avoided "the drain of life on the part of the man. . . . the exhaustion which follows."

With this invention, things moved fast. Noyes had set up a small communal group, the Putney Community, whose dozen or so members shared ev-

erything *except* sex. Now they began to share that, too, the males all practicing "continence" under Noyes's tutorship. Unfortunately, the rest of Putney became aware of this amatory round robin, and Noyes was promptly charged with adultery. While sturdily denying that he had done anything wrong, he decided it was time to establish the Kingdom of Heaven elsewhere. With some money Harriet had inherited, the group bought forty good acres on Oneida Creek, New York, almost exactly in the middle of the state. And there, in 1848, they began to build the Oneida Community.

Oneida grew rapidly and prospered. Noyes was careful about who was allowed to join the community, and he and his lieutenants were shrewd about the means of making Oneida self-supporting. By 1851 they had more than two hundred members, and all of the adults were thoroughly capable workers. They sold their canned fruits and vegetables to the world "outside"; they manufactured straw hats, luggage, and the best steel traps ever seen in the Northeast. Their internal economy was strictly communistic: everyone shared and shared alike in food, shelter, clothing, education, and entertainment.

And love. Far from retreating in his advocacy of multiple love affairs for all, Noyes put the scheme on a regular basis. Boys were trained in it—by women who had passed menopause, for obvious reasons—as soon as they reached fourteen; so were girls. Nobody was forced into unwanted relationships, but Noyes recommended wide circulation for the sake of community coherence. It was all part of their religion, which he called Bible Communism, and it was permissible only for the pure in heart: "Holiness must go before free love." It had practical advantages for the community, too: during the first two decades, when Oneida was struggling to get on its feet, there were very few births. Later, when it was decided that the time had come to raise a new generation of Oneidans, mates

were chosen deliberately in order to form "scientific combinations," with Noyes doing most of the choosing. (He chose himself as the appropriate male in nine cases, although he was by now in his sixties.) This extraordinary experiment in eugenics resulted in fifty-four children, none of them defective and most of them extremely bright.

It was because of alarming innovations like this that Thomas Wentworth Higginson, the impeccable Boston reformer, visited Oneida in 1870. He expected to be appalled, since "some of their main principles seem to me false, and others actually repulsive." His reaction, published in *The Woman's Journal,* was quite otherwise: "I am bound to say, as an honest reporter, that I looked in vain for the visible signs of either . . . suffering or . . . sin. The Community makes an impression utterly unlike that left by the pallid joylessness of the Shakers, or the stupid sensualism which impressed me in the few Mormon households I have seen. . . . The fact that the children of the Community hardly ever wish to leave it; that the young men whom they send to Yale College, and the young women whom they send for musical instruction to New York, always return eagerly and devote their lives to the Community: this proves a good deal. . . ."

Residents of the surrounding towns and cities, although they came to Oneida to gawk on visitors' days and no doubt did a great deal of tsk-tsking, were remarkably tolerant of all this until the early 1870's. Then, a professor at nearby Hamilton College began a campaign of persecution by denunciation. He built up a following, and in 1879 Noyes, at the age of sixty-eight, moved to Canada to avoid legal action. He tried to direct the affairs of Oneida by remote control, but it worked badly. Community sex was given up, and many Oneidans picked themselves mates and married, thus legitimizing most of the children. Nor could economic communism be maintained: the Oneida factories were transformed into a joint-stock company that eventually became famous for its production of silverware. Noyes died, still an exile, in 1886. The most revolutionary and promising alternative community of the nineteenth century had, after all, come to a rather early end.

Commenting on the brief existence of a California commune of World War I vintage, that perennial utopian Aldous Huxley observed:

Except in a purely negative way, the history of Llano is sadly uninstructive. All that it teaches is a series of don'ts. Don't pin your faith on a water supply which, for half the time, isn't there. Don't settle a thousand people on territory which cannot possibly support more than a hundred. Don't admit to your fellowship every Tom, Dick, and Harry who may present himself. Don't imagine that a miscellaneous group can live together, in closest physical proximity, without rules, without shared beliefs, without private and public "spiritual exercises" and, without a magnetic leader.

Generalized somewhat, that list of "don'ts" could be used to explain the failure of a number of the nineteenth-century communal efforts, just as it could be used as a caveat for intentional communities today. But Huxley had this, also, to say: ". . . for anyone who is interested in human beings and their so largely unrealized potentialities, even the silliest experiment has value. . . . And many of the recorded experiments were far from silly. Well planned and carried out with skill and intelligence, some of them have contributed significantly to our knowledge of that most difficult and most important of all the arts—the art of living together in harmony and with benefit for all concerned."

Travels with Tocqueville: Traces of his America persist

Joseph Barry

Mr. Barry has written Passions and Politics *and also* SMITHSONIAN *articles. Paul Hogarth illustrated our* Royal Dublin Society *story in August 1971.*

A young Frenchman lost his heart to the young republic of 1830. Today his notes elicit recognition from our matronly nation

As political computers and campaigners calculate the various doomsdays facing us, it is the best of times for a fresh look at a famous young traveler in 19th-century America. He described his experiences, discoveries, hopes, fears and predictions. To wit:

"For a long while before the appointed time has come, the election becomes the important and, so to speak, the all-engrossing topic of discussion. Factional ardor is redoubled. . . . [The President] no longer governs for the interest of the state, but for that of his re-election. . . . The citizens are divided into hostile camps . . . the election is the daily theme of the press, the subject of private conversation, the end of every thought and every action. . . ."

Thus Alexis de Tocqueville speaks directly to us in his classic *Democracy in America,* though it was published for the French in 1835. Repeatedly this young aristocrat, who was not 26 when he landed on our shores and who left before he was 27, addresses our condition, our minds, our admiration. Above all, for those who think this the worst of times, Tocqueville's words of optimism and hope are worth recalling:

". . . The great advantage of the Americans consists in their being able to commit faults which they may afterwards repair." And later, ". . . Perhaps, after all it was God's wish to spread a mediocre happiness

throughout mankind, and not to concentrate a great amount of happiness on a few and bring a small number near to perfection."

He was small, dignified and reserved, delicate of feature and body. He was Alexis Charles Henri Clérel de Tocqueville, born on July 29, 1805. His father was a member of the minor nobility of Normandy. His grandfather had been guillotined during the Revolution, his father and mother imprisoned. When he was born, Napoleon was mobilizing for victory at Austerlitz. After Waterloo, his father served the restored Bourbon dynasty as departmental prefect.

Alexis studied at the lycée in Metz. He discovered the agnostic works of the *philosophes* in his father's library and at 15 his Catholic faith was shaken, though not shattered. He remained religious, if without dogma. He studied law in Paris and at 21 began a career as *juge auditeur* in the court at Versailles, where his father was now a count. He had the independence of lifetime doubt and met a like-minded young nobleman and fellow magistrate of similarly liberal principles, Gustave de Beaumont.

Together the young Frenchmen attended François Guizot's lectures, listening to the future statesman expound on the march of the middle class to ascendent power. Clearly for them the Bourbon monarchy of Charles X had no program for a modern France and when the Revolution of 1830 occurred, they both accepted, if they did not welcome, his Orleanist successor, Louis Philippe, the "bourgeois monarch." "At war with myself" (his father and class were Bourbonist), Tocqueville took the oath of allegiance, as did Beaumont, but was suspected, quite rightly, of deep reservations, and he was demoted in the magistracy.

The two petitioned to depart for America to study prison reforms. "I have long had the greatest desire to visit North America," Tocqueville explained in a letter. "I shall go see there what a great republic is like; my only fear is lest, during that time, they establish one in France."

Permission was granted. The young Frenchmen collected letters of introduction from Tocqueville's illustrious cousin, Vicomte de Chateaubriand, who had

 Copyright 1972 from *SMITHSONIAN*, Smithsonian Institution, November 1972.

Drawings by Paul Hogarth

Alexis de Tocqueville: ". . . small, dignified and reserved, delicate of feature and body."

been to America, and solicited others from Beaumont's even more famous cousin, the Marquis de Lafayette. They packed. Tocqueville's baggage included two hats (one silk), five pairs of boots, a fowling piece and, one might declare, a French genius for analysis, synthesis and generalization. Beaumont took along two sketchbooks, his flute and a gun as well.

They sailed on the *Havre* on April 2, 1831, and at sea Tocqueville practiced his English with a pretty American girl. They landed May 9 at Newport and noted four or five banks clustered in the small town.

Truly, Americans appeared a commercial people. The big steamer that took them to New York was their first impression of America's magnitude and power. Excitement had allowed them little sleep. "No sooner do you set foot upon American ground than you are stunned by a kind of tumult," he wrote later in *Democracy*.

They read in the New York *Mercantile Advertiser* that "two magistrates"—one of them Tocqueville—had been sent by their French government "to examine the various prisons in our country, and make a report on their return to France." The story was picked up in papers from Boston to Baltimore, and beyond. "Our arrival in America," Beaumont wrote home, "has *created a sensation. . . .*" It was the America of Andrew Jackson's first term, a young raw republic of 13 million (less than half the population of France) with its 24 states almost entirely east of the Mississippi. William Lloyd Garrison had just begun his abolition crusade, temperance societies were springing into being, and James Fenimore Cooper was Europe's conception of an American writer.

On May 13, the governor of New York received the French visitors in the parlor of the boarding house where he stayed when in New York. "The authorities," Tocqueville wrote his mother, "seem extraordinarily approachable."

They were wined and dined, and they winced at the inevitable toasts to Lafayette, whom they deemed an irresponsible demagogue at home, and perhaps at their hostesses' invariable turn at the piano. When they traveled on invitation to the new prison of Sing Sing, in their eagerness they forgot to take their guns for the fine hunting in that vicinity. (America's prisons, they found, were penitentiaries, that is, places for penitence and reform, not simply as in France for punishment.)

Put off initially by the "national conceit" (Tocqueville's phrase), they soon warmed as the free-and-easy democratic air affected them—as it had, they concluded, the national character. ". . . The smallest conversations are instructive," Tocqueville wrote to his father, "and we can say there is not a man, on whatever rung of society he finds himself, who cannot teach us something." To a friend: ". . . I envy this people . . . the ease with which they do without government."

They covered thousands of miles of America and part of Canada. Doggedly Tocqueville drove his frail body the great distances. Between Albany and Buffalo he brooded over the fate of the Indians he met. "One might say that the European is to the other races of man what man in general is to the rest of animate nature. When he cannot bend them to his use or make them indirectly serve his well-being, he destroys them."

Tocqueville's words: "No sooner do you set foot on American ground than you are stunned by a kind of tumult." The notation is as apt today, attested by anyone who has alighted on this soil amid the chaos of an international airlines terminal

"Hard Cider" campaign of 1840 and modern dispute between longhair and hard-hat (opposite):

He saw in the pioneer "the representative of a race to which belongs the future of the new world," if not the entire world, because of his "perseverance and a scorn for life," his single-minded drive for wealth and land. And if the young French nobles met swarms of mosquitoes on their way through the wilderness to Saginaw, Michigan, they also boated on the Great Lakes when their waters were so clear they could follow a white, peeled potato dropped by a crewman down to a depth of 40 feet. And there is another nostalgic note in Tocqueville's diary: "In the steamboats we at first wanted to give a tip to the steward. [Fellow passengers] prevented us, claiming that this would be to humiliate him."

Back in Boston, Beaumont reflected in a letter that "people throw themselves less at the head of strangers than in New York"—and both Frenchmen, as a consequence, felt at home. But Bostonian doors opened soon enough to fellow aristocrats, and they stayed for three-and-a-half weeks. They met Daniel Webster (who "cares only for power," Tocqueville quickly concluded), John Quincy Adams, William Ellery Channing, Edward Everett. Jared Sparks first suggested the possibility of a "tyranny of the majority" in a democracy, but he also indicated the political importance of the township, "founded," Sparks said, "before the [American] state."

Meticulously the travelers composed questionnaires

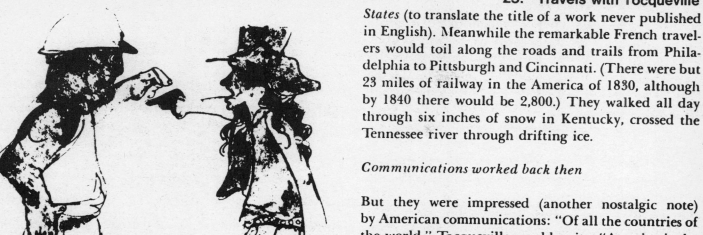

States (to translate the title of a work never published in English). Meanwhile the remarkable French travelers would toil along the roads and trails from Philadelphia to Pittsburgh and Cincinnati. (There were but 23 miles of railway in the America of 1830, although by 1840 there would be 2,800.) They walked all day through six inches of snow in Kentucky, crossed the Tennessee river through drifting ice.

Communications worked back then

But they were impressed (another nostalgic note) by American communications: "Of all the countries of the world," Tocqueville would write, "America is the one where the movement of thought and human industry is the most continuous and swift."

On the way to New Orleans they listened to Sam Houston; in Washington they were unimpressed by Andrew Jackson; and finally they went on to New York, where they boarded the boat for France, February 20, 1832, having spent nine months in America. Back home they encountered cholera and indifference. Beaumont was dismissed from his magistracy and Tocqueville indignantly resigned his. However, their prison report, published in 1833 spurred controversy over the need for penal reform in Europe.

In January 1835, Part I of Tocqueville's *De la démocratie en Amérique* (Concerning Democracy in America) appeared. The acclaim was gratifying and general, not only abroad, but at home. A more philosophical Part II would be published five reflective years later.

Just after the publication of Part I, Tocqueville revealed his purpose in a letter to a friend: "To those who [have fancied] an ideal democracy, a brilliant vision which they think easy to realize, I undertook to show that they have arrayed their future in false colors; that the democratic government they advocate can . . . only be maintained on certain conditions of intelligence, private morality, and religious faith which we do not [as a nation] possess. . . .

"To those for whom the word *democracy* is synonymous with disturbance, anarchy, spoliation, and murder, I have attempted to show . . . that, if democratic government is less favorable [than other governments] to some of the finer parts of human nature, it has also great and noble elements. . . ."

Democracy in America (Tocqueville's own title is more tentative) reveals that by *démocratie* the author invariably meant equality, popular rule, representative government and even participatory democracy. Only an intelligent, alert citizenry, he insisted, might prevent a democracy from falling under "the tyranny

which they presented or mailed to all who might illuminate America for them. From John Quincy Adams, Tocqueville learned the importance of the open lands of the west for siphoning off the discontented, and it would lead to his anticipating historian Frederick Jackson Turner on the influence of the frontier in American history.

Baltimore was the travelers' first contact with the South and the "problem" of the blacks, which Tocqueville swiftly recognized as primarily the problem of the whites. Contrasting the prosperity and enterprise of a free Ohio with the backward condition of adjacent slave Kentucky, he would write that slavery, if it brutalizes the black population, more gravely debilitates the white. Bleakest of Tocqueville's prophecies is his prediction of conflict:

". . . I do not regard the abolition of slavery as a means of warding off the struggle of the two races in the Southern states. The Negroes may long remain slaves without complaining; but if they are once raised to the level of freemen, they will soon revolt at being deprived of almost all their civil rights. . . ."

The black plus the Indian dilemma of America would be Beaumont's impassioned subject in a semi-documentary novel, *Marie, or Slavery in the United*

of the majority" or from its surrender to a demagogue ruling by plebiscite as "guardian" of the people's welfare. (" 'The danger for a democracy' is not the tyrant but the good shepherd." Thus Pierre Mendès-France, in the time of De Gaulle, would loosely quote Tocqueville.)

Religious belief and private morality were, for Tocqueville, the societal restraints when power is the people's. They would moderate the rashness or injustice of the majority. How then might the state encourage morality in the people of a democracy? By the example of moral government, Tocqueville replies.

"My answer," he wrote in Part II of his work, "will do me harm in the eyes of politicians." And one reads on with the routine political prayer meetings at the White House in one's mind: "I believe that the sole effectual means which governments can employ in order to have the doctrine of the immortality of the soul duly respected is always to act as if they believed in it themselves; and I think that it is only by scrupulous conformity to religious morality in great affairs that they can hope to teach the community at large to know, to love, and to observe it in the lesser concerns of life."

Tocqueville makes an important distinction between

Hogarth interprets Tocqueville's religious hope "to know, to love . . ." (above).

Pioneer American steam locomotive "Tom Thumb" races a horse in 1830, the year Tocqueville noted that open competition produces a restless society. Today, grass grows through Chicago tracks (right) as a jet flies above: In a subtler sense, the Frenchman's thoughts are still as valid.

centralized or federal *government* and decentralized or local *administration*. "The partisans of centralization," he wrote, "maintain that the government can administer the affairs of each locality better than the citizens can do it for themselves. . . . But I deny that it is so when the people are as enlightened, as awake to their interests, and as accustomed to reflect on them as the Americans are." These capacities, he felt, grew only with their local exercise: "Town meetings are to liberty what primary schools are to science; they bring it within the people's reach, they teach men how to use and how to enjoy it." The jury system, too, he held, served the same purpose.

Above all, Tocqueville was a believer in the freedom of the individual. He had a view verging on the tragic of the individual in unequal combat with society—wherefore his insistence on decentralization to give the individual a fighting chance. His experience in America persuaded him that here were the elements of a model for the world: federal government and local administration, judicial review by an independent judiciary, private morality and the daily practice of self-rule and self-responsibility; also, a free press.

He foresaw "tyranny of the executive"

Tocqueville visited America before the extension of Presidential powers. But he was farsighted enough to quote Thomas Jefferson on both aspects of American government: "The tyranny of the legislature is really the danger most to be feared, and will continue to be so for many years to come. The tyranny of the execu-

tive power will come in its turn, but at a more distant period." It was the egalitarian aspect of democracy —the sense of its leveling down rather than up—which disturbed Tocqueville. He finally defended it as the spreading of general welfare versus the heaping of culture and fortune upon the few. Yet Tocqueville's taste, training and instinct were elitist. He deplored, as he traveled through Tennessee, the election of "an individual named David Crockett," who could barely read or write. But he was resigned to the victory of middle-class democracy at the inevitable price of lowered culture, customs and manners.

However, Tocqueville's attitude towards the future of culture requires a closer look than usually accorded. "I think that in no country in the civilized world is less attention paid to philosophy than in the United States," he begins Part II. But he immediately swings into an analysis of the self-reliant character and mind of the American (he had not met Emerson on his trip, then obscure, a slow ripening 28) and concludes, "America is therefore one of the countries where the precepts of Descartes are least studied and are best applied."

Similarly Tocqueville looked freshly at the churning that was America, the "restless ambition that equality begets," the "number of those who cultivate science, letters, and the arts," the stirring of the "intellectual world . . . into prodigious activity . . . ," the creation of the audience and marketplace for a science, literature and art. He foretold a new American language and poetry in which Man would be the theme—and within the next decade Whitman would be singing the continental, mind-blowing adventure of the American.

As for the consumer society (as we, not he, term it), other than as audience, Tocqueville was far less sanguine. He remarked the dark streak in American pros-

3. NATIONAL CONSOLIDATION AND EXPANSION

Tocqueville mistrusted the overweening materialism that even then marked the American dream.

He found a melancholy in the "image of chance . . . open to ambition" that beckoned Americans.

perity, the restlessness created by an open, competitive society, of the melancholy of its beckoning "image of chance . . . open to ambition." When the American is not urged on by his wants, he noted, he is at least by his desires, for of all the possessions that he sees around him, none are wholly beyond his reach.

In a democracy, Tocqueville continues, "men easily attain a certain equality of condition, but they can never attain as much as they desire. It perpetually retires from before them, yet without hiding itself from their sight, and in retiring draws them on. . . . To these causes must be attributed that strange melancholy which often haunts the inhabitants of democratic countries in the midst of their abundance, and that disgust at life which sometimes seizes upon them in the midst of calm and easy circumstances." He found the materialism in the American dream to be overly burdensome. He dryly remarks that "Religious insanity is very common in the United States."

"The business of America is business," said Calvin Coolidge. It might have been Tocqueville. "The passions that agitate the Americans most deeply," he wrote, "are not their political, but their commercial passions." The desire for physical gratifications, he noted, drove Americans from agriculture into industry in the pursuit of quicker returns. In the process a second drive developed: "love of the constant excitement occasioned by that pursuit."

Tocqueville also warned of a growing "manufacturing aristocracy." He thought it "one of the harshest that ever existed in the world; but at the same time it is one of the most confined and least dangerous. Nevertheless," he adds, "the friends of democracy should keep their eyes anxiously fixed in this direction; for if ever a permanent inequality of conditions and aristocracy again penetrates into the world, it may be predicted that this is the gate by which it will enter." He further warned of a large army and a protracted war, as a source of danger for a democracy.

Tocqueville perceived the atomization of American life, the loneliness and isolation in the midst of the American crowd and at the same time the compensatory urge to club together and form associations which are part of the democratic structure.

And if, in Tocqueville's America, "the independence of woman is irrecoverably lost in the bonds of matrimony," she surrenders it "without a struggle and without a murmur when the time comes for making the sacrifice." (Susan B. Anthony was not yet a teen-ager at the time of his visit.)

One returns to Tocqueville with some malaise. How would today's American democracy measure up to his? How have the hopes and fears he expressed fared 140 years later? There is some relief, comfort and reassurance (at least in one American's rereading) along with remembered delights. One finds greater grounds for optimism than for despair, as many insights into tomorrow's America as into yesterday's and today's.

The cure for the problems of democracy, said Whitman, and it might have been Tocqueville, is more democracy, not less. The young Frenchman who analyzed a pre-industrial America has a great deal to say to a rapidly approaching post-industrial America, whose problem is no longer production, but rather the producer—the reorganization of society for an improved quality of life through the direct exercise and practice of the democracy Tocqueville describes and advocates. The decentralization he admired is at the top of the agenda of today's futurologists.

Tocqueville's America is not Paradise Lost. It was never paradise and it is not lost. ". . . From this extreme limit of my task," he wrote in concluding his great work, "[I find myself] full of apprehensions and of hopes. I perceive mighty dangers which it is possible

Tocqueville warned of a growing "manufacturing aristocracy," for "if ever a permanent inequality of conditions . . . again penetrates . . . this is the gate by which it will enter."

to ward off, mighty evils which may be avoided or alleviated; and I cling with a firmer hold to the belief that for democratic nations to be virtuous and prosperous, they require but to will it. . . . It is true that around every man a fatal circle is traced beyond which he cannot pass; but within the wide verge of that circle he is powerful and free; as it is with man, so with communities."

TEXAS GIANT OF CONTRADICTIONS: SAM HOUSTON

Joe B. Frantz

Joe B. Frantz *is Walter Prescott Webb Professor of History and Ideas at the University of Texas and a former president of the Western History Association.*

HE WAS a man of extremes.

A giant of a man by the standards of the nineteenth century, Sam Houston would be a big man nowadays. Six feet two, says his army record; six feet six, said an admirer. No matter, he was large. He bore himself like a titan, always a commanding presence without being overbearing. A two-fisted drinker through half of his life, he turned abstemious after his third marriage and gave frequent temperance lectures during his remaining years. A storied Indian fighter, he lived with the Cherokees as a boy and returned to them after he exiled himself from Tennessee. A hater of Mexicans with continuing plans to take over their nation, he treated his captured enemy, General Antonio López de Santa Anna, with magnanimity at a time when Texans were crying for the Mexican generalissimo's blood.

He was a man of contradictions.

According to Texas folklore, you could trace Old Sam's route through the countryside nine months or more after he traveled past: every thirty miles (or a day's journey) you could find a blue-eyed Indian, a sure sign that Sam had camped there. He married an Indian woman while he had an undivorced wife back in Nashville. He married a teen-aged girl when he was a bachelor in his mid-thirties, and he married a girl who was barely twenty when he was pushing fifty.

Nothing in his early life indicated that Houston was headed for empire building. Born on March 2, 1793, near Timber Ridge Church toward the southern end of upland Virginia's Shenandoah Mountains (his home county, Rockbridge, still had only 16,637 inhabitants in 1970), he attended school sporadically until his widowed mother moved her nine children to a wilder frontier west of Maryville, Blount County, Tennessee, in 1807. The teen-ager showed no aptitude for farming or clerking, soon ran away

to the far side of the Tennessee River to live with the Cherokees for a year, returned home (apparently less repentant than the Prodigal Son), was fined for beating a drum with such fervor that he upset the workings of a local court, and ducked out on the fine by returning to the Indians, who promptly adopted him and gave him a name, "the Raven." Up to this point Houston sounds like an 1810 version of any rebellious youth of the past twenty years, the worry of his mother, and the despair of her established, nosy neighbors.

Houston again left the Indians to teach school between May and November in 1812. Although he probably had no more than a year of schooling himself, he seems to have been a successful teacher (which ought to give certification boards some pause). But he could spell and he could read, though he was deficient in mathematics, and he had educated himself in frontier lore and military tactics, which should have kept his back-country kids in awe, if nothing else.

In March of 1813 Houston joined the Creek Indian War by enlisting as a private in the Thirty-ninth Infantry, and began a fairly rapid rise to officer status. A year later he met General Andrew Jackson, a man who would give as much direction as anyone could to the erratic flight of this Raven. When in late March, 1814, Houston showed extraordinary leadership at the Battle of Horseshoe Bend, Jackson commended his young third lieutenant, his words undoubtedly helping to assuage the pain of Houston's severe shoulder and leg wounds. The injured shoulder would pain him periodically for the remainder of his life.

After furloughs for his health and a stint on the state adjutant's staff in Nashville, Houston was named subagent to the Cherokees. An unexpected spin-off from this assignment resulted in a lifelong dislike for one of the South's sainted heroes, John C. Calhoun. After the secretary of war had received Houston and a Cherokee delegation to Washington with his outward southern courtesy, he called the young officer aside to upbraid him for appearing before a cabinet officer in the dress of a savage. Houston's retort that the Indians were more likely to accept him as a true

This article first appeared in the July/August 1980 issue of THE AMERICAN WEST. Reprinted by permission.

son if he dressed as they did made no dent on Calhoun's rigid sense of etiquette.

Shortly Calhoun summoned Houston to charge him with complicity in slave smuggling. Houston's answer that, far from smuggling, he had actually attempted to break up a smuggling ring brought an investigation that exonerated him but implicated several congressmen friendly with the ring. When Calhoun failed to follow up on the disclosures or even to express regret to Houston for having accused him wrongly, Houston in a huff (not his last one) resigned his commission in the army, renouncing a career that he had apparently intended to follow for life. Such impulsiveness would not disappear with age.

To MANY of his friends, Sam Houston was through. His beloved Cherokees were being moved to the Arkansas River, his army commission was gone, and at the age of twenty-five he owned only a hatful of debts.

The Raven promptly sold his possessions to liquidate his indebtedness, returned to Nashville, and at an age when most men were getting entrenched in their careers, started to read law in the office of Judge James Trimble in 1818. Although the reading should have required a minimum of eighteen months, Houston passed admission to the bar six months later. Meanwhile he played several roles in productions of Nashville's Dramatic Club, including one prophetic run as a drunken porter that brought praise from the audience and the press. In the words of the club's stage manager, Noah M. Ludlow, he had "never met a man who had a keener sense of the ridiculous . . . nor one who could more readily assume the ludicrous or the sublime." Forty years later both his Texas critics and admirers would have repeated this verdict.

After a brief fling as a lawyer in Lebanon, thirty miles east of Nashville, where he existed at first on near charity, he returned to Nashville as state adjutant general, with the rank of colonel. Less than three years later his fellow field officers would elect him major general. Meanwhile in October, 1819, with Jackson's help, Houston was named attorney general for the Nashville district, after having turned down an offer from the despised Secretary Calhoun, again recommended by Jackson, to be agent to the Cherokees. With Jackson's assistance Houston was becoming a man to notice.

Houston was paying back the old Chief's sponsorship by loyal support of Jackson's presidential ambitions. He stood for Congress, unopposed, in the late summer of 1823, in part to have a wider forum from which to present Jackson's record to the people. Foreshadowing a later stand, he made his maiden speech in Congress a call for recognition of Greek independence. As Llerena Friend, Houston's most nearly definitive biographer, so succinctly summed up, "In general, he supported in the House the measures which Jackson approved in the Senate." When Houston's first term was completed, he was easily reelected. He had not been an outstanding congressman on

the issues of the day, but he had been devoted to his constituency and to his mentor. That type of congressman gets returned forever.

Houston tried to marry about this time, and traveled all the way from Washington to South Carolina for the event. There a Miss M—was waiting, but the couple decided to postpone such a step until Houston could quit campaigning for reelection and settle some "*personal* difficulties." Later he wrote a relative that he was continuing "the full enjoyments of the sweets of single blessedness." History does not record what became of the romance, except that it never came off.

In 1827, when he was thirty-four years old, Houston decided to make his big jump. With Jackson's support he announced for governor of Tennessee. Basically he ran a one-issue campaign; like most westerners he believed that his section was suffering for lack of internal improvements. Houston was elected governor handily by a four-to-three margin (57 percent) over his opponent. Meanwhile he pushed Jackson's candidacy for president. He was achieving a reputation as the one man who could handle the fractious Jackson. In one case, for instance, he refused to deliver a letter from Jackson to Samuel L. Southard, secretary of the navy, because he thought the old Chief was unnecessarily inflammatory. Like an obedient pupil, Jackson rewrote a milder version acceptable to his protégé.

Houston's first term as governor, while not spectacular, moved along harmoniously enough so that he was considered a shoo-in for a second term. In fact, his name was being bandied about as a possible successor to Andrew Jackson as president whenever Old Hickory should be elected and serve out his years. The idea was not far fetched. Tennessee, a developing western state, had captured the public's imagination. Over the next several decades three Tennesseans would advance to the White House—Jackson, James K. Polk, and Andrew Johnson. In the late 1820s Houston's star shone as brightly as any of them except Jackson's. The governorship of the Volunteer State just might lead to the presidency, as it did for one of Houston's contemporaries, Polk. Why not the same path to national greatness for Houston?

The roadblock was romance. First, the American electorate does not like bachelors for its leaders, especially those with a reputation for being attractive to the ladies. As Houston wrote once in exasperation, "What the devil is the matter with the gals I can't say but there has been hell to pay and no pitch hot!" Everyone had a candidate for his marriage vows; he was, as a thirty-six-year-old bachelor governor, the catch of Tennessee, perhaps of the nation.

Before he completed his campaign, unopposed, for a second term, Houston fell in love. The affair was the kind that Victorian novelists often mooned about—an older half saint, half devil just waiting to be gentled by a pure woman barely come of age. The plot was straight out of

171

St. Elmo. For years Houston had dropped by the home of Colonel John Allen at Gallatin during his travels through upper middle Tennessee. At first Colonel Allen had a thirteen-year-old daughter, Eliza, described as having "large blue eyes and yellow hair." Houston, ever gallant, undoubtedly talked to little Eliza each time he visited her father.

The trouble with thirteen-year-old girls is that they grow up, and one day when she was eighteen, Houston, according to one of his biographers, "looked into Eliza's blue eyes and ceased to speak to her of childish things." Despite the disparity of age, Eliza's parents and other relatives were undoubtedly thrilled by the prospect of the attraction becoming serious. At eighteen Eliza could be the first lady of Tennessee; in her middle twenties she might be the first lady of the United States. Few parents ambitious for good marriages for their offspring could resist being swept up in the enthusiasm of such prospects.

Today Eliza would have laughed and said, "Forget it, you dirty old man." But those were the days when daughters did as their parents bade them; in addition, every old crone in Gallatin was advising Eliza that a brilliant future was unfolding. Apparently Eliza confused prospects with love. She gave Houston her hand. On January 22, 1829, they were married by candlelight in a Presbyterian ceremony in Gallatin, and moved to the Nashville Inn where Houston continued his campaign for a second gubernatorial term. Aside from Houston's political necessities, he seemed to be the most attentive of husbands, and the two of them made a most affectionate couple. They went out little socially, evidently content in each other's company.

But in mid-April it was all over. Houston took his bride, "the only earthly object dear to me," back to her parents and announced that he would never disclose the reasons "to a living person." As he told a boyhood friend, Willoughby Williams: "I can make no explanation. I exonerate this lady [Eliza] freely, and I do not justify myself. I am a ruined man." He promptly resigned as governor of Tennessee. The express to the White House had been derailed.

His silence has left gossips and historians frustrated for a century and a half. They still don't know what happened. A good guess is that Eliza told Houston that she had actually been in love with another man when she had been dazzled by his proposal of marriage, and that she did not love her husband. In keeping silence throughout the remainder of his life, Houston showed restraint that few other heads of households or heads of state would have observed, then or now. His silence is particularly noteworthy in an era when the male was king, and this particular male was the kingliest in his state.

Human nature in the 1820s was not different from human nature in the 1980s. Most of Houston's friends rushed to see who could desert him most quickly. A "howling crowd" burned him in effigy on Gallatin's courthouse lawn. Tennessee buzzed, and the nation quivered with the excitement of a good scandal. The *Richmond* (Virginia) *Inquirer* wrote of "rumors about Gen. Houston . . . too unpleasant . . . to be repeated." *Niles' Register* in Washington was more sympathetic as it lamented his "deeply wounded spirit."

And what of Eliza Allen? None of Houston's more than fifty biographers has probed her feelings. After all, she was a mere eighteen years old, thrown out—in effect—by her governor-husband. But Eliza was no teen-aged slender reed. Like Houston she too could keep silent, and did. The feeling persists that she may have been the one who spurned Houston, rather than the other way around. Houston wrote to his father-in-law after the separation: "I . . . do love Eliza . . . she is the only earthly object dear to me God will bear witness."

After the unexplained break with his wife, Houston resigned as governor and exiled himself to live with the Cherokees again, this time beyond the western end of Arkansas, not far from the kicker grounds of today's Okies from Muskogee. As *Niles' Register* noted at the end of May, 1829, Houston had "caused much surprise among the people." Or as William Carroll, a former supporter turned enemy, observed: "His conduct, to say the least, was very strange and charity requires us to place it to the account of insanity. I have always looked upon him as a man of weak and unsettled mind . . . incapable of manfully meeting a reverse of fortune."

The Cherokees received Houston as a brother, a restless soul who had gone away to the white man's world, who had succeeded by the white man's standards, who had drunk the bitter tea of white perfidy, and who had returned to relatives who asked no questions and demanded no justifications. To them, his broken marriage to Eliza Allen did not matter, for in the Cherokee world a marriage to a white woman was no marriage at all, just a temporary convenience. The Cherokee's basic attitude was similar to the whites', which held that a marriage to a red woman (or later, to a Japanese or a Nicaraguan or a Vietnamese) was a convenience to be ignored whenever the Yankee returned to his homeland. As a boy Sam Houston had learned freedom and acceptance from the Cherokees. Now as a man who had lost his compass—a man with no goals, no future, no love, and few friends—he turned to his Indian companions again.

At once Houston found friends. Almost as quickly he found love. He had known Tiana Rogers on that first sojourn—as the ten-year-old, half-naked, half-sister of his closest Cherokee boyhood chums, John and James Rogers. Now she was a tall, graceful "widow" of thirty, somewhat mysterious herself, for no one knew what had become of her first husband, David Gentry. Perhaps he was dead, killed in a fight against the Osage; perhaps the pair had split the blanket. Never mind. She was eligible, and Houston was in no position to ask questions.

In Cherokee society it was a splendid marriage for Houston. Tiana (to use just one of a dozen variations of her name) was the daughter of the Supreme Chief, Ol-loo-te-ka, who himself was descended in part from a British soldier of the Revolution. And Houston was his adopted son. Tiana's half-brother John would be the next head chief, and her grand-nephew, William Charles Rogers, would become the last chief of the Cherokee nation. Although no official record exists of the marriage, the Cherokees accepted Houston and Tiana as man and wife rather than a temporary liaison.

So Houston married into the inner, upper councils of the Cherokee. He and Tiana set up in a large log house near the Neosho River, planted an apple orchard, and started living in Houston's accustomed good style, entertaining and trading. He began to write articles for the *Arkansas Gazette* over in Little Rock (a fine paper then, a superior one today), inveighing against the systematic defrauding of the Cherokees by the white man. These repeated charges did not endear Houston to Americans along the frontier, many of whom thought he ought to be lynched as a bigamist anyway. Although he signed his articles "Standing Bear," no one doubted Houston's authorship.

When official Washington reached out to demand that Houston comply with requirements that all American traders with Indians be licensed, Houston refused. American laws had no validity where he was concerned, he retorted. He was no longer a citizen of the United States. He was a Cherokee. To extend the law to him would be to enter a wedge whereby a free Cherokee nation might eventually succumb to vassalage. First the attorney general in Washington and then the United States Supreme Court, in a parallel case, declared that Houston's position was untenable.

For a year Houston was a model Indian and husband. Then in 1831 without warning, grief from his troubled life overflowed, and for six months he tried to drink his way to oblivion. He dueled with an employee; he struck his father-in-law and was beaten unconscious by bystanders, only to have the chief bathe and nurse him. The Indians gibed at him. They nicknamed him "Big Drunk." Perhaps it was because he would never drink with them.

And then in September Sam went to the bedside of his dying mother in Tennessee. He left the funeral sober. The Raven was ready to fly again.

THREE MONTHS LATER he was back in the East, an unofficial member of a Cherokee delegation to present grievances to President Jackson. On this trip, in 1831, Congressman William Stanbery of Ohio wrongly accused Houston of having connived with Secretary of War John Eaton at a fraudulent contract for Indian rations. Houston sent Representative Cave Johnson of Tennessee to Stanbery to open negotiations for a duel. When Stanbery retorted that he did not recognize Sam Houston, the Raven announced, "I'll introduce myself to the damned rascal."

Chancing on Stanbery on a Washington street one night, Houston proceeded to cane the congressman about the head. When Stanbery drew a pistol which misfired against Houston's chest, Houston lifted Stanbery's feet in the air and "struck him elsewhere," which must be interpreted as a Victorian euphemism.

The affray brought Houston before the House of Representatives, though he was not a member. Francis Scott Key, the poet-lawyer, represented him before Congress. Meanwhile, Houston gave Washington society and its press the sort of sideshow in which it glories to this day.

Typically for that period in his life Houston sat up drinking with friends on the night before his own appearance before the House. The next morning he couldn't even hold down coffee. But when his turn came to speak, he stood straight and faced a standing-room-only crowd that included the diplomatic corps, the military, and highly placed civilians. Houston spoke without straining: "I can never forget that reputation, however limited," he said in an almost conversational tone that reached to the galleries, "is the high boon of heaven. . . . Though the plowshare of ruin has been driven over me and laid waste to my brightest hopes . . . I have only to say . . . 'I seek no sympathies, nor need;/The thorns which I have reaped are of the tree/I planted; they have torn me and I bleed.' "

The gallery was with him. One woman was heard to say, "I had rather be Sam Houston in a dungeon than Stanbery on a throne!" For half an hour Houston talked seriously, intensely, showing no evidence of a monumental hangover. He cited Julius Caesar, Oliver Cromwell, Napoleon Buonaparte, William Blackstone, and St. Paul; he retraced the tyrannies that had brought down Greece and Rome. He had committed, he said, only a crime of "impulse" after being almost driven to it by his opponent's charges. Otherwise he was guilty of no crime for which Congress could punish him without invading his private rights.

Finally, as Houston gazed at the American flag framing Lafayette's portrait, his declamation soared to new heights: "So long as that flag shall bear aloft its glittering stars . . . so long . . . shall the rights of American citizens be preserved safe and unimpaired—till discord shall wreck the spheres—the grand march of time shall cease—and not one fragment of all creation be left to chafe the bosom of eternity's waves."

At this point the gallery would have given Houston the White House. But Congress, more deliberate, debated four days before deciding that Sam Houston should be reprimanded. The Speaker announced, "I do reprimand you accordingly."

Stanbery wasn't through. He brought criminal charges of assault and then chaired an investigating committee into the fraud charge. For the assault Houston was fined $500, which he never paid. By a split decision the investigating committee acquitted him of fraud in a protracted trial that threatened to become the Watergate of the 1830s.

Stanbery lost more than just two cases out of three. He resurrected Sam Houston. Before the trials Houston was, in his terms, "a man of broken fortune and blasted reputation." But Houston, who had an actor's and a politician's (redundant terms possibly?) instinct for knowing when an audience turns in one's favor, later observed: "I was dying out and had they taken me before a justice of the peace and fined me ten dollars it would have killed me; but they gave me a national tribune for a theatre, and that set me up again." With his trial Sam Houston had returned in triumph to the white man's world. Redemption was his.

WHILE HOUSTON was on trial for caning Stanbery, he annoyed President Jackson's enemies by coming and going at will in the White House. If the president's relationship was not that of a surrogate father, it was at least avuncular and sponsoring, as it had been since the two men had endured the Indian wars together earlier in the century.

The other place that Houston seemed to come and go at will was Texas, which was geographically intimate with Houston's new residence in Arkansas Territory. What was he doing there? The answers are as numerous as the people interrogated. He wrote a Tennessee cousin that he had business in Texas "of importance to his pecuniary interest," and that "I will practice law, and with excellent prospects of success." He also wrote of "several minor matters I am engaged in." Houston knew how to write and talk without really revealing anything. Today's press would have had a field day interviewing him; he would have raised all kinds of possibilities, filling newspapers and the air with speculations while seldom contributing any hard news. He reminds me of the late Dizzy Dean, who during one day gave three New York reporters "exclusive" interviews, each with a contradictory set of facts regarding his background. Sportswriters haven't resolved the confusion yet! Houston would have approved of that boy.

In one memoir Houston is quoted as intending to become a herdsman and spend the rest of his life "in the tranquillity of the prairie solitudes." He could no more have tolerated a herdsman's life than his twentieth-century opposite number Lyndon Johnson could have remained a lifetime, high school debate coach. Houston was created for action.

"Several minor matters" were the operative words in Houston's remark above. Results of the "minor matters" are too well known to detail. Sam Houston showed up in Texas in time for a fight. He had been in the region only a few months when he was chosen to represent Nacogdoches as one of five delegates to a convention to decide on Texas policy toward mother Mexico. At the convention of 1833 he aligned himself with the "war party" opposed to Stephen F. Austin, often hailed as the "father of Texas," though a bachelor. Austin advocated a patient policy toward Mexico. Houston was named chairman of the committee to frame a constitution for a state of Texas, if it should be separated from its current status as an appendage of Coahuila. And he reflected the antibank bias of his mentor, Jackson, by helping to obtain a provision in the proposed constitution that no bank or any other moneyed corporation should be chartered. (In fact, Texas did not legalize banking until the end of Reconstruction, so deep was the antibank feeling.)

As the rift between Mexico and Texas deepened, Houston began urging his fellow Texans to break their connections with Mexico City. Older Texans urged moderation, believing that Mexico's excesses were caused by its inability to stabilize its own government and pointing out that the Mexicans had been unbelievably generous and usually tolerant toward the Anglo-American settlers. But the newer Texans had little patience, coupled with a huge dosage of yanqui intolerance for anything and anybody who was different. Although Houston could be extremely understanding of Indian inconsistencies, he detested the erratic Mexican government and joined the hotspurs in demanding separation.

By the spring of 1836 many Texans were ready to declare their independence of Mexico. Houston's name was put up as a delegate to represent Nacogdoches at the independence convention to be held at the beginning of March. He was defeated. But he was elected as a delegate from Refugio, more than three hundred miles away, despite his having been there only once as a military scout. Thus does chance intervene to forward careers.

When at the beginning of February Houston arrived at Washington-on-the-Brazos, where the convention was to be held, he "created more sensation than . . . any other man. He . . . seems to take pains to ingratiate himself with everybody." The convention met while Santa Anna was besieging the Alamo, whose defenders thought they were fighting for restoration of the liberal Mexican constitution of 1824. But the delegates, 150 miles behind the battle line, had their eyes on independence. They made their declaration on March 2, 1836, Houston's forty-third birthday, and presented Old Sam with a birthday present of the rank of major general and a mandate to organize and command an army, plus an intimation that he was to hold that command until he had defeated the Mexicans. As a leading newspaper in Texas observed, "No general ever had more to do."

Again, Houston provoked controversy. The jury is still out on his abilities as a field commander. At first he was roundly denounced, for all he did was retreat and avoid battle, which as subsequent leaders have discovered, does not fit the yanqui psyche. Did he withdraw, Fabian fashion, until he lured Santa Anna into a trap? Or did he retreat until he had nowhere else to hide, after which the luck of the cornered took over? Whichever side you choose, the one indisputable fact is that Sam Houston led his troops to their only significant victory in the Texas revolution, but it proved to be the last battle—at San Jacinto in a bayou bend twenty-five miles east of present-day Houston on April 21, 1836. In eighteen brief minutes the Texans captured 730 and killed 630 Mexicans against 9 of their own killed and 34 wounded. The next day Santa Anna himself was taken, the war was over, Texas was actually if not officially free, and Sam Houston was being idolized by most Texans and once again by a host of people back in the United States.

THE EIGHTEEN MINUTES at San Jacinto rescued Houston once and for all from the oblivion that had faced him when he walked out of the governor's chair in Tennessee and out of the United States. For years more sedate people east of the Mississippi had clucked about how he had chucked his one golden opportunity. Now at forty-three years of age he was back as a man of action, a noticeable man. Again, redemption, as the Victorians viewed it, was his. While the idolatry ran high, Houston became the first president of the infant Republic of Texas.

And now that Houston was a Texan his Cherokee marriage to Tiana Rogers was no longer observed. With a private divorce from Eliza Allen following shortly, he was a free man. Most of his advisers thought he should remain that way.

However, Houston's third marriage, in 1840, proved happy and lasting. He really got two women for the price of one. On a swing through Alabama he met Margaret Lea, tall, brown-haired, violet-eyed and twenty. He was forty-seven. They both fell, though evidence exists that Margaret had kept an eye on Houston ever since he had debarked on crutches in New Orleans amid a wild demonstration of welcome a month after his victory at San Jacinto. He had been dressed in tatters, with a stinking rag wrapped around his still-bloody ankle wound. As attendants tried to lift him onto a litter, he had fainted. Instead of being repulsed by his dishevelment, Margaret had found him romantic. Evidently she had decided that this wild man was fated for her, though the odds against a young girl from Alabama getting acquainted with the hero of far-off Texas were almost insurmountable, akin to those of all the young girls in Ogallala and Ogden who know that the Prince of Wales remains a bachelor because he was meant for one of them.

But a couple of years later Houston and Margaret did meet through relatives, and the only barrier to their pursuit of happiness was Margaret's mother, Nancy, widow of a Baptist minister, who did not want anyone with as storied a past as Houston hanging around her daughter. After an intensive exchange of love letters, the couple decided to wed. Margaret wrote Houston that she was coming to Texas and named the boat. Houston was in Galveston to meet it. As he stepped from a dory to greet his intended, he saw only his prospective mother-in-law. Where was Margaret? In Alabama still. "General Houston, my daughter . . . goes forth in the world to marry no man. The one who receives her hand will receive it in my home," said Nancy.

And so Houston wound up in Marion, Alabama, where Margaret was firm in her intention to marry this rascal. The fact was, her mother liked Houston. But unlike the Allen parents, she saw the pitfalls as clearly as she felt the glamour of such a union. As the wedding was about to take place in the Lea residence on May 9, 1840, still another Lea relative pulled Houston aside to say that no wedding would take place until Houston explained the Eliza Allen debacle. The fiddlers were already tuned and ready to start the wedding music. But Houston told Margaret's relative to "call his fiddlers off." He would never break his silence on that subject.

Margaret did not care about Eliza, at least not enough to deny herself Sam Houston as a husband. The wedding took place, and Houston gave Texas a new heroine. Bernard Bee, Houston's former secretary of war, predicted the marriage wouldn't last six months. "In all my acquaintances with life," he wrote to a friend, "I have never met an Individual more totally disqualified for domestic happiness" than Houston.

Bee was wrong. Margaret and Sam lived together until his death a quarter of a century later, Nancy proved to be a doting if somewhat dictatorial mother-in-law, and Houston quit his notorious carousing habits. The raven was finally caged, and he liked it.

AS PRESIDENT of the Republic of Texas, Houston showed a talent for organization and an ability to keep problems from aggravating into major quarrels. Most Texans felt he was too lenient with the captive Santa Anna. They wanted the Mexican leader hanged, quartered, stoned, anything but alive. Houston saw Santa Anna as an extension of Texan diplomacy and sent him to Washington under guard as a representative of Texas's hopes for independence. Nor could most Texans ever figure where Houston stood on annexation to the United States; most still can't.

After lying out a term, as required by the constitution of the Republic of Texas, Houston came back for a second round as president at the beginning of the 1840s, with annexation to the United States the crucial topic in most people's minds. By now Jackson was long gone as president, which considerably reduced Houston's influence in Washington. When Houston's second term ended, he was succeeded by Dr. Anson Jones, his hand-picked choice, while in Washington James K. Polk, another Tennesseean and Jacksonian, was bearing down on the American presidency. The good-old-boy system is not a twentieth-century invention.

Uneven as ever, Houston refused to encourage a filibustering expedition into Mexico and turned down requests—nay, demands—to rescue Texans held prisoner as a result of the Mier foray below the Rio Grande. Observed Houston, "The true interest of Texas is to maintain peace . . . and to cultivate her soil." When an outbreak of citizens' meetings insisted that Houston had the wide discretionary powers to order an invasion, Old Sam retorted, "The indulgence of intemperate expressions and feelings can produce no possible good." Indeed, he insisted, "No calamity has ever befallen Texas . . . but what has been caused by a disregard of law and substituting in its place a 'wide discretion.' " Still he called the Mexicans "an imbecile and ignorant people," too "vain" to consider consequences.

Truth was, though Texas was the size of continental France with considerably more geographical resources, the republic was having a hard time staying afloat. It needed the United States more than the United States needed it, and Houston was pragmatist enough to realize the situation. Houston threatened. Either annex Texas now or forget it, he warned.

Still his dream of a Texas empire persisted. In May, 1844, he wrote William S. Murphy, the United States chargé to Texas, of his vision of Texas's destiny—a nation of Europeans, all committed to working and planning, stretching across northern Mexico all the way to Oregon. Oh, what a nation that could be! But in 1845 Texas joined the United States, and Houston saw it become just another star in a flag that now contained twenty-eight such stars. The dream should have died. Still, like many Americans, he couldn't resist the idea that "the Anglo-Saxon race [must] pervade the whole southern extremity of this vast continent."

After Texas became a state, Houston served as one of its United States senators, and was regularly touted for the presidency by people, both North and South, who favored strong leadership. He was caught up in national issues, particularly the Compromise of 1850 and the Kansas-Nebraska bill. He regularly voted opposite to the thinking of his natural constituency, which had a strong southern drift. Most southern politicians in Washington looked on him as a traitor to his section, but he always replied that Texas had joined the United States, not the South. Furthermore, he was explicit in branding southern radicals as unfit for leadership.

And in 1858 Houston set the Senate's teeth on edge when he introduced a resolution proposing that the United States establish a protectorate over Mexico and Central America. Piously he told his fellow senators that he did not offer "this resolution . . . with a view to extending our dominion, but with a view of improving our neighborhood. The mixture of races [in the United States] causes an irresistible impetus, that must overshadow and overrule that whole region" from Mexico through Costa Rica. The resolution never reached a vote. But he kept bringing it up, like a small boy pestering his mother for more cookies.

So incensed were members of the Texas legislature by his constant ridiculing of Jefferson Davis, the secretary of war, and by his stand for union that despite his vote for the proslavery Lecompton Constitution of Kansas in 1858, they chose his successor as senator ahead of the usual election time. It was a studied insult to the old leader.

Texans then overruled their legislature by electing Houston as governor, where he again fell quickly into disfavor because he opposed secession. To him, the United States came first. In the interim between his deposition as senator and his election as governor, Houston resumed talk of pastoral pursuits but still dreamed of being president. He saw two ways to achieve that honor, by saving the Union from the suicide of secession and fratricidal war, and by extending the power of the United States over Mexico.

Houston hid his grand designs behind a cloak of reason —Mexico by 1858 was in the throes of its fourteenth revolution in a little more than a third of a century of existence. (Houston alleged twenty-five revolutions, but he was making a point.) The United States, he argued, could bring Mexico into good government and the good life that goes with such an institution. Despite his adamance against southern secession, he hinted at Texas secession to carry out his plan if the United States should be indisposed to go along. When the Senate refused to vote on his resolution advocating a protectorate, he not only threatened independent Texas action but a movement by unidentified "humane men" who would be willing to "arrest the cruelties on, and to stop the murders of, a defenseless people."

On another occasion, when a Pacific railroad bill was under consideration in 1859, Houston interjected a prediction that Texas would soon extend its borders to Mexico City, where it would run into California moving down the Pacific coast to the same terminus. He further predicted a harmonious union of the two potential empires.

Texas newspapers took up the cry in behalf of Houston's plan, as did English holders of Mexican bonds (Mexico was in arrears on payments of interest). Encouraged, Houston made a speech, the only one in his gubernatorial campaign of 1859, in which he asserted that a protectorate over Mexico would show the United States as "a nationality in which freedom exists" with "strength to maintain it."

Mexico was vulnerable to filibustering at this point. Mexican liberals under Benito Juárez were attempting to overthrow a reactionary central government, while Juan Cortina was depredating both sides of the Texas-Mexico border without declaring for much of anyone except himself. Houston knew he could get money to mount an expedition; could he get the men and materiel? The Texas Rangers were a possibility, and he had always kept the Indians in his camp.

The Rangers may have staved off a Texas invasion of Mexico by pacifying the border in late 1859 and early 1860. But in February, 1860, Houston sent two emissaries to sound out Colonel Robert E. Lee, then in command of federal troops in the area, whether he would be "willing to aid . . . to pacificate Mexico" as a protector in case Houston became president of the United States. Lee, ever correct, replied that he was opposed to filibustering and would act only "in conformity to the Constitution and laws of the country." Despite this refusal, which was really a rebuke from the high-minded Lee, Houston kept the heat on

Washington, sending men and letters indicating that Texas would raise ten thousand men on thirty days' notice, and suggesting that the federal government should send proportionately more.

From Kentucky, from Pennsylvania, from New Jersey came offers to help Houston lead troops into Mexico, each with a prediction that such a grand filibuster would so inflame the American spirit as to promote its originator to the nation's highest office. Volunteers applied from most of the northern states and some of the southern ones. A man in New Orleans volunteered ten thousand muskets; a man in Philadelphia, $50,000. Another group promised that an expedition would be financed by British capitalists, who in addition would grant an annuity to Houston's wife. Houston had struck a national, even an international, chord, and he must have been mesmerized by the sound. The cause of empire was a sacred charge throughout the nineteenth century.

BUT THERE in the late spring of 1860 the threat ended. Whether Houston was sincere in wishing to extend the American flag over Mexico or whether he was fanning a fire of manifest destiny into a presidential draft cannot be ascertained. A disruptive fire that was smoldering within the United States would create a convulsion more nearly justifying Mexico's establishing a protectorate over the United States than the reverse.

Houston would go down fighting, augmenting his pragmatic, patriotic oratory of the 1850s with new bursts of rhetoric supporting the Union. The legislature demanded a special session to denounce the federal and northern state governments, but Houston stood firm. One reporter from the *Galveston News* obtained the statement from Houston that while he had rescued Texas several times in the past, this time it could go to hell by itself; "he would not go with her."

Houston took one last look at empire. To the burgeoning Confederacy he issued the warning that sooner than join the disunionists, Texas would travel in a third direction—her own "separate Nationality. . . . Texas has views of expansion not common to many of her sister States. Although an empire within herself, she feels that there is an empire beyond, essential to her security. She will not be content to have the path of her destiny clogged. The same spirit of enterprise that founded a Republic here, will carry her institutions Southward and Westward." When that sentiment became known, Houston lost the support of both the secessionists and the federal-minded.

But Texas was hell-bent on destruction along with the other secessionists, and in early 1861 left the Union. Undoubtedly Houston, although sixty-eight years old, could have mustered support for separate nationhood, but he did not want to shed the blood of brothers. Rumor held that the new president, Abraham Lincoln, would offer the old warrior a position in his cabinet, perhaps secretary of war, as a reward for his steadfast unionist sentiments. And Lincoln did offer troops to keep the governor in office. But Houston was tired of Texans' rebellious inclinations and determined to leave office and let the state sink without him. And sink it did, along with the other ten states of the Confederacy.

Out of office, Houston came around. Two months after being deposed as governor, he said in a speech at Independence, Texas, "The time has come when a man's section is his country. I stand by mine."

He had two more years, holding his family together by selling firewood. Sometimes Houston was mentioned as the next governor, but he was getting too old and ill for the political wars. Right after Vicksburg and Gettysburg, on July 26, 1863, he died of pneumonia. One of his everlasting enemies, E. H. Cushing, summed him up in an editorial in the *Houston Tri-Weekly Telegraph*: "He has not always been right, nor has he always been successful, but he has always kept the impress of his mind upon the times in which he has acted."

That he did.

Big Drunk. Big Dealer. Big Dreamer. Great Designer, in Llérena Friend's phrase. From the 1820s to 1861 Sam Houston was like a larger-than-life stink bug in America's life. No matter how many times you plugged his hole and pressed him down, he always reappeared somewhere else, as tangible a factor as ever. With his cool blue eyes, his Roman senator's brow, and his oversize but graceful frame, he could stare down the most formidable antagonist. But he had a dreamer's heart connected with a doer's organizational skill, and each shared in making him Texas's most noteworthy adopted son.

No, that's wrong. Typically Houston adopted Texas, for in many ways he was larger than the infant republic and the fledgling state. He was the parent, and Texas was his offspring. As a parent, though he himself was often personally undisciplined, he scolded, spanked, cajoled, and threatened Texas until he shaped it into a wayward entity that still hasn't lived up to the standards and images he set for it.

BIBLIOGRAPHIC NOTE

The best books on Houston are Llerena B. Friend, *Sam Houston, the Great Designer* (1954); Marquis James, *The Raven* (1929); John F. Kennedy, *Profiles in Courage* (1956); *Sam Houston & the Senate* (a reprint of the Kennedy chapter on Houston, 1970); and Amelia Williams and Eugene C. Barker, eds., *Writings of Sam Houston* (8 vols., 1938–1943).

Jacksonian Democracy: Myth or Reality?

Benjamin G. Rader

In American history the 1825 to 1845 era has long been hailed as "The Age of Jacksonian Democracy," "The Age of the Common Man," and the "Egalitarian Age." These concepts, like any other interpretative devices, are only useful to the extent that they simplify the historical record so that it can be better understood. Unfortunately for historical purposes the concepts associated with the Jacksonian era have always been so loosely defined as to be in danger of losing their utility and becoming inimical to sound historical thinking. Without precise definition, for example, "democracy" is subject to many implicit connotations, all heavily weighted with normative and subjective content. Textbooks, as well as heavy tomes of research, are guilty of describing Puritan New England, Revolutionary America, the Jeffersonian era, and the age of Jackson, all as democratic. Using the term in this indiscriminate fashion gives the student an ahistorical notion of the evolution of American political institutions and behavior. If there were important social and political changes between the settlement of Jamestown and the presidency of Jackson, these changes are totally obscured by describing all of these epochs as democratic. To avoid confusion and misunderstanding the concepts associated with the Jacksonian era must be defined so that logical comparisons can be made between historical eras.

Jacksonian democracy as implicitly used by textbook authors appears to have two fundamental meanings. First, it seems to mean a political system in which all or almost all adult white males have approximately equal opportunities and power to influence political decision-making. Presumably this power accrued to the "common man" because he was able to, and did, vote for one party or candidate instead of another. Secondly, it seems to mean that Jacksonian democracy included a social system in which all white men had almost unlimited opportunities and freedom to change their social status. The common man could move freely up or down the social ladder. Hence the wide usage of the term "the rise of the common man" apparently refers to an open, exceptionally mobile social system.

While textbooks do not use exactly the same evidence, and vary in their emphases, there is agreement among them that certain bodies of facts support the concept of the Jacksonian era as democratic. One group of facts includes the changes in the formal political processes of the era—the expansion of suffrage, the transference of the choice of presidential electors from the state legislatures to the electorate, and the replacement of "King Caucus" by nominating conventions. A second body of facts includes ostensible changes in political behavior and power—increased voter turnout, the victories of Andrew Jackson, the Bank war, and sometimes the "spoils system." In short the Jacksonian era supposedly witnessed the end of elite rule in American politics. The New Democratic Party represented the common man against the privileged; in 1840 the Whigs came to see the folly of their ways and also capitulated to the power of democracy. Finally, textbook writers include a group of imprecise facts to support the idea that general social equality existed in the Jacksonian era.

Recent research in the Jacksonian era has

Reprinted by permission from *The Social Studies*, Vol. LXV, No. 1, January 1974. Published by Heldref Publications, Washington, D. C.

shown that much if not most of the evidence used to demonstrate the democratization of the era has been misunderstood or misinterpreted. Viewed from the perspective of the definitions of democracy heretofore offered, this research makes the continued use of the term "Jacksonian Democracy" logically indefensible.

Changes in formal political processes are obviously poor criteria for determining the existence of a democracy. If merely the proportion of the population having the right to vote is the standard, the Soviet Union and Castro's Cuba are among the most democratic countries in the world. The more crucial question is how much actual influence did the voters have in selecting candidates and ultimately on political decision-making. Did the voters in the Jacksonian era have approximately equal influence? Historians have long assumed that one qualified voter had about as much political clout as another. This assumption arose from the reports of contemporary foreign travellers and the political rhetoric employed during the Jacksonian era. Candidates paid extravagant lip service to the common man—to his incomparable wisdom, practicality, guilelessness and moral principles. They even assumed a deferential posture toward the voter, reversing the order of deference from what it had been in Colonial politics.

But the rhetoric and style of Jacksonian politics obscures the actual flow of political power. Recent studies provide extensive evidence supporting the notion that the voters continued to be manipulated and controlled by the upper class or elite. The office-holders themselves came from the richer segment of the population and enjoyed distinctly more social prestige than the average voter. "The fault, if fault it was, lay not with the suffrage . . . ," Edward Pessen has asserted, "but with a party system that for all its flattery of the common man effectively insulated him from the sources of power and decision making." The common man may well have enjoyed less real political power at the end of the Jacksonian era, Pessen concludes, than he did at the beginning.

Other changes made in the formal political system failed to increase the effective power of the average voter. The selection of presidential electors by popular vote rather than state legislatures was well under way prior to 1824. By 1824 the legislatures chose the electors in only six states; by 1828 in only one. While this reform encouraged the development of the "new" or "second" party system, tightly controlled cliques selected the electoral nominees.

The innovation of the national party convention for nominating the presidential candidates did come in the Jacksonian era, but the honor goes to a minority party, the Antimasonic Party in 1831. The Whig and Democratic parties soon followed. The destruction of King Caucus, according to the traditional interpretation, was a great victory for the common man. But careful reconstruction of the political history of the era from county courthouses to the National Capitol, discloses that the conventions at all levels were controlled by small elite groups. Richard P. McCormick concludes that the conventions "gave the appearance of representing party sentiment whereas, in fact, they usually did little more than follow the dictates of party leaders. Made up in large measure of office-holders and party activists, they were readily susceptible to manipulation and control." The dedication of party leaders to winning office, maintaining party discipline, and using office to support policies in the interests of party "insiders" or influential constituents far outweighed their commitment to the interests of the avarage voter. Except as a rhetorical device to flatter constituents, appeals to ideology or an abstract national interest played negligible roles in the behavior of political parties in the age of Jackson.

Reputedly the election of Jackson in 1828 represented a victory of the common man over the well-to-do elite who had presumably ruled American politics prior to 1828. It is no secret, however, that Jackson himself was a wealthy Tennessee land speculator who owned a large plantation with slaves. Prior to his ascension to the Presidency his public career had been one of consistent opposition to cheap money and favoritism to the creditor rather than the debtor class. In short by American standards he was a western aristocrat. Jackson's reputation as the champion of the common man rests on what he had come to symbolize. He was self-made, thereby fulfilling a central American myth, and he along with the "noble" frontiersmen had won a great military victory over the "effete" British. The natural man had triumphed over the artificial man. Thus it is argued that Jackson was perceived by contemporaries as the representative of a vast popular movement resting on the interests of the common man. When he became President, again in the interest of the common man, he fought the mighty Second Bank of the United States, an agency of the Eastern elite.

A reexamination of the election of 1828 and the Bank issue throws serious doubt on the assumption that Jackson was viewed by contemporaries as being uniquely the knight of the common man pitted against the dragons of the privileged. Jackson's position on the issues in 1828 was totally ambiguous. More significantly, the voter turnout in 1828, while double that of the confused election of 1824, was hardly a "mighty democratic outpouring." "There was in 1828 a voter turnout that approached—but in only a few places matched or exceeded—the maximum levels that had been attained before the Jacksonian era." Pessen adds that "for all the clamor and propaganda directed at them, American voters did not rush to the polls to install the alleged great champion of popular rights." Almost half the qualified voters did not bother to go to the polls.

Neither was Jackson's war with the BUS perceived as a clear issue between the common man and those who enjoyed special economic privileges. All of the recent research indicates that the average man was either unconcerned about the issue of the Bank or, when he was interested, divided his support evenly in favor or opposition to the Bank. For most voters ethnic, religious, and other social issues were more paramount than the Bank issue. Despite all of the hullabaaloo over the BUS, the voter turnout in 1832, after Jackson had vetoed the recharter bill, was even less than in 1828.

Given our definition for a political democracy—a political system in which almost all adult males have aproximately equal opportunities *and* power to influence political decision-making—it is then inaccurate and deceptive to describe the politics of the Jacksonian era as democratic. The new system of politics involved an unequal distribution of power; those with more money and status also had more political influence. The style of elite rule had changed, but the elite still ruled. What had changed in the Jacksonian era was the frank recognition by political leaders that their constituency had been enlarged. Thus to win elections they had to flatter the voter and develop issues which offended as few voters as possible, particularly those who enjoyed more status. Elections in the era thus turned more on personalities, ethnic and religious divisions within the population, and effective propaganda than on programs designed specifically to benefit the common man. Crude but concrete parallels exist between the political style and behavior of the Jacksonian era and modern American politics. If we want to describe the present political system as democratic, then a good case can be made for calling Jacksonian politics democratic. But the implicit definitions employed by textbook writers provide an ideal standard for democracy, one probably no society has achieved in practice. For the term to be logically related to the politics of the era it must be abandoned as an interpretative catchword or carefully redefined so that it is empirically valid for the era it is supposed to describe.

Neither does the research of the last ten years support the contention of an egalitarian social and economic system in the

Jacksonian era. By reputation Americans in the Jacksonian era—with, of course, the exception of Negroes and Indians—were overwhelmingly middle class and enjoyed a society in which upward social mobility was frequent and easy. The evidence to support the egalitarian thesis rests in large part on the changing political style, the genuine material well-being of most Americans in comparison with other countries, the development of equalitarian social manners, and numerous reports by foreign travellers. Foreign visitors, usually with a firm European frame of reference and preconceived notions of America as a social and political democracy, were inordinately impressed by the lack of an hereditary aristocracy and the crude, undeferential manners of the average American which they perceived as evidence of equalitarianism. Alexis de Tocqueville, for example, asserted in the very first sentence of his classic study of American democracy that "Among the novel objects that attracted my attention during my stay in the United States, nothing struck me more forcibly than the general equality of condition among the people." Until recently Tocqueville's conclusion was treated by scholars as almost sacrosanct.

Partly because of Tocqueville and other foreign visitors, textbook authors have tended to overlook an abundance of impressionistic evidence that would suggest a different conclusion. Labor historians long ago reported that the plight of the lower classes, particularly immigrant workers, was unenviable in the Jacksonian era. Glaring disparities in housing conditions in American cities were the rule. City workers labored from daybreak to dark, faced the recurrent spectre of unemployment, and suffered under working conditions that differed little from their European counterparts. During the Jacksonian era real wages appear to have remained stable. The burgeoning appearance of reform groups concerned with labor problems in the age of Jackson also testifies to a general inequality of conditions. To the ex-

tent that evidence is known, inequalities among farmers were common and the conditions of work involved a great deal of gruelling, monotonous drudgery.

Only recently, however, have historians made careful and detailed studies of wealth distribution and class structure in the Jacksonian era. Perhaps if social and economic equality existed anywhere, we would expect it in the West. But Richard Wade has found that a class system quickly emerged in western cities. Headed by the local merchants, the white social structure in descending order included the professional class, the workingmen with some skills plus store clerks, and at the bottom a large number, extremely difficult to estimate, of transients and ne'er-do-wells. And, of course, free blacks held a social status even lower than the transients. De facto residential segregation reflected these class lines. Even though whites could cross class lines by acquiring or losing wealth, this phenomenon became increasingly difficult. Class lines in the Jacksonian era in western cities, Wade concludes, became more stratified and rigid.

Similarly, in eastern cities Pessen has found that the distribution of wealth was grossly unequal. The degree of inequality increased in the Jacksonian era. For example, in Boston in 1833 one per cent of the taxpaying population owned thirty-three per cent of the city's non-corporate wealth; in 1838 their share increased to thirty-seven per cent. The top four per cent in Boston owned fifty-nine per cent in 1833; sixty-four per cent in 1848. At the bottom of the wealth ladder eighty-six per cent of those who had taxable wealth had only fourteen per cent of the total in 1833 and only four per cent in 1848. In Brooklyn, in 1841, sixty-six per cent of the taxable residents had noncorporate wealth under $100 and their combined wealth was less than one per cent of the total. While apparently the poor and middle classes were silghtly improving their standard of living in the Jacksonian era, all of Pessen's data indicates that the distribution of wealth was becoming more skewed in favor of the rich. Pessen's findings are also consistent with a growing body of statistics which show that the distribution of wealth was highly unequal in the Colonial and late nineteenth century eras, but ironically less so than in the Jacksonian era.

While equality of economic conditions did not prevail in the Jacksonian era neither did equality of opportunity. According to legend, the Jacksonian era provided unparalleled opportunities for the poor boy to make good. Presumably many of the rich came from lowly origins. Pessen has found that changes in status from the middle or poorer classes to the rich were quite rare. For example, of those who were assessed for property worth $100,000 and upward in New York City in 1828 and $250,000 or more in 1845, about ninety-five per cent came from wealthy families; about five per cent from middle and poor backgrounds. Similar mobility patterns were found in Philadelphia, Brooklyn, and Boston. Pessen concludes that "only about two per cent of the Jacksonian era's urban economic elite appear to have actually been born poor, with no more than about six per cent of middling social and economic status." While many of those born into affluence became richer in the age of Jackson, this hardly supports the notion of general social mobility for the non-rich. The phenomenon of "rags to riches" was as much a myth in the Jacksonian era as it has been in other periods of American history.

If economic and social democracy be defined as a social system in which white men have almost unlimited opportunities to change their social status, one in which the "rags to riches" phenomenon is common, and one that is overwhelmingly middle class, then the Jacksonian era cannot qualify. But, of course, such standards are ideal ones which have never been attained in practice. A more realistic definition of social democracy might be a social system in which there are ample opportunities to make minor advances or declines in social status and income, say an improvement in wealth of $100 to $1,000 during two generations. Though this is not egalitarianism as commonly defined, it appears that many families may have had such experiences in the antebellum period. Moreover, they commonly perceived America as providing the opportunity for such minor improvements in status. If we use this kind of precise criterion for defining the existence of social democracy, then we can salvage the concept. But we must use extreme care to avoid using the term both as an ideal standard and in a descriptive, empirical sense.

In summary, the recent research requires a rethinking of the traditional concepts popularly used to describe the Jacksonian era. If the concepts Jacksonian democracy, common man, egalitarianism, and the like are going to be used at all, they should be carefully redefined to square with the evidence. Since the terms are intimately associated with cherished American ideals and are loaded with deeply emotive connotations, only precise definition and comparisons will allow us to distinguish between the rhetoric and reality, and changes that were substantive and those which were ephemeral. Only in this way can we teach an authentic American history and thereby correctly inform the present.

Melville and Hawthorne

Although of dissimilar personality, and fifteen years apart in age, the two writers developed a friendship that would have profound effects on each other's work— especially on the creation of *Moby Dick.*

BY R. L. LOWE

I met Melville the other day, and liked him so much that I have asked him to spend a few days with me before leaving these parts." Thus wrote Nathaniel Hawthorne to his friend Horatio Bridge on August 7, 1850.

Melville, for his part, also took a great liking to Hawthorne and wrote an article about him which was published anonymously in the *Literary World.* In it he described Hawthorne as a man capable of "mystical depths of meaning" and as having a "profound, nay appalling moral shrouded in a blackness ten times black . . . Not a very great deal more and Nathaniel were verily William . . . But I already feel that this Hawthorne has dropped germinous seeds into my soul."

Melville was then living on his farm, Arrowhead, near Pittsfield, Massachusetts, and Hawthorne lived a few miles away at Lenox. Riding over from Pittsfield on horseback, accompanied by his great Newfoundland dog, Melville became a frequent and welcome visitor at the little red house in which Hawthorne then lived. Sitting up until all hours the two men talked about "time and eternity, things of this world and of the next, and all possible and impossible matters."

Yet it is surprising that a friendship of some warmth should have developed between two such dissimilar men—the one a semi-recluse, the other a man of action who had seen more danger in a few years in the South Pacific than the other was to experience in a lifetime. A brief perusal of the careers of the two writers up to the time of their meeting may help to explain why they were so attracted to each other.

Melville, a son of a large family constantly beset by financial worries, lost his father while he was still in his early teens and had to go to work in a bank to help support his family. Restless, yearning for a wider experience of life, Melville tried unsuccessfully to get work on the construction of the Erie Canal, and then signed on the *St. Lawrence* for a voyage to Liverpool. He liked the seaman's life, hated the vile slums of Liverpool, and returned home again only to find his family in worse financial difficulties than before. It was at this point that Melville first tried his hand at writing, publishing an account of his trip in the *Democratic Press & Lansingburgh Advertiser.*

Next, in another effort to widen his horizon, he and a friend named Fly decided to "go West," but got no further than Galena, Illinois, before giving up the notion and returning to Boston. From there Melville shipped out on a whaler, the *Acushnet,* for an extended voyage to the Pacific, and despite the dangers and hardships of a sailor's life, he flourished on backbreaking work, salt meat and hardtack. One of the sailors with whom he shared the forecastle told a story of the ship Essex which in 1819 was sunk by an infuriated whale—a tale which young Melville was later to remember. On June 23, 1842, the *Acushnet* dropped anchor in Taio Hae Bay, Nuku Hiva, and Melville, accompanied by another sailor called Toby, jumped ship and made for the interior of the island, only to fall into the hands of the cannibal Typee. Fortunately the Typee treated and fed them well (perhaps too well—were they fattening the lads for a feast?) and after several weeks let them go back to the coast where Melville signed on for another voyage, this time in an Australian whaler named *Lucy Ann.* Conditions aboard this vessel were abominable, so that Melville jumped ship again in Tahiti. After a short time in jail, he joined the crew of the *Charles and Henry* for a two-year voyage to the whaling grounds, and it was in this ship that he became intimately acquainted with the whaling trade, serving, by his own account, as a harpooner.

When his two years were up, he joined the U.S. Navy in Honolulu and shipped to Boston on the *U.S.S. United States.* Once home, he decided to write up his experiences and settled down at Lansingburgh, Massachusetts, to write *Typee,* an account of his adventures in Nuku Hiva. Without much difficulty he found a publisher for the book both in England and the U.S. and wrote a second book, *Omoo (The Wanderer),* which was also published and well received. Now launched as an author, Melville produced three other works—*Mardi, Redburn* and *White Jacket*—which all did quite well and established him firmly as an American writer of consequence. Even though his books brought him a modest income, it was not enough to live on and raise a family, so that Melville took up farming in a small way, at Arrowhead, a farm near Pittsfield.

In 1850 he began work on what was to become the finest book of his career—*Moby Dick*—and it was while he was at work on this book that he read *Mosses from an Old Manse* and a little later met Hawthorne.

"Melville and Hawthorne," by R.L. Lowe, *Mankind,* November 1979. Reprinted by permission.

3. NATIONAL CONSOLIDATION AND EXPANSION

The life of Hawthorne up to the year that he and Melville became friends was of a totally different nature. The son of a sea captain who died in Surinam while Hawthorne was a small boy, he was raised by his mother. At the age of nine he injured one of his feet and was a semi-invalid for two years thereafter, which undoubtedly increased his self-absorption and habit of introspection. Later, in college at Bowdoin, he made a few friends—Longfellow was one of his classmates but the two did not become close—and viewed his graduation with considerable apprehension: what was he to do, what profession should he follow, what work should he do to earn his living? His choice was to become a writer, and for nearly four years he shut himself up in his room under the eaves at Herbert Street, Salem, writing, writing, writing.

He could not have found a more severe apprenticeship for, lacking any experience that could be used as a background or substance for a book, he was forced to conjure up material for writing entirely from his imagination. Unfortunately he could find no publisher for his first work, *Seven Tales from My Native Land,* and in a fit of disgust, he burnt the manuscript. His self-esteem severely shaken, he wrote: "A writer of story-books! What kind of business in life—what mode of glorifying God or being serviceable to mankind in his day and generation—may that be? Why, the degenerate fellow might as well have been a fiddler."

His next book, *Fanshawe,* Hawthorne published at his own expense, and it was in this way that his work came to the attention of Samuel Goodrich, the publisher of a magazine called *The Token,* who invited him to contribute. Over the next few years Hawthorne published some 30 tales in *The Token,* without, however, making any impression, as far as he was aware, on the reading public. Worse still, he found himself losing respect for his art, writing to his friend Bridge that he felt like a man drifting towards a cataract. "I'm a doomed man, and over I must go."

Then at last, in 1837, came the breakthrough. Bridge, in association with Goodrich, urged him to collect in book form the best of his tales that had appeared in *The Token* and other magazines. The result was the publication of *Twice-told Tales.* The volume was favorably reviewed by Longfellow in *The North-American.* Hawthorne had arrived.

However, the publication of *Twice-told Tales* brought him very little money and he had to look for work of another kind. After some fruitless searching, he was able to secure a patronage appointment in the Boston customhouse. At first he welcomed his new job inasmuch as it meant doing "real" work instead of writing in solitude, but after a while he became tired of measuring cargoes of coal and salt and found his labors "a grievous thralldom." He stuck it out for two years and then resigned.

Meanwhile he had become engaged to Sophia Peabody and it was through her that he became interested in Brook Farm, a quasi-communistic community at West Roxbury on the Charles River. Brook Farm hoped to bring about a "more natural union between intellectual and manual labor than now exists." It seemed to him to be just what he was looking for, and for a while he threw himself enthusiastically into cutting hay for the cattle, milking, planting vegetables, carting firewood and pitchforking manure. Inevitably, though, he decided that the community was not for him and he resigned in November, 1841. (However, Brook Farm was later to furnish him with material for *The Blithedale Romance.)*

In the meantime he had married his Sophia and the couple settled down in the Old Manse at Concord, where Hawthorne went back to writing full time, producing a second volume of tales which he called *Mosses from an Old Manse.* But, as before, his writing did not produce enough money to live on, so that he was obliged to accept another patronage appointment, this time as a surveyor at the Salem custom-house. It was here, one rainy afternoon, that he came across a mysterious object in a musty, unused room, an object which on closer examination assumed the shape of the letter "A." "My eyes," he wrote later, "fastened themselves upon the old scarlet letter and would not be turned aside. Certainly there was some deep meaning in it, most worthy of interpretation." If ever an author received a direct inspiration for a book, this was it. The result was, of course, Hawthorne's masterpiece, *The Scarlet Letter,* published in 1850.

It was at this point that Melville and Hawthorne met and became warm friends. Inevitably, one asks, why? Why would the author of *Typee* feel drawn to the author of *Mosses from an Old Manse*? Why would the man who had written *White Jacket* reach out in friendship to the man who had written *The Scarlet Letter*? There is no simple answer. But the two men had this in common—they both felt isolated and estranged from life, for in spite of its bustle, Melville had lived through his experience of the world in a solitariness no less bleak than Hawthorne's. The "dismal chamber" under the eaves in which Hawthorne had shut himself up in Salem was the rough equivalent of the stinking forecastle of Melville's adventures in the South Seas. Not for nothing had he requested the reader to "call me Ishmael."

The most immediate effect of Melville's and Hawthorne's friendship was that Melville absorbed from the older man a view of life which demanded that *Moby Dick,* the first version of which he was then completing, be recast. In the beginning Melville had conceived Ahab as a romantic hero a la Manfred, but his reading of Hawthorne's *Mosses from an Old Manse* led him to the discovery of the black truth which had lain at the bottom of his mind without his recognizing it: the understanding that the heart creates its own evil, that men seek or can be led to seek their own worst fate, and that the noblest and grandest appearance of heroism and manhood may be but a sham.

Two tales from *Mosses from an Old Manse* particularly impressed Melville: "Young Goodman Brown" and "Earth's Holocaust." In the former story the hero, or rather the anti-hero, is a young man in Puritan times who is drawn to the dark forest to attend a black mass, and there discovers among the devil worshippers the leading men and women of his village. The Fiend himself conducts the business in hand and roars at the assembled throng: "Lo, there ye stand, my children. Depending upon one another's hearts ye had still hoped that virtue were not all a dream. Now you are undeceived.

Evil is the nature of mankind. Evil must be your only happiness. Welcome again, my children, to the communion of your race." In "Earth's Holocaust," Hawthorne's message is even stronger.

What but the human heart itself? And unless they hit upon some method of purifying that foul cavern, from it will reissue all the shapes of wrong and misery . . . How sad a truth, if truth it were, that mankind's age-long endeavor for perfection had served only to render him the mockery of the evil principle, from the fatal circumstance of an error at the very root of the matter! The heart, the heart—there was the little boundless sphere wherein existed the original wrong of which the crime and misery of this outward world were merely types.

With these words fresh in his mind, Melville was moved to write, "There is the grand truth about Nathaniel Hawthorne. He says no, in thunder; but the devil himself cannot make him say, yes. For all men who say yes, lie. . . "

Reshaping the character of Ahab meant accepting Hawthorne's interpretation of human nature. Leon Howard, a biographer of Melville, quotes two passages from *Moby Dick* which help to explain what Melville thought he had to do. The first passage is from the chapter entitled "The Quarter Deck," in which it is Ahab himself who speaks.

All visible objects, man, are but as pasteboard masks. But in each event—in the living act, the undoubted deed—there some unknown but still reasoning thing puts forth the moulding of its features from behind the unreasoning mask. If a man will strike, strike through the mask! How can the prisoner reach outside except by thrusting through the wall? To me the whale is that wall, shoved near to me. Sometimes I think there is naught beyond. But t'is enough. He tasks me; he heaps me; I see in him outrageous strength, with inscrutable malice sinewing it. That inscrutable thing is chiefly what I hate; and be the whale agent, or be the whale principal, I will wreak that hate upon him.

The second passage occurs in the chapter named "Moby Dick," wherein the narrator makes this explanation of Ahab's character.

Ahab had cherished a wild vindictiveness against the whale, all the more fell for that in his frantic nervousness he at last came to identify with him all his bodily woes, but all his intellectual and spiritual exasperations. The White Whale he saw before him as the monomaniac incarnation of all those malicious agencies, which some deep men feel eating in them, till they are left living on with half a heart and half a lung. The intangible malignity which has been from the beginning; to whose dominion even the modern Christians ascribe one half of the world; which the ancient Ophites of the east reverence in their statue devil. Ahab did not fall down and worship it like them; but deliriously transferring its idea to the abhorred white whale, he pitted himself, all mutilated, against it. All that most maddens and torments; all that stirs up the lees of things; all truth with malice in it; all that cracks the sinews and cakes the brain; all the subtle demonisms of life and thought; all evil, to crazy Ahab were visibly personified and made practically assailable in Moby Dick.

In modern terms, Melville had made Ahab insane, whereas previously he had ascribed to him mere Byronic moodiness.

"Shall I send you a fin of the Whale by way of a specimen mouthful?" Melville wrote to Hawthorne. "The tail is not yet cooked—though the hellfire in which the whole book is broiled might not unreasonably have cooked it all ere this. This is the book's motto—(the secret one), *Ego non baptiso te in nomine.*[1]"

If Ahab's morbidness had remained as it was suggested in the first version of *Moby Dick* the whole drama would have rested in the author's rhetoric and eloquence, but Melville, under the influence of Hawthorne, proceeded to give a symbolism to his character's

nature, and this raised the level of tragedy to Elizabethan heights. The revised version of Ahab did indeed have its baptism of fire in the name of the devil and his savage spirit of defiance finally brought about the death of himself and all his crew save one.

In dedicating *Moby Dick* to Hawthorne, Melville as much expressed his thanks for his friendship as acknowledged the debt he owed him for deepening the work. Melville's reaction to Hawthorne's praise of the work was truly extravagant. "Your joy-giving and exultation–breeding letter[2] is not my reward for ditcher's work with that book, but is the good goddess' bonus over and above what was stipulated for. . . A sense of unspeakable security is in me at this moment, on account of your having understood the book."

The two men met only once more, five years later, when Hawthorne was U.S. Consul in Liverpool and Melville passed through that city on his way to London. Of that meeting Hawthorne wrote with characteristic detachment: "It is strange how he persists—and has persisted, ever since I knew him, and probably long before—in wandering to and fro over these deserts. . . He can neither believe nor be comfortable in his unbelief. . . If he were a religious man he would be one of the most truly religious and reverential; he has a very high and noble nature, and is better worth immortality than any of us."

The friendship of the two writers, had friendship been all, would have rated a page or two in their biographies, but since Hawthorne's view of human character as seen by Melville, brought about the metamorphosis of Captain Ahab from a Byronic hero to one of Shakespearean dimensions and to a symbolism as profound as any in literature, the relationship between the two men deserves a much fuller treatment. Unquestionably, in seeking out the fifteen year older Hawthorne, Melville was searching for a father from who he wanted to receive a kind of benediction for *Moby Dick*, and it is to his everlasting credit that Hawthorne supplied that role, if only half-conscious of what was expected of him.

---

[1]The full quotation reads: *"Ego non baptiso te in nomine Patris, Filii et Spiritus sancti—sed in nomine Diaboli."*

[2]Hawthorne's letters to Melville have not survived.

Eden Ravished

The Land, Pioneer Attitudes, and Conservation

Harlan Hague

Harlan Hague teaches history of the American West and American environmental history at San Joaquin Delta College, Stockton, California. He is the author of Road to California: The Search For a Southern Overland Route *and articles on western exploration and trails.*

IN O. E. RÖLVAAG'S *Giants in the Earth,* a small caravan of Norwegian immigrants stopped on the prairie, and the riders got down from their wagons. They scanned the landscape in all directions and liked what they saw. It was beautiful, all good plowland and clean of any sign of human habitation all the way to the horizon. After so much hoping and planning, they had finally found their place in the new land. One of the men, Per Hansa, still had difficulty comprehending what was happening:

"This vast stretch of beautiful land was to be his—yes, his. . . . His heart began to expand with a mighty exaltation. An emotion he had never felt before filled him and made him walk erect. . . . 'Good God!' he panted. 'This kingdom is going to be mine!'"

Countless others who went to the West reacted like Rölvaag's Per Hansa. They entered the Promised Land with high expectations, possessed the land and were possessed by it. They changed the land and in time were changed by it.

The influence of the West on the American mind has interested historians ever since Frederick Jackson Turner read his momentous essay in 1893 to a meeting of the American Historical Association. In the essay, Turner concluded: "The existence of an area of free land, its continuous recession, and the advance of American settlement westward, explain American development." Turner went on to describe in some detail the various ways the western environment changed the frontiersman, molding him into the American. The processes and result of this evolution were in the end, by implication, favorable.

Writing in the early 1890s, Turner did not detect one of the most important themes, if not the most important, of the westward movement, a theme which would have immense impact on the shaping of the American character. This was the belief that the resources of the West were inexhaustible. Henry Nash Smith, in his influential *Virgin Land,* caught the point that Turner missed:

"The character of the American empire was defined not by streams of influence out of the past, not by a cultural tradition, nor by its place in a world community, but by a relation between man and nature—or rather, even more narrowly, between American man and the American West. This relation was thought of as unvaryingly fortunate."

This cornucopian view of the West was the basis of the frontiersman's attitude toward and his use of the land.

The typical trans-Mississippi emigrant in the last half of the nineteenth century accepted the assumption of inexhaustible resources. Yet the view of the West as an everlasting horn of plenty had been proven false long before the post-Civil War exodus. For example, commercial hunting of the sea otter along the California coast, which had begun in 1784, reached its peak around 1815; by the mid-1840s, the numbers of the animals had declined alarmingly, and the otter was soon hunted almost to extinction. The beaver's fate was similar. Soon after Lewis and Clark told about the teeming beaver populations in western streams, trappers moved westward to harvest the furs. They worked streams so relentlessly that the beaver began to disappear in areas where it had always been plentiful. By 1840, the beaver had been trapped virtually to oblivion. No mountain man in the 1820s would have dreamed there could ever be an end to the hardy little animal. Yet unbridled exploitation had nearly condemned the beaver to extinction. The lesson was lost on Westerners.

Pioneers were not noticeably swayed by the arguments of the naturalists, who publicized the wonders of nature or went further and pled for its preservation. William Bartram, a contemporary of Jefferson, wrote eloquently about the beauty of American nature in his *Travels.* Originally published in 1791, his book was more popular in Europe than in the United States, which had yet to discover its aesthetic environment. John James Audubon had more influence in this country upon publication of his *Birds of America* series (1827–1844) and his subsequent call for protection of wildlife. Francis Parkman, while not famed as a naturalist, wrote firsthand accounts about the scenic West and the Indian inhabitants who lived in harmony with nature. It is no wonder that Parkman, who was enthralled with the outdoors, admired Indians and mountain men more than the settlers he encountered during his western travels.

 From *The American West* magazine, May/June 1977. Copyright by the American West Publishing Company, Tucson, Arizona. Reprinted by permission of the author.

The romantic optimism of the westward movement is reflected in the faces of the pioneers in Westward the Course of Empire Takes Its Way, *a fervent celebration of Manifest Destiny painted by German artist Emanuel Leutze about 1861.*

There was indeed a whole body of romantic literature and art during the first half of the nineteenth century that might have persuaded Americans that environmental values could be measured in terms other than economic. William Cullen Bryant wrote with such depth of feeling about the simple pleasures of the outdoors that he is still known as one of our foremost nature poets. The founding spirit of transcendentalism, Ralph Waldo Emerson, wrote in his first book, *Nature:*

"In the presence of nature, a wild delight runs through the man. . . . In the woods, is perpetual youth. . . . In the woods, we return to reason and faith. . . . The currents of the Universal Being circulate through me; I am part or particle of God. . . . In the wilderness, I find something more dear and connate than in streets or villages."

Emerson's contemporary, Henry David Thoreau, was even less restrained in his adoration of untamed nature when he wrote: "In Wildness is the preservation of the World." At the same time, Thomas Cole and the Hudson River school of landscape painters captured on canvas the essence of nature that the romantic writers had recorded in prose and poetry. And farther west, beyond the Missis-

sippi River, George Catlin, Karl Bodmer, and Alfred Jacob Miller were painting the exotic wilderness that increasingly drew the attention of Americans.

Unmoved by praise of the aesthetic quality of the environment, frontiersmen were even less impressed by warnings that its resources were not without end. Every American generation since the colonial period had been told of the virtue of using natural resources wisely. An ordinance of Plymouth Colony had regulated the cutting of timber. William Penn had decreed that one acre of trees be left undisturbed for every five acres cleared. In 1864, only a moment before the beginning of the migration that would cover the West within one generation, George Perkins Marsh published his book *Man and Nature,* the most eloquent statement up to that time of the disastrous result that must follow careless stewardship of the land. "Man has too long forgotten," he wrote, "that the earth was given to him for usufruct alone, not for consumption, still less for profligate waste." That is, man could and should both cherish and use the land, but he should not use it up. The significance in Marsh's warning was the recognition that the land could be used up.

3. NATIONAL CONSOLIDATION AND EXPANSION

While American ambassador to Italy, Marsh had theorized that ancient Rome's fall could be traced to the depletion of the empire's forests. He predicted a like fate for the United States if its resources were similarly squandered. Marsh's book appears to have been widely read by American intellectuals and probably favorably influenced the movements for national parks and forestry management. In it, indeed, were the seeds of the conservation movement of the early twentieth century. Yet it is unlikely that many frontiersmen read or were aware of—or at least they did not heed—Marsh's advice.

Pioneers heard a different drummer. They read descriptions about the West written by people who had been there. Lansford W. Hastings's glowing picture of California and Oregon thrilled thousands:

"In view of their increasing population, accumulating wealth, and growing prosperity, I can not but believe, that the time is not distant, when those wild forests, trackless plains, untrodden valleys, and the unbounded ocean, will present one grand scene, of continuous improvements, universal enterprise, and unparalleled commerce: when those vast forests, shall have disappeared, before the hardy pioneer; those extensive plains, shall abound with innumerable herds, of domestic animals; those fertile valleys, shall groan under the immense weight of their abundant products: when those numerous rivers shall team [sic] with countless steam-boats, steam-ships, ships, barques and brigs; when the entire country, will be everywhere intersected, with turnpike roads, rail-roads and canals; and when, all the vastly numerous, and rich resources, of that now, almost unknown region, will be fully and advantageously developed."

Once developed, hopeful emigrants learned, the area would become the garden of the world. In the widely-distributed *Our Western Empire: or the New West Beyond the Mississippi*, Linus P. Brockett wrote that "in no part of the vast domain of the United States, and certainly in no other country under the sun, is there a body of land of equal extent, in which there are so few acres unfit for cultivation, or so many which, with irrigation or without it, will yield such bountiful crops."

Other books described the routes to the Promised Land. The way west was almost without exception easy and well-watered, with plenty of wood, game, and grass.

There was not just opportunity on the frontier. Walt Whitman also saw romance in the westward migration:

> *Come my tan-faced children,*
> *Follow well in order, get your weapons ready,*
> *Have you your pistols? have you your sharp-edged*
> *axes?*
> *Pioneers! O pioneers!*
>
> *For we cannot tarry here,*
> *We must march my darlings, we must bear the brunt*
> *of danger,*

> *We the youthful sinewy races, all the rest on us*
> *depend,*
> *Pioneers! O pioneers! . . .*
>
> *We primeval forests felling,*
> *We the rivers stemming, vexing we and piercing deep*
> *the mines within,*
> *We the surface broad surveying, we the virgin soil*
> *upheaving*
> *Pioneers! O pioneers! . . .*
>
> *Swift! to the head of the army!—swift! spring to your*
> *places, Pioneers! O Pioneers!*

The ingredients were all there: danger, youth, virgin soil. Well might frontiersmen agree with Mark Twain who wrote that the first question asked by the American, upon reaching heaven, was: "Which way West?" Thoreau also thought a westward course the natural one:

"When I go out of the house for a walk . . . my needle . . . always settles between west and south-southwest. The future lies that way to me, and the earth seems more unexhausted and richer on that side. . . . westward I go free. . . . I must walk toward Oregon."

Emigrants felt this same pull but for different reasons. Thoreau's West was a wild region to be enjoyed for itself and preserved untouched, while the West to the emigrants was a place for a new start. The pioneers would conquer the wilderness and gather its immeasurable bounty. This did not imply that Westerners were oblivious to the beauty of the land. Many were aware of the West's scenic attractions but felt, with the influential artist Thomas Cole, that the wilderness, however beautiful, inevitably must give way to progress. In his "Essay on American Scenery," Cole described the sweet joys of nature—the mountains, lakes, rivers, waterfalls, and sky. The essay, dated 1835, is nostalgic. Cole closed his paean with an expression of "sorrow that the beauty of such landscapes are quickly passing away . . . desecrated by what is called improvement." But, after all, he added, "such is the road society has to travel." Clearly, Cole, like most of his nineteenth-century readers, did not question the propriety of "improvement" or the definition of "progress."

THE BELIEF in the inexhaustibility of western resources was superimposed on an attitude toward the land that Americans had inherited from generations past. In the Judeo-Christian view, God created the world for man. Man. was the master of nature rather than a part of it. The resources of the earth—soil, water, plants, animals, insects, rocks, fish, birds, air—were there for his use, and his proper role was to dominate. It was natural then for God's children to harvest the rich garden provided for them by their Creator. They went into the West to do God's bidding, to use the land as he willed, to fulfill a destiny.

This attitude of man-over-nature was not universal. Like most primitive cultures throughout history, it was not held by the American Indian. The Indian saw himself as a part of nature, not its master. He felt a close kinship with the earth and all living things. Black Elk, a holy man of the Oglala Sioux, for example, believed that all living things were the children of the sky, their father, and the earth, their mother. He had special reverence for "the earth, from whence we came and at whose breast we suck as babies all our lives, along with all the animals and birds and trees and grasses." Creation legends of many tribes illustrate the Indian's familial attachment to the earth and his symbiotic relationship with other forms of life.

The land to Indians was more than merely a means of livelihood for the current generation. It belonged not only to them, the living, but to all generations of their people, those who came before and those who would come after. They could not separate themselves from the land. Of course, there were exceptions. Some Indians fell under the spell of the white trader who offered them goods that would make their lives easier, not to say better. As they became dependent on white man's goods, the land and its fruits began to assume for them an economic value that might be bartered for the conveniences produced by the white man's technology. This is not to say that the Indian attitude toward the land changed. Rather it illustrates that some Indians adopted the white man's view.

To European-Americans, the western Indians' use of the land was just another proof of their savagery. The pioneers had listened to the preachers of Manifest Destiny, and they knew that the nomadic tribes must stand aside for God's Chosen People who would use the land as God intended.

And so they returned to Eden. While some went to California and some to Oregon, the most coherent migration before the rush for California gold began in 1849 was the Mormon exodus to Salt Lake Valley. The latter was not typical of the westward movement. The persecuted saints entered the West not so much for its lure as because of its inaccessibility. In 1830, the same year that the Mormon Church was founded, Joseph Smith announced a revelation which would lead eventually to—or at least foresaw —the great migration:

"And ye are called to bring to pass the gathering of mine elect . . . unto one place upon the face of this land . . . [which] . . . shall be on the borders by the Lamanites [Indians]. . . . The glory of the Lord shall be there, and it shall be called Zion. . . . The righteous shall be gathered out from among all nations, and shall come to Zion, singing with songs of everlasting joy."

Mormons who trekked to the Utah settlements in the late 1840s and 1850s knew they were doing God's bidding.

Other emigrants were just as sure that the Lord had prepared a place for them. "Truly the God in Heaven," wrote an Oregon-bound traveler in 1853, "has spread in rich profusion around us everything which could happify man and reveal the Wisdom and Benevolence of God to man." Oregon Trail travelers often noted in their journals that they were going to the "Promised Land." In A. B. Guthrie's *The Way West,* Fairman, who would be leaving Independence shortly for Oregon, proposed a toast "to a place

where there's no fever." McBee, another emigrant, impatient to get started, responded:

" 'Y God, yes, . . . and to soil rich as anything. Plant a nail and it'll come up a spike. I heerd you don't never have to put up hay, the grass is that good, winter and all. And lambs come twice a year. Just set by and let the grass grow and the critters birth and get fat. That's my idee of farmin.' "

It seems that most emigrants, in spite of the humor, did not expect their animals or themselves to wax fat in the new land without working. God would provide, but they must harvest.

Following close on the heels of the Oregon Trail farmers, and sometimes traveling in the same wagon trains, were the miners. This rough band of transients hardly thought of themselves as God's children, but they did nevertheless accept the horn-of-plenty image of the West. Granville Stuart wrote from the California mines that "no such enormous amounts of gold had been found anywhere before, and . . . they all believed that the supply was inexhaustible." Theirs was not an everflowing cornucopia, however, and each miner hoped to be in the right spot with an open sack when the horn tipped to release its wealth.

The typical miner wanted to get as rich as possible as quickly as possible so he could return home to family, friends, and a nabob's retirement. This condition is delightfully pictured in the frontispiece illustration in Mark Twain's *Roughing It.* A dozing miner is seated on a barrel in his cabin, his tools on the floor beside him. He is dreaming about the future: a country estate, yachting, carriage rides and walks in the park with a lady, an ocean voyage and a tour of Europe, viewing the pyramids. The dreams of other miners, while not so grand, still evoked pleasant images of home and an impatience to return there. This yearning is obvious in the lines of a miner's song of the 1850s:

> *Home's dearest joys Time soon destroys,*
> *Their loss we all deplore;*
> *While they may last, we labor fast*
> *To dig the golden ore.*
> When the land has yielded its riches:
> *Then home again, home again,*
> *From a foreign shore,*
> *We'll sing how sweet our heart's delight,*
> *With our dear friends once more.*

Miners' diaries often reflected these same sentiments, perhaps with less honeyed phrases but with no less passion.

A practical-minded argonaut, writing in 1852 from California to his sister in Alabama, explained his reason for going to the mines: "I think in one year here I can make enough to clear me of debt and give me a pretty good start in the world. Then I will be a happy man." What then? He instructed his sister to tell all his friends that he would soon be "back whare [sic] I can enjoy there [sic] company." Other miners thought it would take a little longer, but the motives were the same. A California miner later reminisced:

"Five years was the longest period any one expected to stay. Five years at most was to be given to rifling California of her treasures, and then that country was to be thrown aside like a used-up newspaper and the rich adventurers would spend the remainder of their days in wealth, peace, and prosperity at their eastern homes. No one talked then of going out 'to build up the glorious State of California.'"

The fact that many belatedly found that California was more than worked-out diggings and stayed—pronouncing the state glorious and themselves founding fathers—does not change their motives for going there.

There was a substantial body of miners, perpetually on the move, rowdies usually, the frontier fraternity boys, whose home was the mining camp and whose friends were largely miners like themselves. They rushed around the West to every discovery of gold or silver in a vain attempt to get rich without working. Though they had no visions of returning east to family and fireside, they did believe that the West was plentifully supplied with riches. It was just their bad luck that they had not found their shares. Their original reason for going to the mining camps and, though they might enjoy the camaraderie of their fellows, their reason for staying, was the same as that of the more genteel sort of miner who had come to the western wilderness, fully expecting to return to the East. More than any other emigrant to the West, the miner's motive was unabashed exploitation. For the most part, he did not conserve, preserve, or enrich the land. His intention, far from honorable, was rape.

THE CATTLEMAN was a transition figure between the miner who stripped the land and the farmer who, while stripping the land, also cherished it. The West to the cattleman meant grass and water, free or cheap. The earliest ranchers on the plains raised beef for the eastern markets and for the government, which had decreed that the cow replace the buffalo in the Plains Indians' life-style. The Indians, except for a few "renegades," complied, though they were never quite able to work the steer into their religion.

It was not long before word filtered back to the East that fortunes could be made in western stock raising. James Brisbin's *Beef Bonanza; or, How to Get Rich on the Plains,* first published in 1881, was widely read. Readers were dazzled by the author's minutely documented "proof" that an industrious man could more than double his investment in less than five years. Furthermore, there was almost no risk involved:

"In a climate so mild that horses, cattle, and sheep and goats can live in the open air through all the winter months, and fatten on the dry and apparently withered grasses of the soil, there would appear to be scarcely a limit to the number that could be raised."

Experienced and inexperienced alike responded. Getting rich, they thought, was only a matter of time, not expertise.

Entrepreneurs and capital, American and foreign, poured into the West. Most of the rangeland was not in private ownership. Except for small tracts, generally homesteaded along water courses or as sites for home ranches, it was public property. Though a cattleman might claim rights to a certain range, and though an association of cattlemen might try to enforce the claims of its members, legally the land was open, free, and available.

By the mid-1880s, the range was grossly overstocked. The injury to the land was everywhere apparent. While some began to counsel restraint, most ranchers continued to ravish the country until the winter of 1886–1887 forced them to respect it. Following that most disastrous of winters, which in some areas killed as much as 85 percent of range stock, one chastened cattle king wrote that the cattle business "that had been fascinating to me before, suddenly became distasteful. . . . I never wanted to own again an animal that I could not feed and shelter." The industry gradually recovered, but it would never be the same. More land was fenced, wells dug, and windmills installed. Shelters for cattle were built, and hay was grown for winter feeding. Cattle raising became less an adventure and more a business.

In some cattlemen there grew an attachment, if not affection, for the land. Some, especially after the winter of 1886–1887, began to put down roots. Others who could afford it built luxurious homes in the towns to escape the deficiencies of the countryside, much as twentieth-century townsmen would build cabins in the country to escape the deficiencies of the cities. Probably most cattlemen after the winter of 1886–1887 still believed in the bounty of the West, but a bounty which they now recognized would be released to them only through husbandry.

Among all those who went into the West to seek their fortunes, the frontier farmers carried with them the highest hopes and greatest faith. Their forebears had been told for generations that they were the most valuable citizens, chosen of God, and that their destiny lay westward. John Filson, writing in 1784 about frontier Kentucky, described the mystique of the West that would be understood by post-Civil War emigrants:

"This fertile region, abounding with all the luxuries of nature, stored with all the principal materials for art and industry, inhabited by virtuous and ingenious citizens, must universally attract the attention of mankind." There, continued Filson, "like the land of promise, flowing with milk and honey, a land of brooks of water, . . . a land of wheat and barley, and all kinds of fruits, you shall eat bread without scarceness, and not lack any thing in it."

By 1865 the Civil War had settled the controversy between North and South that had hindered the westward movement, the Homestead Act had been passed, and the Myth of the Garden had replaced the Myth of the Desert. By the grace of God and with the blessing of Washington, the frontier farmer left the old land to claim his own in the new:

> Born of a free, world-wandering race,
> Little we yearned o'er an oft-turned sod.
> What did we care for the father's place,
> Having ours fresh from the hand of God?

Farmers were attracted to the plains by the glowing accounts distributed by railroads and western states. Newspapers in the frontier states added their accolades. The editor of the *Kansas Farmer* declared in 1867 that there were in his state "vast areas of unimproved land, rich as that on the banks of the far famed Nile, . . . acres, miles, leagues, townships, counties,—oceans of land, all ready for the plough, good as the best in America, and yet lying without occupants." Would-be emigrants who believed this sort of propaganda could sing with conviction:

> Oh! give me a home where the buffalo roam,
> Where the deer and the antelope play;
> Where never is heard a discouraging word,
> And the sky is not clouded all day.

There was a reason for the sky's clarity, the emigrants learned when they arrived on the plains. It was not long before many had changed their song:

> We've reached the land of desert sweet,
> Where nothing grows for man to eat;
>
> I look across the plains
> And wonder why it never rains.

And, finally, sung to the cadence of a "slow, sad march":

> We do not live, we only stay;
> We are too poor to get away.

It is difficult to generalize about the experience of pioneer farmers. Those who continued their journeys to the Pacific Coast regions were usually satisfied with what they found. It was those who settled on the plains who were most likely to be disillusioned. Their experience was particularly shattering since they had gone to the West not just to reap in it but also to live in it. Most found not the land of milk and honey they expected, but, it seems, a life of drudgery and isolation.

The most persistent theme in the literature of the period is disenchantment. This mood is caught best by Hamlin Garland. In *Main-Travelled Roads,* Garland acknowledged two views of the plains experience when he wrote that the main-travelled road in the West, hot and dusty in summer, muddy and dreary in fall and spring, and snowy in winter, "does sometimes cross a rich meadow where the songs of the larks and bobolinks and blackbirds are tangled." But Garland's literary road is less cluttered: "Mainly it is long and wearyful, and has a dull little town at one end and a home of toil at the other. Like the main-travelled road of life it is traversed by many classes of people, but the poor and the weary predominate."

The opposite responses to the plains are more pronounced in O. E. Rölvaag's *Giants in the Earth,* one of the most enduring novels of the agricultural West. Per Hansa meets the challenge of the new land, overcomes obstacles and rejoices in each success, however small. He accepts the prairie for what it is and loves it. Meanwhile, his wife, Beret, is gradually driven insane by that same prairie. Where Per Hansa saw hope and excitement in the land, Beret saw only despair and loneliness. "Oh, how quickly it grows dark out here!" she cries, to which Per Hansa replies, "The sooner the day's over, the sooner the next day comes!" In spite of her husband's optimistic outlook, Beret's growing insanity dominates the story as it moves with gloomy intensity to its tragic end. It is significant that Per Hansa dies, a victim of the nature that he did not fear but could not subdue.

Willa Cather, the best-known novelist of nineteenth-century prairie farm life, treated relationships between people and their environment more sensitively than most. While her earlier short stories often dwell on themes of man against the harsh land, her works thereafter, without glossing over the severity of farm life, reveal a certain harmony between the land and those who live on it and love it. Her characters work hard, and suffer; but they are not immune to the loveliness of the land.

The histories of plains farming dwell more on processes than suffering, but accounts that treat the responses of the settlers to their environment generally verify the novelists' interpretations. According to the histories, the picture of desperation painted by Garland and Rölvaag applies principally to the earliest years of any particular frontier region. By the time sod houses acquired board floors and women were able to visit with other women regularly, Cather's images are more accurate.

The fact that pioneer farmers were not completely satisfied with what they found in the Promised Land does not alter their reasons for going there. They had gone into the West for essentially the same reason as the trappers, miners, and cattlemen: economic exploitation. Unlike their predecessors, they also had been looking for homes. Yet, like them, they had believed fervently in the Myth of Superabundance.

THE IRRATIONAL BELIEF that the West's resources were so great that they could never be used up was questioned by some at the very time that others considered it an article of faith. George Perkins Marsh in 1864 warned of the consequences of a too rapid consumption of the land's resources. In 1878, John Wesley Powell attacked the Myth of the Garden when he pointed out that a substantial portion of western land, previously thought to be cultivable by eastern methods, could be farmed successfully only by irrigation. Overgrazing of grasslands resulted in the intrusion of weeds and the erosion of soil, prompting many ranchers, especially after the devastating winter of 1886–1887, to contract their operations and practice range management. Plowing land where rainfall was inadequate for traditional farming methods resulted in wind and water erosion of the soil. Before the introduction of irrigation or dry farming techniques, many plains

3. NATIONAL CONSOLIDATION AND EXPANSION

farmers gave up and returned eastward. The buffalo, which might have numbered fifty million or more at mid-century, were hunted almost to extinction by 1883. Passenger pigeons were estimated to number in the billions in the first half of the nineteenth century: around 1810, Alexander Wilson, an ornithologist, guessed that a single flock, a mile wide and 240 miles long, contained more than two billion birds. Yet before the end of the century, market hunting and the clearing of forest habitats had doomed the passenger pigeon to extinction. Examples of this sort led many people to the inescapable conclusion that the West's resources were not inexhaustible.

At the same time a growing number of people saw values other than economic in the West. Some plains farmers struggling with intermittent drought and mortgage could still see the beauty of the land. Alexandra in Cather's *O Pioneers!* could see it: "When the road began to climb the first long swells of the Divide, Alexandra hummed an old Swedish hymn. . . . Her face was so radiant" as she looked at the land "with love and yearning. It seemed beautiful to her, rich and strong and glorious. Her eyes drank in the breadth of it, until her tears blinded her."

Theodore Roosevelt wrote often of the "delicious" rides he took at his Badlands ranch during autumn and spring. He described the rolling, green grasslands; the prairie roses; the blacktail and whitetail deer; the songs of the skylark; the white-shouldered lark-bunting; and the sweet voice of the meadowlark, his favorite. Of a moonlight ride, he wrote that the "river gleams like running quicksilver, and the moonbeams play over the grassy stretches of the plateaus and glance off the wind-rippled blades as they would from water." Lincoln Lang, a neighbor of Roosevelt's, had the same feeling for the land. He called the Badlands "a landscape masterpiece of the wild, . . . verdant valleys, teeming with wild life, with wild fruits and flowers, . . . with the God-given atmosphere of truth itself, over which unshackled Nature, alone, reigned queen."

Even miners were not immune to the loveliness of the countryside. Granville Stuart, working in the California mines, was struck by the majestic forests of sugar pine, yellow pine, fir, oak, and dogwood. He described the songs and coloration of the birds and the woodpeckers' habit of storing acorns in holes that they meticulously pecked in tree limbs. He delighted in watching a covey of quail near his cabin each day. "Never was I guilty of killing one," he added. Bret Harte lived among the California miners, and his stories often turn to descriptions of the picturesque foothills of the Sierra Nevada. After the birth of "The Luck" in Roaring Camp, the proud, self-appointed godfathers decorated the baby's "bower with flowers and sweet-smelling shrubs, . . . wild honey-suckles, azaleas, or the painted blossoms of Las Mariposas. The men had suddenly awakened to the fact that there were beauty and significance in these trifles, which they had so long trodden carelessly beneath their feet."

Success of some sort often broadened the frontiersman's viewpoint. The miner, cattleman, or farmer who had succeeded in some way in his struggle with the land had more time and inclination to think about his relationship with it. Viewing his environment less as an adversary, the Westerner began to see what was happening to it.

At times, concern for the environment led to action. The mounting protests of Californians whose homes and farms had been damaged by the silt-laden runoff from hydraulic mining finally led to the outlawing of this mindless destruction of the land. Frederick Law Olmsted, who had designed New York's Central Park, initiated an era in 1864 when he and some friends persuaded Congress to grant to the state of California a piece of land in California's Sierra Nevada for the creation of a park, merely because the land, which included Yosemite Valley and the Mariposa Big Trees, was beautiful and the public would enjoy it. The idea took hold, and other parks soon followed, Yellowstone in 1872 being the first public "pleasuring ground" under federal management. The new art of landscape photography showed Easterners the wonders of the West, without the hardships of getting there, and revealed to many Westerners a land they inhabited but had never seen. With the improvement in transportation, principally railroads, more and more people ventured into the West to see these wonders firsthand.

A growing awareness that unrestrained exploitation was fast destroying the natural beauty of the West and that its resources, by the end of the nineteenth century widely acknowledged to be finite, were being consumed at an alarming pace led to considerable soul-searching. Frederick Jackson Turner, who had most eloquently described the influence that the great expanses of western land had on the shaping of American character, also hinted that the disappearance of available land was likely to cause some serious disruptions in American society. "The frontier has gone," he wrote, "and with its going has closed the first period of American history."

If the first phase of American history, in which a dominant theme was the advance of the frontier, ran from 1607 to 1890, the second phase began with the emergence of the conservation movement which would lead to the alteration of fundamental attitudes toward the land nurtured during the first phase. While based generally on concern for the environment, the movement split in the early twentieth century into two factions. One faction argued for wise management of the country's resources to prevent their being wasted. This "utilitarian conservation" was not a break with the frontier view of exploitation. It was a refinement. While the frontier view was one of rapid exploitation of inexhaustible resources, the utilitarian conservationists rejected the myth of inexhaustibility and advocated the careful use of finite resources, without rejecting the basic assumption that the resources were there to be exploited. This view of conservation led to the setting aside and management of forest reserves, soil and water conservation projects, and irrigation and hydroelectric programs.

The other faction, whose ideology has been called "aesthetic conservation," clearly broke with the frontier past when its members argued for the preservation of areas of natural beauty for public enjoyment. This group's efforts bore fruit in the establishment of national and state parks, monuments and wilderness areas. There are indications that the two factions are drawing closer together in the umbrella ecology movement of the 1970s, perhaps eventually to merge.

It is senseless to compare nineteenth-century frontier attitudes toward the land with today's more enlightened views. Faced seemingly with such plenty—billions of passenger pigeons, millions of buffalo, innumerable beaver,

endless seas of grass, vast forests of giant trees, mines to shame King Solomon's—excess was understandable and probably inevitable. Excess in this case meant waste. Here the Turner thesis is most meaningful, for the belief in the inexhaustibility of resources in the West generated the unique American acceptance of waste as the fundamental tenet of a life-style. For this, the frontiersman is not entirely blameless. But certainly, he is less blameworthy than the neo-pioneer who continues, against reason and history, to cling hopefully to the myth of inexhaustibility. Yet there were examples, however few, and voices, however dim, that the frontiersman might have heeded. It remains to be seen whether Americans today have learned the lesson their ancestors, four generations removed, failed to comprehend.

BIBLIOGRAPHIC NOTE

There are few comprehensive surveys of the evolution of American attitudes toward the environment. Three useful sources are Stewart L. Udall, *The Quiet Crisis* (New York: Holt, Rinehart, 1963); Hans Huth, *Nature and the American: Three Centuries of Changing Attitudes* (Berkeley: University of California, 1957); and Roderick Nash, *Wilderness and the American Mind,* rev. ed. (New Haven: Yale University, 1973), the last particularly concerned with the American response to wilderness. Frederick Jackson Turner's frontier thesis, which inevitably must be considered in any study of the relationship between Americans and their environment, is in his *The Frontier in American History* (New York: Henry Holt, 1921). Invaluable to an understanding of what Americans thought the West was is Henry Nash Smith, *Virgin Land: The American West as Symbol and Myth* (New York: Vintage Books, 1950). The most influential book of the twentieth century in the development of a land ethic is Aldo Leopold, *A Sand County Almanac* (New York: Oxford University, 1949).

Selections from historical materials and literature were blended in this study to illustrate western emigrants' expectations for and responses to the new country. In addition to titles listed in the text, literary impressions of nature are in Wilson O. Clough, *The Necessary Earth: Nature and Solitude in American Literature* (Austin: University of Texas, 1964) and John Conron, *The American Landscape: A Critical Anthology of Prose and Poetry* (New York: Oxford University, 1974). Useful bibliographies of the literature of the westward movement are Lucy Lockwood Hazard, *The Frontier in American Literature* (New York: Thomas Y. Crowell, 1927) and Richard W. Etulain, *Western American Literature* (Vermillion, S.D.: University of South Dakota, 1972). Bibliographies of historical materials are in Ray Allen Billington, *Westward Expansion,* 4th ed. (New York: Macmillan, 1974), and Nelson Klose, *A Concise Study Guide to the American Frontier* (Lincoln: University of Nebraska, 1964).

Lucretia Mott
'A Woman of Sufficient Confidence'

Dana Greene

Dana Greene is associate professor of history at St. Mary's College of Maryland.

If the stereotyping of women seems pervasive and intractable today, imagine the situation faced by the 19th century foremothers of the women's rights movement. Every institution—the schools, the church, law, medicine, and daily custom—confirmed what was deemed to be the divinely ordained role for women. Rich or poor, she was to be helpmeet of man. Marriage was her primary goal; upon its fulfillment the husband and wife became one and, as the English jurist William Blackstone indicated, that one was the husband. A woman who believed otherwise was alone in her unorthodoxy. There were few models for independent women. No consciousness-raising groups banded for support; no popular literature challenged women's role; no organizations lobbied to change her condition.

Of course, there have always been women who broke out of that powerful stereotype, but they were not members of the respectable middle class. The poor and the deviant were considered outside the pale of society. The broad latitude of behavior allowed them was purchased at tremendous price. The very rich had their own kind of protection; money and social status assured them a limited immunity from criticism. But for respectable white women of the middle class, those who came to make up the ranks of the woman's rights movement in the 19th century, there was no such protection. They, above all others, were expected to conform. How was it, then, that they were able to break through the stereotype and risk their respectability?

Obviously, the vision of each of those women was her own. However, for many of the earliest feminists (1830 to 1850), their religious experience provided the basis for a new vision of womankind.

On its surface, that fact does not seem too surprising given the

---

The religious veneration of woman has been so misdirected by her religious training, that she needs to be taught to judge for herself. She will find, when she does so, that the Scriptures have been perverted and that the customs of society are not always founded in truth and justice. Nor will her veneration for the good, the true, and the divine be lessened when she learns to respect the divinity of her own nature; nor will she be ashamed of this new Gospel of truth, or afraid to declare it before the people.
—Lucretia Mott, 1856

---

enormous female participation in the evangelical revivals of the early part of the 19th century. However, while the religious rebirth led many women to involvement in a whole series of reform movements, it was fundamentally hostile toward feminism. In fact many early feminists rejected ortho-

dox Christianity or were members of minority sects, such as the Society of Friends (Quakers) and Unitarians, who were outside the mainstream of religious expression in America. If religious experience was an important influence on early feminists, their activity was frequently labeled as heretical by established religious institutions.

Perhaps the clearest bond between religious experience and the pioneer feminist movement is found in the person of Lucretia Mott, a Quaker minister and early supporter of abolition and feminism. Hailed through the 1860s as the guiding light of the woman's rights movement, Mott was the most respected of American feminists. Her lifelong commitment to freedom for American Negroes won her the sobriquet, the black man's goddess. In 1980, the centennial of her death, she is recognized as a profoundly religious woman who inspired others to strive, as she did, for a just society. Abolitionist and feminist, Mott was also a pacifist, a supporter of temperance, and an advocate for the rights of Indians and immigrants. She was a prophetic orator and preacher; yet her manner radiated total serenity. She used her wit and extensive command of scripture to demolish the arguments of her opponents. Her blameless life brought respectability to unpopular causes, and her personal presence was powerful and compelling—qualities that were remarked by admirers and adversaries alike.

It is immediately obvious that Mott was an undivided woman. She believed steadfastly in her work, and once a cause or person won her support she remained a constant defender. She was always able to maintain her position without personally rejecting her antagonist. Disagreements

Copyright 1981 American Association of University Women; reprinted from Graduate Woman.

among friends and fellow reformers were painful for her; she frequently served to reconcile dissident reformist factions.

When the Equal Rights Association began to disintegrate in the late 1860s, she tried to mediate between those who believed that the 15th Amendment and votes for black males must be supported at all costs and those who maintained that suffrage must be extended to females as well. She defended an old friend, abolitionist Wendell Phillips, against the attacks of Elizabeth Cady Stanton and Susan B. Anthony, but she nonetheless agreed with the feminist position that women should have the vote as well. She also condemned the sometimes racially-tainted arguments of her staunch friend, Stanton.

There was no sense of inner turmoil in Lucretia Mott's life. Unlike many feminists, she saw no conflict between her activities as a reformer and her demanding domestic life as the mother of five and the emotional center of a large extended Quaker

---

When woman shall be properly trained, and her spiritual powers developed she will find in entering the marriage union nothing necessarily degrading to her. The independence of the husband and wife should be equal, and the dependence reciprocal.
—Lucretia Mott, 1853

---

family. Since she was not wealthy, Mott did most of her household work herself. There is every indication that she thrived on cooking, cleaning, and sewing; she frequently entertained 30 for dinner. Quakers, literati, abolitionists, runaway slaves, feminists, and beggars—all were welcome at her table.

Her personal qualities of inner serenity and unlimited energy helped Mott endure the rough and tumble of 19th century reform politics. But what vision drove her to participate in

such a wide range of humanitarian causes? A refusal to participate in secular reform activities would have been sanctioned by members of the Society of Friends on the grounds that such involvement might corrupt her spiritual values. But Lucretia Mott did not choose the option of quiet respectability; she threw herself into reformist activities, pitting her vision of the world against the formidable forces of custom, superstition, and orthodox Christianity.

Mott's Early Life
Mott was raised by Quaker parents on the island of Nantucket, a place of strong women who supported and sustained their families while their husbands were at sea. Most of her education was acquired at Nine Partners School, a coeducational Quaker boarding school where females were provided with an education that almost equaled that given to males. At Nine Partners, she learned of the horrors of the slave trade and experienced the inequities endured by women. There too she met her future husband, James Mott, a fellow Quaker with whom she shared years of tender mutual support and a common commitment to reform in American society.

After the death of her second child, Mott turned increasingly to religion. At 28, she was recognized as a minister in the Society of Friends. Mott's Quakerism, more than any other single factor, provided the basic assumptions for her vision of a just society and her commitment to reform.

During the early 19th century a schism occurred within the Society of Friends over questions of religious authority and the role of the church's members in the world. Lucretia Mott joined the Hicksite branch, largely because she believed that the ideals of primitive Quakerism were best realized among that group. Throughout her ministerial life she was often at odds with the Hicksites, but she managed to deflect efforts to disown her and committed herself to staying within the Quaker fold. She believed she could do more good within the Society than outside of it.

The Hicksite understanding of religious experience was particularly influential for Mott. Hicksites emphasized the presence of the "inner light"

and reaffirmed the early Quaker notion that religious authority was internal, not necessarily contained in the teachings of ministers and elders. Revelation was considered personal and continuous, and scripture was understood to be open to reinterpretation under the guidance of the spirit. Those notions of the nature of religious experience were to have profound implications for Mott's understanding of her own religious experience and her view of religion's role in society.

Quakerism also gave Mott a positive attitude toward the role of women. From its inception in the 17th century the Society of Friends had always recognized the validity of women ministers. If there was "that of God in everyone," as the Society's founder George Fox claimed, then women must not be denied the opportunity to speak and preach. Furthermore, female Quakers organized their own business meetings to raise money for and carry out a whole range of service activities. That is not to say that Quaker women were considered totally equal with Quaker

---

I have no idea, because I am a Non-Resistant, of submitting tamely to injustice inflicted either on me or on the slave. I will oppose it with all the moral powers with which I am endowed.
—Lucretia Mott, 1860

---

men. In matters of church governance they were clearly subordinate. But relative to their status in other denominations, Quaker women had extraordinary independence as the spiritual equals of men.

Abolitionist to Feminist
Although Mott's feminism was securely rooted in Quaker tradition, she came to woman's rights (as did a number of early feminists) through her activities as an abolitionist. Mott was a strong supporter of William Lloyd Garrison, who promoted the idea of unconditional and immediate emancipation of the slaves. Like Garrison, she was committed to the belief

that intellectual and moral agitation were necessary to achieve concrete reform. Mott's work as an abolitionist catapulted her into an examination of the degraded condition of women. Excluded on account of her sex from a delegate's seat at the 1840 World Anti-Slavery Convention in London, she became acutely aware of the limitations placed on female reformers. In 1848 she joined with Elizabeth Cady Stanton in calling the first woman's rights convention in Seneca Falls, NY, to examine the political, social,

---

The question is often asked, 'what does woman want, more than she enjoys?' What is she seeking to obtain? Of what rights is she deprived? What privileges are withheld from her? I answer, she asks nothing as favor, but as right, she wants to be acknowledged a moral, responsible being.
—Lucretia Mott, 1849

---

economic, and religious condition of women.

For the next 20 years, Mott labored to build support for the fledgling woman's rights movement. Her life was intimately linked with those of all the important feminists of the mid-19th century. As one of the oldest, she often served as their mentor. Elizabeth Cady Stanton, younger than Mott by 22 years, wrote of their first meeting in the *History of Woman Suffrage:* "Thus came Lucretia Mott to me, at a period in my young days when all life's problems seemed inextricably tangled. . . . I often longed to meet some woman who had sufficient confidence in herself to frame and hold an opinion in the face of op-

position, a woman who understood the deep significance of life to whom I could talk freely; my longings were answered at last."

Susan B. Anthony attested, in the same chronicle, that when Lucretia Mott was on her side she knew she was right.

As the antislavery issue had occupied Mott's early life, the question of women came to dominate her middle years. Toward the end of her life, she became increasingly interested in peace and antisectarianism, but she continued to raise the question of woman's rights at every opportunity.

Mott was above all a preacher, an orator, an agitator. She wrote almost nothing for publication and her sermons and speeches were all given extemporaneously at religious, peace, women's rights, or abolitionist meetings. Preserved in the minutes and proceedings of those many organizations, her words stand as a testimony to the power of religious insight in the reform of society.

In her speeches, Mott's analysis of the condition of women and the causes of their subordination is clearly articulated. In the famous *Discourse on Woman* delivered in 1849, she maintained that the present condition of women was paralyzing and enervating and that such a condition was neither natural nor divinely ordained. She offered numerous examples of strong women, both biblical and contemporary, whose lives refuted the stereotype of the frivolous, empty-headed female.

For Mott, males and females were created equal by God. One of the wages of sin was the subordination of women. When spiritually reborn, women would stand again as men's equals, and consequently any work to establish that divinely ordained equality became a religious work.

Again and again Mott brought the churches under heaviest attack, claiming that they were one of the greatest obstacles to changing the condition of women. Not only did institutional religion subordinate wom-

en and exclude them from its ministry, but it justified that subordination on religious grounds.

Mott urged women to be wary of ministers and sects and faithful to their own God-given powers. She admonished them to respect the divinity within, to stop "pinning [their] faith on other peoples' sleeves," and to examine the scriptures and their beliefs themselves.

In her analysis of women's condition, Mott never claimed female superiority. "I believe," she said in a sermon in Boston in 1841, "that, when truth directs us, there will be no longer assumed authority on one side, or admitted inferiority on the other; but that as we advance in the cultivation of all our powers, . . . we shall see that our independence is equal, our dependence mutual, and our obligations reciprocal."

The fact that women's equality with men could not be proven did not dismay her. She found women so crushed by law, custom, and perverted Christianity, that their bondage was complete; they did not even desire liberty or equality. Only if they were taught to rely on their own God-given powers would they come to regard themselves and to behave as equal, moral, responsible beings. In that same 1841 sermon she proclaimed, "I long for the time when my sisters will rise and occupy the sphere to which they are called by their high nature and destiny. What a change would then appear in the character of woman! We should no longer find her the mere plaything of man, and a frivolous appendage of society."

Mott's religious experience led her to a life of reformist activities, but her unorthodox beliefs provided the vision of a just society, a source of personal courage, and the authority to challenge the status quo. Driven by her own truth, she contested the untruth of the world around her. After more than a century, Lucretia Mott looms out of the past, an indomitable personality, a source of courage and inspiration for contemporary women.

The Green & the Gold

Brian McGinty

Brian McGinty *is a San Francisco attorney and writer who contributes frequently to* The American West. *His most recent book is* The Palace Inns: A Connoisseur's Guide to Historic American Hotels.

Early in the nineteenth century, an Irish priest, returning from a pilgrimage to Rome, happened on a Christian church somewhere in the remote deserts of Tunisia. At the church, the priest was greeted by a sun-bronzed patriarch, a seer who told him of a strange vision. "I behold," said the patriarch, "a great exodus from the confines once known as Hibernia, a million of her distracted natives leaving their thatched cabins on the fens and the moors, and dragging their emaciated forms to the western shores, and there the tall-masted ships bear them over the wide bosom of the ocean called Atlantic. . . . And I see out on the western coast of America, where nature smiles the whole year through, a glorious new empire spring into existence as if by magic, where there is golden treasure in the hills if they but dig for it, and wealth in the valleys if they but nourish and harvest it."

Because the priest was an Irishman, he was neither suprised nor unsettled by this fanciful North African vision. The Irish have been mystics, visionaries, and dreamers at least as long as they have been warriors and saints. Far away from the knobby summit of Tara of the Kings and the murky waters of the River Liffey, they have carried their faith in spirits and wraiths, their mystical trust in the shadowy forces that transcend the here and now and commune with the heretofore and the hereafter, to remote corners of the civilized and uncivilized earth.

Visions have a way of becoming realities—or so it seems to believers. And for the Irish, at least, the pioneer experience in Western America was in many respects a vision come true, for the treasures they found on the slopes of the Sierra Nevada and along the sandy shore of the Pacific were only slightly less wonderful than those described by the North African seer.

The Irish migration to California in the 1850s was part of a much larger movement that swept up the peoples of a score of nations and sent them scurrying halfway round the world in an impulsive pursuit of wealth and a more desperate search for relief from the oppressive conditions of their Old World lives. The bloody revolutions which swept the capitals of continental Europe in 1848 uprooted tens of thousands of Germans, Frenchmen, Italians, Austrians, and Hungarians, forcing them to flee tyrannical governments and abandon tired lands. Blight struck the potato crops of Ireland—a staple of the national diet—in 1845 and 1846. As the smell of potatoes rotting in the fields mingled with the stench of death that rose from cottages and hedgerows, hordes of hungry immigrants crowded like cattle into creaking ships that filled the harbors of Dublin and Cork. The ships were destined for England or South America, for Australia or New Zealand—for any stretch of halfway hospitable soil where the Irish might find food and a chance for a decent life.

As the famine continued through 1847 and 1848, many Irish refugees found their way to the United States, particularly to the cities of the Northeast, where they crowded tenements and pounded cobbled pavements in a frantic search for food and work. News of the discovery of gold in the tailrace of a sawmill on the American River in faraway California electrified the Irish as much as—perhaps more than—any other people. California was a Hispanic land, inhabited by warm-blooded Latins who, like the Irish, worshipped at candlelit altars and acknowledged the spiritual authority of the Bishop of Rome. Since the days of the Norman conquest of Ireland, the English rulers of the Emerald Isle had been heartily hated by Irish patriots. Like Ireland, Boston and New York were dominated by an Anglo-Saxon elite who had little use and less respect for the "shanty Irish" surrounding them. There were Anglo-Americans in numbers in California in 1848, but the country still bore the strong imprint of the padres and the missions. There was, moreover, gold to be had almost for the taking in the foothills of the Sierra. The rush to California began in earnest in 1849, and, from the beginning, it had a strong Hibernian flavor.

THERE WERE, of course, Irish settlers in California before the Gold Rush. Joseph O'Cain, an Irish-born sailor on an English ship that stopped at Santa Barbara in 1795, was probably the first non-Spanish European to

Copyright 1978 by American West Publishing Co. Reprinted from *The American West,* March/April 1978 by permission of the author.

apply for permission to live in California. His petition was rejected, but he continued to frequent the coast, hunting sea otters with a crew of Aleut oarsmen and dividing his profits with the Russian colonists in Alaska. The first non-Spaniard to settle in California may well have been John Milligan, a native of Ireland's County Down, who arrived early in 1814. Milligan taught weaving to the mission Indians and acquired an interest in a rancho in the Salinas Valley. A more prominent Irish settler was Timothy Murphy, a Wexford-born shipping clerk who came to California in 1828, settled on a sprawling rancho in Marin County, and, as Don Timoteo, became one of the country's wealthiest landowners.

Paralleling Murphy's experience north of San Francisco Bay was that of two Irish brothers who, in the 1840s, acquired large estates in Southern California. Nicholas Den, born in Kilkenny in 1812, arrived at Monterey on an American ship in 1836. He settled at Santa Barbara, married the daughter of a Yankee captain and a Spanish woman, and acquired large ranchos. When he died in 1862, he was one of the richest and most respected of the Santa Barbara dons. Den's younger brother Richard was a physician and surgeon trained in Dublin. He came to California in 1843, received a license to practice his profession in Los Angeles, and for more than half a century ministered to the medical needs of the largely Spanish pueblo population.

Jasper O'Farrell was another Irishman who achieved prominence in pre-Gold Rush California. Born in Dublin in 1817, he came to California in 1843, found he liked the country around San Francisco Bay, and determined to settle there. Trained as a surveyor, O'Farrell found steady employment plotting the boundaries of the large ranchos that bordered the bay. In 1847, the alcalde of the village of Yerba Buena asked the Irishman to lay out the town's streets. Working north as far as North Beach and west as far as Taylor Street, O'Farrell adopted an unusual plan for the area south of the town plaza, where he laid out a grid of streets at an oblique angle to the plaza grid. Cutting a broad avenue through the intersection of the two grids, he created the thoroughfare known as Market Street. Years after Yerba Buena became San Francisco, the Dublin-born surveyor was remembered by pedestrians and motorists who traversed the busy surface of downtown O'Farrell Street. But long before that, O'Farrell had retired to a large estate in Sonoma County, where he lived in a princely style that would have done justice to any of a hundred English squires in the Emerald Isle.

The Murphys, the Dens, and the O'Farrells found the pastoral setting of Spanish and Mexican California a congenial one in which to live and to work. Though they were men of ability, they were not (like the Yankees who visited the coast in ever-increasing numbers) driven by consuming ambitions, determined to build empires beside the Pacific. They were men of charm and humor, with a gift for words and an endearing warmth of manner, and, as

such, they were eagerly sought after by the country's many marriage-minded *señoritas*.

The great flood of Irish immigrants who came to California in the wake of the potato famine and the gold discovery were spurred by different forces from those that motivated the Murphys, Dens, and O'Farrells. The new immigrants were, for the most part, impoverished farmers and artisans, hungry men with hungry wives, children, mothers, and fathers—many of whom remained in New York or Boston while their sons, fathers, and husbands made the hazardous continental or Isthmian crossing to seek new stakes in the land of gold. They looked with pride to the Hibernians who had settled in the West before them (and to such prominent Irish-Americans as Brigadier General Stephen W. Kearny, who led American troops to New Mexico and California during the Mexican War and served as military governor of California, and Brigadier General Bennett Riley, Kearny's successor as governor, who called the convention which drafted a constitution for the state in 1849). But the experiences of such men offered more inspiration than example to the droves who now poured into San Francisco and the gold fields.

*I*N CALIFORNIA, the new Irish immigrants found themselves awash in a sea of strangers speaking diverse languages. Of the nearly 22,000 foreign-born residents of California in 1850, only about 2,500 were Irish. More than 3,000 were English, about the same number Germans, 1,500 French, and the rest mostly Chinese, Italians, Mexicans, and Portuguese. But Irish immigration increased rapidly in the next few years, strengthened by an influx of American-, Canadian-, and Australian-born Irish. Writing to friends in Dublin in 1858, a San Francisco priest estimated that no less than one-third of the city's population was Irish. If the priest's reckoning was exaggerated, the calculations of the U.S. Census were not. They showed that in 1860 there were 33,000 Irish-born residents in California—22 percent of the total foreign-born population.

Despite their numbers, the Irish sensed a certain hostility in the Gold Rush environment. The prejudices which sustained centuries of English misrule in Ireland also flourished in the United States, and many Yankees carried them to the gold fields. The Vigilance Committees of 1851 and 1856 had a strong anti-Irish bent (the best-known victim of the 1856 Committee was an Irishman, James P. Casey), as did the nativist or Know-Nothing movement of 1854–58. The same priest who in 1858 estimated that one-third of San Francisco's population was Irish noted that most of the local Irish tried to deny their origins. "Mixing among Americans," he wrote, "they think it is a disgrace to be an Irishman."

Others formed associations to preserve their Irish identity and to ease the shock of adjustment to life in new and largely unfriendly surroundings. As early as 1854, there was a Hibernia Society of San Francisco and a Sons of the Emerald Isle. There were parades to celebrate Saint Patrick's Day, and wakes to ease the passage of the dead from

198

this life to the next. The procession that formed in the plaza in San Francisco on March 17, 1854, was typical of Saint Patrick's Day festivities throughout the decade. Nearly a thousand marchers joined the parade, hundreds on horseback. All were gaily dressed, many wearing green sashes. "A fine band of music," wrote one observer, "and a beautifully painted flag, showing the wolf-dog and harp of Erin, headed the procession. There was much excitement among the Irish citizens, and *Erin go bragh* ['Ireland forever'] was the order of the day." When the parade concluded, the celebrants crowded into one of the city's largest saloons to quench their thirst and partake of a sumptuous dinner.

Though a few of the Irish immigrants to California were Protestants, most were Roman Catholics, and the Church of Rome was an Irish-American bastion throughout the Gold Rush. Some of the Spanish mission padres remained at their posts after 1850, but Irish priests early assumed the principal pastoral duties of the region. San Francisco's Saint Patrick's Church, founded by an Irish priest in 1851, was one of the state's largest parishes throughout the 1850s. Saint Mary's Cathedral, opened on California Street in 1854, was built mostly with Irish labor. Even Mission Dolores, ancient seat of San Francisco's Spanish Catholicism, was entrusted to the care of an Irish priest. Up into the gold fields, doughty Hibernians carried the sacraments to remote placers and swarming pit mines—to Nevada City, Columbia, Hangtown, and the new silver capital of the West, Virginia City, Nevada. When the Spanish-born Archbishop Joseph Sadoc Alemany retired from his San Francisco see in 1884, the Irish Patrick William Riordan succeeded him. To celebrate Riordan's succession, the city's Hibernians built a second and even more glorious Saint Mary's Cathedral, which opened on Van Ness Avenue in 1891.

The religious fervor of the Irish was nearly matched by their passion for politics. In New York in the 1840s, a handful of Irish-Americans had made an attempt to win elective office by alternately cultivating the establishment and organizing their own ethnic community. Resisted by the older and more established English and Dutch aristocracy, they met with little success. In California, where the native Spanish-speaking population was quickly outnumbered by foreign-born immigrants, there was no entrenched aristocracy to stem the Irish surge. The Irish organized many of the volunteer fire companies that throughout the fifties protected the burgeoning metropolis from fire. The companies were social clubs as much as fire-fighting organizations, and they quickly became centers of political recruiting.

The most dynamic politician in California in the 1850s was an Irish tavern-keeper-turned-assayer named David Broderick. Born in Washington, D.C., in 1820, Broderick was the son of an Irish-born stonecutter who had emigrated to Baltimore in 1817 and later helped to build the capitol in Washington. Raised in New York City, Broderick operated a tavern and joined a volunteer fire company before declaring himself a candidate for Congress in 1846. His defeat was not unexpected, but the fact that he ran a strong second in a field of four candidates persuaded many observers that the Irish had become a force to be reckoned with in big city politics.

Joining the Gold Rush to California, Broderick became an assayer in San Francisco. He bought and sold real estate and soon acquired a substantial fortune, but business success could not keep him from his first love—politics. A talented orator and an indefatigable organizer, with Tammany connections and Jacksonian ideals, he quickly rose to the political leadership of San Francisco. After his election to the state senate in 1850, he was widely regarded as the most powerful single politician in the state. Condemned by his opponents as a "ruffian" and "state plunderer," Broderick was praised by his admirers as a faithful friend of the working man and a resolute opponent of slavery. He opposed the extra-legal Vigilance Committees of 1851 and 1856, once going so far as personally to attack a lynch mob in a vain attempt to save the life of an alleged burglar. Elected to the United States Senate in 1857 (he was perhaps the first Irish-American Catholic to become a member of that exclusive "club"), Broderick established himself as an outspoken critic of the Southern policies of President James Buchanan. When, in 1859, the chief justice of the California Supreme Court, Kentucky-born, pro-Dixie Democrat David Terry, challenged him to a duel, Broderick accepted reluctantly. The senator lived only three days after Terry put a fatal bullet in his chest, but it was long enough for him to leave a ringing condemnation of his political opponents: "I die because I was opposed to a corrupt administration and the extension of slavery."

*I*RISH-AMERICANS continued to play leading roles in California politics after Broderick's passing. Two of their number—John Conness and Eugene Casserly—became United States senators, and a third—John G. Downey—served as governor. In San Francisco in 1878, no less than eight of the twelve supervisors, the sheriff, most of the deputy sheriffs, the postmaster, one-third of the police force, and an estimated nine-tenths of the city's firemen were Irish-born or of Irish extraction.

A bright if short-lived meteor in the western political sky was the Irish drayman-turned-sandlot orator Denis Kearney. Born in County Cork in 1847, Kearney settled in San Francisco in 1872 and, five years later, became leader of the Chinese-baiting Workingmen's Party. Kearney's supporters made a strong showing in the elections of 1878 and played a prominent role in drafting the state constitution that was adopted the following year. Anti-Chinese feeling had been strong among the Irish since the beginning of the Gold Rush (Irish workingmen saw cheap Chinese labor as a threat to their own livelihoods), and the new constitution placed restrictions on Chinese employment in the state.

3. NATIONAL CONSOLIDATION AND EXPANSION

Though they were unusually active in politics and in religion, the Irish of the Gold Coast also achieved success in the arts. J. Ross Browne, born in Dublin in 1821 and a California resident after 1849, was perhaps the most prominent western writer of Irish background. His popular stories, travel journals, and essays presaged the style of broad, exaggerated humor that was later perfected by Mark Twain. One of the most popular, if controversial, actresses of the Gold Rush was the self-styled Lola Montez, whom the mad King Ludwig I of Bavaria, in a fit of erotic passion, named Countess of Landsfeld. Montez claimed a noble Spanish ancestry, but those who knew her best recalled that she was born Dolores Gilbert in Limerick, Ireland, and that her current husband was the thoroughly Irish California newspaperman, Patrick Purdy Hull. Until the mid-seventies, an Irishman named Tom Maguire was the West's leading theatrical impresario. In 1851, Maguire built the Jenny Lind Theatre on San Francisco's plaza—a building so large and handsome that the city fathers bought it and made it into the city hall. Maguire then put up Maguire's Opera House and the Academy of Music, in which he introduced such stage luminaries as Junius Brutus Booth, Adah Isaacs Menken, and Edwin Forrest to western audiences. In 1866, Mark Twain made his auspicious debut as a lecturer on the stage of Maguire's Academy of Music.

Though most of the Irish who came to California in the ten years after 1849 probably expected to make their fortunes in the gold fields, few made more than modest livings there, and none acquired great wealth. Those who sought their fortunes in San Francisco generally did better than those who braved the placers and pit mines.

Peter Donahue and his brother, James, set up a blacksmith and boilermaker shop in San Francisco in 1850, opened an iron works a year later, and, in 1852, organized the San Francisco Gas Company, which installed the city's first gas-fueled street-lighting system. James Phelan, who emigrated from Ireland as a youth, opened a saloon soon after arriving in San Francisco in 1849. By 1870, his extensive investments in local real estate and banks had made him one of the city's ten richest men. John Sullivan, Edward J. Martin, and Richard Tobin organized the Hibernia Savings and Loan Society in 1859, later reorganizing it as the Hibernia Bank, which became one of the state's most influential financial institutions.

*P*ROSPEROUS as were the Donahues, Phelans, and Tobins, their success stories paled before those of the four Irishmen who became known as the "Silver Kings of the Comstock." John W. Mackay, James G. Fair and William S. O'Brien were all born in Dublin, though there is no record that they were acquainted before they met in California, while James Clair Flood, who first saw the light of day in New York City in 1826, was the son of poor Irish refugees who had recently crossed the Atlantic on an emigrant ship. Mackay and Fair spent most of the fifties hunting gold in the Sierra, Flood and O'Brien operating a saloon on the San Francisco waterfront. Then in 1859, two

itinerant Irish prospectors named Patrick McLaughlin and Peter O'Riley happened on a rich vein of gold and silver in the alkali desert of western Nevada—a vein later known throughout the world as the Comstock Lode. The prospectors sold their claims too early to realize any great wealth from them, but other Irishmen were to profit wonderfully from the discoveries. When the Sierra miners Mackay and Fair formed a partnership with the San Francisco saloonkeepers Flood and O'Brien (who had recently become members of the San Francisco Mining Exchange), the stage was set for one of the most spectacular success stories in the history of Irish-American finance. Gaining control of the Comstock through shrewd stock manipulations, Mackay, Fair, Flood, and O'Brien began the not-unpleasant task of dividing among themselves an estimated $400,000,000 worth of gold and silver bullion. Flood used his share of the treasure to build fabulous mansions on San Francisco's Nob Hill and on the peninsula south of the city. The bachelor O'Brien bought elegant gowns and carriages for his sisters. Fair acquired substantial chunks of western real estate and, in 1879, got himself elected United States senator from Nevada. Mackay founded the Postal Telegraph Company and financed his social climbing wife's successful assault on the citadels of European society.

Flaunting their new wealth as flagrantly as any of their Yankee counterparts, the Irish millionaires began to shop for "suitable matches" for their marriageable daughters. One of John Mackay's sisters-in-law became the bride of the Italian Count Telfner, while Mackay's adopted daughter married Ferdinand Julian Colonna, Prince of Galarto. Anna Donahue, daughter of Peter, married the German Baron Henry von Schroeder. Though James Fair's daughters married Americans, their matches were quite as stunning as the foreign alliances. Tessie Fair became Mrs. Herman Oelrichs of New York and Newport, Rhode Island, and settled down to life in a palatial mansion on Manhattan's Fifth Avenue. Tessie's sister, Birdie, married William K. Vanderbilt, Jr., in the process becoming the sister-in-law of the Duke of Marlborough.

Several years before the Fair-Vanderbilt nuptials, a writer for San Francisco's weekly *Argonaut* laughed at the posturing of the Irish *nouveau riche,* writing: "We have a millionaire among us! . . . His name is MacDooligan. . . . The present partner of the joys and sorrows of MacDooligan was once the beautiful Bridget MacShinnegan. . . . The MacShinnegan coat of arms is a spalpeen rampant on a field of gold; their motto '*De profundis saltare!*' The family is going to Paris while father remains to superintend the erection of a palatial mansion on Nob Hill. . . . *Louis Quatorze?* Renaissance? . . . Their manner is now *distingué,* their society *recherché,* their appearance *debonnaire,* their actions breathe a *savoir faire.*" To be satirized in the press was the unmistakable mark of social success in the Gilded Age. If the *Argonaut*'s words proved anything, it was that the Gold Coast Irish had "arrived."

Or at least some of them had. Others—perhaps most— had found the Gold Rush a gorgeous but exquisitely fragile bubble. As the nineteenth century closed, most of the Irish in the West were still working men, still carrying lunch pails to dreary jobs six days a week, still drinking riotously on Saturday nights and suffering remorsefully through Sunday mass. In his old age, an Irish prospector who once struck it rich but later lost his fortune recalled his rise and fall by the names he had been called during his western career:

"Quinn
Pat Quinn
C. Patrick Quinn
Col. Cornelius Patrick Quinn
Col. C. P. Quinn
Patrick Quinn
Pat Quinn
Old Quinn"

The experiences of many of Pat Quinn's countrymen were parallel to his own. For some, the Irish migration to the West was fully as wonderful as, years before, the Tunisian patriarch had promised it would be. If the experience of others only hinted at the glory of the seer's prediction, the hint was enough to renew the promise, to sustain the vision, to perpetuate the mystical faith. For it was the vision that nurtured the faith, and the faith that sustained the people. That alone was glory enough for most of the Irish of the Gold Coast.

BIBLIOGRAPHIC NOTE

The history of the Irish in America has been well summarized by William V. Shannon in *The American Irish* (New York: Macmillan, 1966) and Carl Wittke in *The Irish in America* (New York: Louisiana State University, 1956). An early, laudatory view of the Irish in Western America is *The Irish Race in California and on the Pacific Coast* (San Francisco, 1878) by Father Hugh Quigley. A later volume, only slightly less laudatory than Quigley's, is Judge Thomas F. Prendergast's *Forgotten Pioneers: Irish Leaders in Early California* (reprint, Freeport, New York: Arno, 1972).

David Broderick's meteoric career and tragic death are recorded by David A. Williams in *David C. Broderick: A Political Portrait* (San Marino, California: Huntington Library, 1969). The activities of the Irish Catholics in nineteenth-century California are traced in *Hallowed Were the Gold Dust Trails* (Santa Clara, California: University of Santa Clara, 1946) by Henry L. Walsh, S.J., and in *Documents of California Catholic History, 1784–1963* (Los Angeles: Dawson's Book Shop, 1965) by Frances J. Weber.

Lola Montez's legendary exploits have inspired many biographers, notable among whom are Ishbel Ross, *The Uncrowned Queen: The Life of Lola Montez* (New York: Harper & Row, 1972) and Horace Wyndham, *The Magnificent Montez, From Courtesan to Convert* (London: Hutchinson & Company, 1935). Tom Maguire's long and interesting career has been traced by Lois Foster Rodecape in "Tom Maguire, Napoleon of the Stage," *California Historical Society Quarterly,* Vol. XX, No. 4 (December 1941), pages 289–314.

John G. Downey's biography may be found in Benjamin F. Gilbert and H. Brett Melendy's *Governors of California, Peter H. Burnett to Edmund G. Brown* (Georgetown, California: Talisman Press, 1965). The Comstock Kings—Fair, Mackay, Flood, and O'Brien—have inspired many books, the best of which is Oscar Lewis's *Silver Kings* (New York: Knopf, 1947).

Statistical data about the Irish (and other ethnic groups) can be found in Allyn Campbell Loosely's *Foreign Born Population of California, 1848–1920* (thesis, Berkeley: University of California, 1927). The Saint Patrick's Day parade of 1854 is described in *The Annals of San Francisco* by Frank Soulé, John H. Gihon, M.D., and James Nisbet (New York: Appleton, 1854).

Estelle Kleiger

George Washington wore a perfumed, powdered wig at his inauguration, and very likely rouge as well. Most of the other men present were similarly bedecked; it was standard fashion for upper-class men of that period. Women of the same class were more elaborately adorned and went to greater extremes to be fashionable. Their ghostly pallor was not always due to delicate health, but to ceruse, a white lead paint, known to be toxic. In spite of the horror stories about the slow death and ruined complexions of its users, some women braved the consequences. They used rouge, too, and their hair—real and false, powdered and pomaded—reached heights of a foot or more above their heads. A Philadelphia newspaper of that time advertised hair dressing with "construction of rolls" to raise heads to the desired "pitch." No attempt was made by either sex to conceal the wearing of cosmetics, since their use was the mark of the aristocrat.

Of course, such fashions were not for rural New Englanders, whose intense concern was with the state of their souls and with eking a living from the land, and whose moral codes forbade such frivolities. Those who used these artificialities were plantation owners, wealthy residents of Southern cities, especially New Orleans where the extravagant French influence was very strong, and some in the upper classes of New York, Boston, and Philadelphia.

Americans copied Euro-

pean styles, but they usually ran a year or so behind the times because of slow communications. Also, the most extreme fashions were shunned because they did not suit the temper of the country. The "macaronis," whose fashion originated in Italy and spread to other European countries, affected an exaggerated, heavily made-up style, and wore tiny hats atop enormous powdered wigs. Although they were severely criticized in Europe, they had some adherents. In the colonies they were merely ridiculed and gained fame through "Yankee Doodle."

Yet, Americans were surely fashion conscious. Most wealthy homes reserved a special room or closet for hair powdering, a distinctly messy process. The powder was distributed by means of a bellows which dusted the hair and everything else in sight. Two people were involved: the subject of the powdering, who kept a cone or similar object over his eyes, nose, and mouth; and a second person, usually a valet or a barber, who operated the bellows. Many men had their hair powdered and curled daily, but women whose elaborate coiffures took many hours to complete had their hair arranged only once in several months, and neither combed nor washed their heads between times. When one considers the infrequency of shampoos and the fact that powder was applied over oil or pomade to make it stick, the charm of this fashion rapidly fades. Wigs, powdered or not, were much eas-

Wigged, perfumed, and probably rouged, Washington takes the oath as President on April 30, 1789, on the site of the present Treasury Building, New York. ("Century Magazine," April 1889)

From *American History Illustrated*, August 1979. Reproduced through the courtesy of The National Historical Society, publishers of *American History Illustrated*, P.O. Box 1831 Harrisburg, PA 17105.

ier to maintain, and were as popular here as in England.

The French Revolution sent tremors throughout the Western World. Here, our own Revolution began a leveling process, with political power slowly slipping from the hands of the aristocrats who founded the country. One by one the states discarded property qualifications for voting and moved toward universal suffrage for white men. The old guard was dying off and being replaced by men of the people. By the beginning of the 19th century, as part of the growing resentment against class distinctions, there was a gradual building of social pressures against the use of cosmetics.

Carry-overs from previous years, however, persisted, and despite warnings of the hazards of white paint containing bismuth and lead, some women still used it. Hair styles for the upper classes of both sexes became simpler, although men, even more than women, continued to be perfumed and powdered. Describing her husband's appearance at James Monroe's Inaugural Ball, Mrs. Robert Goodloe Harper wrote in a letter that he had been "perfumed like a milliner." The North was more restrictive about the use of cosmetics than the South, where the wealthy clung to aristocratic ways for a longer period. Before John Adams' Administration, Philadelphia was the nation's Capital, and when it moved to Washington, a change in decor was evident. State entertaining became more elaborate and the wealthy Southerners who flocked there were more heavily made-up, their clothes showing the French influence. Eight years later when the gay and beautiful Dolley Madison moved into the White House, the use of cosmetics throughout the country was already more subdued. Tongues wagged about whether or not the first lady "rouged," but the momentous question was never really settled.

The voice of the common man grew louder as the century progressed and the modes and manners of the aristocrats were more roundly criticized. Andrew Jackson, a Westerner whose cruder speech and bearing dismayed his predecessors, was elected President. Men who used cosmetics were ridiculed and labeled effeminate. President Martin Van Buren's career suffered even when a political opponent revealed that he installed a bathtub in the White House. A President who insisted on "the pleasures of a warm or tepid bath" might also perfume his whiskers with "Double Extract of Queen Victoria"! The mere mention of this toilet preparation in connection with President Van Buren was enough to make him a laughingstock.

The stress on respectability during Queen Victoria's reign extended to this country, and cosmetics for women, too, fell into disfavor. Some older women, set in their habits, continued to paint and also to powder their hair. The writer of a mid-century book on perfumes, while conceding that it was passé, nevertheless stated his belief that powder imparted "a degree of softness to the features."

Occasionally during the early years of the Victorian era, articles appeared urging the use of cosmetics, at least for the elderly, but most commentators took the opposite view, as did Mrs. Merrifield in a mid-century *Godey's Lady's Magazine*. She berated the attempt to conceal or repair the "ravages of time" with paint and false hair, calling it a violation of the "laws of nature," and, as if that were not enough, "a positive breach of sincerity." Besides, she continued, this "acting a lie" deceives nobody but "the unfortunate perpetrator of the would-be deceit." Lip rouge was condemned to an even greater degree than cheek rouge. M.M. Marberry wrote that Victoria Woodhull, the notorious 19th-century free-wheeler, was accused by some of using lipstick, but that most people refused to believe she would go *that* far. Cheek rouge ("false bloom") was permissible under certain very special circumstances, such as the case of a pale invalid who wished to spare the feelings of loved ones. For the rest, women could go on pinching their cheeks and biting their lips to give them color.

In spite of public censure, cosmetics were still used, but furtively, and to avoid scorn they were often invested with health-giving or healing qualities. For example, an 1853 *Godey's* gave a formula for "Carnation Lip Salve" with alkanet root as a coloring agent. Ostensibly designed to prevent or soothe chapped lips, that it also reddened them was only incidental. "Tri-cosian Fluid," imported from England, was a hair dye for women, and aside from its primary purpose, it was advertised as being "highly beneficial in nervous headaches or weakness of the eyes." Some cosmetic preparations appeared in pharmacies and barbershops, and these included Pearl Powder, Florida Water, Orange Flower Water, Bear's Oil, and Macassar Oil. The last two were hair dressings for men, Bear's Oil being used mostly by frontiersmen, with Macassar Oil the preference of the wealthy. Both were greasy, and antimacassars (doilies to protect the backs of chairs) soon became popular.

Hair dye for men was also available. An 1897 Sears, Roebuck catalogue advertised "Old Reliable Hair and Whisker Dye" which, it claimed, had been in use since 1860. The price was forty cents a bottle.

Until the last quarter of the 19th century, however, most cosmetic preparations were made in the home. Women concocted all sorts of mixtures, some of them sounding good enough to eat. Fresh strawberries steeped for seven days in white wine produced a solution which was supposed to make the skin firmer. Cucumber juice rubbed on the face and left there to dry would keep the complexion soft and white. New milk, skimmed milk, and buttermilk each had special healing and beautifying effects (some of the claims are still in favor), but a 19th-century author was quick to specify that he referred only to the "milk of healthy, grass-fed cows, not the washy, unwholesome liquid given by the stall fed animals kept in the crowded districts of large cities."

3. NATIONAL CONSOLIDATION AND EXPANSION

The editor of *Godey's Lady's Magazine*, Sarah Josepha Hale, shared with her readers her special beauty secret: She believed that brown butcher's paper soaked in fresh apple vinegar, applied to the temples and left there overnight, would prevent crow's-feet. Freckles were considered a bane and attempts at erasing them ranged from frequent applications of lemon juice to powerful lotions containing hydrochloric and sulphuric acid. *Godey's* stated that the favorite Parisian lotion for removing freckles was "an ounce of alum and an ounce of lemon juice in a pint of rose water."

For men, beards and mustaches were the fashion news of the 19th century. Following a long period of relative beardlessness, facial hair burst into view in a profusion of styles and shapes, from the trim goatee to the long and flowing full beard. Side whiskers appeared first in the early part of the century, gradually becoming longer and fuller. The American army, disapproving of the lack of uniformity, issued a directive in 1835 forbidding side whiskers that extended below the ear lobe. For the most part the order was not strictly enforced and in 1840, in an effort to go along with the times, the army issued another one permitting the wearing of mustaches. Each commanding officer was to set his own fashion rules. But this, again, proved to be too restrictive, and in 1853 the army threw up its hands: Beards, too, were declared within regulations, and all objection on the army's part had to be set aside when President Lincoln decided to join the ranks of the bearded. Just why he did so has often been a matter of speculation. A young woman urged him "for heaven's sake, to raise side-whiskers to fill out the lantern jaw," but Carl Sandburg suggested that a desire to appear graver and more responsible may have been the reason. But for whatever reason, the President did grow a beard—and set a style.

Lincoln's results were so successful that a cartoon appeared advertising jars of "Lincoln Whiskeropherous," guaranteed to grow whiskers in a few weeks. Actually, the selling of unguents to stimulate the growth of facial hair was a thriving business, and full-grown beards and mustaches were lovingly rubbed with oils and pomades. In addition to those purchased in the store, many preparations for men came from home, made by the housewife along with her own toiletries. The famous Macassar Oil consisted chiefly of oil of almonds, colored red with alkanet root and scented with oil of cassia. It could be made at home for a fraction of its barbershop price. Nitrate of silver was used to dye hair black, but it had the disadvantage of imparting a tell-tale iridescent quality which resembled, according to one description, the feathers on "the neck of a pigeon."

After the Civil War the mood of the country changed. Many of those who found themselves in a better financial position, stressed frivolities. The old families looked down upon these *nouveau riche* who, in many cases, had made their money through unscrupulous means. They were offended by the lavish entertaining of this group. Suffragette Matilda Joslyn Gage blasted politicians in the Grant Administration for giving parties which, she said, rivaled foreign ones. The wealthy traveled in greater numbers to Europe and returned home with the latest in fashion and beauty aids. There was a brief revival of hair powdering for women, only now gold and silver dust were used. Some of the more daring used mascara which, it is believed, Empress Eugenie introduced. At about this time a new method of making face powder was discovered. Previously, it had been made with chloride of bismuth, arsenic salts, or lead, the constant use of which was harmful. The new powder had a zinc oxide base, was harmless, and did not discolor. Also it was cheap, and women of limited means could purchase it.

In the 1880's, the glamorous Harriet Hubbard Ayer, with an estranged husband, two children, and no money, began to sell a face cream that she said she herself had

Mrs. Ayer advertises (1887) her miraculous complexion cream, endorsed by Adelina Patti, Sarah Bernhardt, Lily Langtry, Helena Modjeska, and others. (AHI Collection)

204

been using for many years. She wrote and publicized the story that originally the cream had been made for Julie Récamier, a great French beauty, and that she, Mrs. Ayer, had come upon it quite by accident. She explained that while in Europe she suffered a severe sunburn and believed that her complexion was "irretrievably injured." An unidentified countess, sympathizing with her predicament, gave her a pot of the cream. The improvement it brought about was almost miraculous, Mrs. Ayer wrote, thus stressing the curative powers of the cream as well as its beautifying effects.

From the start, the cream sold well here and in England, and soon Mrs. Ayer hit on another advertising scheme, one that started a whole new trend: She asked famous beauties to endorse her cream—for a consideration, of course. At first only actresses, who were on the far side of respectability anyway, would agree to do so, but eventually Mrs. James Brown Potter of Tuxedo Park, a socialite, lent her name to Mrs. Ayer's product. Her testimonial, the first to feature a name from the Social Register, caused a storm of consternation among members of that group, but it was not long before others entered the field, making certain to let it be known that the proceeds from such arrangements went to charity.

The Victorian era was drawing to a close. A few older men kept their beards, though no longer fashionable. A highly imaginative variety of styles in mustaches flourished in the 1890's, but at the turn of the century they, too, vanished and men became clean shaven once again. Women were still surreptitious about their use of cosmetics. The dictates of respectability decreed that soap and water were sufficient to keep their complexions glowing and to allow their inner beauty to shine. Despite the scandals of the period and the effective and growing political activity of the suffragists, mawkish sentimentality, at least in song and verse, kept women on their pedestals.

Then bleached blonde hair became popular with actresses, and the term "peroxide blonde" came into being, but no "nice" woman succumbed to this fashion, or, as a

writer in an 1892 *Ladies Home Journal* grimly put it, "It goes without saying that a well-bred woman does not dye her hair." Yet a sizable number of them did, though they often tried to avoid detection by taking months to complete the process. Harriet Hubbard Ayer placed the blame for the blonde craze on the men who, "from the beginning of the world," have sung of the beauty of golden-haired women. She discouraged bleaching of the hair because, she wrote, it never remains the same color and because a woman with bleached hair is "regarded lightly." But for those who "hurl anathemas" at the artful use of cosmetics, she wrote, let men show their devotion and loyalty to "sallow-faced, pale-lipped, dull, thin-haired women," and the application of these substances would soon cease.

Advertisers played on people's natural desire to improve their appearance. The 1897 Sears, Roebuck catalogue declared that it is

in the nature of the human family from the savage to the most civilized to use the best means obtainable, by which they can render themselves more pleasing and attractive to others. It is almost a duty and a pleasure we owe to one another. It is almost criminal to go about with a repulsive complexion, etc., when the means to render yourself attractive are so easily obtainable.

In spite of this and similar rhetoric, and the great increase in commercial preparations available, the social attitude toward cosmetics remained restrictive. Not until after WW I was there general acceptance of their use.

In her first article for AHI Estelle Kleiger, of Scarsdale, New York, gives us an interesting and often humorous view of the use of cosmetics in the 19th century. For those interested in reading more on this subject, she recommends Richard Corson's Fashions in Make-Up *(1972) and* Fashions in Hair *(1965), and Gilbert Miller Vail's* A History of Cosmetics in America, *though the latter is an old edition and difficult to find.*

The Civil War and Reconstruction

The institution of slavery plagued this nation from its birth, as can be seen in those sections relating to it in the constitution. Major efforts to "compromise" the issue were made again in 1820 and in 1850. Still the matter would not cease. In general, professional politicians in both the North and South tried to keep the struggle offstage because they recognized that it would tear the political parties, if not the nation, apart. Despite their efforts, attitudes on both sides hardened over the decades until genuine negotiations became impossible. To the extent that slavery came to be seen primarily as a moral issue, rather than merely a political or economic one, confrontation became inevitable. Unlike tariffs or internal improvements, issues which also divided the sections, slavery could not be handled by "splitting the difference."

The Whigs broke apart first, to be replaced by the exclusively Northern Republican party. Although this organization was a coalition ranging all the way from ardent abolitionists to those who were indifferent if not actually hostile to Blacks, Southerners tended to see it as a clear threat to their way of life. When the Republican candidate, Abraham Lincoln, won the presidential election in 1860, one by one the Southern states began to secede. Lincoln, like the lame duck President Buchanan before him, tried to avoid hostilities but failed. There followed four years of the bloodiest war in this nation's history.

Historians have debated the causes of the war and its outcome ever since. The North had clear advantages in areas such as population, industrial production, and naval power, to name a few. The South, on the other hand, fought largely on its own soil and had only to keep the North at bay to achieve its goals. Whether the North won because of superior political and military leadership, or because it simply had more of everything is not clear. In any event the Civil War ended by force of arms the debates over slavery and the right to secede.

A number of questions may be raised about the Civil War and Reconstruction. Could better statesmanship have avoided conflict, or were the issues too fundamental for compromise? Was the institution of slavery doomed anyway? What were the goals of the "radicals" with regard to former slaves? with regard to southern whites? To what extent might it be said that radical reconstruction was doomed to fail?

Sojourner Truth:

"a self-made woman"

Elizabeth Shafer

Elizabeth Shafer is a freelance author, as well as associate editor of Earth Science *magazine. Her sources for this article include* Sojourner Truth, an Ebony Classic, *and* Journey Toward Freedom, *by Jacqueline Bernard.*

She was over 6 feet tall, rawboned, black, and—for the first forty years of her life—a slave. The next forty-six years she spent becoming, as she said, "a self-made woman."

Sojourner Truth was a powerful and eloquent speaker against slavery and for women's rights, lecturing in twenty-one states and the District of Columbia from 1843 until 1878, when she was 81. She was a friend and co-worker of the great names among the abolitionists and fighters for women's rights. She was a guest of Harriet Beecher Stowe, who celebrated her as "The Libyan Sibyl" in *The Atlantic Monthly*; and she was received at the White House by Abraham Lincoln.

Those who heard her speak and sing in her deep, strong voice never forgot her nor her shrewd wit, simple wisdom, and droll humor. Mrs. Stowe wrote of the "power and sweetness in that great warm soul and that vigorous frame," adding, "I do not recall ever to have been conversant with anyone who had more of that silent and subtle power which we call personal presence than this woman." From the sister of the famous preacher and spellbinder, Henry Ward Beecher, this was the ultimate compliment.

She was born in 1797 in Ulster County, New York, the twelfth child of Bomefree and Mama Bett, slaves of a Dutchman, Charles Hardenbergh. (New York and New Jersey were the last of the northern states to keep slaves; the other states had abolished slavery following the Revolution.) When Sojourner was about 11, Hardenbergh died, and "Isabella," as she was then called, was sold at an auction of "slaves, horses, and other cattle" to a Yankee storekeeper, John Nealy. Nealy paid a hundred dollars for the gawky child and a herd of sheep.

Years later she was to say, "Now the war begun." For Isabella spoke only Low Dutch, and the Nealys spoke only English. When her father learned how they beat her, he begged a local tavernkeeper to buy her. She lived eighteen months with the Scrivers, working in the house and in the fields and serving customers in the tavern. She was 13 now, and already 6 feet tall.

She was happy those brief months, but in 1810 John J. Dumont of nearby New Paltz bought her for $300. (As a sturdy young woman, her value was going up.) Dumont was a large slaveholder by New York standards, keeping ten slaves. They all lived in a large room behind the kitchen called the slave kitchen.

Isabella was a good worker—too good in the opinion of her fellow slaves, who called her "white man's nigger." She fell in love with "Catlin's Robert," as slaves were identified in those days. But Robert's master beat him terribly and forced him to marry one of the Catlin slaves. Isabella, in turn, was married to old Thomas, one of Dumont's slaves. They were to have five children.

While she was chiefly a house slave for Mrs. Dumont, she also worked in the fields. She would put her latest baby in a basket, tie a rope to the handles, and suspend it in a tree, where a small child was set to swinging it.

Meanwhile, New York State had passed a new law. All slaves born before July 4, 1799, were to be freed on July 4, 1827. All slaves younger than 28 were "free" —but had to work as unpaid servants until the boys were 28, the girls 25. Because she was such a faithful worker, Dumont promised Isabella he would free her

From AMERICAN HISTORY ILLUSTRATED, January 1974. Reproduced through the courtesy of The National Historical Society, publishers of AMERICAN HISTORY ILLUSTRATED, P. O. Box 1831, Harrisburg, Pa. 17105.

a year early. But in the summer of 1826, he refused to fulfill his promise.

Isabella remembered the Quaker, Levi Rowe, who had said to her once, years before, "Thou should not be a slave." She took her youngest child, Sophia, leaving the others at Dumont's with Thomas, and walked to Rowe's farm.

Rowe was dying, but he sent her on to Mr. and Mrs. Isaac S. Van Wagener. When Dumont followed, demanding his property, the Van Wageners agreed to buy Isabella's services for the rest of the year for twenty dollars, and the child's services until she was 25 for five dollars. However, they instructed Isabella not to call them "master" and "mistress," and she was treated as a paid servant.

Once she became homesick and almost agreed to accompany Dumont back to his farm, but as she was heading for the gate she heard a voice: "Not another step!" She quickly returned to her room, where she prayed for strength. Her mother had long ago taught her the Lord's prayer in Low Dutch, and had told her solemnly, "There is a God, who hears and sees you." It was at this crisis in her life that Isabella discovered Jesus. But she was afraid, she said afterwards, that the whites would discover that Jesus was her friend and take him from her as they had taken everything else, so she kept her new friend a secret.

There was a small island in a nearby stream. Here she wove a wall of willows and conducted private talks with God and Jesus. She was to continue this very personal dialog for the rest of her life.

On "freedom day," July 4, 1827, Isaac and Maria Van Wagener conducted a small private ceremony, reading from the Bible. Maria kissed Isabella on the cheek. "Take thy Sophia, too, into freedom," she said, handing her the child. They agreed upon wages for her labor, and Isabella and the child lived with them for another two years.

Her son, Peter, had disappeared, and Isabella finally learned that Dumont had sold the boy to a family whose daughter had taken Peter south to Alabama. This meant, of course, that he would never be free.

When Isabella spoke to Mrs. Dumont about Peter, the woman jeered at her. Isabella drew herself to her full height and cried in her deep voice, "I'll have my child again!" She was to recall afterwards, "When I spoke to my mistress that way, I felt so tall within. I felt as if the power of a nation was within me."

An abolitionist advised her to go to a certain Quaker for help. She arrived at night, and was given a room of her own with a tall poster bed. She remembered later, "I was scared when she left me alone with that great white bed. I had never been in a real bed in my life. It never came into my mind she could mean me to sleep on it. So I just camped under it, and I slept pretty well there on the floor."

Next morning, she took her case to the grand jury at Kingston. This was the first of many battles she was to undertake and win. The woman who was to become Sojourner Truth believed in the power of the law and used it effectively for herself and for her people.

Peter was returned to her, and the two went to New York City in 1829. But the boy fell into bad company and she was finally forced to send him to sea. He sent her several letters, saying he had received none of her. Then he stopped writing; she never heard from him again.

While in New York she learned English, which she always spoke with a heavy Dutch accent, and worked as a domestic for various families and for a religious group called The Kingdom. But in 1843, she had a vision. She took her clothes, some bread and cheese, and twenty-five cents for the ferry to Brooklyn. "I am no longer Isabella," she said. "I am Sojourner." But Sojourner what? She gave the matter some thought. Remembering that a slave always took the name of her master, she said, "Oh, God, thou art my last master, and they name is Truth, so shall Truth be my abiding name until I die."

And so, at 46, Sojourner Truth was born.

The year 1843 was a time of great religious revival. Reform was in the air. Abolitionists were calling for an end to slavery. Talk of women's rights would culminate in the first Women's Rights Convention at Seneca, New York in 1848. Men and women were setting up religious communities. Camp meetings were held everywhere.

In her wanderings, Sojourner came upon her first camp meeting. She began to speak and sing at many such gatherings. Later, she advertised and conducted meetings of her own. Olive Gilbert, who was the first to help Sojourner put her story into print (*Narrative of Sojourner Truth: A Northern Slave*, 1850) commented, "All who have ever heard her sing . . . will probably remember it as long as they remember her."

At one such camp meeting, a group of rowdies threatened to disrupt the proceedings. Sojourner walked to one side, on a little knoll, and began to sing. The rowdies gathered around her, begging her to sing some more, and became quiet. They even laughed appreciatively when she told them, "Well, there are two congregations on this ground. It is written that the sheep shall be separated from the goats. The other preachers have the sheep, I have the goats. I have a few sheep among my goats, but they are very ragged." Both meetings went on without incident after that.

She met all the great figures of the abolition movement: Samuel Hill, Wendell Phillips, Parker Pillsbury, Frederick Douglass, and William Lloyd Garrison. These men also worked with women in organizing the first women's rights convention.

Sojourner knew Lucretia Mott, Susan B. Anthony, Elizabeth Cady Stanton, and Lucy Stone. She was the only black delegate to the Worcester, Massachusetts women's rights convention in 1850. Men jeered, newspapers called it the Hen Convention, and one minister even threatened to expel from his congregation any member daring to attend.

It was at this convention that Sojourner, ever the militant, asked, "If women want any rights more'n they've got, why don't they just take 'em and not be talking about it?"

She was a faithful fighter for all women's rights, but she drew the line at the current fad of wearing "bloomers." Recalling her days as a slave who got only a single length of cloth to cover her long frame and so had to stitch it up the legs for modesty, she declared, "Tell *you*, I had enough of bloomers in them days!"

With the passage of the Fugitive Slave Act in 1850, the abolitionists redoubled their activities. Sojourner was invited to join them on their speaking tours.

She often traveled alone, in a borrowed buggy loaded with copies of her book, song sheets of her own composing, and copies of her photograph ("I sell the shadow to support the substance.") She would give the horse its head, saying, "God, you drive." It always seemed to turn out right. She would stop at a crossroads or in a village square, unfold the freedom banner which the Akron, Ohio women's rights convention had given her, and speak and sing.

One of her own songs, eleven stanzas long, began:

> "I am pleading for my people—
> A poor, down-trodden race,
> Who dwell in freedom's boasted land
> With no abiding place.
>
> I am pleading that my people
> May have their rights restored,
> For they have long been toiling
> And yet have no reward."

Uncle Tom's Cabin had received instant acclaim in 1852, and, wanting to meet the author, Sojourner appeared at Harriet Beecher Stowe's home in Andover, Massachusetts. Harriet was so taken with her visitor that she invited her to stay for several days.

"An audience was what she wanted," Harriet was to write later. "It mattered not whether high or low, learned or ignorant. She had things to say, and was ready to say them at all times, and to anyone."

In 1857 the Dred Scott decision ruled that a slave could not be a citizen, and that Congress had no power to exclude slavery from the western territories. This precipitated new abolitionist activity. Sojourner went into Indiana with Parker Pillsbury. It was during this speaking tour that a hostile doctor rose and demanded that she show her breasts to a group of women from the audience. He said, "Your voice is not the voice of a woman, it is the voice of a man, and we believe you are a man."

Silently, Sojourner Truth, now 60, undid her Quaker kerchief and opened her dress, displaying her breasts

Sojourner Truth (Library of Congress)

to the whole congregation. "It is not my shame but yours that I do this," she said.

Events began moving more swiftly now. In 1859, John Brown raided Harpers Ferry. In 1860, Lincoln was elected President. And by April 1861, Fort Sumter had been fired upon.

Josephine Griffing of Ohio asked Sojourner to accompany her on an anti-slavery lecture tour into Indiana, where Copperheads (pro-slavery forces) controlled the legislature. This was a dangerous undertaking, but Sojourner agreed at once. Two miles across the Ohio-Indiana border, she was arrested. Josephine got a court order for her release. Hecklers broke up their first meeting and they were taken into protective custody by a member of the Union home guard, who escorted them to Angola. Here, the Copperheads threatened to burn the building where Sojourner was to speak.

"Then I will speak upon the ashes," she said firmly.

The women of the town dressed her in a red, white, and blue shawl with a sash and apron to match. She wore a cap with a star, and a star on each shoulder.

Sojourner remembered: "When we were ready to go, they put me into a large, beautiful carriage with the captain and other gentlemen, all of whom were armed. The soldiers walked by our side and a long procession followed. As we neared the court house, looking out of the window I saw that the building was surrounded by a great crowd. I felt as I was going against the Philistines and I prayed the Lord to deliver me out of their hands. But when the rebels saw such a mighty army coming, they fled, and by the time we arrived they were scattered over the fields, looking like a flock of frightened crows, and not one was left but a small boy, who sat upon the fence, crying, 'Nigger, nigger!'"

The procession marched into the court house, everyone sang, and she spoke without interruption.

The tour was a triumph, but it exhausted her. She was ill for some time, and there were rumors she was dead. But the Emancipation Proclamation of January 1, 1863 heartened her; she declared that she must get well.

Slowly, over the years, she had been gathering her family about her in Battle Creek, Michigan—her daughters and grandsons Sammy and James, who sometimes acted as escorts on her journeys. When she was not lecturing, she earned her living as she always did, cooking, cleaning house, doing laundry, and caring for the sick.

Grandson James Caldwell had joined the Union Army now that they were accepting Negroes. At Thanksgiving in 1863, Sojourner visited the 1st Michigan Colored Infantry at Detroit, taking them donations of good things to eat. She taught them to sing her latest song, to the tune of *John Brown's Body:*

We are the valiant soldiers who've 'listed for the war;
We are fighting for the Union, we are fighting for the law;
We can shoot a rebel farther than a white man ever saw,
    As we go marching on . . . .

From Detroit, she went to New York, speaking to Henry Ward Beecher's Brooklyn congregation at Plymouth Church. And on October 29, 1864, she met Abraham Lincoln at the White House. The President signed her "Book of Life," an autograph book containing the signatures of many of the most famous people of her time.

She found plenty to do in Washington. She spoke to the Colored Soldiers' Aid Society. She worked at Arlington Heights, Virginia as a counselor for the National Freedmen's Relief Association, and that autumn she was asked to help the surgeon in charge of the Freedmen's Hospital to "promote order, cleanliness, industry, and virtue among the patients."

Before the war, the streetcars in Washington had been segregated. After Lincoln signed a law outlawing discrimination in Washington public transportation, many conductors simply refused to stop for black passengers. One day Sojourner Truth stood in the middle of the street and shouted three times at the top of her lungs, "I WANT TO RIDE!" She nearly panicked the horses, but she managed to get on, then refused to stand on the platform behind the horses, "I am a passenger and shall sit with the other passengers."

In a later incident, an irate conductor slammed her against the door, pushing her shoulder out of joint. Again, she went to court. The Freedmen's Bureau lawyer sued the company, the conductor lost his job, and from then on blacks rode the Washington streetcars.

In 1867, escorted by grandson Sammy, she traveled through western New York, seeking jobs for freed slaves. Journalist Theodore Tilton asked permission to write her life story. She replied, "I am not ready to be writ up yet, for I have still lots to accomplish." And in 1870 she set out on "the last great mission of her life"—petitioning Congress for free land for the former slaves. But Senator Charles Sumner, who had worked for passage of the bill, died. Then grandson Sammy fell ill and died. Sojourner herself suffered a stroke and a lengthy illness. The petition for free land failed, one of the few failures in her long and productive life.

In the nation's centennial year, she celebrated her eightieth birthday. Her paralysis had disappeared, her hair began to grow in black instead of its former gray, and as writers of the period commented, her deep voice had lost none of its power. When she was 81, she spoke in thirty-six different towns in her home state of Michigan. And in July of that year, she was one of three Michigan delegates to the 30th anniversary meeting of the Women's Rights Convention.

While her dream of free land had not been realized, she was to see 60,000 freedmen take up homesteads in Kansas by the end of 1879.

Sojourner Truth died at her home in Battle Creek on November 26, 1883 with her family around her. She was buried at Oak Hill Cemetery. Many of her early friends were dead or too old to attend the services, but Frederick Douglass sent a message, as did Wendell Phillips. A thousand friends and neighbors filed past her coffin. Among the floral offerings was a great sheaf of ripened wheat from the freedmen of Kansas.

Once when a friend had asked, "But Sojourner, what if there is no heaven?" she had replied, "What will I say if I don't get there? Why, I'll say, 'Bless the Lord! I had a good time thinking I would!'"

The Myth of the UNDERGROUND RAILROAD

Larry Gara

Larry Gara is a member of the history department at Wilmington (Ohio) College. An acknowledged authority on the underground railroad, he based this article on his book The Liberty Line: The Legend of the Underground Railroad *(1967), published by University of Kentucky Press.*

Of all the legends growing out of the Civil War era and the slavery struggle preceding it, none has taken deeper root in popular thought than that of the underground railroad. Although details are usually indistinct, the term still suggests a widespread, highly secret conspiracy to transport slaves from southern bondage to northern freedom. The railroad operated a very busy line, despite the constant dangers its employees faced. And the abolitionist operators usually outwitted the road's would-be sabateurs with such tricks as secret rooms and passageways, instant disguises, and many other devices based on ingenuity and daring. It was an abolitionist institution and most of its willing passengers would have been helpless without the road's many services.

The underground railroad of legend, like most legendary institutions, is a blend of fiction and fact. Most of the historical source material which provided the basis for the traditional view of the institution was not recorded until long after the events took place, much of it in the post-Civil War era when abolitionists and their descendants wrote their reminiscences or handed down the anecdotes of exciting times by word of mouth. With one major exception, the books published after the Civil War containing first-hand underground railroad accounts view the events from the standpoint of the white abolitionists. As all historical sources reflect the bias of their writers, abolitionist sources tended to view the ante bellum past as a morality play with themselves in the role of righteous crusaders, Southerners as the villains, and the fugitive slaves as helpless, passive recipients of aid. The former antislavery activists were recalling a time of high danger and excitement. When Professor Wilbur H.

Siebert contacted hundreds of abolitionists in the 1890's for material for his history of the underground railroad, one wrote him: "There was a peculiar *fascination* about that 'U.G.R.R.' biz., that *fires me up*, even now when I recall the scenes of excitement and danger."

In retrospect, the romance of underground railroad work inevitably led to some exaggeration. There was some organized assistance provided in a few northern communities for fleeing slaves, but there was nothing resembling a nationally organized effort, and much of the aid was rendered on a temporary and haphazard basis. With the passage of time one or two well-known incidents concerning fugitives and those who helped them sometimes created a popular image of a busy underground line in a particular locale. Well-known figures in the anti-slavery movement were often associated with underground railroad activity, whether or not they had actually participated in that phase of the effort. When Professor Siebert contacted the Reverend Joshua Young of Groton, Massachusetts for his experiences, Young replied that he could tell very little. "Perhaps my connection with the U.G.R.R. has been exaggerated," he explained, "owing to the circumstances of my being the only present and officiating clergyman at John Brown's funeral, which gave me some prominence among abolitionists."

Not all the former abolitionists were as modest as the Reverend Young; in the postwar period individuals and their relatives sometimes expanded on their actual adventures in underground railroad work. Thus family pride contributed to the legend. Among other things, those people who had been scorned and ridiculed in many communities now had their position vindicated. Thrilling stories were recounted at gatherings of northern local historical societies, repeated in hundreds of newspapers, and often found their way into the county histories which were published in the 1880's. Communities as well as individuals claimed an unblemished record of sacrificial service to the victims of slavery who were fleeing from its toils. Hardly a town in the North was with-

From *American History Illustrated*, January 1978. Reproduced through the courtesy of The National Historical Society,

out its local legends or a house reputed to have been a major depot on the underground line. Very few such places have had their historical reputations verified, and in some instances even houses built after the Civil War came to share an underground railroad reputation.

One of the more serious distortions caused by the legend of the underground railroad concerns the role of the fugitives themselves. An overemphasis on the amount of assistance rendered by white abolitionists has tended to make the people the railroad was designed to aid — the fugitive slaves — either invisible or passive and helpless without aid from others. In fact, they were anything but passive. The thousands of slaves who left the South usually planned and carried out their own escape plans. They were careful, determined, and imaginative in devising such plans.

Some slaves merely ran off, traveling by night and resting by day, with assistance from other slaves, free black persons, and occasionally sympathetic whites, not necessarily abolitionists. Others made contact with and paid ship captains running from southern to northern ports to hide them among the cargo. When viewed from the perspective of the slave narratives dictated or written by the former slaves themselves, the whole fugitive slave epoch takes on a different emphasis with more attention to the fugitives' own self-help efforts, though credit is accorded abolitionist assistance when it was given.

Often there was no help available, either in planning or carrying out slave escapes, and in light of such circumstances a successful escape was a major accomplishment of the human spirit. In 1838 Charles Ball traveled 1,200 miles from Alabama to New York, unaided by any underground railroad. Ball journeyed at night, living mostly on roots and berries, and contacted abolitionists only after he reached New York. Another slave took an entire year to reach Cincinnati from Alabama. The scant records which are available indicate that many escaping slaves were afraid to trust any outside assistance, preferring to rely as little as possible on others.

Since free blacks were legally obligated to carry certificates of freedom at all times, the fugitives frequently borrowed free papers or had them forged. When Frederick Douglass succeeded in leaving slavery he borrowed the "protection papers" of an American sailor, but it was only in the postwar edition of his autobiography that he revealed his method of escape. Disguise was also commonly used by fugitives. Light-colored slaves sometimes posed as white travelers. When Lewis Clarke left Kentucky slavery, he wore only dark glasses to disguise himself. Clarke stayed in hotels and taverns along the way and reached Ohio safely, later continuing his journey to Canada.

One of the most imaginative and daring of slave escape plans was that devised and carried out by William and Ellen Craft of Macon, Georgia. Ellen, who was the daughter of her own master and of very light complexion, posed as an elderly and infirm southern gentleman with

a bandaged head and one arm in a sling. The Crafts used the sling in order to make it impossible for the traveling "master" to sign necessary forms and to register at hotels, a ploy to hide Ellen's illiteracy. William played the part of a loyal personal servant. He was a skilled cabinetmaker who had earned enough of his own money to purchase a railroad ticket from Georgia to Philadelphia. The Crafts played their roles well. Except for a brief moment of near-disaster in Baltimore when a railroad ticket agent wanted Ellen to sign a form and provide a bond for her servant, the couple had no trouble along the way.

A free black fellow passenger gave the Crafts the name of an abolitionist in Philadelphia; this was their first knowledge of any possible aid from such a source. They rested briefly in Philadelphia before going on to Boston, where they made their home until they fled the country to elude agents of their former owner. The Crafts recorded their remarkable escape story in a pamphlet, "Running a Thousand Miles for Freedom, or the Escape of William and Ellen Craft from Slavery," published in England.

Henry Brown, a slave in Richmond, Virginia, used an equally daring method to escape from slavery. He decided to have himself crated and shipped north by railway express. The plan was Brown's, but of course it required an accomplice. Brown contacted Samuel A. Smith, a sympathetic white man, who followed instructions and, for a fee of $40, sent the crate to the Philadelphia Anti-Slavery Office. Brown's safe arrival was hailed as a miracle in the antislavery press. Later he spoke to numerous abolitionist gatherings, exhibiting the box used in his flight from slavery, along with a powerful diorama showing many scenes of southern slave life, painted for him by Benjamin Roberts, a black artist from Boston. Meanwhile, Samuel Smith helped several others to escape and was apprehended and convicted for his efforts, serving eight years in a Virginia prison. Henry "Box" Brown and the Crafts were frequently referred to as "passengers" on the underground railroad, even though their escapes were planned and largely carried out by themselves, certainly not according to the usual transportation service that institution brings to mind.

When fugitive slaves did receive aid it was mostly by chance and after they had succeeded in completing the most dangerous part of their journey through the southern states. There were abolitionists who made the underground railroad a kind of special concern though the aid they provided was on a regional rather than a national basis. Two who were very active in this phase of the antislavery work were Levi Coffin and Thomas Garrett, both Quakers. Coffin lived and worked in Newport, Indiana for more than twenty years, then moved to Cincinnati, where he added a degree of local organization to the efforts of those who were already helping runaway slaves. Coffin and his friends transported fugitives in wagons from one town to another, on occasion having to elude slave hunters. They also provided the former

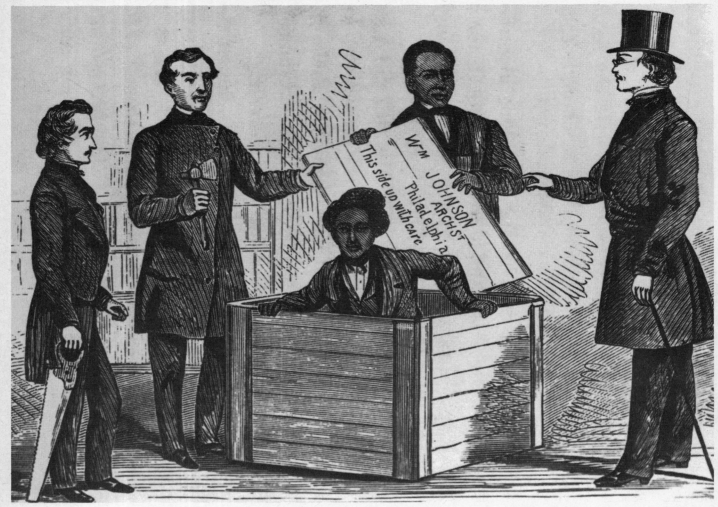

Henry "Box" Brown emerging from the crate in which he was shipped to Philadelphia. ("Ebony" Collections)

slaves with clothing and other necessities, and sometimes boarded them until they could be transported or sent by themselves farther north. Much of Levi Coffin's underground railroad work was aboveboard, especially as antislavery sentiment strengthened in the years just preceding the Civil War. He recorded in his memoirs, written many years later, that public opinion in his neighborhood became so strongly antislavery that he kept fugitives at his house "openly, while preparing them for their journey to the North."

Thomas Garrett provided skillful leadership in assisting fugitive slaves in and around Wilmington, Delaware, working closely with others in Chester County, Pennsylvania and the Philadelphia area. Garrett spared neither time nor expense in his efforts, which usually involved sheltering fugitives, making arrangements for their transportation, and paying necessary expenses. Several times he assisted Harriet Tubman, who, having escaped herself, made trips into the South to rescue others. Although Delaware was a slave state, Garrett capitalized on its unusual degree of free speech and freedom of the press and he seldom worked in secrecy. Sued for damages by a number of slave

owners who won verdicts against him totalling nearly $8,000, Garrett eventually settled for a quarter of that amount, still a considerable sum of money.

Thomas Garrett, Levi Coffin, and other abolitionists involved in the work of assisting fugitive slaves nearly always concentrated their efforts in their own localities. With very few exceptions, such locally organized assistance was unavailable in the South, and even the more militant abolitionists declined to entice slaves from their bondage. Levi Coffin made frequent business trips into the South, but never had any trouble while there. Although he spoke openly of his opposition to slavery, he assured his southern acquaintances that it was not his business while in the South "to interfere with their laws or their slaves." Others believed the risk outweighed the benefits. James H. Fairchild, president of Oberlin College, recalled that the majority of Oberlin abolitionists did not consider it "legitimate to go into the Slave States and entice the slaves from their masters." While they denied the master's ownership they looked upon venturing into the South as a "reckless undertaking, involving too much risk, and probably doing more harm than good." It is no wonder then that the former slaves who recorded their escape accounts tell of plans and daring journeys involving only themselves.

—VOL. 1. No. 4.—

THE
AMERICAN
ANTI-SLAVERY
ALMANAC,
FOR
1839,

BEING THE THIRD AFTER BISSEXTILE OR LEAP-YEAR, AND THE 63D OF AMERICAN INDEPENDENCE. CALCULATED FOR BOSTON; ADAPTED TO THE NEW ENGLAND STATES.

What has the North to do with Slavery?

" Have no *fellowship* with the unfruitful works of darkness, but rather *reprove* them."

NEW YORK & BOSTON:
PUBLISHED FOR THE AMERICAN ANTI-SLAVERY SOCIETY.
NEW YORK: — S. W. BENEDICT, 143, NASSAU ST.
BOSTON: — ISAAC KNAPP, 25, CORNHILL.

Frontispiece of "The American Anti-Slavery Almanac" depicting a fugitive slave being apprehended by the dreaded slave-catchers. (Library of Congress)

All of the prosecutions under the Federal Fugitive Slave Act of 1850 were for acts allegedly committed in the North. Although only about a dozen cases were prosecuted, they received a great deal of public attention and did much to popularize antislavery and anti-southern sentiment. The act itself met with widespread criticism and opposition in the northern states. As part of the Compromise of 1850 it was designed to mollify the slave interests, but its blatant violation of the rights of anyone accused of being a fugitive slave gave a powerful propaganda weapon to the antislavery forces. They pointed out that there was no provision for a jury trial for alleged fugitives and that in fact the law, which they usually referred to as a "bill," denied the protection of free soil

to fleeing slaves and made slavery a national rather than a sectional institution. Many Northerners who had little concern for the slaves themselves resented this intrusion of the slave power into their free society.

When fugitives were captured and returned to slavery the effect on northern public opinion was even stronger. Anthony Burns, a former Virginia slave living in Boston, was arrested on May 24, 1854, only days after the Senate passed the unpopular Kansas-Nebraska Bill opening new territories to slave expansion. A group of people, most of them black, tried to break into the courthouse where Burns was held and rescue him. In the scuffle one officer was killed and later there were arrests for that act, but no conviction. With extraordinary security the Government was able to try Burns and order his return to slavery.

The day Anthony Burns left Boston the church bells tolled and the line of march was draped in mourning crepe. Thousands of disgusted citizens watched while contingents of police, twenty-two companies of Massachusetts soldiers, and a battery of artillery guarded the fugitive. One scholar estimated that Burns's rendition cost $100,000, yet the nationally publicized event converted many to the antislavery point of view. One abolitionist urged William Lloyd Garrison to publish the entire Burns history, believing that "it furnishes far more important materials for History, than it would have furnished had the man been rescued."

Much of the publicity concerning Anthony Burns was promoted by the Boston Vigilance Committee, one of several such committees founded or reactivated in response to the Fugitive Slave Law of 1850. The work of these committees contributed substantially to the popular image of the underground railroad, though much of their work was aboveboard and routine. Some were founded by Negroes and all of them used black sympathizers as contacts and workers. One of the more active was the Philadelphia Vigilance Committee with William Still, a black abolitionist, as chairman. Approximately 100 fugitives a year received assistance from the committee during the eight-year period when William Still kept records of its work. Still and committee members also interviewed each of the former slaves, carefully recorded essential facts, and preserved the organization's financial records and some of its correspondence. William Still later used this and other first-hand material in compiling his important book, *The Underground Rail Road.* As a Negro he was concerned that the fugitives receive credit as well as those whites who risked much to help them. Still wrote, promoted, and sold his book through agents. He hoped the work would inspire other blacks to greater efforts until they could gain wealth and produce literary works of quality. As the only book-length account of the underground railroad written by a black author, Still's volume is unique.

4. THE CIVIL WAR AND RECONSTRUCTION

RIGHT: Map illustrating the route to Canada on the underground railroad. (From "Anti-Slavery" by Dwight Lowell Dumond, University of Michigan Press, 1961)

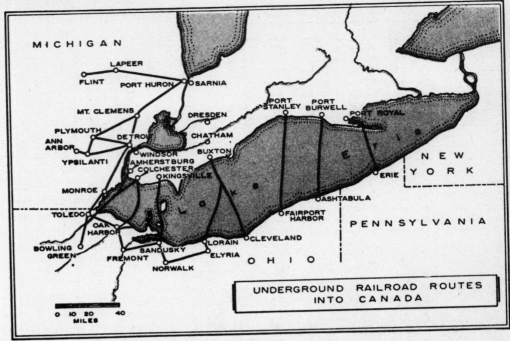

In the years before the Civil War the underground railroad also provided a wealth of propaganda material for the antislavery cause. Incidents concerning fugitives and their rescue, often by black crowds, were frequently reported in the reform press. Abolitionists boasted of their underground railroad activity and published details of escapes to arouse further sympathy for the fugitives and the antislavery cause. Sometimes escaped slaves were exhibited at abolitionist meetings. Available assistance was even listed in some of the antislavery newspapers along with the narratives of former slaves. Nearly every aspect of the activity had potential for winning new free soil or antislavery converts. The fugitives aroused sympathy, for their treatment by southern slave hunters and by the courts violated all sense of decency and respect for civil liberties. All of this contributed to a growing resentment of the encroachments and demands of what Northerners referred to as the slave power.

It was in the years after the Civil War had destroyed the slave power and its hold on the nation that the underground railroad assumed the character of a cherished American legend. Many Northerners viewed the past and the defeated slave interests with a vision distorted by the course of events. The immorality of slavery became obvious with its defeat, and some who had had only marginal connections with free soil or antislavery efforts were prone to exaggerate their contributions. As early as 1864 abolitionist Lydia Maria Child remarked to William Lloyd Garrison that new antislavery friends were "becoming as plenty as roses in June," and she marveled "at

their power of keeping a secret so long!" A year later an abolitionist reported that it was "rare to meet one who has ever wished well to slavery, or desired anything but its final abolition."

The romantic nature of underground railroad activity virtually assured its place in Civil War tradition. In the 1890's, when Professor Siebert corresponded with hundreds of abolitionists and their descendants, only a few denied having valid recollections of the institution. Journalists and local historians in many northern communities took for granted an underground railroad record, and to some Northerners the thousands of slaves who escaped became millions.

A pattern of action emerged in these accounts, with emphasis on the role of white abolitionists, a pattern which was repeated in a number of works of fiction as well as in some historical writing. Consequently, the black participants became virtually invisible in the underground railroad of legend. Exposing the distortions and oversimplifications associated with the underground railroad in the years since the Civil War should not denigrate those abolitionists who were actively involved, nor should it minimize the importance of their efforts. The historical picture, however, is much more complex and vastly different from the legendary accounts with their heroes and villains participating in a noble crusade to free helpless victims of slavery. Underground railroad operators did aid some slaves in their escape, but such aid must not overshadow or obliterate the efforts of the slaves to free themselves.

Johnny Reb and Billy Yank

The men (and boys) who opposed each other in the American Civil War had more similarities than differences. But those differences were enough to keep our bloodiest conflict going for four years.

By Bell I. Wiley

Dr. Bell I. Wiley, one of the truly great military historians of our Nation, who is acclaimed also for his work as a teacher, editor, and publisher, has specialized on studies of military personnel, particularly of soldiers in the Civil War. He is a regular contributor to "CIVIL WAR TIMES Illustrated."

THE COMMON SOLDIERS of North and South during the American Civil War were very much alike. As a general rule they came from similar backgrounds, spoke the same language, cherished the same ideals and reacted in like manner to the hardships and perils of soldiering. They hated regimentation, found abundant fault with their officers, complained often about army rations and hoped earnestly for speedy return to civilian life. Even so, men of the opposing sides presented some notable and interesting differences.

In the first place, Billy Yanks were more often of foreign background than were their opposites in gray. During the decades preceding the Civil War several million Europeans migrated to America and because of convenience, economic opportunity, and other influences, most of them settled in the North. In 1861 there were about four million persons of alien birth living in the states adhering to the Union as against only about one fourth of a million residing in the Southern Confederacy. Because the immigrants tended to identify themselves with the section in which they settled, far more of them donned the Union blue than the Confederate gray. Probably one out of every four or five Billy Yanks was of foreign birth and only one out of every twenty or twenty-five Johnny Rebs.

On the northern side the Germans, aggregating about 200,000, were the most numerous of the foreign groups. Next were the Irish, numbering about 150,000, then Canadians and Englishmen each totalling about 50,000 and, down the line, lesser numbers of Scandinavians, Frenchmen, Italians, and other nationalities.

It has been estimated that 15,000 to 20,000 Irishmen marched in Confederate ranks and they apparently outnumbered any other foreign group on the Southern side. But Canada, England, France, and Italy were well represented among wearers of the gray.

ON BOTH sides most of the foreigners were enlisted men, but many served as company and field grade officers and a considerable number attained the rank of general. Forty-five of the North's 583 general officers were of foreign birth, and among them were twelve Germans and twelve Irishmen. Among the Confederacy's 425 generals, there were nine foreigners of whom five were Irish.

In both armies the foreign groups added color and variety to camp life by singing their native songs, celebrating festive days, and observing customs peculiar to their homeland. St. Patrick's Day was always

Irish-born Major General Patrick Ronayne Cleburne, CSA, killed in the bloody Battle of Franklin, November 30, 1864. (KA)

German-born Major General Peter Joseph Osterhaus. (U. S. Signal Corps photo No. 111-B-2778 in the National Archives)

From AMERICAN HISTORY ILLUSTRATED, April 1968. Reproduced through the courtesy of The National Historical Society, publishers of AMERICAN HISTORY ILLUSTRATED, P. O. Box 1831, Harrisburg, Pa. 17105.

a great occasion among Irish units, featuring horse races, athletic contests, and consumption of large quantities of alcohol. As Pat and Mike lingered at flowing bowls their pugnacious tendencies were accentuated, and before night guardhouses were crowded with men suffering from cuts, bruises, or broken bones. Indeed, St. Patrick's Day sometimes produced more casualties among sons of Erin than did encounters on the battlefield.

In combat the foreigners gave a good account of themselves. Meagher's Irish Brigade was one of the best fighting units in the Civil War. Ezra J. Warner in *Generals in Blue* rates Prussian-born Peter J. Osterhaus as "certainly the most distinguished of the foreign-born officers who served the Union," and few, if any, division commanders of any nationality on either side had a better battle record than the Confederacy's beloved Irishman, Patrick R. Cleburne.

Among native participants two groups deserving special mention were the Indians and Negroes. The Confederacy had three brigades of redmen, mostly Cherokees, Choctaws, and Seminoles. One of the Cherokees, Stand Watie, became a brigadier general. The Union Army had one brigade of Indians, most of whom were Creeks. Muster rolls of Indian units, filed in the National Archives, contain such names as Private Sweetcaller, Private Hog Shooter, Private Hog Toter, Private Flying Bird, and Lieutenant Jumper Duck. At the Battle of Honey Springs in 1864, Yankee Indians fought Rebel Indians. In combat Indians acquitted themselves well, but between battles they were poor soldiers, since they had only vague ideas of discipline and regimentation.

ON THE Confederate side, Negroes served almost exclusively in accessory capacities, as cooks, hostlers, musicians, and body servants. On March 13, 1865 after prolonged and acrimonious discussion the Confederate Congress passed a law authorizing recruitment of 300,000 slaves to serve as soldiers. A few companies were organized but the war ended before any of them could get into combat. It seems unreasonable to think that slaves would have fought with any enthusiasm for the perpetuation of their bondage. More than 188,000 Negroes, most of whom were ex-slaves, wore the Union blue. Despite discriminations in pay, equipment, and association with fellow soldiers, and notwithstanding the fact that they had to do far more than their share of labor and garrison duty, Negro Yanks fought well at Port Hudson, Milliken's Bend, Fort Wagner, the Crater, and other Civil War battles in which they participated.

Billy Yanks were better' educated than Johnny Rebs, owing to the North's better schools and greater emphasis on public education. In some companies from the rural South, half of the men could not sign

During the Civil War both sides enlisted Indians. This drawing shows a group of Delawares resting after a reconnaissance for the Union army somewhere in the West.

the muster rolls. Such companies were exceptional, but so were those that did not have from one to twenty illiterates. Sergeant Major John A. Cobb of the 16th Georgia Regiment wrote a kinsman on September 8, 1861: "Paying off soldiers is a good deal like paying off negroes their cotton money . . . about one third of the men in the regiment can't write their names, so the Pay Roll has a good many X (his mark) on it, and about one half of those that write them you can't read, nor could they themselves." Among Yanks the rate of illiteracy was highest in Negro units, but the typical Union regiment seems to have had no more than a half-dozen illiterates and many had none at all. On both sides, however, spelling and grammar frequently fell far below schoolroom standards. In soldier letters pneumonia sometimes appeared as *new mornion* or *new mony*, once as *wonst*, uneasy as *oneasy*, fought as *fit*, your as *yore* or *yourn*, and not any as *nary*. Other common usages were *tuck* for took, *purty* for pretty, *laig* for leg, and *shore* for sure. Long words were often divided, sometimes with strange results. One Reb complained about the "rashens" issued by the *comma sary;* another stated that he hoped to get a *fur low* when some more *volen teares* joined the *ridge ment*. A Yank wrote that he had been marching through mud that was *nea deap*. Another reported shortly after Lincoln ordered the organization of McClellan's forces into corps: "They are deviding the army up into corpses." While reading the letter of an Illinois soldier I was puzzled by the statement "I had the camp diary a few days ago," for I had not previously found indica-

tion that Civil War organizations kept unit journals. But my confusion was cleared up by the rest of the sentence which stated "but now I am about well of it." This soldier was suffering from a malady commonly known as the "Tennessee Quickstep."

A Yank who served under General Frederick Lander wrote in one of his letters: "Landers has the ganders." I read it just as it appeared, with a hard "g." On reflection I realized that the "g" was soft and that what the general really had was the jaundice. Landers was very unpopular with this particular Yank, so he added "I hope the old so and so dies." The next letter began: "Well old Landers is dead, and I'll bet he is down in hell pumping thunder at three cents a clap."

Soldiers in both armies frequently spelled hospital as "horsepittle," and that was a place which they abhorred almost as much as the devil himself. A Reb wrote that the hospital which served his unit "outstinks a ded horse."

BECAUSE of differences in Northern and Southern economy, Billy Yanks were more often town dwellers and factory workers than were Johnny Rebs. The contrast is vividly demonstrated in company descriptive rolls. The occupation columns on typical Southern rolls consist of a monotonous repetition of "farmer," while Northern rolls, except in the case of units recruited from agricultural communities, listed a wide assortment of occupations, including carpenters, clerks, coopers, shoemakers, bricklayers, printers, tinsmiths, mechanics. miners, plumbers,

ABOVE: Negro troops in Yankee blue. These are 107th U.S. Colored troops at Fort Corcoran, Washington, D. C. (LC)

A recruiting office in Boston, as sketched by Charles W. Reed, a bugler in the 9th Massachusetts Light Battery. (LC)

tailors, and boatmen. This diversity of skills among the rank and file gave the North a considerable advantage in what proved to be the first great modern war. It meant that if a wagon, steamboat, or locomotive broke down, or if a railroad needed rebuilding, or if a gun failed to function, a Northern commander could usually find close at hand soldiers who knew how to do the job.

Both during and after the war many people believed that the Confederate forces contained more boys and old men than did those of the Union. Study of descriptive rolls and other records indicates that this was an erroneous impression. There were many boys and old men on both sides. Charles Carter Hay enlisted in an Alabama regiment when he was 11 years old, and when four years later he surrendered at Appomattox he had not celebrated his 15th birthday. He had a counterpart on the Union side in the case of Johnny Clem, who began service as a drummer boy at age 9 in 1861, and who graduated to the fighting ranks after the Battle of Shiloh. E. Pollard enlisted in the 5th North Carolina Regiment at 73, but the oldest Civil War soldier apparently was 80-year-old Curtis King of the 37th Iowa, a noncombatant regiment known as the "Graybeards" because on its rolls there were 145 men who had passed

their 60th birthday. But on both sides, most soldiers were neither very young nor very old. The largest single age group were the 18-year-olds, and three-fourths of the men fell in the age bracket 18-30.

Billy Yanks manifested a livelier interest in politics than did the men whom they opposed. This was due in part to the greater literacy of the Northern soldiers and their easier access to newspapers. On the national level the nature of politics was a contributing factor. Because the Confederate Constitution provided a single term of six years for the Chief Executive, there was only one Presidential campaign in the South during the war. This was a very dull affair because Jefferson Davis had no opposition. But in the North the campaign of 1864 between Lincoln and McClellan was a hard-fought contest, and most Yanks thought that the outcome would have a great impact on the prosecution of the war. Electioneering was lively in many units, and soldiers voted in impressive numbers. When ballots were tabulated it was found that the overwhelming majority had voted for "Uncle Abe" and continuance of war until the Union was restored.

Few, if any, other campaigns generated as much enthusiasm among Billy Yanks as did the Lincoln-McClellan contest, but even in the choice of governors, Congressmen, and lesser officials, the men in blue in their letters and diaries revealed considerably more interest than did wearers of the gray.

Billy Yanks' greater involvement in politics reflected a healthier interest in things intellectual. Owing to the North's better schools, the more cosmopolitan character of its population, the more varied pattern of its economy, the presence in its borders of more large cities, the greater prosperity of its citizens, better communication, easier access to books and papers, greater freedom of thought and discussion, and sundry other advantages, Union soldiers manifested greater curiosity about things past and present than their opposites in Confederate service. Common soldiers on either side who showed a deep concern for philosophic aspects of the conflict were rare. But the North appears to have had considerably more than its share of the exceptions.

IN THEIR religious attitudes and activities Billy Yanks and Johnny Rebs manifested some notable contrasts. Letters and diaries of Southern soldiers contain more references to religion than do those of the men in blue, and Rebs were more emotional in their worship than were Billy Yanks. During the last two years of the conflict, great revivals swept over both the Eastern and Western armies of the Confederacy and men made open confessions of their sins, sought forgiveness at mourners' benches, and raised shouts of joy when relieved of the burden of guilt. Seasons of revival sometimes extended for several weeks as leading ministers from Richmond, New Orleans, Nashville, and other cities joined the army chaplains in promoting the cause of salvation. Revivals also took place in Northern units, but rarely did they extend beyond brigade or division. Certainly, the Union forces experienced no army-wide outbreaks of emotionalism such as occurred among Confederates.

The greater interest in religion manifested by Confederates and their greater susceptibility to revivalism was due to a combination of circumstances. The fact that Southerners were a more homogeneous people than Northerners and more often members of evangelistic sects made for greater religious zeal and emotionalism in Confederate camps. Another factor working to the same end was the South's greater ruralism. Still another factor was the example of high-ranking leaders. Robert E. Lee, Stonewall Jackson, and Leonidas Polk were deeply religious men and they showed far more interest in the spiritual welfare of their commands than did Grant, Sherman, and Sheridan. Jefferson Davis proclaimed more days of fasting and prayer and was more of a church man than was Abraham Lincoln.

The fortunes of war played a part in revivalism. The flood tides of emotionalism that swept over the Southern armies came after Vicksburg and Gettysburg, and to some extent they represent the tendency of a religiously rooted people in times of severe crises

Arrival of newspapers in camp as drawn by Civil War artist Edwin Forbes. Union soldiers were better read and better informed than Confederates because of the mass distribution of Northern weeklies like "Harper's" and "Frank Leslie's."

to seek supernatural deliverance from the woes that beset them.

The greater religiosity of the Confederates does not seem to have produced a higher level of morality in Southern camps. Comments of soldiers, complaints of chaplains, court-martial proceedings, and monthly health reports indicate that profanity, gambling, drunkenness, fornication, and other "sins" flourished as much among Rebs as among Yanks.

THE Northern soldiers generally were of a more practical and prosaic bent of mind than were Johnny Rebs. This difference was reflected in the Northerners' greater concern for the material things of life. Billy Yanks more often engaged in buying and selling and other side activities to supplement their army pay. Their letters contain far more references to lending their earnings at interest, investing for profit, and other financial ventures than do those written by the men in gray. Admittedly, Yanks had more money to write about, but their better remuneration, important though it was, was not enough wholly to account for the difference.

Billy Yanks' letters were not so fanciful or poetic as those of Johnny Rebs, nor were they as rich in humor and banter. The Northerners did not so frequently address wives and sweethearts in endearing terms as did their Southern counterparts. Correspondence of the men in blue contains much delightful humor, but I have yet to find any matching that exemplified by the following selections from Confederate sources: A Georgia Reb wrote his wife after absence of about a year in Virginia: "If I did not write and receive letters from you, I believe that I would forgit that I was married. I don't feel much like a maryed man, but I never forgit it so far as to court enny other lady but if I should you must forgive me as I am so forgitful." Another Georgian while on tour of duty in East Tennessee wrote his spouse: "lis, I must tell you that I have found me a Sweat hart heare. . . . I had our pitures taken with her handen me a bunch of flowers . . . she lets on like she thinks a heep of me and when I told her I was marred she took a harty cry about it . . . she ses that she entends to live singel the balance of her days." A Tar Heel wrote a male friend at home: "Thomy I want you to be a good boy and tri to take cear of the wemmen and children tell I get home and we'll all have a chance. . . . I want you to go . . . and see my wife and children but I want you to take your wife with you [when you go]."

BILLY Yanks' reasons for fighting were different from those of Johnny Rebs. Some Yanks went to war

ABOVE: Typical Union infantry company. (National Archives)

BELOW: Confederate artillery (Palmetto Battery) near Charleston, S. C. from an 1863 photo by George S. Cook. (LC)

to free the slaves. One of these was Chauncey Cooke of the 25th Wisconsin Regiment, who wrote home before he heard of Lincoln's issuance of the Emancipation Proclamation: "I have no heart in this war if the slaves cannot be free." But Cooke represented a minority. The overwhelming majority of those who donned the blue did so primarily to save the imperilled Union. Devotion to the Union found eloquent expression in some of their letters. Private Sam Croft, a youth from Pennsylvania, wrote his homefolk after a hard march in September 1861: "I have never once thought of giving out. . . . I am well, hardy, strong, and doing my country a little service. I did not come for money and good living. My Heart beats high and I am proud of being a soldier. When I look along the line of glistening bayonets with the glorious Stars and Stripes floating over them . . . I am proud and sanquine of success." Croft died at Gettysburg.

Most Rebs who commented on their individual motivation indicated that they were fighting to protect their families and homes against foreign invaders, and they envisioned the invaders as a cruel and wicked foe. "Teach my children to hate them with that bitter hatred that will never permit them to meet without seeking to destroy each other," wrote a Georgia Reb to his wife in 1862.

Georgia Private Edwin F. Jennison, died at Malvern Hill. (LC)

MANY Confederates were fighting for slavery, though this was rarely indicated in their letters. Usually they represented themselves as fighting for self-government, state rights, or "the Southern way of life." There is no doubt in my mind that most Southerners, non-slaveholders as well as planters, were earnestly desirous of maintaining slavery, not primarily as an economic system, but rather as an established and effective instrument of social control. A North Carolina private wrote a friend in 1863: "You know I am a poor man having none of the property said to be the cause of the present war. But I have a wife and some children to rase in honor and never to be put on an equality with the African race." Thus did one Reb who owned no Negroes avow that he was fighting for slavery; there were many others like him.

Billy Yanks were better fed and better clothed than Johnny Rebs. In the latter part of the war they frequently were better armed. Each side experienced ups and downs of morale, but generally speaking Confederate morale was higher than that of the Northerners during the first half of the war and lower during the second half. The nadir of Union morale came early in 1863, in the wake of Grant's reverses in Mississippi and Burnside's bloody defeat at Fredericksburg. Confederate morale plummeted after Vicksburg and Gettysburg, rose slightly in the spring and summer of 1864 and began its final unabated plunge after the re-election of Lincoln.

WHAT of the combat performance of Johnny Rebs and Billy Yanks? The Southerners apparently fought with more enthusiasm than their opponents; and, after battle, in letters to the folk at home, they wrote more vividly and in greater detail of their combat experiences. In a fight they demonstrated more of dash, elan, individual aggressiveness, and a devil-may-care quality than Billy Yanks. But the men in blue seemed to have gone about the business of fighting with greater seriousness than Johnny Rebs, and they manifested more of a group consciousness and team spirit. In other words, the Rebs thought a battle was a thrilling adventure in which each man was to a large extent on his own; to Yanks it was a formidable task requiring the earnest and coordinated exertion of all those involved—not a game-shooting experience as some Rebs seemed to regard it, but a grim and inescapable chore that ought to be performed with as much efficiency and expedition as possible.

These differences were reflected in the battle cheers of the opposing forces. Southerners charged with the "Rebel yell" on their lips. This was a wild, high-pitched, piercing "holler," inspired by a combination of excitement, fright, anger, and elation. The standard Yankee cheer, on the other hand, was a regularly intoned huzza or hurrah. The contrast between Southern and Northern cheering was the subject of much comment by participants on both sides. A Federal officer observed after the second battle of Manassas: "Our own men give three successive cheers and in concert, but theirs is a cheering without any reference to regularity of form—a continual yelling." A Union surgeon who was in The Wilderness Campaign of 1864 stated: "On our side it was a resounding, continuous hurrah, while the famous dread-inspiring "Rebel yell" was a succession of yelps staccato and shrill."

UNQUESTIONABLY Johnny Rebs made a better showing in combat during the first half of the war. This was due mainly to better leadership, particularly on the company and regimental levels. On both sides these officers were elected, and in the South, owing largely to the prevalence of the caste system, the successful candidates were usually planters or their sons—privileged persons, recognized community leaders, habituated to the direction of slaves, products of the military academies on which the region principally relied for education of its boys, and strongly indoctrinated with the spirit of *noblesse oblige*.

In the more democratic North, on the other hand, men were chosen as officers because of their effectiveness in persuading neighbors to sign up for military service. In many instances they were deficient in the essentials of leadership. By the summer of 1863, incompetent officers on both sides generally had been weeded out by resignation, dismissal, or hostile bullets. By that time also the Northerners had overcome the initial handicap of being less familiar with firearms than their opponents. During the last two years of the war, there was no discernible difference in the combat performance of Johnny Rebs and Billy Yanks. There was never any significant difference in their determination, pride, courage, devotion to cause, loyalty to comrades, and other basic qualities that go to make good soldiers. From the beginning to the end of the conflict the common soldiers of both sides acquitted themselves in a manner that merited the pride of their descendants and won for them a high standing among fighting men of all time.

Well-armed Illinois Private George W. Crane. (From Logan Collection, courtesy of Illinois State Historical Library)

HOW 'THE LOST CAUSE' WAS LOST

At the start of the Civil War, the South held the trump cards. How then, did it lose?

Henry Steele Commager

Henry Steele Commager is professor of history and American Studies at Amherst.

Looking back now through the mists of 100 years at the prodigious story of Gettysburg and Vicksburg, we are lost in admiration for the gallantry of those who led the ranks of gray in what we have come to call "the Lost Cause." And we know just when it was lost. It was lost in those fateful days of July, 1863, when Lee's bold thrust into Pennsylvania, which was to have threatened the capital and brought recognition of the Confederacy from Britain and France, was blunted and turned back, and when Vicksburg fell and the Father of Waters went again unvexed to the sea. It was high tide and ebb tide; it was the beginning of the end.

So, at least, most of us suppose. As we contemplate the fall of the Confederacy, we conclude that it was indeed inevitable and that the Confederacy was but a dream:

Woe! woe! is us, how strange and sad,
That all our glorious visions fled,
Have left us nothing real but our dead,
In the land where we were dreaming.

To most of us it is inconceivable that the Civil War should have had any outcome but that registered at Appomattox. It is inconceivable that the territory which now constitutes the United States should have been fragmented—like that of Latin America—into 20 states. It is inconceivable that the Confederacy should have made good its bid for independent nationhood.

But the doctrine of inevitability confronts us with two insuperable difficulties. If it was clear from the beginning that the South must lose, how can we explain the fact that men like Jefferson Davis, Judah P. Benjamin, R. B. Rhett, Howell Cobb and scores of others, men who were upright, virtuous, intelligent and humane, were prepared to lead their people to certain destruction? If defeat was inevitable, they must have discerned this, too, and their conduct takes on the character of criminal imbecility. And second, how can we explain the widespread assumption in Europe—and even in parts of the North—that the South would make good her bid for independence? How does it happen that so many otherwise sensible and judicious men were misled?

It is not too much to say that the South held—or appeared to hold—at least two trump cards in 1861. The first was what we would now call grand strategy or ultimate war aims. For the fact is that the Confederacy did not need to win in order to win; it was enough if she held the field long enough to weary the North with the war. But the North, in order to win, had to conquer the South, had to invade and hold an area as great as Western Europe minus Italy and Scandinavia—an achievement as yet without parallel in modern history. The Confederacy could afford to lose all the battles and all the campaigns if only she could persuade the North that the price of victory was too high. The South asked merely to be left alone, and she proposed to make the war so costly that the North would in the end prefer to leave her alone. After all, The American colonies, and the United Netherlands, had won their independence against even heavier odds than those which faced the Confederacy.

And this suggests the second trump card: foreign intervention. The leaders of the Confederacy had read well the history of the American Revolution, or had heard it from their fathers and their grandfathers—for the Virginians of 1860 were psychologically closer to the generation of Washington than were the Yankees of Massachusetts to the generation of Sam Adams. They knew that the intervention of France and then of other European nations had turned the tide in favor of the Americans, and they assumed that history would repeat itself. They counted with confidence on the intervention of Britain and France—intervention at a practical level on behalf of cotton, intervention at a higher level on behalf of freedom and self-determination.

Quite aside from these two major strategic considerations, the South held other advantages. She commanded interior lines and therefore the ability to shift her smaller forces rapidly from one front to another. She fought on the defensive, and that position (so it was thought) more than made up for her numerical inferiority, since offensive operations, with their implacable demands of transportation, supply and occupation, required a greater superiority than she felt the Union forces could muster. She had a long and deeply indented coastline, one which presented almost insuperable obstacles to a successful block-

From *The New York Times Magazine*, August 4, 1963. ©1963 by The New York Times Company. Reprinted by permission.

President Davis, left, with General Lee and members of his Cabinet.

TWO REASONS FOR DEFEAT—Despite the South's strengths, says Professor Commager, its leaders failed to develop a sense of national unity, while the "peculiar institution" of slavery stifled self-criticism, offended public opinion in the North and prevented possible foreign help.

ade—and, after all, the Union Navy was not above contempt. She had, in her 3,000,000 Negro slaves, a large and, on the whole, loyal labor force which might relieve Southern whites of many civilian duties and permit them to fight in the ranks. She had, at the beginning, the best generals and a long military tradition. And she boasted—mistakenly as it proved—a broader and deeper unity than the heterogeneous North.

With all these advantages, why did the South lose? Since 1865, students and historians have speculated about this question but no one has answered it. Curiously enough, the leaders of the Lost Cause had little to say about the reasons for defeat. The greatest of them, R. E. Lee, preserved a dignified silence after Appomattox. President Davis wrote two ponderous volumes but they say nothing about the underlying causes of defeat except to blame his political enemies. Vice President Stephens also produced two unreadable volumes on the Confederacy and the war but failed

conspicuously to speculate on the question (in his case, speculation might have proved too embarrassing). Judah P. Benjamin, the most philoso-phical mind in the Confederate Government, might have given us a really penetrating analysis of the problem, but he chose to forget his American past in a more glamorous English present.

Nor do the lesser figures help us much. The literature is voluminous but mostly elegiac and almost all of it is unreflective. Perhaps the Southerner of that generation was, as Henry Adams wrote of his classmate Rooney Lee, by nature unreflective: "Stricly," said Adams, "the Southerner had no mind; he had temperament. He was not a scholar, he had no intellectual training, he could not analyze an idea, and he could not even conceive of admitting two."

Or, more probably, reflection on the responsibility for so great a catastrophe was simply too uncomfortable. And as for the Northerners, by and large they were content with

victory, or with easy assumptions about their superiority in arms and in men, or the righteousness of their cause, or the wickedness of the South, or the preference of Providence for the Union.

Why *did* the South lose? Was it because the Confederacy was hopelessly outnumbered? Until 1864, it was able to put almost as many soldiers into battle as the Union—in fact, the South had a numerical superiority at First Bull Run, Pea Ridge, Gaines's Mill, Seven Days, Corinth, Chickamauga, Peach Tree Creek and Atlanta. Was it for reasons of finance? Lack of money had not prevented the Americans from making good their bid for independence. (And besides, a financial explanation merely begs another question: *Why* did the Confederacy lack money?) Was it due to poor transportation? The South had a much smaller railroad mileage than the North, but she enjoyed interior lines and the advantage of a system of inland waterways. Southern transportation facilities were not, in fact, inadequate in themselves—or at least not irremediably inadequate. The real question is, why did the South fail to use what she had or to develop what she needed?

Was defeat attributable to the failure of the Confederacy to win the

THE LOST CAUSE—Lee's final surrender

border states—Maryland, Kentucky, Missouri? These were, after all, slave states and Southern in culture and social structure. There was every reason to suppose that they would throw in their lot with the South.

"Come! For thy shield is bright and strong, Come! for thy dalliance does thee wrong, Maryland, my Maryland."

But she did not come, nor did the other border states—though Kentucky and Missouri were represented in the Confederate Congress! Why not? Was it lack of military skill or political prescience, or simply bad luck? Why did this calculation—like so many others—go wrong?

Or was the underlying fault, perhaps, in Jefferson Davis —so brittle, so temperamental, so arrogant? He took the conduct of the war into his own hands; he interfered with the military; he had favorites (like the wretched Braxton Bragg) and enemies (like the brilliant Joseph Johnston). He alienated state Governors and Congressmen and he never won the affections of the Southern people. Yet on balance Davis emerges as a reasonably good President—probably as good as any the Confederacy could have selected at that time. He was tireless, high-minded, courageous, intelligent, indomitable and more often right on major issues than his critics. The real question is why there were so few alternatives to Jefferson Davis.

Or was the South beaten by the blockade? This is perhaps the favorite of all explanations, for ever since Mahan, seapower has been the glamorous key to history. But at the beginning of the war, the North had only an excuse for a navy; not until 1863 was the blockade effective. Why did not the Confederacy bring in whatever she needed before that time? Why did she not utilize her swift privateers to the best advantage? And, why for that matter, were Britain and France willing to respect what was, for a long time, a mere paper blockade? If Cotton was King, why did Europeans refuse to recog-

FINAL DEFEAT—Surrendering Confederate troops hold their muskets butt upward. This sketch, "The Last of Ewell's Corps," was drawn April 6, 1865, by Alfred R. Waud. Three days later, he pictured Gen. Robert E. Lee (right) after his surrender at Appomattox. Waud, considered the greatest of Civil War illustrators, worked for Harper's Weekly, covering the campaigns of the Union Army of the Potomac from its formation to Grant's final victory.

nize its sovereignty? If Cotton was *not* King, why did Southerners so delude themselves?

When we have considered, and dismissed, these surface reasons for the failure of the Confederacy, we come to more fundamental causes. Three of these, all interrelated, command our attention.

The first was the failure of Southern nationalism. Almost all the ingredients of nationalism were there—indeed, the Confederacy in 1860 had more of the ingredients of nationalism than the Colonies in 1775—but somehow the Confederacy never really became a nation. For all its passionate devotion to Dixie Land, it seemed to lack a sense of nationalism and the will to nationalism. Given the circumstances of its birth, this is not surprising. The Southern states had broken away from the old Union because the Federal Government—so

they alleged—threatened their rights, and they defiantly founded their new nation on states' rights and state sovereignty. The new nation was therefore based on a repudiation of nationalism.

Even its political institutions, reflected this, perhaps unconsciously. Military leadership in the South was splendid, but political leadership was weak and vacillating. The Confederacy had its Lee and its Jackson to match—perhaps to outmatch—Grant and Sherman, but where was its Lincoln? Where for that matter were its Seward, its Stanton, its Stevens, its Sumner, its Trumbull; its diplomats like Charles Francis Adams; its war Governors like Andrew of Massachusetts or Morton of Indiana? There were local factions but no political parties, and therefore no safety valve for political discontent. There were strong state supreme courts, but notwithstanding the provision of the Confederate constitution, Congress never created a Confederate Supreme Court.

State sovereignty is not necessarily fatal to nationalism or to union in time of peace and order, when no grave problems confront a government and no stern crises challenge the people. Had the North permitted the "wayward sisters to depart in peace," the Confederacy might have survived long enough to develop the essential institutions, political habits and administrative practices. But to build a nation on state sovereignty in time of war is to build upon a foundation of quicksand.

The second fundamental cause of failure was, in fact, this very issue of states' rights, which steadily eroded the strength of the Confederacy. State Representatives at Richmond devoted their energies to thwarting Jefferson Davis. Vice President Stephens retired to his Georgia home to wage relentless war on the President. State supreme courts nullified Confederate laws, and there was, as we have seen, no Confederate Supreme Court to which to appeal. States put their own interests ahead of the interests of the embryo nation. Even in the first year of the war, the states jealously held on to their arms and supplies. Had they surrendered them to the Confederacy at the beginning of the war, it could have put 600,000 men into the field instead of 400,000, and that might have made all the difference.

State Governors like Brown of Georgia and Vance of North Carolina exempted thousands of their citizens from conscription and their judges protected deserters and refugees from capture and restoration to the ranks of the Confederate armies. The Governor of Mississippi exempted over 4,500 militia officers and others in his state from the operation of the conscription laws, and the Governor of Alabama almost the same number.

All through the war, state Governors withheld desperately needed supplies. Thus Brown of Georgia not only kept his Georgia troops well supplied with uniforms and blankets but had a surplus in his warehouses sufficient to have outfitted the whole of Lee's army—and kept it there! At a time when "Lee's Miserables" were going barefoot and freezing in the terrible trenches of Petersburg, Governor Vance of North Carolina had 5,000 complete uniforms and an equal quantity of shoes and blankets in his warehouses—and kept them there!

States' rights, instead of being the rock on which the nation was built, was the reef on which the nation foundered. There is a moral here, even for our own time.

The third fundamental cause of Southern defeat was slavery itself— that "peculiar institution," as the South euphemistically called it. It was slavery that the war was ultimately about; it was slavery that ultimately doomed the South to defeat. For it was slavery that decisively prevented the one move which might have saved the South, even after Vicksburg and Gettysburg—European intervention. As late as 1863, British aristocrats— a Cecil, a Halifax, a Gregory, a Lindsay, a Vansittart—organized the Southern Independence Association which dedicated itself to intervention. It was in the summer of 1863 that the British navy yards were building the famous Laird rams that almost got away—almost, but not quite!

Had Britain intervened to break the blockade—and France would have followed her lead, and Mexico, of course—there is every likelihood that the Confederacy would have won her independence. With Britain ready to provide the Confederacy with money, arms, munitions, food and drugs, and ready to buy her cotton and other produce, the Confederacy could have fought on indefinitely, just as the Americans did once they had supplies and money from France after 1777. And had the Union Government responded to such intervention by a declaration of war—as it almost certainly would have done—it would probably have signed its own death warrant.

What prevented intervention from abroad? Not the failure of the South on the battlefield, for that failure was not decisive until after the midsummer of 1863. And it was not sympathy for the Government of the Union, for there was very little of that in the ruling circles of Britain or France. No, more than anything else, it was slavery. The upper classes might be sympathetic to the Confederacy, but the powerful middle and working classes were passionately on the side of the North. It was not merely that the North represented democracy—although that was a consideration; it was, far more, that the South represented slavery. Public opinion, that newly emerging and still amorphous thing, simply would not tolerate going in on the side of slavery.

But, it will be asked, why did not the South see what we now see? Why did not Southerners see the necessity of a strong national government in time of war and create one? Why did they not see the pernicious consequences of states' rights in time of crisis and restrict them? Why did they not see the blight of slavery and move against it, move to win public opinion abroad by some dramatic gesture of gradual emancipation?

Here we come to something very fundamental, indeed—to the psychology, the philosophy associated— perhaps inevitably associated—with slavery.

Slavery was the foundation of the South, and slavery carried with it the enslavement of the mind of a people. For 30 years the South had felt herself misunderstood, condemned and beleaguered. For 30 years she had rallied her resources to defend the "peculiar institution," and she had finally convinced herself that slavery was not a necessary evil but a positive good, not a curse but a blessing. She realized, however, that she was almost alone in this opinion and, feeling herself increasingly isolated, she withdrew into her own intellectual and moral fortress.

Whoever criticized slavery in the South was an enemy of society, a traitor to the Southern way of life.

habit of critical inquiry. When you stop agitation, you guarantee complacency. We have learned in our own time the price that a society pays when it intimidates the liberal mind, when it silences criticism.

The habit of independent inquiry and criticism all but disappeared in the South of the eighteen-fifties and sixties—and has not yet really returned. There was no real discussion of slavery, and because there was no discussion there was no probing of alternatives. There was no real debate over secession—at least, not on the principles at stake. As Southern political thought had gone slowly bankrupt after Calhoun, so Southern political discussion went bankrupt—in the Confederate Congress and in the newspapers of the Confederacy. There were a few bold spirits who questioned secession; there were some who doubted the ability of the South to win a war against the North; there were some who saw that slavery would become the Achilles' heel of the Confederacy. But there was no discussion of real issues, as in the North, and no statesman to lead the people out of the labyrinth in which they found themselves and on to a high plateau from which they could see their life and their society in perspective.

There is, perhaps, a certain poetic justice in all this. The Confederacy, which was founded on state sovereignty, was destroyed by state sovereignty. The Confederacy, which was founded on slavery, was destroyed by the state of mind which slavery imposed upon its other victims—the white people of the South. The failure of the Confederacy was ultimately a monument not to a failure of resolution or courage or will, but of intelligence and morality.

Preachers who questioned slavery from their pulpits were deprived of their churches; teachers who criticized slavery were driven out of their colleges and universities; editors who dared raise their voices against slavery saw their presses destroyed. If the United States mails carried abolition or antislavery literature, the mails were rifled, the pernicious literature burned. Libraries were purged of offensive books—even Hinton Helper's "The Impending Crisis of the South"

was publicly burned. The whole South, in short, closed ranks to defend and exalt the "peculiar institution."

Now when you prevent the free discussion of the greatest of public issues, you prevent the discussion of almost all issues. When you drive out critics, you leave behind the noncritics. When you silence dissent, you assure only approval. When you intimidate criticism, you discourage the

THE TRAGIC LEGEND OF RECONSTRUCTION

Kenneth M. Stampp

Kenneth M. Stampp is professor of American history at the University of California (Berkeley) and a specialist on the Civil War. He is the author of among other books, The Peculiar Institution *(1956) and* And the War Came *(1950). The present piece is a chapter of his book,* The Era of Reconstruction 1865-1877.

In much serious history, and in a durable popular legend, two American epochs—the Civil War and the reconstruction that followed—bear an odd relationship to one another. The Civil War, though admittedly a tragedy, is nevertheless often described as a glorious time of gallantry, noble self-sacrifice, and high idealism. Even historians who have considered the war "needless" and have condemned the politicians of the 1850's for blundering into it, once they passed the firing on Fort Sumter, have usually written with reverence about Civil War heroes—the martyred Lincoln, the Christlike Lee, the intrepid Stonewall Jackson, and many others in this galaxy of demigods.

Few, of course, are so innocent as not to know that the Civil War had its seamy side. One can hardly ignore the political opportunism, the graft and profiteering in the filling of war contracts, the military blundering and needless loss of lives, the horrors of army hospitals and prison camps, and the ugly depths as well as the nobility of human nature that the war exposed with a fine impartiality. These things cannot be ignored, but they can be, and frequently are, dismissed as something alien to the essence of the war years. What was real and fundamental was the idealism and the nobility of the two contending forces: the Yankees struggling to save the Union, dying to make men free; the Confederates fighting for great constitutional principles, defending their homes from invasion. Here, indeed, is one of the secrets of the spell the Civil War has cast: it involved high-minded Americans on both sides, and there was glory enough to go around. This, in fact, is the supreme synthesis of Civil War historiography and the great balm that has healed the nation's wounds: Yankees and Confederates alike fought bravely for what they believed to be just causes. There were few villains in the drama.

But when the historian reaches the year 1865, he must take leave of the war and turn to another epoch, reconstruction, when the task was, in Lincoln's words, "to bind up the nation's wounds" and "to do all which may achieve and cherish a just and lasting peace." How, until recently, reconstruction was portrayed in both history and legend, how sharply it was believed to contrast with the years of the Civil War, is evident in the terms that were used to identify it. Various historians have called this phase of American history "The Tragic Era," "The Dreadful Decade," "The Age of Hate," and "The Blackout of Honest Government." Reconstruction represented the ultimate shame of the American people—as one historian phrased it, "the nadir of national disgrace." It was the epoch that most Americans wanted to forget.

Claude Bowers, who divided his time between politics and history, has been the chief disseminator of the traditional picture of reconstruction, for his book, *The Tragic Era,* published in 1929, has attracted more readers than any other dealing with this period. For Bowers reconstruction was a time of almost unrelieved sordidness in public and private life; whole regiments of villains march through his pages: the corrupt politicians who dominated the administration of Ulysses S. Grant; the crafty, scheming Northern carpetbaggers who invaded the South after the war for political and economic plunder; the degraded and depraved Southern scalawags who betrayed their own people and collaborated with the enemy; and the ignorant, barbarous, sensual Negroes who threatened to Africanize the South and destroy its Caucasian civilization.

Most of Bowers's key generalizations can be found in

From *Commentary*, June 1965. Originally from THE ERA OF RECONSTRUCTION, 1865-1877, by Kenneth M. Stampp. Copyright © 1965 by Kenneth M. Stampp. Reprinted by permission of Alfred A. Knopf, Inc.

his preface. The years of reconstruction, he wrote, "were years of revolutionary turmoil, with the elemental passions predominant. . . . The prevailing note was one of tragedy. . . . Never have American public men in responsible positions, directing the destiny of the nation, been so brutal, hypocritical, and corrupt. The constitution was treated as a doormat on which politicians and army officers wiped their feet after wading in the muck. . . . The southern people literally were put to the torture . . . (by) rugged conspirators . . . (who) assumed the post of philanthropists and patriots." The popularity of Bowers's book stems in part from the simplicity of his characters. None is etched in shades of gray; none is confronted with complex moral decisions. Like characters in a Victorian romance, the Republican leaders of the reconstruction era were evil through and through, and the helpless, innocent white men of the South were totally noble and pure.

If Bowers's prose is more vivid and his anger more intense, his general interpretation of reconstruction is only a slight exaggeration of a point of view shared by most serious American historians from the late 19th century until very recently. Writing in the 1890's, James Ford Rhodes, author of a multi-volumed history of the United States since the Compromise of 1850, branded the Republican scheme of reconstruction as "repressive" and "uncivilized," one that "pandered to the ignorant negroes, the knavish white natives and the vulturous adventurers who flocked from the North." About the same time Professor John W. Burgess, of Columbia University, called reconstruction the "most soul-sickening spectacle that Americans had ever been called upon to behold." Early in the 20th century Professor William A. Dunning, also of Columbia University, and a group of talented graduate students wrote a series of monographs that presented a crushing indictment of the Republican reconstruction program in the South—a series that made a deep and lasting impression on American historians. In the 1930's, Professor James G. Randall, of the University of Illinois, still writing in the spirit of the Dunningites, described the reconstruction era "as a time of party abuse, of corruption, of vindictive bigotry." "To use a modern phrase," said Randall, "government under Radical Republican rule in the South had become a kind of 'racket.' " As late as 1947, Professor E. Merton Coulter, of the University of Georgia, reminded critics of the traditional interpretation that no "amount of revision can write away the grievous mistakes made in this abnormal period of American history." Thus, from Rhodes and Burgess and Dunning to Randall and Coulter the central emphasis of most historical writing about reconstruction has been upon sordid motives and human depravity. Somehow, during the summer of 1865, the nobility and idealism of the war years had died.

A synopsis of the Dunning School's version of reconstruction would run something like this: Abraham Lincoln, while the Civil War was still in progress, turned his thoughts to the great problem of reconciliation; and, "with malice toward none and charity for all," this gentle and compassionate man devised a plan that would restore the South to the Union with minimum humiliation and maximum speed. But there had already emerged in Congress a faction of radical Republicans, sometimes called Jacobins or Vindictives, who sought to defeat Lincoln's generous program.

Motivated by hatred of the South, by selfish political ambitions, and by crass economic interests, the radicals tried to make the process of reconstruction as humiliating, as difficult, and as prolonged as they possibly could. Until Lincoln's tragic death, they poured their scorn upon him—and then used his coffin as a political stump to arouse the passions of the Northern electorate.

The second chapter of the Dunning version begins with Andrew Johnson's succession to the Presidency. Johnson, the old Jacksonian Unionist from Tennessee, took advantage of the adjournment of Congress to put Lincoln's mild plan of reconstruction into operation, and it was a striking success. In the summer and fall of 1865, Southerners organized loyal state governments, showed a willingness to deal fairly with their former slaves, and in general accepted the outcome of the Civil War in good faith. In December, when Congress assembled, President Johnson reported that the process of reconstruction was nearly completed and that the old Union had been restored. But the radicals unfortunately had their own sinister purposes: they repudiated the governments Johnson had established in the South, refused to seat Southern Senators and Representatives, and then directed their fury against the new President. After a year of bitter controversy and political stalemate, the radicals, resorting to shamefully demagogic tactics, won an overwhelming victory in the congressional elections of 1866.

Now, the third chapter and the final tragedy. Riding roughshod over Presidential vetoes and federal courts, the radicals put the South under military occupation, gave the ballot to Negroes, and formed new Southern state governments dominated by base and corrupt men, black and white. Not satisfied with reducing the South to political slavery and financial bankruptcy, the radicals even laid their obscene hands on the pure fabric of the federal Constitution. They impeached President Johnson and came within one vote of removing him from office, though they had no legal grounds for such action. Next, they elected Ulysses S. Grant President, and during his two administrations they indulged in such an orgy of corruption and so prostituted the civil service as to make Grantism an enduring symbol of political immorality.

The last chapter is the story of ultimate redemption. Decent Southern white Democrats, their patience exhausted, organized to drive the Negroes, carpetbaggers, and scalawags from power, peacefully if possible, forcefully if necessary. One by one the Southern states were redeemed, honesty and virtue triumphed, and the South's natural leaders returned to power. In the spring of 1877, the Tragic Era finally came to an end when President Hayes withdrew the federal troops from the South and restored home rule. But the legacy of radical reconstruction remained in the form of a solidly Democratic South and embittered relations between the races.

This point of view was rarely challenged until the 1930's, when a small group of revisionist historians began to give new life and a new direction to the study of reconstruction. The revisionists are a curious lot who sometimes quarrel with each other as much as they quarrel with the disciples of Dunning. At various times they have counted in their ranks Marxists of various degrees of orthodoxy, Negroes seeking historical vindication, skeptical white Southerners, and latter-day Northern abolitionists. But among them are numerous scholars who have the wisdom to know that the history of an age is seldom simple and clear-cut, seldom without its tragic aspects, seldom without its redeeming virtues.

Few revisionists would claim that the Dunning interpretation of reconstruction is a pure fabrication. They recognize the shabby aspects of this era: the corruption was real, the failures obvious, the tragedy undeniable. Grant is not their idea of a model President, nor are the Southern carpetbag governments worthy of their unqualified praise. They understand that the radical Republicans were not all selfless patriots and that Southern white men were not all Negro-hating rebels. In short, they have not turned history on its head, but rather, they recognize that much of what Dunning's disciples have said about reconstruction is true.

Revisionists, however, have discovered that the Dunningites overlooked a great deal, and they doubt that nobility and idealism suddenly died in 1865. They are neither surprised nor disillusioned to find that the Civil War, for all its nobility, revealed some of the ugliness of human nature as well. And they approach reconstruction with the confident expectation that here, too, every facet of human nature will be exposed. They are not satisfied with the two-dimensional characters that Dunning's disciples have painted.

What is perhaps most puzzling in the legend of reconstruction is the notion that the white people of the South were treated with unprecedented brutality, that their conquerors, in Bowers's colorful phrase, literally put them to the torture. How, in fact, *were* they treated after the failure of their rebellion against the authority of the federal government? The great mass of ordinary Southerners who voluntarily took up arms, or in other ways supported the Confederacy, were required simply to take an oath of allegiance to obtain pardon and to regain their right to vote and hold public office. But

what of the Confederate leaders—the men who held high civil offices, often after resigning similar federal offices; the military leaders who had graduated from West Point and had resigned commissions in the United States Army to take commissions in the Confederate Army? Were there mass arrests, indictments for treason or conspiracy, trials and convictions, executions or imprisonments? Nothing of the sort. Officers of the Confederate Army were paroled and sent home with their men. After surrendering at Appomattox, General Lee bade farewell to his troops and rode home to live his remaining years undisturbed. Only one officer, a Captain Henry Wirtz, was arrested; and he was tried, convicted, and executed, not for treason or conspiracy, but for "war crimes." Wirtz's alleged offense, for which the evidence was rather flimsy, was the mistreatment of prisoners of war in the military prison at Andersonville, Georgia.

Of the Confederate civil officers, a handful were arrested at the close of the war, and there was talk for a time of trying a few for treason. But none, actually, was ever brought to trial, and all but Jefferson Davis were released within a few months. The former Confederate President was held in prison for nearly two years, but in 1867 he, too, was released. With a few exceptions, even the property of Confederate leaders was untouched, save, of course, for the emancipation of their slaves. Indeed, the only penalty imposed on most Confederate leaders was a temporary political disability provided in the Fourteenth Amendment. But in 1872 Congress pardoned all but a handful of Southerners; and soon former Confederate civil and military leaders were serving as state governors, as members of Congress, and even as Cabinet advisers of Presidents.

What, then, constituted the alleged brutality that white Southerners endured? First, the freeing of their slaves; second, the brief incarceration of a few Confederate leaders; third, a political disability imposed for a few years on most Confederate leaders; fourth, a relatively weak military occupation terminated in 1877; and, last, an attempt to extend the rights and privileges of citizenship to Southern Negroes. Mistakes there were in the implementation of these measures— some of them serious—but brutality almost none. In fact, it can be said that rarely in history have the participants in an unsuccessful rebellion endured penalties as mild as those Congress imposed upon the people of the South, and particularly upon their leaders. After four years of bitter struggle costing hundreds of thousands of lives, the generosity of the federal government's terms was quite remarkable.

If Northern brutality is a myth, the scandals of the Grant administration and the peculations of some of the Southern reconstruction governments are sordid facts. Yet even here the Dunningites are guilty of distortion by exaggeration, by a lack of perspective, by superficial analysis, and by overemphasis. They make corruption a central theme of their narratives, but they overlook constructive accomplishments. They give insufficient attention to the men who transcended the greed of an age when, to be sure, self-serving politicians and irresponsible entrepreneurs were all too plentiful. Among these men were the humanitarians who organized Freedmen's Aid Societies to help four million Southern Negroes make the difficult transition from slavery to freedom, and the missionaries and teachers who went into the South on slender budgets to build churches and schools for the freedmen. Under their auspices the Negroes first began to learn the responsibilities and obligations of freedom. Thus the training of Negroes for citizenship had its successful beginnings in the years of reconstruction.

In the 19th century most white Americans, North and South, had reservations about the Negro's potentialities—doubted that he had the innate intellectual capacity and moral fiber of the white man and assumed that after emancipation he would be relegated to an inferior caste. But some of the radical Republicans refused to believe that the Negroes were innately inferior and hoped passionately that they would confound their critics. The radicals then had little empirical evidence and no scientific evidence to support their belief—nothing, in fact, but faith. Their faith was derived mostly from their religion: all men, they said, are the sons of Adam and equal in the sight of God. And if Negroes are equal to white men in the sight of God, it is morally wrong for white men to withhold from Negroes the liberties and rights that white men enjoy. Here, surely, was a projection into the reconstruction era of the idealism of the abolitionist crusade and of the Civil War.

Radical idealism was in part responsible for two of the most momentous enactments of the reconstruction years: the Fourteenth Amendment to the Federal Constitution which gave Negroes citizenship and promised them equal protection of the laws, and the Fifteenth Amendment which gave them the right to vote. The fact that these amendments could not have been adopted under any other circumstances, or at any other time, before or since, may suggest the crucial importance of the reconstruction era in American history. Indeed, without radical reconstruction, it would be impossible to this day for the federal government to protect Negroes from legal and political discrimination.

If all of this is true, or even part of it, why was the Dunning legend born, and why has it been so durable? Southerners, of course, have contributed much to the legend of reconstruction, but most Northerners have found the legend quite acceptable. Many of the historians who helped to create it were Northerners, among them James Ford Rhodes, William A. Dunning, Claude Bowers, and James G. Randall. Thus the legend cannot be explained simply in terms of a Southern literary or historiographical conspiracy, satisfying as the legend has been to most white Southerners. What we need to know is why it also satisfies Northerners—

how it became part of the intellectual baggage of so many Northern historians. Why, in short, was there for so many years a kind of national, or inter-sectional, consensus that the Civil War was America's glory and reconstruction her disgrace?

The Civil War won its place in the hearts of the American people because, by the end of the 19th century, Northerners were willing to concede that Southerners had fought bravely for a cause that they believed to be just; while Southerners, with few exceptions, were willing to concede that the outcome of the war was probably best for all concerned. In an era of intense nationalism, both Northerners and Southerners agreed that the preservation of the federal Union was essential to the future power of the American people. Southerners could even say now that the abolition of slavery was one of the war's great blessings—not so much, they insisted, because slavery was an injustice to the Negroes but because it was a grievous burden upon the whites. By 1886, Henry W. Grady, the great Georgia editor and spokesman for a New South, could confess to a New York audience: "I am glad that the omniscient God held the balance of battle in His Almighty hand, and that human slavery was swept forever from American soil—the American Union saved from the wreck of war." Soon Union and Confederate veterans were holding joint reunions, exchanging anecdotes, and sharing their sentimental memories of those glorious war years. The Civil War thus took its position in the center of American folk mythology.

That the reconstruction era elicits neither pride nor sentimentality is due only in part to its moral delinquencies—remember, those of the Civil War years can be overlooked. It is also due to the white American's ambivalent attitude toward race and toward the steps that radical Republicans took to protect the Negroes. Southern white men accepted the Thirteenth Amendment to the Constitution, which abolished slavery, with a minimum of complaint, but they expected federal intervention to proceed no further than that. They assumed that the regulation of the freedmen would be left to the individual states; and clearly most of them intended to replace slavery with a caste system that would keep the Negroes perpetually subordinate to the whites. Negroes were to remain a dependent laboring class; they were to be governed by a separate code of laws; they were to play no active part in the South's political life; and they were to be segregated socially. When radical Republicans used federal power to interfere in these matters, the majority of Southern white men formed a resistance movement to fight the radical-dominated state governments until they were overthrown, after which Southern whites established a caste system in defiance of federal statutes and constitutional amendments. For many decades thereafter the federal government simply admitted defeat and acquiesced; but the South refused to forget or forgive those years of humiliation when Negroes came close to winning equality. In Southern mythology, then, reconstruction was a horrid nightmare.

As for the majority of Northern white men, it is hard to tell how deeply they were concerned about the welfare of the American Negro after the abolition of slavery. If one were to judge from the way they treated the small number of free Negroes who resided in the Northern states, one might conclude that they were, at best, indifferent to the problem—and that a considerable number of them shared the racial attitudes of the South and preferred to keep Negroes in a subordinate caste. For a time after the Civil War the radical Republicans, who were always a minority group, persuaded the Northern electorate that the ultimate purpose of Southern white men was to rob the North of the fruits of victory and to re-establish slavery and that federal intervention was therefore essential. In this manner radicals won approval of, or acquiescence in, their program to give civil rights and the ballot to Southern Negroes. Popular support for the radical program waned rapidly, however, and by the middle of the 1870's it had all but vanished. In 1875 a Republican politician confessed that Northern voters were tired of the "worn-out cry of 'southern outrages,' " and they wished that "the 'nigger,' the 'everlasting nigger' were in—Africa." As Northerners ceased to worry about the possibility of another Southern rebellion, they became increasingly receptive to criticism of radical reconstruction.

The eventual disintegration of the radical phalanx, those root-and-branch men who, for a time, seemed bent on engineering a sweeping reformation of Southern society, was another important reason for the denigration of reconstruction in American historiography. To be sure, some of the radicals, especially those who had been abolitionists before the war, never lost faith in the Negro, and in the years after reconstruction they stood by him as he struggled to break the intellectual and psychological fetters he had brought with him out of slavery. Other radicals, however, lost interest in the cause—tired of reform and spent their declining years writing their memoirs. Still others retained their crusading zeal but became disenchanted with radical reconstruction and found other crusades more attractive: civil service reform, or tariff reform, or defense of the gold standard. In 1872 they repudiated Grant and joined the Liberal Republicans; in subsequent years they considered themselves to be political independents.

This latter group had been an important element in the original radical coalition. Most of them were respectable, middle-class people in comfortable economic circumstances, well educated and highly articulate, and acutely conscious of their obligation to perform disinterested public service. They had looked upon Senator Charles Sumner of Massachusetts as their political spokesman, and upon Edwin L. Godkin of the New York *Nation* as their editorial spokesman. Like

most radicals they had believed that the Negro was what slavery had made him; give the Negro equal rights and he would be quickly transformed into an industrious and responsible citizen. With the radical reconstruction program fairly launched, they had looked forward to swift and dramatic results.

But reconstruction was not as orderly and the Negro's progress was not nearly as swift and dramatic as these reformers had seemed to expect. The first signs of doubt came soon after the radicals won control of reconstruction policy, when the *Nation* warned the Negroes that the government had already done all it could for them. They were now, said the *Nation,* "on the dusty and rugged highway of competition"; henceforth "the removal of white prejudice against the Negro depends almost entirely on the Negro himself." By 1870 this bellwether of the reformers viewed with alarm the disorders and irregularities in the states governed by Negroes and carpetbaggers; by 1871 it proclaimed: "The experiment has totally failed. . . . We owe it to human nature to say that worse governments have seldom been seen in a civilized country." And three years later, looking at South Carolina, the *Nation* pronounced the ultimate epithet: "This is . . . socialism." Among the former radicals associated with the *Nation* in these years of tragic disillusionment were three prewar abolitionists: Edmund Quincy of Massachusetts, James Miller McKim of Pennsylvania, and the Reverend O.B. Frothingham of New York.

Finally, in 1890, many years after the reconstruction governments had collapsed, the *Nation,* still accurately reflecting the state of mind of the disenchanted reformers, made a full confession of its past errors. "There is," said the *Nation,* "a rapidly growing sympathy at the North with Southern perplexity over the negro problem. . . . Even those who were not shocked by the carpetbag experiment . . . are beginning to 'view with alarm' the political prospect created by the increase of the negro population, and by the continued inability of southern society to absorb or assimilate them in any sense, physical, social, or political . . . . The sudden admission to the suffrage of a million of the recently emancipated slaves belonging to the least civilized race in the world . . . was a great leap in the dark, the ultimate consequences of which no man now living can foresee. No nation has ever done this, or anything like this for the benefit of aliens of any race or creed. Who or what is . . . [the Negro] that we should put the interest of the 55,000,000 whites on this continent in peril for his sake?" Editor Godkin answered his own question in a letter to another one-time radical: "I do not see . . . how the negro is ever to be worked into a system of government for which you and I would have much respect."

Actually, neither the obvious shortcomings of reconstruction nor an objective view of the Negro's progress in the years after emancipation can wholly explain the disillusionment of so many former radicals. Rather, their changed attitude toward the Negro and the hostile historical interpretation of reconstruction that won their favor were in part the product of social trends that severely affected the old American middle classes with whom most of them were identified. These trends had their origin in the Industrial Revolution; they were evident in the early 19th century but were enormously accelerated after the Civil War. Their institutional symbols were the giant manufacturing and railroad corporations.

In the new age of industrial enterprise there seemed to be no place for the old families with their genteel culture and strong traditions of disinterested public service. On the one hand, they were overshadowed by new and powerful industrial capitalists whose economic strength brought with it vast political influence. Legislative bodies became arenas in which the political vassals of oil, steel, and railroad barons struggled for special favors, while the interests of the public—and the old middle classes liked to think of themselves as *the public*—counted for nothing. On the other hand, they were threatened by the immigrants who came to America to work in the mines and mills and on the railroads—Italians, Slavs, and Jews from Poland and Russia. The immigrants crowded into the tenements of eastern cities, responded to the friendly overtures of urban political bosses, and used their ballots to evict the old middle-class families from power. Here was a threat to the traditional America that these families had loved—and dominated; to that once vigorous American nationality that was Protestant, Anglo-Saxon, and pure. Henry James commented bitterly about the people he met on Boston Common during a stroll one Sunday afternoon: "No sound of English, in a single instance escaped their lips; the greater number spoke a rude form of Italian, the others some outland dialect unknown to me.... The types and faces bore them out; the people before me were gross aliens to a man, and they were in serene and triumphant possession."

Soon the new immigrant groups had become the victims of cruel racial stereotypes. Taken collectively it would appear that they were, among other things, innately inferior to the Anglo-Saxons in their intellectual and physical traits, dirty and immoral in their habits, inclined toward criminality, receptive to dangerous political beliefs, and shiftless and irresponsible.

In due time, those who repeated these stereotypes awoke to the realization that what they were saying was not really very original—that, as a matter of fact, these generalizations were *precisely* the ones that Southern white men had been making about Negroes for years. And, in their extremity, the old middle classes of the North looked with new understanding upon the problems of the beleaguered white men of the South. Perhaps all along Southerners had understood the problem better than they. Here, then, was a crucial part

of the intellectual climate in which the Dunning interpretation of reconstruction was written. It was written at a time when xenophobia had become almost a national disease, when the immigration restriction movement was getting into high gear, when numerous Northern cities (among them Philadelphia and Chicago) were seriously considering the establishment of racially segregated schools, and when Negroes and immigrants were being lumped together in the category of unassimilable aliens.

Several other attitudes, prevalent in the late 19th century, encouraged an interpretation of reconstruction that condemned radical Republicans for meddling in Southern race relations. The vogue of social Darwinism discouraged governmental intervention in behalf of Negroes as well as other underprivileged groups; it encouraged the belief that a solution to the race problem could only evolve slowly as the Negroes gradually improved themselves. A rising spirit of nationalism stimulated a desire for sectional reconciliation, and part of the price was a virtual abdication of federal responsibility for the protection of the Negro's civil and political rights. An outburst of imperialism manifested in the Spanish-American War and the annexation of the Hawaiian Islands, found one of its principal justifications in the notion that Anglo-Saxons were superior to other peoples, especially when it came to politics. In the words of Senator Albert J. Beveridge of Indiana: "God has not been preparing the English-speaking and Teutonic people for a thousand years for nothing but vain and idle self-admiration. No! He has made us the master organizers of the world to establish system where chaos reigns.... He has made us adepts in government that we may administer government among savages and senile peoples." What folly, then, to expect Italians and Slavs to behave like Anglo-Saxons—or to accept the sentimental doctrine that Negroes deserve to be given the same political rights as white men!

Finally, at this critical juncture, sociologists, anthropologists, and psychologists presented what they regarded as convincing evidence of innate racial traits—evidence indicating that Negroes were intellectually inferior to whites and had distinctive emotional characteristics. The social scientists thus supplied the racists of the late 19th and early 20th centuries with something that ante-bellum pro-slavery writers had always lacked: a respectable scientific argument. When, in 1916, Madison Grant, an amateur cultural anthropologist, published *The Passing of the Great Race,* his racism was only a mild caricature of a point of view shared by numerous social scientists. Examining the history of the United States, Grant easily detected her tragic blunder:

Race consciousness ... in the United States, down to and including the Mexican War, seems to have been very strongly developed among native Americans, and it still remains in full vigor today in the South, where the presence of a large negro population forces this question upon the daily attention of the whites. . . . In New England, however . . . there appeared early in the last century a wave of sentimentalism, which at that time took up the cause of the negro, and in so doing apparently destroyed, to a large extent, pride and consciousness of race in the North. The agitation over slavery was inimical to the Nordic race, because it thrust aside all national opposition to the intrusion of hordes of immigrants of inferior racial value, and prevented the fixing of a definite American type. . . . The native American by the middle of the nineteenth century was rapidly becoming a distinct type. . . . The Civil War, however, put a severe, perhaps fatal, check to the development and expansion of this splendid type, by destroying great numbers of the best breeding stock on both sides, and by breaking up the home ties of many more. If the war had not occurred these same men with their descendants would have populated the Western States instead of the racial nondescripts who are now flocking there.

In this social atmosphere, armed with the knowledge of race that the social scientists had given them, historians exposed the folly of radical reconstruction. At the turn of the century, James Ford Rhodes, that intimate friend of New England Brahmins, gave his verdict on Negro suffrage—one that the Dunningites would soon develop into the central assumption, the controlling generalization, of the reconstruction legend. "No large policy in our country," concluded Rhodes, "has ever been so conspicuous a failure as that of forcing universal negro suffrage upon the South. . . . From the Republican policy came no real good to the negroes. Most of them developed no political capacity, and the few who raised themselves above the mass did not reach a high order of intelligence. . . . The negro's political activity is rarely of a nature to identify him with any movement on a high plane. . . . (He) has been politically a failure and he could not have been otherwise."

In the course of time the social scientists drastically revised their notions about race, and in recent years most of them have been striving to destroy the errors in whose creation they themselves played so crucial a part. As ideas about race have changed, historians have become increasingly critical of the Dunning interpretation of reconstruction. These changes, together with a great deal of painstaking research, have produced the revisionist writing of the past generation. It is dangerous, of course, for a historian to label himself as a revisionist, for his ultimate and inevitable fate is one day to have his own revisions revised.

But that has never discouraged revisionists, and we may hope that it never will, especially those who have been rewriting the history of the reconstruction era. One need not be disturbed about the romantic nonsense that still fills the minds of many Americans about their Civil War. This folklore is essentially harmless. But the legend of reconstruction is another matter. It has had serious consequences, because it has exerted a powerful influence upon the political behavior of many white men, North and South.

The Bluecoats

Robert M. Utley

Robert M. Utley, Deputy Director of the President's Advisery Council on Historic Preservation, is the author of a two-volume history of the bluecoats, 1850-90, entitled Frontiersmen in Blue *and* Frontier Regulars. *His latest book is* Life in Custer's Cavalry: Diaries and Letters of Albert and Jennie Barnitz, 1867-68. *He is a member of the Board of Advisers of the National Historical Society.*

The surrender ceremony at Appomattox Court House on April 9, 1865, marked the resolution of the sectional conflict that had so long divided Americans. Now was the time, Abraham Lincoln declared, to bind up the nation's wounds. Part of the healing would take place in the West. By the thousands Northerners and Southerners alike faced west, seeking fortune, adventure, or simply a new start. The overland trails teemed with white-topped wagons, freight trains, and stagecoaches, and beside them twin bands of steel went down to link Pacific to Atlantic by rail. Conspicuous among all these westering migrants were the bluecoats of the new Regular Army.

The postwar Regulars belonged distinctively to wild-eyed, scraggly bearded William Tecumseh Sherman. Cantankerous, fiercely independent, the hero of Atlanta and the March to the Sea got along with almost no one outside the Army—especially newspaper reporters and Secretaries of War—but he won a near-mystic devotion from his Regulars out West, and he dedicated his stormy tenure as commanding general to their welfare. The Regulars also belonged to stocky Philip H. Sheridan, the fiery and profane Irishman who held command over the Great Plains and a good portion of the Rocky Mountains until he replaced Sherman as general in chief in 1883.

If the peacetime Army took its tone from "Cump" Sherman and "Little Phil" Sheridan, it marched or rode behind a cadre of ambitious colonels who had been generals in the Civil War Volunteers and now wanted to be generals again in the Regulars. Sherman labeled them "the young vigorous colonels, who are moving heaven and earth to secure promotion." They included vain, pompous but aggressively able Nelson A. Miles; the music teacher turned cavalryman Benjamin H. Grierson; hard-driving, eccentric, emotionally troubled Ranald S. Mackenzie; sturdy, taciturn John Gibbon; and the flamboyant cavalier whose Civil War exploits had made him a general at 23, George Armstrong Custer.

When it finally shook out after several years of congressional tinkering, the line of the new Army consisted of ten regiments of cavalry, twenty-five of infantry, and (mainly to garrison coastal defenses) five of artillery. Of special interest were the 9th and 10th Cavalry and 24th and 25th Infantry, black units led by white officers. Victims of a racism made worse by attitudes born of the military caste system, the "buffalo soldiers" nevertheless compiled a notable record on the frontier.

Conventional methods continued to characterize the Army's approach to its frontier mission. "Regimental commanders in these latter days are not much wiser than Braddock in the olden times," observed the 7th Cavalry's Captain Albert Barnitz, "and refuse to fight Indians or even follow Indians in Indian fashion." One who urged that the Army profit by Braddock's mistakes was the quietly competent General George Crook. A skilled outdoorsman and student of Indian psychology, Crook advocated recruiting Indians to fight Indians. In campaigns in Idaho and Arizona, he showed what could be accomplished with them when properly managed. He also pioneered in increasing mobility by substituting mule trains for wagon trains. But few officers heeded his example. The Army remained, as an officer observed, a "chained dog," always held back by its supply and transportation system.

The Army's Western task was vastly complicated by a continuing feud with the Indian Bureau, the

From *American History Illustrated*, November 1979. Reproduced through the courtesy of The National Historical Society, publishers of *American History Illustrated*, P.O. Box 1831, Harrisburg, PA 17105.

arm of government charged with managing Indians on the reservations. In the postwar years the government's policy of "concentration" moved swiftly to a conclusion. In treaties that the Indians rarely understood, they promised to move to defined tracts of territory and there, under the guidance of the Great Father's agents, tried to support themselves by farming while also getting "civilized." When the full implications of this revolutionary change finally dawned, the Indians rose in protest. A war often followed. Such was the pattern of almost all the postwar hostilities. Soldiers campaigned against Indians who had promised to go to a reservation but were having second thoughts or who had already tried a reservation and found it intolerable. Military officers bitterly objected to fighting wars they regarded as caused by civilian mismanagement, railed against divided responsibilities that confused the Indians and prompted incessant quarreling between military and civilian officials, and championed a system that would place all Indians, peaceful or hostile, under military control.

The Sioux, inflamed by General Patrick Connor's harsh offensive of 1865, gave the Regulars their first serious test. The Army tried to open the Bozeman Trail, a link between the Oregon-California Trail and the Montana gold fields, against the fierce resistance of Red Cloud's Sioux. On a wintry day in December 1866 they struck with devastating ferocity at Fort Phil Kearny, one of three posts along the trail.

The Indians used the hoary decoy trick. A small party under a rising young warrior named Crazy Horse fell on a wagon train hauling logs to the fort. Colonel Henry B. Carrington at once organized a relief party. Captain William J. Fetterman demanded to lead it. Carrington distrusted Fetterman, who had ridiculed the Indians' fighting prowess and boasted that he could ride through the whole Sioux nation with eighty men, but acceded because of his seniority. Cautioned not to get beyond sight of the fort, Fetterman at once disappeared from view, pursuing the decoy party over a hilltop and into a well-laid ambush. Hundreds of Sioux burst upon the little band of bluecoats and slaughtered them to a man. Fetterman had got his chance: Exactly eighty men perished with him.

Despite two brilliant victories the following summer—the Wagon Box and Hayfield fights—the Army had to relinquish the Bozeman Trail and its guardian forts. The Treaty of Fort Laramie in 1868 gave Red Cloud all he demanded. Or so it seemed to the humiliated and resentful Regulars. Actually the treaty contained the seeds of the ultimate conquest of the Sioux.

The Fetterman Massacre was the opening gun in more than a decade of fighting on the Great Plains. To the south Kiowas and Comanches continued to ravage the Texas frontier and strike deep into Mexico on plundering forays that occurred with predictable regularity. Cheyennes and Arapahos fought back as settlers pushed up the fertile valleys of Kansas and Nebraska and the government tried by both military and diplomatic means to shove them southward onto reservations in Indian Territory (today's Oklahoma).

Part of this effort was Phil Sheridan's winter campaign of 1868-69. Hardened frontiersmen warned of disaster in winter operations, but the daring Custer justified his chief's strategy and also gained fame as an Indian fighter. On November 27, 1868, two days short of four years after Sand Creek, Custer led his 7th Cavalry in a slashing surprise attack on Black Kettle's Cheyenne village, sleeping in fancied security under a thick blanket of snow in the Washita Valley. The victory was total, and this time the chief did not survive. Again there was debate over whether Black Kettle's people were hostile or peaceful, but with the evidence less conclusively in their favor than at Sand Creek.

The Plains War of 1868-69 also featured clashes at Beecher's Island, Soldier Spring, and Summit Spring. In the latter, a wild charge by Major Eugene A. Carr's 5th Cavalry on Tall Bull's camp of Cheyenne Dog Soldiers, a daredevil young scout began to build a notoriety that would one day make the name "Buffalo Bill" Cody legend throughout the country. Sheridan's operations forced the Southern Plains tribes to accept their reservations, but it would take another war to make the acceptance lasting.

This was the Red River War. It had its origins in increasingly intolerable conditions on the reservations, and it broke out in the summer of 1874 when discontented Kiowas, Comanches, and Cheyennes left their agencies and, moving west, gathered among the brakes along the eastern base of the Staked Plain, in the Texas Panhandle. The first shot, at Adobe Walls, was a celebrated but unsuccessful attack on a party of buffalo hunters, hated symbols of the destruction of the Indians' way of life.

General Sheridan mounted a comprehensive campaign. Modeled after his offensive of 1868-69, it featured a convergence strategy that sent blue columns at the war zone from five directions. Nelson Miles dueled with Cheyennes and Comanches on the Canadian River and Ranald Mackenzie stormed through a big village in Palo Duro Canyon, but mainly it was a war of harassment. From a parched summer through a soggy autumn to a blizzardy winter the columns cut back and forth on the Staked Plain and the valleys that radiated from it. Kept always on the move, always fearful of a sudden attack, the Indians grew tired and disheartened. In small groups and large they drifted eastward. By the spring of 1875 all had surrendered.

The Red River War ended hostilities on the

Southern Plains. Never again did Kiowas and Comanches strike terror in Texas and Mexico. Never again did Cheyennes waylay travelers on the Santa Fe and Smoky Hill trails or sweep through the settlements of Kansas' Saline and Solomon valleys.

Although the postwar decade was dominated by President Grant's "Peace Policy" toward the Indians, there was little peace. The wars of 1868-69 and 1874-75 kept Kansas, Indian Territory, and Texas in turmoil. In the Southwest the Apache wars dragged on year after year, although the vigorous and unorthodox operations of General Crook produced a breathing space from 1873 to 1875. In California a handful of Modocs under Captain Jack, holed up in fortress-like lava beds, held a sizable army at bay for seven months in 1872-73; during a Good Friday peace conference they assassinated General Edward R.S. Canby, the only Regular Army general killed in all the Indian wars [see "The Modoc Indian War," *AHI* August 1978]. And as the Grant Administration drew to a close in 1876, another Sioux war burst over the northern Plains.

The Treaty of 1868 had set aside reservations for the Sioux and Cheyennes on which Red Cloud and other people tired of fighting settled. But to the west, in the "unceded" plains country drained by the Missouri and Yellowstone rivers, chiefs such as Sitting Bull, Black Moon, Crazy Horse, and Gall vowed never to yield the old buffalo-hunting life. Advancing railroads and a gold rush to the Black Hills, sacred Sioux country supposedly guaranteed by treaty, put this vow to the test. In 1876 General Sheridan launched another of his convergence operations as columns under George Crook, Alfred Terry, and John Gibbon marched into the country of these "hostiles" from three directions.

With Terry rode the dashing, yellow-haired Custer, splendid in fringed buckskins. In a sequence of events and decisions that experts still fiercely debate, Custer and his 7th Cavalry discovered a combined Sioux and Cheyenne village on Montana's Little Bighorn River and on June 25 attacked from two directions. Some 2,000 well-armed warriors, buoyed by a victory over Crook the week before and now defending their families, leaped to the fray. Among the broken ridges above the valley they overwhelmed Custer and about 225 men in five troops under his personal command. Not a man survived. Four miles away the rest of the regiment, almost 400 strong, withstood a two-day siege until relief arrived.

In "Custer's Last Stand" lay the seeds of the Indians' own defeat. A stunned nation lashed back. Fresh regiments hastened to the Sioux country. Through the autumn and a bitter winter Crook, Miles, Mackenzie, and others pressed the beleaguered foe.

Exhausted and destitute, many gave up and accepted the reservation. The diehards, under Sitting Bull, took refuge in Canada. But hunger progressively eroded their ranks. An embittered Sitting Bull finally laid down his rifle at Fort Buford, Montana, in 1881.

In the summer of 1877, before the Sioux had been fully run down, hostilities broke out with the Nez Perces in Idaho when the government forced Joseph, White Bird, Looking Glass, and other chiefs to take their followers to a reservation. The pious, one-armed "Christian general," Oliver O. Howard, mobilized his troops. At White Bird Canyon and Clearwater, the Indians beat off the soldiers, then in one of history's most dramatic treks faced east in search of security on the Montana plains.

Across the Bitterroot Mountains the people hurried, with Howard in pursuit. Gibbon cut them off at Big Hole but was pushed aside with severe casualties. On the east edge of Yellowstone National Park they tricked the 7th Cavalry under Colonel Samuel D. Sturgis, then fought it off in a rearguard fracas at Canyon Creek. Exhausted, Howard and his column pushed on, never able to come up with the fugitives as they headed northward across Montana toward sanctuary in Canada. From Fort Keogh, to the east, Nelson Miles raced to intercept them. At Bear Paw Mountain, a heartbreaking forty miles from Canada, he succeeded. After a bloody battle and five-day siege, the Nez Perces surrendered. "From where the sun now stands," declared Chief Joseph in a memorably eloquent speech to Miles, "I will fight no more forever."

Crook's reassignment from the Southwest in 1875 had been followed almost at once by a resumption of Apache hostilities. Cochise had been persuaded to call off his war by General Howard in 1872 and had died two years later. The most formidable adversary the troops faced now was the wily Victorio, heir to the mantle of Mangas Coloradas. After his death in battle with Mexican troops in 1880 the distinction passed to a squat, thick-set fighter whose face seemed fixed in a perpetual scowl—Geronimo. His rise to prominence coincided with Crook's return to Arizona in 1882.

Like almost all Indian wars of 1866-90, the Geronimo wars were fought to return people to a reservation from which they had broken loose. It was at San Carlos, a barren and baked tract on Arizona's Gila River, that the government was attempting to concentrate all Apaches. The proximity of the wild mountain wilderness of Mexico vastly complicated the task, for the "renegades" could take refuge there, strike at targets north of the border, then vanish swiftly into their Mexican hideaways.

Crook's answer was to plunge into these mountains himself. In the spring of 1883, with units of Indian scouts and supplied by mule trains, he marched into

4. THE CIVIL WAR AND RECONSTRUCTION

Mexico. High in the Sierra Madre he came face to face with Geronimo and other Apache leaders. So alarmed were they by this audacious penetration of their hitherto impregnable lairs that, after suspenseful negotiations, they agreed to return to San Carlos.

But the peace was fragile, and in 1885 Geronimo "busted out" again and raced for Mexico. Again Crook sent his scout units in pursuit. All winter they combed the Mexican mountains and again, in March 1886, brought about another tense confrontation between Crook and Geronimo, at Canyon de los Embudos. Again Geronimo agreed to give up, but this time the agreement came apart and the Apaches faded into the mountains. Discouraged, his methods assailed by General Sheridan, Crook asked to be relieved. Nelson Miles, now a brigadier general, took his place and in an exhausting summer's campaign brought Geronimo to a conference in which he once more agreed to give up.

This time was the last time. As the 4th Cavalry Band rendered "Auld Lang Syne" on the Fort Bowie parade ground, Geronimo and his people were loaded in wagons to be hauled to the railroad and transported to prisons in faraway Florida.

That ceremony on the Fort Bowie parade ground might have marked the close of the Indian wars.

There was to be another gasp of resistance, however, as Sioux excited by the mystical teachings of the Ghost Dance religion so frightened Nebraska and Dakota settlers that they cried for soldiers. In November 1890 General Miles moved a good portion of the U.S. Army onto the Sioux reservations. At Wounded Knee Custer's old regiment clashed with Big Foot's Sioux band in one of the most tragic episodes of the Indian wars. Despite the passions kindled by Wounded Knee, the massive military buildup quickly brought about the surrender of the Ghost Dancers.

Wounded Knee closed out four centuries of Indian warfare in North America. It occurred, moreover, in the very year in which the Census Bureau could no longer trace a frontier of settlement on the map of the West. Not the ceremony at Fort Bowie but a grand review at Pine Ridge Indian Agency celebrated the last services of the frontier army. Regiment after regiment paraded before General Miles. Finally, sabers flashing and yellow-lined capes flying in the wind, the 7th Cavalry, decimated by Wounded Knee, trooped by. The 1st Infantry Band struck up "Garryowen," Custer's battle air, and with these rollicking strains rather than "Auld Lang Syne" the bluecoats ended their contribution to the opening of the West.

Now they belonged to Remington, Schreyvogel, Charles King, and John Wayne—and to history.

WHO'S WRITING AND WRITTEN ABOUT

INDEX

Credits/Acknowledgments

Cover design by Charles Vitelli.

Cover photo: National Gallery of Art, Washington, D.C.

1. The New Land
Facing overview—Courtesy, New York Public Library picture collection. 23—Harper's New Monthly Magazine.
2. Revolutionary America
Facing overview—"Battle of Monmouth Court House" from *The American Revolution,* a picture sourcebook. 55—Library Company of Philadelphia. 58—John Trumbull "Benjamin Franklin", Yale University Art Gallery. 74—The Bettmann Archive.
3. National Consolidation and Expansion
Facing overview—"Indians and the Frontier" from *The American Revolution,* a picture sourcebook. 166—(right) The Bettman Archive. 187—The Bettmann Archive.
4. The Civil War and Reconstruction
Facing overview—"Civil War: A Recruiting Station in City Hall Park" (1864) from *New York in The Nineteenth Century.*
226—The Bettmann Archive. 227-228—Library of Congress.

WE WANT YOUR ADVICE

ANNUAL EDITIONS: AMERICAN HISTORY, VOLUME I
Article Rating Form

Here is an opportunity for you to have direct input into the next revision of this reader. We would like you to rate each of the 38 articles listed below, using the following scale:

1. **Excellent: should definitely be retained**
2. **Above average: should probably be retained**
3. **Below average: should probably be deleted**
4. **Poor: should definitely be deleted**

Your ratings will play a vital part in the next revision. So please mail this prepaid form to us just as soon as you complete it.
Thanks for your help!

Rating	Article	Rating	Article
	1. Christopher Columbus' Quest for God, Glory and Gold. And Japan.		19. The Jay Treaty: Crisis Diplomacy in the New Nation
	2. Indentured Servants		20. Experiment at Nashoba Plantation
	3. Bacon's Rebellion		21. Gabriel's Insurrection
	4. The Devil in Salem		22. The War Against Demon Rum
	5. Battling the Red Death		23. The Trail of Tears
	6. The Trial of Peter Zenger		24. Our Forefathers in Hot Pursuit of the Good Life
	7. The Great Earthquake		25. Travels with Tocqueville
	8. The Revolution as a World Ideal		26. Sam Houston
	9. The Spirit of '74		27. Jacksonian Democracy, Myth or Reality?
	10. Meet Dr. Franklin		28. Melville and Hawthorne
	11. England's Vietnam: The American Revolution		29. Eden Ravished
	12. Common Sense		30. Lucretia Mott
	13. The Revolution Remembered		31. The Green and the Gold
	14. Brave Women		32. Vanity in the 19th Century
	15. The Founding Fathers and Slavery		33. Sojourner Truth: "A Self-Made Woman"
	16. The American World Was Not Made for Me: The Unknown Alexander Hamilton		34. The Myth of the Underground Railroad
	17. George Washington and the "Guilty, Dangerous and Vulgar Honor"		35. Johnny Reb and Billy Yank
			36. How "The Lost Cause" Was Lost
	18. Do We Care If Johnny Can Read?		37. The Tragic Legend of Reconstruction
			38. The Bluecoats

(continued on back)

About you

Name _____ Date _____

Address _____

City _____ State _____ Zip _____

Telephone _____

1. What do you think of the Annual Editions concept?

2. Have you read any articles lately that you think should be included in the next edition?

3. Which articles do you feel should be replaced in the next edition? Why?

4. In what other areas would you like to see an Annual Edition? Why?

AMERICAN HISTORY, VOLUME I

BUSINESS REPLY MAIL

First Class   Permit No. 84   Guilford, Ct.

Postage Will Be Paid by Addressee

Attention: Annual Editions Service
The Dushkin Publishing Group, Inc.
Sluice Dock
Guilford, Connecticut 06437

NO POSTAGE
NECESSARY
IF MAILED
IN THE
UNITED STATES